The Art of SQL

計利以聽，乃爲之勢，以佐其外。

While heeding the profit of my counsel, avail yourself also of any helpful circumstances over and beyond the ordinary rules.

—*Sun Tzu,* The Art of War

Other resources from O'Reilly

Related titles

SQL in a Nutshell
SQL Tuning
SQL Pocket Guide
SQL Cookbook™

oreilly.com

oreilly.com is more than a complete catalog of O'Reilly books. You'll also find links to news, events, articles, weblogs, sample chapters, and code examples.

oreillynet.com is the essential portal for developers interested in open and emerging technologies, including new platforms, programming languages, and operating systems.

Conferences

O'Reilly brings diverse innovators together to nurture the ideas that spark revolutionary industries. We specialize in documenting the latest tools and systems, translating the innovator's knowledge into useful skills for those in the trenches. Visit *conferences.oreilly.com* for our upcoming events.

Safari Bookshelf (*safari.oreilly.com*) is the premier online reference library for programmers and IT professionals. Conduct searches across more than 1,000 books. Subscribers can zero in on answers to time-critical questions in a matter of seconds. Read the books on your Bookshelf from cover to cover or simply flip to the page you need. Try it today for free.

The Art of

SQL

Stéphane Faroult with Peter Robson

O'REILLY®

Beijing • Cambridge • Farnham • Köln • Paris • Sebastopol • Taipei • Tokyo

SHROFF PUBLISHERS & DISTRIBUTORS PVT. LTD.

Mumbai Bangalore Chennai Kolkata New Delhi

The Art of SQL

by Stéphane Faroult with Peter Robson

 ISBN: 0-596-00894-5
Originally printed in the United States of America.

Published by O'Reilly Media Inc., 1005 Gravenstein Highway North, Sebastopol, CA 95472.

O'Reilly books may be purchased for educational, business, or sales promotional use. Online editions are also available for most titles (*safari.oreilly.com*). For more information, contact our corporate/institutional sales department: (800) 998-9938 or *corporate@oreilly.com*.

Editor: Jonathan Gennick

Production Editor: Jamie Peppard and Marlowe Shaeffer

Copyeditor: Nancy Reinhardt

Indexer: Ellen Troutman Zaig

Cover Designer: Mike Kohnke

Interior Designer: Marcia Friedman

Illustrators: Robert Romano, Jessamyn Read, and Lesley Borash

Printing History:

March 2006: First Edition.

Second Indian Reprint: June 2008

ISBN 10: 81-8404-141-1
ISBN 13: 978-81-8404-141-5

Published by **Shroff Publishers and Distributors Pvt. Ltd.** C-103, MIDC, TTC Industrial Area, Pawane, Navi Mumbai 400 705, Tel: (91 22) 2763 4290, Fax: 2768 3337, e-mail: spdorders@shroffpublishers.com. Printed at Rose Fine Art, Mumbai.

The French humorist Alphonse Allais (1854–1905), once dedicated one of his short stories as follows:

To the only woman I love and who knows it well.

. . . with the following footnote:

This is a very convenient dedication that I cannot recommend too warmly to my fellow writers. It costs nothing, and can, all at once, please five or six persons.

I can take a piece of wise advice when I meet one.

Stéphane Faroult

CONTENTS

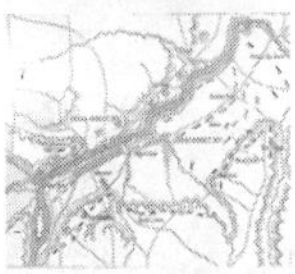

PREFACE

There used to be a time when what is known today as "Information Technology" or IT was less glamorously known as "Electronic Data Processing." And the truth is that for all the buzz about trendy techniques, the processing of data is still at the core of our systems—and all the more as the volume of data under management seems to be increasing even faster than the speed of processors. The most vital corporate data is today stored in databases and accessed through the imperfect, but widely known, SQL language—a combination that had begun to gain acceptance in the pinstriped circles at the beginning of the 1980s and has since wiped out the competition.

You can hardly interview a young developer today who doesn't claim a good working knowledge of SQL, the lingua franca of database access, a standard part of any basic IT course. This claim is usually reasonably true, if you define knowledge as the ability to obtain, after some effort, functionally correct results. However, enterprises all over the world are today confronted with exploding volumes of data. As a result, "functionally correct" results are no longer enough: they also have to be fast. Database performance has become a major headache in many companies. Interestingly, although everyone agrees that the source of performance issues lies in the code, it seems accepted everywhere that the first concern of developers should be to provide code that works—which seems to be a reasonable expectation. The thought seems to be that the database access part of their code should be as simple as possible, for maintenance reasons, and that "bad SQL" should be given to senior database administrators (DBAs) to tweak and make run faster, with the help of a few magic database parameters. And if such tweaking isn't enough, then it seems that upgrading the hardware is the proper course to take.

It is quite often that what appears to be the common-sense and safe approach ends up being extremely harmful. Writing inefficient code and relying on experts for tuning the "bad SQL" is actually sweeping the dirt under the carpet. In my view, the first ones to be concerned with performance should be developers, and I see SQL issues as something encompassing much more than the proper writing of a few queries. Performance seen from a developer's perspective is something profoundly different from "tuning," as practiced by DBAs. A database administrator tries to get the most out of a system—a given hardware, processors and storage subsystem, or a given version of the database. A database administrator may have some SQL skills and be able to tune an especially poorly performing statement. But developers are writing code that may well run for 5 to 10 years, surviving several major releases (Internet-enabled, ready-for-the-grid, you name it) of the Database Management System (DBMS) it was written for—and on several generations of hardware. Your code must be fast and sound from the start. It is a sorry assessment to make but if many developers "know" SQL, very few have a sound understanding of this language and of the relational theory.

Why Another SQL Book?

There are three main types of SQL books: books that teach the logic and the syntax of a particular SQL dialect, books that teach advanced techniques and take a problem-solving approach, and performance and tuning books that target experts and senior DBAs. On one hand, books show how to write SQL code. On the other hand, they show how to diagnose and fix SQL code that has been badly written. I have tried, in this book, to teach people who are no longer novices how to write *good* SQL code from the start and, most importantly, to have a view of SQL code that goes beyond individual SQL statements.

Teaching how to use a language is difficult enough; but how can one teach how to efficiently use a language? SQL is a language that can look deceivingly simple once you have been initiated. And yet it allows for an almost infinite number of cases and combinations. The first comparison that occurred to me was the game of chess, but it suddenly dawned on me that chess was invented to teach war. I have a natural tendency to consider every new performance challenge as a battle to be fought against an army of rows, and I realized that the problem of teaching developers how to use databases efficiently was similar to the problem of teaching officers how to conduct a war. You need knowledge, you need skills, and you need talent. Talent cannot be taught, but it can be nurtured. This is what most strategists, from Sun Tzu, who wrote his *Art of War* 25 centuries ago, to modern-day generals, have believed—so they tried to pass on the experience acquired on the field through simple maxims and rules that they hoped would serve as guiding stars among the sound and fury of battles. I have tried to apply this method to more peaceful aims, and I have mostly followed the same plan as Sun Tzu—and I've borrowed his title. Many respected IT specialists claim the status of scientists; "Art" seems to me more appropriate than "Science" when it comes to defining an activity that requires flair, experience, and creativity, as much as rigor and understanding.* It is quite likely that my fondness for Art will be frowned upon by some partisans of Science, who claim that for each SQL problem, there is one optimal solution, which can be attained by rigorous analysis and a good knowledge of data. However, I don't see the two positions at odds. Rigor and a scientific approach will help you out of *one* problem *at one given moment*. In SQL development, if you don't have the uncertainties linked to the next move of the adversary, the big uncertainties lie in future evolutions. What if, rather unexpectedly, the volume of this or that table increases? What if, following a merger, the number of users doubles? What if we want to keep several years of data online? How will a program behave on hardware totally different from what we have now? Some architectural choices are gambles on the future. You will certainly need rigor and a very sound theoretical knowledge—but those qualities are prerequisites of any art. Ferdinand Foch, the future Supreme Commander of the Allied armies of WWI, remarked at a lecture at the French Ecole Supérieure de Guerre in 1900 that:

> The art of war, like all other arts, has its theory, its principles—otherwise, it wouldn't be an art.

This book is not a cookbook, listing problems and giving "recipes." The aim is much more to help developers—and their managers—to raise good questions. You may well still write awful, costly queries after having read and digested this book. One sometimes has to. But, hopefully, it will be knowingly and with good reason.

Audience

This book is targeted at:

- Developers with significant (one year or, preferably, more) experience of development with an SQL database
- Their managers
- Software architects who design programs with significant database components

* One of my favorite computer books happens to be D.E. Knuth's classic *Art of Computer Programming* (Addison Wesley).

Although I hope that some DBAs, and particularly those that support development databases, will enjoy reading this book, I am sorry to tell them I had somebody else in mind while writing.

Assumptions This Book Makes

I assume in this book that you have already mastered the SQL language. By *mastering* I don't mean that you took SQL 101 at the university and got an A+, nor, at the other end of the spectrum, that you are an internationally acknowledged SQL guru. I mean that you have already developed database applications using the SQL language, that you have had to think about indexing, and that you don't consider a 5,000-row table to be a big table. It is not the purpose of this book to tell you what a "join" is—not even an outer one—nor what indexes are meant to be used for. Although you don't need to feel totally comfortable with arcane SQL constructs, if, when given a set of tables and a question to answer, you are unable to come up with a functionally correct piece of code, there are probably a couple of books you had better read before this one. I also assume that you are at least familiar with one computer language and with the principles of computer programming. I assume that you have already been down in the trenches and that you have already heard users complain about slow and poorly performing systems.

Contents of This Book

I found the parallel between war and SQL so strong that I mostly followed Sun Tzu's outline—and kept most of his titles.* This book is divided into twelve chapters, each containing a number of principles or maxims. I have tried to explain and illustrate these principles through examples, preferably from real-life cases.

Chapter 1, *Laying Plans*
: Examines how to design databases for performance

Chapter 2, *Waging War*
: Explains how programs must be designed to access databases efficiently

Chapter 3, *Tactical Dispositions*
: Tells why and how to index

Chapter 4, *Maneuvering*
: Explains how to envision SQL statements

Chapter 5, *Terrain*
: Shows how physical implementation impacts performance

* A few titles were borrowed from Clausewitz's *On War*.

Chapter 6, *The Nine Situations*

Covers classic SQL patterns and how to approach them

Chapter 7, *Variations in Tactics*

Explains how to deal with hierarchical data

Chapter 8, *Weaknesses and Strengths*

Provides indications about how to recognize and handle some difficult cases

Chapter 9, *Multiple Fronts*

Describes how to face concurrency

Chapter 10, *Assembly of Forces*

Addresses how to cope with large volumes of data

Chapter 11, *Stratagems*

Offers a few tricks that will help you survive rotten database designs

Chapter 12, *Employment of Spies*

Concludes the book by explaining how to define and monitor performance

Conventions Used in This Book

The following typographical conventions are used in this book:

Italic

Indicates emphasis and new terms, as well as book titles.

`Constant width`

Indicates SQL and, generally speaking, programming languages' keywords; table, index and column names; functions; code; or the output from commands.

`Constant width bold`

Shows commands or other text that should be typed literally by the user. This style is used only in code examples that mix both input and output.

`Constant width italic`

Shows text that should be replaced with user-supplied values.

This icon signifies a *maxim* and summarizes an important principle in SQL.

NOTE

This is a tip, suggestion, or general note. It contains useful supplementary information about the topic at hand.

Using Code Examples

This book is here to help you get your job done. In general, you may use the code in this book in your programs and documentation. You do not need to contact O'Reilly for permission unless you're reproducing a significant portion of the code. For example, writing a program that uses several chunks of code from this book does not require permission. Selling or distributing a CD-ROM of examples from O'Reilly books *does* require permission. Answering a question by citing this book and quoting example code does not require permission. Incorporating a significant amount of example code from this book into your product's documentation *does* require permission.

O'Reilly, Media Inc. appreciates, but does not require, attribution. An attribution usually includes the title, author, publisher, and ISBN. For example: "*The Art of SQL* by Stéphane Faroult with Peter Robson. Copyright © 2006 O'Reilly Media, 0-596-00894-5."

If you feel your use of code examples falls outside fair use or the permission given above, feel free to contact the publisher at *permissions@oreilly.com*.

Comments and Questions

Please address comments and questions concerning this book to the publisher:

O'Reilly Media, Inc.
1005 Gravenstein Highway North
Sebastopol, CA 95472
(800) 998-9938 (in the U.S. or Canada)
(707) 829-0515 (international or local)
(707) 829-0104 (fax)

The publisher has a web page for this book, where we list errata, examples, and any additional information. You can access this page at:

http://www.oreilly.com/catalog/artofsql

To comment or ask technical questions about this book, send email to:

bookquestions@oreilly.com

For more information about our books, conferences, Resource Centers, and the O'Reilly Network, see O'Reilly's web site at:

http://www.oreilly.com

You can also visit the author's company web site at:

http://www.roughsea.com

Safari® Enabled

When you see a Safari® Enabled icon on the cover of your favorite technology book, that means the book is available online through the O'Reilly Network Safari Bookshelf.

Safari offers a solution that's better than e-books. It's a virtual library that lets you easily search thousands of top tech books, cut and paste code samples, download chapters, and find quick answers when you need the most accurate, current information. Try it for free at *http://safari.oreilly.com*.

Acknowledgments

Writing a book in a language that is neither your native language nor the language of the country where you live requires an optimism that (in retrospect) borders on insanity. Fortunately, Peter Robson, whom I had met at several conferences as a fellow speaker, brought to this book not only his knowledge of the SQL language and database design issues, but an unabated enthusiasm for mercilessly chopping my long sentences, placing adverbs where they belong, or suggesting an alternative to replace a word that was last heard in Merry England under the Plantagenets.*

Being edited by Jonathan Gennick, the best-selling author of the O'Reilly *SQL Pocket Guide* and several other noted books, was a slightly scary honor. I discovered in Jonathan an editor extremely respectful of authors. His professionalism, attention to detail, and challenging views made this book a much better book than Peter and I would have written on our own. Jonathan also contributed to give a more mid-Atlantic flavor to this book (as Peter and I discovered, setting the spelling checker to "English (US)" is a prerequisite, but not quite enough).

I would like to express my gratitude to the various people, from three continents, who took the time to read parts or the whole of the drafts of this book and to give me frank opinions: Philippe Bertolino, Rachel Carmichael, Sunil CS, Larry Elkins, Tim Gorman, Jean-Paul Martin, Sanjay Mishra, Anthony Molinaro, and Tiong Soo Hua. I feel a particular debt towards Larry, because the concept of this book probably finds its origin in some of our email discussions.

I would also like to thank the numerous people at O'Reilly who made this book a reality. These include Marcia Friedman, Rob Romano, Jamie Peppard, Mike Kohnke, Ron Bilodeau, Jessamyn Read, and Andrew Savikas. Thanks, too, to Nancy Reinhardt for her most excellent copyedit of the manuscript.

* For readers unfamiliar with British history, the Plantagenet dynasty ruled England between 1154 and 1485.

Special thanks to Yann-Arzel Durelle-Marc for kindly providing a suitable scan of the picture used to illustrate Chapter 12. Thanks too, to Paul McWhorter for permission to use his battle map as the basis for the Chapter 6 figure.

Finally, I would like to thank Roger Manser and the staff at Steel Business Briefing for supplying Peter and me with an office and much-needed coffee for work sessions in London, halfway between our respective bases, and Qian Lena (Ashley) for providing me with the Chinese text of the Sun Tzu quote at the beginning of this book.

CHAPTER ONE

Laying Plans

Designing Databases for Performance

C'est le premier pas qui, dans toutes les guerres, décèle le génie.

It is the first step that reveals genius in all wars.

—Joseph de Maistre (1754–1821)

Lettre du 27 Juillet 1812
à Monsieur le Comte de Front

The great nineteenth century German strategist, Clausewitz, famously remarked that war is the continuation of politics by other means. Likewise, any computer program is, in one way or another, the continuation of the general activity within an organization, allowing it to do more, faster, better, or cheaper. The main purpose of a computer program is *not* simply to extract data from a database and then to process it, but to extract and process data *for some particular goal*. The means are not the end.

A reminder that the goal of a given computer program is first of all to meet some *business requirement** may come across as a platitude. In practice, the excitement of technological challenges often slowly causes attention to drift from the end to the means, from upholding the quality of the data that records business activity to writing programs that perform as intended and in an acceptable amount of time. Like a general in command of his army at the beginning of a campaign, we must know clearly what our objectives are—and we must stick to them, even if unexpected difficulties or opportunities make us alter the original plan. Whenever the SQL language is involved, we are fighting to keep a faithful and consistent record of business activity over time. Both faithfulness and consistency are primarily associated with the quality of the database model. The database model that SQL was initially designed to support is the relational model. One cannot overemphasize the importance of having a good model and a proper database design, because this is the very foundation of any information system.

The Relational View of Data

A database is nothing but a model of a small part of a real-life situation. As any representation, a database is always an imperfect model, and a very narrow depiction of a rich and complex reality. There is rarely a single way to represent some business activity, but rather several variants that in a technical sense will be semantically correct. However, for a given set of processes to apply, there is usually one representation that best meets the business requirement.

The relational model is thus named, not because you can relate tables to one another (a popular misconception), but as a reference to the relationships between the columns *in* a table. These are the relationships that give the model its name; in other words, *relational* means that if several values belong to the same row in a table, they are *related*. The way columns are related to each other defines a relation, and a relation *is* a table (more exactly, a table represents one relation).

The business requirements determine the scope of the real-world situation that is to be modeled. Once you have defined the scope, you can proceed to identify the data that you

* The expression *business requirement* is meant to encompass non-commercial as well as commercial activities.

need to properly record business activity. If we say that you are a used car dealer and want to model the cars you have for sale (for instance to advertise them on a web site), items such as make, model, version, style (sedan, coupe, convertible...), year, mileage, and price may be the very first pieces of information that come to mind. But potential buyers may want to learn about many more characteristics to be able to make an informed choice before settling for one particular car. For instance:

- General state of the vehicle (even if we don't expect anything but "excellent")
- Safety equipment
- Manual or automatic transmission
- Color (body and interiors), metallic paintwork or not, upholstery, hard or soft top, perhaps a picture of the car
- Seating capacity, trunk capacity, number of doors
- Power steering, air conditioning, audio equipment
- Engine capacity, cylinders, horsepower and top speed, brakes (everyone isn't a car enthusiast who would know technical specifications from the car description)
- Fuel, consumption, tank capacity
- Current location of the car (may matter to buyers if the site lists cars available from a number of physical places)
- And so on...

If we decide to model the available cars into a database, then each row in a table summarizes a particular statement of fact—for instance, that there is for sale a 1964 pink Cadillac Coupe DeVille that has already been driven twenty times around the Earth.

Through relational operations, such as joins, and also by filtering, selection of particular attributes, or computations applied to attributes (say computing from consumption and tank capacity how many miles we can drive without refueling), we can derive new factual statements. If the original statements are true, the derived statements will be true.

Whenever we are dealing with knowledge, we start with facts that we accept as truths that need no proof (in mathematics these are known as *axioms*, but this argument is by no means restricted to mathematics and you could call those unproved true facts *principles* in other disciplines). It is possible to build upon these true facts (*proving theorems* in mathematics) to derive new truths. These truths themselves may form the foundations from which further new truths emerge.

Relational databases work in exactly the same way. It is absolutely no accident that the relational model is mathematically based. The relations we define (which once again means, for an SQL database, the tables we create) represent facts that we accept, *a priori*, as true. The views we define, and the queries we write, are new truths that we prove.

NOTE

The coherence of the relational model is a critically important concept to grasp. Because of the inherent mathematical stability of the principles that underlie relational data modeling, we can be totally confident that the result of any query of our original database will indeed generate equally valid facts—if we respect the relational principles. Some of the key principles of the relational theory are that a relation, by definition, contains no duplicate, and that row ordering isn't significant. As you shall see in Chapter 4, SQL allows developers to take a number of liberties with the relational theory, liberties that may be the reasons for either surprising results or the failure of a database optimizer to perform efficiently.

There is, however, considerable freedom in the choice of our basic truths. Sometimes the exercise of this freedom can be done very badly. For example, wouldn't it be a little tedious if every time someone went to buy some apples, the grocer felt compelled to prove all Newtonian physics before weighing them? What must be thought of a program where the most basic operation requires a 25-way join?

We may use much data in common with our suppliers and customers. However, it is likely that, if we are not direct competitors, our view of the same data will be different, reflecting our particular perspective on our real-life situation. For example, our business requirements will differ from those of our suppliers and customers, even though we are all using the same data. One size doesn't fit all. A good design is a design that doesn't require crazy queries.

Modeling is the projection of business requirements.

The Importance of Being Normal

Normalization, and especially that which progresses to the *third normal form* (3NF), is a part of relational theory that most students in computer science have been told about. It is like so many things learned at school (classical literature springs to mind), often remembered as dusty, boring, and totally disconnected from today's reality. Many years later, it is rediscovered with fresh eyes and in light of experience, with an understanding that the essence of both principles and classicism is *timelessness*.

The principle of normalization is the application of logical rigor to the assemblage of items of data—which may then become structured information. This rigor is expressed in the definition of various normal forms, most typically three, although purists argue that one should analyze data beyond 3NF to what is known in the trade as *Boyce-Codd normal form* (BCNF), or even to *fifth normal form* (5NF). Don't panic. We will discuss only the first three forms. In the vast majority of cases, a database modeled in 3NF will also be in BCNF* and 5NF.

You may wonder why normalization matters. Normalization is applying order to chaos. After the battle, mistakes may appear obvious, and successful moves sometimes look like nothing other than common sense. Likewise, after normalization the structures of the various tables in the database may look natural, and the normalization rules are sometimes dismissively considered as glorified common sense. We all want to believe we have an ample supply of common sense; but it's easy to get confused when dealing with complex data. The three first normal forms are based on the application of strict logic and are a useful sanity checklist.

The odds that our creating un-normalized tables will increase our risk of being struck by divine lightning and reduced to a little mound of ashes are indeed very low (or so I believe; it's an untested theory). Data inconsistency, the difficulty of coding data-entry controls, and error management in what become bloated application programs are real risks, as well as poor performance and the inability to make the model evolve. These risks have a very high probability of occurring if we don't adhere to normal form, and I will soon show why.

How is data moved from a heterogeneous collection of unstructured bits of information into a usable data model? The method itself isn't complicated. We must follow a few steps, which are illustrated with examples in the following subsections.

Step 1: Ensure Atomicity

First of all, we must ensure that the characteristics, or attributes, we are dealing with are *atomic*. The whole idea of atomicity is rather elusive, in spite of its apparent simplicity. The word *atom* comes from ideas first advanced by Leucippus, a Greek philosopher who lived in the fifth century B.C., and means "that cannot be split." (Atomic fission is a contradiction in terms.) Deciding whether data can be considered atomic or not is chiefly a question of scale. For example, a regiment may be an atomic fighting unit to a general-in-chief, but it will be very far from atomic to the colonel in command of that regiment, who deals at the more granular level of battalions or squadrons. In the same way, a car may be an atomic item of information to a car dealer, but to a garage mechanic, it is very far from atomic and consists of a whole host of further components that form the mechanic's perception of atomic data items.

* You can have 3NF but *not* BCNF if your table contains several sets of columns that are unique (candidate keys, which are possible unique identifiers of a row) and share one column. Such situations are not very common.

From a purely practical point of view, we shall define an *atomic attribute* as an attribute that, in a `where` clause, can always be referred to in full. You can split and chop an attribute as much as you want in the select list (where it is returned); but if you need to refer to parts of the attribute inside the `where` clause, the attribute lacks the level of atomicity you need. Let me give an example. In the previous list of attributes for used cars, you'll find "safety equipment," which is a generic name for several pieces of information, such as the presence of an antilock braking system (ABS), or airbags (passenger-only, passenger and driver, frontal, lateral, and so on), or possibly other features, such as the centralized locking of doors. We can, of course, define a column named `safety_equipment` that is just a description of available safety features. But we must be aware that by using a description we forfeit at least two major benefits:

The ability to perform an efficient search

If some users consider ABS critical because they often drive on wet, slippery roads, a search that specifies "ABS" as the main criterion will be very slow if we must search column `safety_equipment` in every row for the "ABS" substring. As I'll show in Chapter 3, regular indexes require atomic (in the sense just defined) values as keys. One can sometimes use query accelerators other than regular indexes (full-text indexing, for instance), but such accelerators usually have drawbacks, such as not being maintained in real time. Also take note that full-text search may produce awkward results at times. Let's take the example of a `color` column that contains a description of both body and interior colors. If you search for "blue" because you'd prefer to buy a blue car, gray cars with a blue interior will also be returned. We have all experienced irrelevant full-text search results through web searches.

Database-guaranteed data correctness

Data-entry is prone to error. More importantly than dissuasive search times, if "ASB" is entered instead of "ABS" into a descriptive string, the database management system will have no way to check whether the string "ASB" is meaningful. As a result, the row will never be returned when a user specifies "ABS" in a search, whether as the main or as a secondary criterion. In other words, some of our queries will return wrong results (either incomplete, or even plain wrong if we want to count how many cars feature ABS). If we want to ensure data correctness, our only means (other than double-checking what we have typed) is to write some complicated function to parse and analyze the safety equipment string when it is entered or updated. It is hard to decide what will be worse: the hell that the maintenance of such a function would be, or the performance penalty that it will inflict on loads. By contrast, a mandatory Y/N `has_ABS` column would not guarantee that the information is correct, but at least declarative check constraints can make the DBMS reject any value other than Y or N.

Partially updating a complex string of data requires first-rate mastery of string functions. Thus, you want to avoid cramming multiple values into a single string.

Defining data *atoms* isn't always a simple exercise. For example, the handling of addresses frequently raises difficult questions about atomicity. Must we consider the address as some big, opaque string? Or must we break it into its components? And if we decompose the address, to what level should we split it up? Remember the points made earlier about atomicity and business requirements. How we represent an address actually depends on what we want to do with the address. For example, if we want to compute statistics or search by postal code and town, then it is desirable to break the address up into sufficient attribute components to uniquely identify those important data items. The question then arises as to how far this decomposition of the address should be taken.

The guiding principle in determining the extent to which an address should be broken into components is to test each component against the business requirements, and from those requirements derive the atomic address attributes. What these various address attributes will be cannot be predicted (although the variation is not great), but we must be aware of the danger of adopting an address format just because some other organization may have chosen it, before we have tested it critically against our own business needs.

Note that sometimes, the devil is in the details. By trying to be too precise, we may open the door to many distracting and potentially irrelevant issues. If we settle for a level of detail that includes building number and street as atomic items, what of ACME Corp, the address of which is simply "ACME Building"? We should not create design problems for information we don't need to process. Properly defining the level of information that is needed can be particularly important when transferring data from an operational to a decision-support system.

Once all atomic data items have been identified, and their mutual interrelationships resolved, distinct relations emerge. The next step is to identify what uniquely characterizes a row—the primary key. At this stage, it is very likely that this key will be a compound one, consisting of two or more individual attributes. To go on with our used car example, for a customer it's the combination of make, model, version, style, year, and mileage that will identify a particular vehicle—not the current registration number. It isn't always easy to correctly define a key. A good, classic example of attribute analysis is the business definition of "customer." A customer may be identified by a name. However, a name may not be the best identifier. If our customers are companies, the way we identify them may be the source of ambiguities—is it "RSI," "Relational Software," "Relational Software Inc" (with or without a dot following "Inc," with or without a comma after "Relational Software") that identifies this given company? Uppercase? Lowercase? Capitalized initials? We have here all the conditions for storing information inside a database and never seeing it again. The choice of the customer name as identifier is a challenging one, because it demands the strict application of naming standards to avoid possible ambiguities. It may be preferable to identify a customer on the basis of either a standard short name, or possibly by use of a unique code. And one should always keep in mind the impact on related data of Relational Software Inc. changing its name to, say, Oracle Corporation. If we need to keep a history of our relationship, then we must be able to identify both names as representing the same company at different points in time.

As a general rule, you should, whenever possible, use a unique identifier that has meaning rather than some obscure sequential integer. I must stress that the primary key is what characterizes the data—which is not the case with some sequential identifier associated with each new row. You may choose to add such an identifier later, for instance because you find your own `company_id` easier to handle than the place of incorporation and registration number that truly identify a company. You can even promote the sequential identifier to the envied status of primary key, as a technical substitute (or shorthand) for the true key, in exactly the same way that you'd use table aliases in a query in order to be able to write:

```
where a.id =  b.id
```

instead of:

```
where table_with_a_long_name.id = table_even_worse_than_the_other.id
```

But a technical, numerical identifier doesn't constitute a real primary key by the mere virtue of its existence and mustn't be mistaken for the real thing. Once all the attributes are atomic and keys are identified, our data is in *first normal form* (1NF).

Step 2: Check Dependence on the Whole Key

I have pointed out that some of the information that we should store to help used car buyers make an informed choice would already be known by a car enthusiast. In fact, many used car characteristics are not specific to one particular car. For example, all the cars sharing make, model, version, and style will have the same seating and cargo capacity, regardless of year and mileage. In other words, we have attributes that depend on only a part of the key. What are the implications of keeping them inside a `used_cars` table?

Data redundancy

If we happen to have for sale many cars of the same make, model, version, and style (a set of characteristics that we can generically call the *car model*), all the attributes that are not specific to one particular car will be stored as many times as we have cars of the same model. There are two issues with the storage of redundant data. First, redundant data increases the odds of encountering contradictory information because of input errors (and it makes correction more time-consuming). Second, redundant data is an obvious storage waste. It is customary to hear that nowadays storage is so cheap that one no longer needs to be obsessed with space. True enough, except that such an argument overlooks the fact that there is also more and more data to store in today's world. It also overlooks the fact that data is often mirrored, possibly backed up to other disks on a disaster recovery site where it is mirrored again, and that many development databases are mere copies of production databases. As a result, every wasted byte isn't wasted once, but four or five times in the very best of cases. When you add up all the wasted bytes, you sometimes get surprisingly high figures. Besides the mere cost of storage, sometimes—more importantly—there is also the issue of recovery. There are cases when one experiences "unplanned downtime," a very severe crash for which the only solution is to restore the database from a backup. All other things being equal, a database that is twice as big as necessary will take twice the time to restore than would otherwise be needed. There are environments in which a long time to restore can cost a lot of money. In a hospital, it can even cost lives.

Query performance

A table that contains a lot of information (with a large number of columns) takes much longer to scan than a table with a reduced set of columns. As we shall see in other chapters, a full table scan is not necessarily the scary situation that many beginners believe it to be; there are many cases where it is by far the best solution. However, the more bytes in the average row, the more pages will be required to store the table, and the longer it takes to scan the table. If you want to display a selectable list of the available car models, an un-normalized table will require a `select distinct` applied to all the available cars. Running a `select distinct` doesn't mean only scanning many more rows than we would with a separate `car_model` table, but it also means having to sort those rows to eliminate duplicates. If the data is split in such a way that the DBMS engine can operate against only a subset of the data to resolve the query, performance will be significantly better than when it operates against the whole.

To remove dependencies on a part of the key, we must create tables (such as `car_model`). The keys of those new tables will each be a part of the key for our original table (in our example, make, model, version, and style). Then we must move all the attributes that depend on those new keys to the new tables, and retain only make, model, version, and style in the original table. We may have to repeat this process, since the engine and its characteristics will not depend on the style. Once we have completed the removal of attributes that depend on only a part of the key, our tables are in *second normal form* (2NF).

Step 3: Check Attribute Independence

When all data has been correctly moved into 2NF, we can commence the process of identifying the *third normal form* (3NF). Very often, a data set in 2NF will already be in 3NF, but nevertheless, we should check the 2NF set. We now know that each attribute in the current set is fully dependent on the unique key. 3NF is reached when we cannot infer the value of an attribute from any attribute other than those in the unique key. For example, the question must be asked: "Given the value of attribute A, can the value of attribute B be determined?"

International contact information provides an excellent example of when you can have an attribute dependent on another non-key attribute: if you know the country, you need not record the international dialing code with the phone number (the reverse is not true, since the United States and Canada share the same code). If you need both bits of information, you ought to associate each contact with, say, an ISO country code (for instance IT for Italy), and have a separate `country_info` table that uses the country code as primary key and that holds useful country information that your business requires. For instance, a `country_info` table may record that the international dialing code for Italy is 39, but also that the Italian currency is the euro, and so on. Every pair of attributes in our 2NF data set should be examined in turn to check whether one depends on the other. Such checking is a slow process, but essential if the data is to be truly modeled in 3NF. What are the risks associated with not having the data modeled in 3NF? Basically you have the same risks as from not respecting 2NF.

There are various reasons that modeling to the third normal form is important. (Note that there are cases in which designers deliberately choose not to model in third normal form; *dimensional modeling*, which will be briefly introduced in Chapter 10, is such a case. But before you stray from the rule, you must know the rule and weigh the risks involved.) Here are some reasons:

A properly normalized model protects against the evolution of requirements.

As Chapter 10 will show, a non-normalized model such as the dimensional one finds its justification in assumptions about how the data is maintained and queried (the same can be said of the physical data structures that you'll see in Chapter 5; but a physical implementation change will not jeopardize the logic of programs, even if it can seriously impact their performance). If the assumptions prove wrong one day, all you can do is throw everything away and rebuild from scratch. By contrast, a 3NF model may require some query adjustments, but it will be flexible enough to accommodate changes.

Normalization minimizes data duplication.

As I have already pointed out, duplicate data is costly, both in terms of disk space and processing power, but it also introduces a much-increased possibility of data becoming corrupt. Corruption happens when one instance of a data value is modified, but the same data held in another part of the database fails to be simultaneously (and identically) modified. Losing information doesn't only mean data erasure: if one part of the database says "white" while another part says "black," you have lost information. Data inconsistency can be prevented by the DBMS if the modeling allows it—if your atomic attributes let you define column constraints, or if you can declare referential integrity constraints. Otherwise, it has to be prevented by additional programming traps. You then have the choice between using triggers and stored procedures that can grow very complex and add significant overhead, or making programs unnecessarily complicated and therefore costlier to maintain. Triggers and stored procedures must be extremely well documented. Data consistency ensured in programs moves the protection of data integrity out of the database and into the application layer. Any other program that needs to access the same data has the choice between duplicating the data integrity protection effort, or happily corrupting the data painfully maintained in a consistent state by other programs.

The normalization process is fundamentally based on the application of atomicity to the world you are modeling.

To Be or Not to Be, or to Be Null

A very common modeling mistake is to associate large numbers of *possible* characteristics within a relation, which may result in a table with a large number of columns. Some scientific disciplines may require a very detailed characterization of objects under study, and thus require a large number of attributes, but this is rarely the case in business applications. In any case, a sure sign that a database design is flawed is when columns of some prominent tables mostly contain null values, and especially when two columns cannot possibly contain a value at the same time; if one is defined, the other must be null, and vice versa. This condition would undoubtedly indicate a violation of either 2NF or 3NF.

If we admit that a row in a table represents a statement about the characteristics of a given "thing," indicating that "we don't know" for most characteristics seriously downgrades the table as a source of reliable information. This may be a minor inconvenience if the data is stored for informative purpose only. It becomes a major issue if the unknown values are supposed to help us define a result set, and this state of affairs is indicative of a flawed model. All columns in a row should ultimately contain a value, even if business processes are such that various pieces of information are entered from more than one source and/or at different points in time. A stamp collector might likewise keep some room in an album for a series temporarily absent from the collection. But even so, there is a risk of wasting storage if it is actually reserved because one always tailors for the maximum size. There is also a risk of very serious performance problems if only placeholders are used and data goes to some remote overflow area when it is entered at last.

The existence of null values also raises an important point with regard to relational modeling, which is the main foundation for the query optimizer. The completeness of a relational model is founded on the application of *two-valued logic*; in which things *are* or they *aren't*. Any in-between case, a null value, is indeterminate; but in a `where` clause, conditions cannot be indeterminate. They are true or they are false, because you return a row or you don't; you cannot return a row with a "maybe this one answers the question but I'm not really sure" qualifier. The transition from the *three-valued logic* implied by nulls (true, false, or indeterminate) to the two-valued logic of the result set is perilous. This is why all SQL practitioners can recall cases when what looked like a good SQL query failed to return the proper result set because of an encounter with null values. For instance, if a column named color contains the values RED, GREEN, and BLACK, this condition:

```
where color not in ('BLUE', 'BLACK', null)
```

will result in no row being returned, because we don't know what null is and the SQL engine will consider that there is a possibility that it might be RED or GREEN, whereas:

```
where color in ('BLUE', 'BLACK', null)
```

will return all rows for which color is BLACK, and nothing else (remember, we have no BLUE in our table), since there is a possibility that null would be neither RED nor GREEN. As you can see, an SQL engine is even more risk-averse than a banker. Finding an explicit null inside an in ( ) list is, of course, unusual; but such a situation may occur if, instead of an explicit list, we have a subquery and fail to ensure that no null value is returned by that subquery.

A representation of customers can provide a very good example of the difficulties inherent to dealing with missing information. Each customer has an address, which is normally the address that will appear on an invoice to that customer. But what if the address to which we must ship our goods is different? Must we consider the shipping address to be a characteristic of the order? It can make sense if we sell once, only to never see customers again. If we are not a funeral parlor, however, and especially if we repeatedly ship goods to the same address, it makes no sense at all from a business point of view. Entering the same data over and over again, besides being a waste of time, also increases the risk of a mistake—hence goods get sent to the wrong address, creating a dissatisfied customer or perhaps an ex-customer. The shipping address is, obviously, a characteristic of the customer, not of the order. This situation ought to have been resolved in the analysis of dependencies during the original design of the model.

It is also possible to have the accounting department at a location different from the official, customer delivery address if the customer is a company. So, for one customer, we may have one "official" address, a billing address, and also a shipping address. It is quite common to see customer tables with three sets of columns (each set describing one address) for this purpose.

However, if we *can* have all these addresses, what is likely to be the most common case? Well, it is quite possible that in 90% of the cases we shall have only one useful address, the official address. So, what must we do with all our other columns? Two possibilities come to mind:

Set billing and shipping addresses to null.

This is not a very sound strategy, because this will require our programs to use implicit rules, such as "if the billing address is undefined, then send the invoice to the corporate address." The logic of such programs will become much more complicated, with an increased risk of bugs entering the code.

Replicate the information, copying the corporate address to the billing address columns where there is no special billing address.

This approach will require special processing during data entry, by a trigger perhaps. In such a case the overhead may not matter much, but in another case the overhead might matter a lot. Moreover, we must also take care of replicating *changes*—each update of the corporate address must be replicated to those of the other addresses that are identical, for fear of inconsistency.

Both of these scenarios betray a critical lack of understanding on the part of the original modelers. Using null values and implicit rules is a classic fudge to accommodate three-valued logic. The use of nulls inevitably introduces three-valued logic, which immediately introduces semantic inconsistency; no amount of clever programming can remove semantic issues. Replicating data illustrates what happens when dependencies have not been properly analyzed.

One solution to our address conundrum might be to get the address information out of the `customer` table. One design we may contemplate is to store each address in an `address` table, together with a customer identifier and some column (a bit mask, perhaps) indicating the *role* of the address. But this is not necessarily the best solution, because issues such as the true meaning of addresses often appear after programs have been rushed into production and an attempt to remodel the original data as part of a later release can introduce insuperable problems.

We have so far assumed that we have *one* shipping address for each customer, which may or may not be identical to the corporate, registered address. What if we send our invoices to a single place but must ship our goods to many different branches, with several distinct shipments belonging to the same invoice? This is not necessarily unusual! It is no longer workable for our design to have a single (mostly null) "shipping address" (represented by several columns) in the `customer` table. We are, ironically, back to the "shipping address is a characteristic of the order" situation. This means that if we want to refer (especially repeatedly) to addresses in orders, we must associate some kind of purpose-built identifier to our addresses, which will spare us repeating the whole shipping address in each order (normalization in action). Or perhaps we should begin to contemplate the introduction of a `shipments` table.

There is no such thing as the totally perfect design for the customers/addresses conundrum. I have just wandered through likely problems and tried to sketch some of the possible solutions. But there will be one solution that works best in your case, and many other solutions that will lead to the risks of inconsistencies. With an inappropriate solution, code will be at best more complicated than necessary with very high odds of being underperforming as well.

The question of null values is probably the thorniest issue of the relational theory. Dr. E.F. Codd, the father of the relational model, introduced null values early, and explicitly asked in the 3rd of the 12 rules that he published in 1985 for a systematic treatment of null values. (The 12 rules were a concise definition of the required properties of a relational database.) However, the battle is still raging among theorists. The problem is that "not known" may encompass quite a number of different cases. Let's consider a list of famous writers, each with a birth date and a death date. A null birth date would unambiguously mean "unknown." But what does a null death date mean? Alive? We don't know when this author died? We don't know whether this author is alive or not?

I cannot resist the pleasure of quoting the immortal words of the then–U.S. Secretary of Defense, Mr. Donald Rumsfeld, at a February 2002 news briefing of his department:

> As we know, there are known knowns. There are things we know we know. We also know there are known unknowns. That is to say we know there are some things we do not know. But there are also unknown unknowns, the ones we don't know we don't know.

I don't find it unusual to have null values for, to put it in Rumsfeldese, "known unknowns," attributes that are known to exist and have some value we don't know at one point in time, for various reasons. For the rest, speculating leads nowhere. Strangely, some of the most interesting usages of null values may perfectly involve nothing but tables where all columns of all rows contain values: null values can be generated through outer joins. Some efficient techniques for checking the absence of particular values that I discuss in Chapter 6 are precisely based on outer joins and tests on null values.

Nulls can be hazardous to your logic; if you must use them, be very sure you understand the consequences of doing so in your particular situation.

Qualifying Boolean Columns

Even though the Boolean type doesn't exist in SQL, many people feel a need to implement flags to indicate a Boolean true/false status (for instance `order_completed`). You should aim for increasing the density of your data—`order_completed` may be useful information to know, but then perhaps other information would be nice to store too:

when was it completed? Who completed it? So that means that instead of having a single "Y/N" column, we can have a `completion_date` column, and perhaps a `completed_by` column, both of which will tell us more (although we may not necessarily want to see a null value as long as the order isn't completed; a solution may be to use a distinct table to track the various stages of every order from creation to completion). As before, examine the dependencies in the context of your business requirements, and only include those additional columns where the successful operation of the business requires it.

Alternatively, a series of essentially Boolean attributes can sometimes be advantageously combined into a unique `status` attribute. For instance, if you have four attributes that can be either true or false, you can assign a numerical value between 0 and 15 to each of the possible combinations and define the "status" as being represented by this value. But beware—this technique may offend the basic rule of atomicity, so if you must use this approach, do so with considerable caution.

Data for data's sake is a path to disaster.

Understanding Subtypes

Another reason for the appearance of unnecessarily wide tables (as in having too many attributes) is a lack of understanding of the true relationship between data items. Consider the example of subtypes. A company may have a mix of employees, some of whom are permanent, others who are contractors. They all have several properties in common (name, year of birth, department, room, phone number, and so forth), but there are also properties that are unique to each type of employee (for instance, hire date and salary for permanent employees, rate and contract reference for contractors). The manner in which the common attributes can be shared, while ensuring that the distinctive features are kept separate, introduces the topic of subtypes.

We can model this situation by defining three tables. First, the `employee` table contains all information that is common to every employee, regardless of their status. However, an attribute tells the status of each employee. It has as many distinct values as there are distinct employee types, for example "P" (for permanent employee), and "C" (for contract employee). This table uses an employee number as the primary key.

Next, we create additional tables, one for each employee type. In this case, there are two tables. Tables `permanent` and `contract` represent subtypes of the table `employee`, for example. Each permanent or contract employee inherits certain characteristics from the `employee` table, in addition to possessing unique characteristics, as defined in their own tables.

Now let's examine the creation of the primary keys between these two types of tables, as it's the primary key construct that implements the subtype relationships. The unique key for all tables is the unique identifier for each member of staff—the employee number. The set of primary keys of `employee` is the union of the primary keys of the various subtype tables, and the intersection of the primary keys of all subtype tables is by construction empty, because each employee belongs to just one, in this case, of the two categories. The primary keys of subtype tables are also foreign keys, referencing the primary key of `employee`.

Please note that assigning totally independent primary keys to the subtype tables would, of course, be a disastrous mistake. In the real world however, you will certainly find examples in which this disastrous mistake has been perpetrated. Note also that entity sub-types are *not* the same as master-detail relationships. They can quickly be distinguished on examination of their respective primary keys. For those who would think that this type of discussion is a bit academic (associating with the word "academic" some vague, slightly pejorative connotation), I'll just say that whenever different subtypes use a primary key that is not a subset of the primary key of the parent table, the result is almost invariably pathetic performance, from many points of view.

One of the main principles to follow in order to achieve efficient database access is a principle attributed to Philip II of Macedonia, father of Alexander the Great, and that principle is: *Divide and Rule*. It is quite likely that the vast majority of the queries executed by the HR department will belong to either of two categories: they will be either generic queries about all the people working in an organization or specific queries about one category of person. In both cases, by using subtypes correctly,* we will only need to examine that data which is most likely to provide the result that we require, and no time will be wasted examining irrelevant information. If we were to put everything into a single table, the most modest query would have to plow through a much greater quantity of data, most of which is useless in the context of that query.

Tables in which specific columns appear as null indicate the need for subtypes.

* You can use subtypes incorrectly. As one of the reviewers remarked, having a kind of super-generic parent table that is referred to several times in the most innocuous query isn't a model for efficiency. Such a super-generic parent table is hammered by all queries if it stores vital information. Subtypes must be born of logical distinction, not of an ill-conceived desire to implement with tables a strong inheritance scheme inspired from object-oriented techniques.

Stating the Obvious

It is always an unsound situation in which there are implicit constraints on your data—for instance "if the business line is such, then the identifier is numeric (although defined as a string of characters to accommodate other business lines)," or "if the model is T, then the color is necessarily black." Sometimes, such general knowledge information can prove extremely efficient when filtering data. However, if it remains human knowledge, the DBMS engine, unaware of it, will be unable to take advantage of it, and the optimizer will not possess the necessary information to affect the most efficient database access. In the worst case, implicit constraints can even lead to a runtime failure. For instance, you might inadvertently require the database engine to apply an arithmetic process to a character string. This can happen when a character-defined column is used only for storing numeric data, and a non-numeric character slips in.

As an aside, the example of a string identifier that sometimes contains character data and sometimes numerical data illustrates a confusion over domain definitions in the initial database design. It is quite clear that the nature of such a field varies according to circumstances—which is totally unacceptable in a properly designed database. If we need to store, for instance, configuration parameters of various natures (numerical, Boolean, character, and so on), we should not store them in a single table `configuration(parameter_name, parameter_value)`, but rather use a generic table `configuration(parameter_id, parameter_name, parameter_type)` and have as many subtypes as we have parameter types. If we use, for instance, `configuration_numeric(parameter_id, parameter_value)`, where `parameter_value` is a numeric column, any mistyping of the letter "O" instead of zero will be detected by the DBMS when the configuration is changed, instead of resulting in a runtime error when the parameter is used.

Define all the constraints you can. Primary keys are, of course, a *sine qua non* in a relational database. Use alternate key, when they characterize the data and any type of unique constraints. Foreign keys, which ensure that your data is consistent by mapping to master tables, are vital as part of the comprehensive expression of the meaning of the data model. Constraints that control the range of values that can be entered are also valuable. Constraints have two major impacts:

- They contribute to ensuring the integrity of your data, guaranteeing that everything, as far as defined rules are concerned, is consistent with those rules.
- They provide valuable information about your data to the DBMS kernel, and more specifically to the optimizer. Even if today the optimizer does not make full use of all available constraint data, it is likely that in future releases of the database system, that constraint data will become used for more sophisticated processing by the kernel.

The earlier example of the confusion over multiple shipping and billing addresses is a further example of the way semantic information is lost to the database by a fundamentally weak design. This essential information must therefore be placed into an unpredictable number of application programs. "If the billing address is null, then the headquarters address applies" is a rule that is unknown to the database and must therefore be handled in the programs—note the use of the plural *programs* here! Once again, everything that is defined in the database is defined only once, thus guaranteeing that no program will use the data inconsistently. Implicit rules about, for example, address precedence must be coded into every program accessing the data. Because these implicit rules are totally arbitrary, it is not impossible at all that in some cases the billing address will be the shipping address, and not the headquarters address.

Data semantics belong in the DBMS, not in the application programs.

The Dangers of Excess Flexibility

As always, pushing a line of reasoning to the limits (and often past them) can result in a monument to human madness. A great favorite with third-party software editors is the "more-flexible-than-thou" construct, in which most data of interest is stored in some general purpose table, with equally general purpose attributes such as: `entity_id`, `attribute_id`, `attribute_value`. In this "design," everything is stored as a character string into `attribute_value`. The design certainly avoids the risk of having null values. However, the proponents of this type of design usually store the mandatory attributes in `attribute_value` as well. Their mantra, by the way, is usually that this design approach makes it easy to add new attributes whenever they are needed. Without commenting on the quality of a design that makes it necessary to anticipate the necessarily haphazard addition of attributes, let's just remark that it's all very nice to store data, but usually, somehow, one day you will have to retrieve and process that same data (if data retrieval is not being planned, there is something seriously wrong somewhere). Adding a column to a table really pales into insignificance when compared to writing a program to do something useful with the new bits of information that you are given to manage (as enthusiasts that praise the flexibility of the Extensible Markup Language [XML] are bound to understand).

The database cost of such pseudoflexibility rockets sky-high. Your database integrity is totally sacrificed, because you can hardly have a weaker way of typing your data. You cannot have any referential integrity. You cannot, in fact, have any type of declarative constraints. The simplest query becomes a monstrous join, in which the "value table" is joined 10, 15, or 20 times to the very same entity, depending on the number of attributes one wants to select. Needless to say, even the cleverest optimizer is at a loss on such a query, and performance is what one should expect—dismal. (You can try to improve the performance of such a query as described in Chapter 11, but the SQL code is not a pretty sight.) By comparison, the most inept campaign of military history looks like a masterpiece of strategic planning.

True design flexibility is born of sound data-modeling practices.

The Difficulties of Historical Data

Working with historical data is an extremely common condition—the process of *valuation*, or specifying the price of goods or a service at a particular point in time, is based on historical data—but one of the really difficult issues of relational design is the handling of data that is associated with some *period* (as opposed to point) of time.

There are several ways to model historical data. Let's assume that we want to record the successive prices of goods identified by some `article_id`. An obvious way to do so is to store the following items:

```
(article_id, effective_from_date, price)
```

where `effective_from_date` is the date when the new price takes effect, and the primary key of the historical table is `(article_id, effective_from_date)`.

Logically correct, this type of model is rather clumsy to use when working with *current* data, which in many cases will be our main concern. How are we going to identify the current value? It's the one associated with the highest `effective_from_date`, and it will be retrieved by running a query looking like:

```
select a.article_name, h.price
from articles a,
     price_history h
where a.article_name = some_name
  and h.article_id = a.article_id
  and h.effective_from_date =
     (select max(b.effective_from_date)
      from price_history b
      where b.article_id = h.article_id)
```

Executing this query requires two passes over the same data: one in the inner query to identify which is the most recent date we have for a given article, and one in the outer query to return the price from a row that we have necessarily hit in the inner query (Chapter 6 talks about special functions implemented by some DBMS systems that can avoid, to some extent, multiple passes). Executing repeated queries following this pattern can prove very costly.

However, the choice of how to register the validity period for a price is arbitrary. Instead of storing the effective date from which the price applies, why not store the "end date" (e.g., the last date on which the current price prevails), identifying the time intervals by their upper bound instead of by their lower bound?

This new approach may look like an attractive solution. You have two ways to define current values—either that the end date is undefined, which looks neat but isn't necessarily a good idea, or that the end date is something like December 31, 3000.

It's quite obvious that looking for the price of an article as of December 31, 3000 will take you directly to the row you want, in a single pass. Definitely attractive. Is this the perfect solution? Not quite. There may be some practical worries with the optimizer, which I discuss in Chapter 6, but there is also a major logical issue: prices, as any consumer knows, rarely stay constant, and price increases are not usually decided instantly (financial environments may be something different). What happens when, for example, in October, new prices are decided for the next year and duly recorded in the database?

What we get in our valuation table are two records for each item: one stating the current price, valid until December 31, and one giving the price that will be applied from January 1. If we store the first date when the price applies we will have one row with an `effective_from_date` in the past (for instance January 1 of the current year) and another one in the future (say, the next January 1). In effect, what will define the current price is not the highest date, but the highest date before today (returned in Oracle by the system function `sysdate`). The preceding query needs to be modified only slightly:

```
select a.article_name, h.price
from articles a,
     price_history h
where a.article_name = some_name
  and h.article_id = a.article_id
  and h.effective_from_date =
     (select max(b.effective_from_date)
      from price_history b
      where b.article_id = h.article_id
        and b.effective_from_date <= sysdate)
```

If we store the last day when the price applies, we will have one row with an `end_date` set to December 31 and another with `end_date` set either to null or doomsday. Expressing that we want the price for which the `end_date` is the smallest date after the current date is no obvious improvement on the query just shown.

Denormalization is of course a possible solution—one can imagine storing both the date when a price becomes effective and the date when it ceases to be, or one could also argue for storing the `effective_from_date` and the number of days for which the `effective_from_date` price applies. This could allow using either the start or the end of the period, as best suits the query.

Denormalization always implies taking a risk with data integrity—a minor date entry error can leave black holes when no price is defined. You can of course minimize the risk by adding more checks when data is inserted or updated, but there is always a performance penalty associated with such checks.

Another possible solution is to have a *current* table and a *historical* table and plan a migration of rows from current to historical when prices change. This approach can suit some kinds of applications, but may be complicated to maintain. Moreover, the "pre-recording" of future prices fits rather badly into the picture.

In practice, particular storage techniques such as partitioning, which I discuss in Chapter 5, will come to the rescue, making constructs such as the one using the `effective_from_date` less painful than they might otherwise have been, especially for mass processing.

But before settling for one solution, we must acknowledge that valuation tables come in all shapes and sizes. For instance, those of telecom companies, which handle tremendous amounts of data, have a relatively short price list that doesn't change very often. By contrast, an investment bank stores new prices for all the securities, derivatives, and any type of financial product it may be dealing with almost continuously. A good solution in one case will not necessarily be a good solution in another.

Handling data that both accumulates and changes requires very careful design and tactics that vary according to the rate of change.

Design and Performance

It is flattering (and a bit frightening too) to performance specialists to see the faith in their talents devotedly manifested by some developers. But, at the risk of repeating myself, I must once again stress what I said in the introduction to this book: *tuning* is about getting the best possible performance, now. When we *develop*, we must have a different mindset and not think "let's code it, and then have a specialist tune it later in production." The impact of tuning on the structure of programs is usually nil, and on queries, often minimal once the big mistakes have been corrected. There are indeed two aspects to this matter:

- One aspect of tuning is the improvement of the overall condition of the system, by setting some parameters in accordance with the current resources in terms of CPU power, memory available, and I/O subsystems, and sometimes taking advantage of the physical implementation of the DBMS. This is a highly technical task, which may indeed improve the performance of some processes by a significant factor, but rarely by more than 20 or 30 percent unless big mistakes were made.

- The other aspect of tuning is the modification of specific queries, a practice that may, unfortunately, expose the limitations of the query optimizer and changes of behavior between successive DBMS releases.

That is all there is to it.

In my view, adding indexes doesn't really belong to the tuning of production databases (even if some tuning engagements are sometimes a matter of reviewing and correcting the indexing scheme for a database). Most indexes can and must be correctly defined from the outset as part of the designing process, and performance tests should resolve any ambiguous cases.

Performance is no more a question of making a couple of queries faster than war is a question of winning a couple of battles. You can win a battle and lose the war. You can tune your queries and nevertheless have an application with dismal performance that nobody will want to use, except at gunpoint. Your database and programs, as well as your SQL queries, must all be properly designed.

A functionally correct design is not enough. Performance must be incorporated into the design—and down-stream tuning provides for that little surplus of power that can provide peace of mind.

The single largest contributory factor to poor performance is a design that is wrong.

Processing Flow

Besides all the questions addressed earlier in this chapter, the operating mode is also a matter that may have significant impact on the working system. What I mean by *operating mode* is whether data should be processed asynchronously (as is the case with batch programs) or synchronously (as in a typical transactional program).

Batch programs are the historical ancestors of all data processing and are still very much in use today even if no longer very fashionable; synchronous processing is rarely as necessary as one might think. However, the improvement of networks and the increase in bandwidth has led to the "global reach" of an increasing number of applications. As a result, shutting down your online transaction processing (OLTP) application running in the American Midwest may become difficult because of East Asian users connected during one part of the Midwestern night and European users connected during the other part. Batch programs can no longer assume that they are running on empty machines. Moreover, ever-increasing volumes of data may require that incoming data is processed immediately rather than being allowed to accumulate into unmanageably large data sets. Processing streams of data may simply be the most efficient way to manage such quantities.

The way you process data is not without influence on the way you "think" of your system, especially in terms of physical structures—which I talk about more in Chapter 5. When you have massive batch programs, you are mostly interested in throughput—raw efficiency, using as much of the hardware resources as possible. In terms of data processing, a batch program is in the realm of brute force. When you are processing data on the fly, most activity will be small queries that are going to be repeatedly executed a tremendous number of times. For such queries, performing moderately well is not good enough—they have to perform at the maximum possible efficiency. With an asynchronous program, it is easy to notice that something is wrong (if not always easy to fix): it just takes too long to complete. With synchronous processing, the situation is much more subtle, because performance problems usually show up at the worst moment, when there are surges of activity. If you are not able to spot weaknesses early enough, your system is likely to let you down when your business reaches maximum demand levels—the very worst time to fail.

A data model is not complete until consideration has also been taken of data flow.

Centralizing Your Data

For all the talk about grids, clustered servers, and the like, spreading data across many servers means adding a considerable amount of complexity to a system. The more complicated a structure—any type of structure—the less robust it is. Technological advance does indeed slowly push up the threshold of acceptability. In the eighteenth century, clocks indicating the minutes were considered much less reliable than those indicating only the hour, and much more reliable than those showing the day in the month or the phases of the moon. But nevertheless, try to keep the theater of operations limited to that which is strictly required.

Transparent references to remote data are performance killers, for two reasons. First, however "transparent" it may look, crossing more software layers and a network has a heavy cost. To convince yourself, just run a procedure that inserts a few thousands rows into a local table, and another one doing the very same thing across—for instance, an Oracle database link, even on the same database—you can expect performance to be in the neighborhood of five times slower, if not worse, as you see demonstrated in Chapter 8.

Second, combining data from several sources is extremely difficult. When comparing data from source A to data from source B, you have no choice other than literally copying the data from A to B or the reverse. Transfer is one significant overhead. Data drawn from its own carefully constructed environment no longer benefits from the planning which went into establishing that environment (carefully thought-out physical layout, indexes, and so forth). Instead, that data lands in some temporary storage—in memory if the amount of data transferred is modest, otherwise on disk. The management of temporary storage is another major overhead. In a case where nested loops would be, in theory, the most efficient way to proceed when querying local data, an optimizer is left with two unattractive possibilities when some of the data is remotely located:

- Using nested loops and incurring high overhead with each iteration
- Sucking the remote data in, and then operating against the local copy, which has left all indexes behind

Optimizers can be forgiven for not performing at their best under these circumstances.

When it comes to the placement of major data repositories, some of the art is simply keeping a balance. If your company operates worldwide, keeping all the data at one location is unlikely to be a popular solution with people who live and work at the antipodes. Hitting a remote server is certainly no problem when surfing the Internet—it is quite another matter when using an application intensely. It's not a question of bandwidth, it's a question of light speed, for which, unfortunately, not much improvement can be expected from technological progress. Whatever you do, issuing a query against a server located on another continent adds another quarter or half second to response times, depending on the continent—and this at the best of times. If you need everyone to have the global picture, replication solutions and products (as opposed to remote access) should be contemplated. For each group of players, keep their own chessboard right at hand—don't make players reach.

The nearer you are to your data, the faster you can get at it!

System Complexity

Other points to keep in mind when designing are what will happen if some piece of hardware breaks (for example, a disk controller) or if some mistake is made (for instance, the same batch program is applied twice). Even if your administrators are wizards who are doing night shifts to bring everything back on course by dawn, transfer rates are limited; the recovery of a huge database always takes a lot of time. "Spare" backup databases maintained in synch (or with some slight delay) may help. But backup databases will not be of any use in the case of a program inadvertently run twice, especially if the synchronization delay is shorter than the execution time of the program. What is already complicated with one database becomes a nightmare with several related databases, because you must be perfectly certain that all the databases are correctly synchronized after any recovery, to avoid any risk of data corruption.

This particular point of recovery is often a bone of contention between developers and database administrators, because developers tend to consider, not unreasonably, that backups and recoveries belong to administrators, while administrators point out, logically, that if they can guarantee that the container is in working order, they have no idea about the status of the contents. Indeed, any functional check in case of recovery should not be forgotten by developers. The more complicated the overall design, the more important it is for developers to keep in mind the constraints of operations.

Database systems are joint ventures; they need the active and cooperative participation of users, administrators, and developers.

The Completed Plans

We have reviewed the basic foundations for laying plans in constructing a database system. We have reviewed the fundamentals of data modeling, and in particular the broad steps involved in normalizing data to third normal form. We have then proceeded to review a number of scenarios, in which a faulty design can be identified as the road to disaster.

Most examples in this chapter come directly from or are inspired by cases I have encountered in some big companies. And it is always striking to consider how much energy and intelligence can be wasted trying to solve performance problems that are born from the ignorance of elementary design principles. Such performance issues need not be present, yet they are quite common and often made worse by further denormalization of what is already a questionable design, on the unassailable grounds of "performance improvement." One query may, in fact, run much faster, but unfortunately, the nightly batch program now takes twice as long. In this way, and almost without being noticed, a full information system is built on a foundation of sand.

Successful data modeling is the disciplined application of what are, fundamentally, simple design principles.

CHAPTER TWO

Waging War

Accessing Databases Efficiently

Il existe un petit nombre de principes fondamentaux de la guerre, dont on ne saurait s'écarter sans danger, et dont l'application au contraire a été presque en tous temps couronnée par le succès.

There exist a small number of fundamental principles of war, which it is dangerous to ignore: indeed, following these principles has almost invariably led to success.

—*Général Antoine-Henri de Jomini (1779–1869)*

Précis de l'Art de la Guerre

Anybody who has ever been involved in the switch from development to production of a critical system knows how much it can feel like the noise and tumult of battle. Very often, a few weeks before D-Day, performance tests will show that the new system is going to fall short of expectations. Experts are brought in, SQL statements are fine-tuned, and database and system administrators are called to contribute to a succession of crisis meetings. Finally, performance vaguely comparable to the previous system is obtained on hardware that is now twice as expensive as the original installation.

Tactics are often used as a substitute for a strategic approach. The latter demands the adoption of a sound overall architecture and design. As in war, the basic principles here are also few, but too often ignored. Architectural mistakes can prove extremely costly, and the SQL programmer must enter the battle fully prepared, knowing where to go and how to get there. In this chapter, we are going to review the key goals that will increase our chances of success in writing programs that access databases efficiently.

Query Identification

For centuries, the only means that a general had to check the progress of his troops during the heat of battle was to observe the position of his units as indicated by the color of the soldiers' uniforms and the flags they were carrying. When some process in the database environment is consuming an inordinate amount of CPU, it is often possible to identify which piece of SQL code is actually running. But it is very often much more difficult, especially in a large and complicated system that includes dynamically built queries, to identify which precise part of a given application issued that statement and needs reviewing. Despite the fact that many products have good monitoring facilities, it is sometimes surprisingly difficult to relate an SQL statement to its broader environment. Therefore, you should adopt the habit of identifying your programs and critical modules whenever possible by inserting comments into your SQL to help identify where in the programs a given query is used. For instance:

```
/* CUSTOMER REGISTRATION */ select blah ...
```

These identifying comments can be important and helpful in subsequently tracking down any erroneous code. They can also be helpful when trying to determine how much load is put on a server by a single application, especially when some localized increase in activity is expected and when you are trying to assess whether the current hardware can absorb the surge.

Some products have special registration facilities that can spare you the admittedly tedious step of commenting each and every statement. Oracle's `dbms_application_info` package allows you to register a program using a 48-character module name, a 32-character action name, and a 64-character client information field. The content of those fields is left to your discretion. In an Oracle environment, you can use this package to keep track not only of which application is running, but also what that application is doing at any given time. This is because you can easily query the information that your application passes to the package through the Oracle V$ dynamic views that show what is currently happening in memory.

Identifiable statements make the identification of performance issues easier.

Stable Database Connections

A new database connection can be created quickly and easily, but this ease can disguise the high cost of making repeated connections. You must manage the use of database connections with great care. The consequences of allowing multiple connections to occur, perhaps hidden within an application, can be substantial, as the next example illustrates.

Some time ago I came across an application in which numerous small files of up to an arbitrary maximum of 100 lines were being processed. Each line in these small text files contained both data and the identification of the database instance into which that data had to be loaded. In this particular case, there was a single server, but the principle being illustrated is exactly the same as if there were a hundred database instances.

The process for each file was coded as follows:

```
Open the file
Until the end of file is reached
      Read a row
      Connect to the server specified by the row
      Insert the data
      Disconnect
Close the file
```

This process worked quite satisfactorily, except for the occasional circumstance in which a large number of small files would arrive in a very short space of time, and at a rate greater than the ability of the application to process them. This resulted in a substantial backlog, which took considerable time to clear.

I explained the problem of performance degradation as a consequence of frequent connection and disconnection to the customer with the help of a simple program (written in C) emulating the current application. Table 2-1 gives the results from that demonstration.

NOTE

The program generating the results in Table 2-1 used a conventional `insert` statement. I mentioned in passing to the customer the existence of direct-loading techniques that are even faster.

Test	Results
Connect/disconnect for each line in turn	7.4 lines loaded per second
Connect once, all candidate lines individually inserted	1,681 lines loaded per second
Connect once, all candidate lines inserted in arrays of 10 lines	5,914 lines loaded per second
Connect once, all candidate lines inserted in arrays of 100 lines	9,190 lines loaded per second

TABLE 2-1. *Result of connect/disconnect performance tests*

The demonstration showed the importance of trying to minimize the number of separate database connections that had to be made. Thus, there was an obvious and enormous advantage in applying a simple check to determine whether the "next" insert was into the same database as the previous one. The rationalization could go further, as the number of database instances was of course finite. You could likely achieve further performance gain by setting up an array of handlers, one for each specific database connection, opening a new connection each time a new database is referenced, and thus connecting at most once to each database. As Table 2-1 shows, the simple technique of connecting only once (or a very few times) improved performance by a factor of more than 200 with very little additional effort.

Of course, this was an excellent opportunity to show that minimizing the number of round-trips between a program and the database kernel, using arrays and populating them with incoming data, can also lead to spectacular improvements in performance. By inserting several rows at once, the throughput could be radically improved—by another factor of five. The results in Table 2-1 demonstrate that improvements in the process could reach a modest factor of 1,200.

Why such dramatic improvement?

The reason for the first and biggest improvement is that a database connection is fundamentally a "heavy," or high-resource operation.

In the familiar client/server environment (which is still very widely used), the simple connection routine hides the fact that the client program first has to establish contact with a listener program on a remote machine; and then, depending on whether shared servers are being used on this machine, the listener must either spawn another process or thread and make it run some database kernel program, or hand the request, directly or indirectly, to an existing server process.

Whatever the number of system operations (process spawning or thread creation and the start of executions) your database system will need to create a new environment for each session, to keep track of what it does. Your DBMS will need to check the password provided against the encrypted password of the account for which a new session is to be created. Your DBMS may also have to execute the code for some logon trigger. It may have to execute some initialization code for stored procedures or packages the first time they are called. This does not include the base machine handshaking protocols between client and server processes. This is the reason techniques that allow the upkeep of permanent connections to the database, such as connection pooling, are so important to performance.

The reason for the second improvement is that a round-trip between your program (and even a stored procedure) and the database also has its costs.

Even when you are connected and maintain a connection, context switches between your program and the DBMS kernel take their toll. Therefore if your DBMS allows you to communicate through an *array* interface of some kind, you should not hesitate to use it. If, as sometimes happens, the array interface is implicit (the application program interface [API] uses arrays when you use only scalar values), it is wise to check the default array size that is used and perhaps tailor it to your particular needs. And of course, any row-by-row logic suffers the same context-switch mechanisms and is a cardinal sin—as you shall have several opportunities to see throughout this chapter.

Database connections and round-trips are like Chinese Walls—the more you have, the longer it takes to receive the correct message.

Strategy Before Tactics

Strategy defines the tactics, not the other way round. A skillful developer doesn't think of a process in terms of little steps, but in terms of the final result. The most efficient way to obtain that result may not be to proceed in the order specified in the business rules, but rather to follow a less obvious approach. The following example will show how paying too much attention to the procedural processes within a business can distract ones' attention from the most efficient solution.

Some years ago I was given a stored procedure to try to optimize; "try" is the operative word here. Two attempts at optimization had already been made, once by the original authors, and secondly by a self-styled Oracle expert. Despite these efforts, this procedure was still taking 20 minutes to run, which was unacceptable to the users.

The purpose of the procedure was to compute quantities of raw materials to be ordered by a central factory unit, based on existing stocks and on orders that were coming from a number of different sources. Basically, the data from several identical tables for each data source had to be aggregated inside one master table. The procedure consisted of a succession of similar statements simplified as follows. First, all data from each distinct source table were inserted into the single master table. Second, an aggregate/update was applied to each instance of raw material in that master table. Finally, the spurious data not relevant to the aggregate result was deleted from the table. These stages were repeated in sequence inside the procedure for every distinct source table. None of the SQL statements were particularly complex, and none of them could be described as being particularly inefficient.

It took the better half of a day to understand the process, which eventually prompted the question: why was this process being done in multiple steps? A subquery in a `from` clause with a `union` operator would allow the aggregation of all the various sources. A single `select` statement could provide in one step the result set that had to be inserted into the target table. The difference in performance was so impressive—from 20 minutes down to 20 seconds—that it took some time to verify that the final result was indeed identical to that previously obtained.

Extraordinary skills were not required to achieve the tremendous performance improvement just described, but merely an ability to think outside the box. Previous attempts to improve this process had really been hindered by the participants allowing themselves to get too close to the problem. One needed to take a fresh look, to stand back, and try to see the bigger picture. The key questions to ask were "What do we have when we enter this procedure?" and "Which result do we want when we return from it?" Together with some fresh thinking, the answers to those questions led to a dramatically improved process.

Stand back from your problem to get the wider picture before plunging into the details of the solution.

Problem Definition Before Solution

A little knowledge can be a dangerous thing. Frequently, people may have read or heard about new or unusual techniques—which in some cases can indeed be quite interesting—and then they will try to fit their problem to one of these new solutions. Ordinary developers and architects often jump quickly on to such "solutions," which often turn out to be at the root of many subsequent problems.

At the top of the list of ready-made solutions, we usually meet denormalization. Blissfully unaware of the update nightmare that it turns out to be in practice, denormalization advocates often suggest it at an early stage in the hunt for "performance"—and in fact often at a point in the development cycle when better design (or learning how to use joins) is still an option. A particular type of denormalization, the materialized view, is also often seen as being something of a panacea. (Materialized views are sometimes referred to as *snapshots*, a less impressive term, but one that is closer to the sad reality: copies of data at one point in time.) This is not to say that sometimes, as a last resort option, theoretically questionable techniques cannot be used. To quote Franz Kafka: "Logic is doubtless unshakable, but it cannot withstand a man who wants to go on living."

But the immense majority of problems can be solved using fairly traditional techniques in an intelligent manner. Learn first how to get the best of simple, traditional techniques. It's only when you can fully master them that you will be able to appreciate their limitations, and then to truly be able to judge the potential advantage (if any) of new technical solutions.

All technological solutions are merely means to an end; the great danger for the inexperienced developer is that the attractions of the latest technology become an end in themselves. And the danger is all the greater for enthusiastic, curious, and technically minded individuals!

Foundations before Fashion: learn your craft before playing with the latest tools.

Stable Database Schema

The use of data definition language (DDL) to create, alter, or drop database objects inside an application is a very bad practice that in most cases should be banned. There is no reason to dynamically create, alter, or drop objects, with the possible exception of partitions—which I describe in Chapter 5—and temporary tables *that are known to the DBMS to be temporary tables.* (We shall also meet another major exception to this rule in Chapter 10.)

The use of DDL is fundamentally based on the core database data dictionary. Since this dictionary is also central to all database operations, any activity on it introduces global locks that can have massive performance consequences. The only acceptable DDL operation is `truncate table`, which is a very fast way of emptying a table of all rows (without the protection of rollback recovery, remember!).

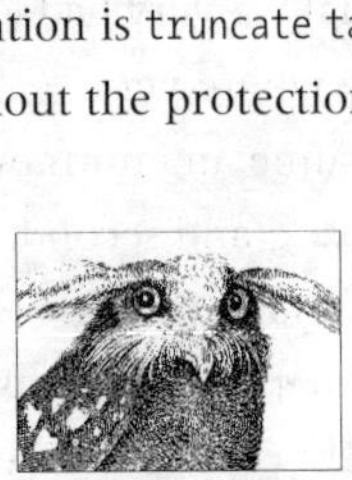

Creating, altering, or dropping database objects belong to application design, not to regular operations.

Operations Against Actual Data

Many developers like to create temporary work tables into which they extract lists of data for subsequent processing, before they begin with the serious stuff. This approach is often questionable and may reflect an inability to think beyond the details of the business processes. You must remember that temporary tables cannot offer storage options of the same degree of sophistication as permanent tables (you see some of these options in Chapter 5). Their indexing, if they are indexed, may be less than optimal. As a result, queries that use temporary tables may perform less efficiently than well-written statements against permanent tables, with the additional overhead of having to fill temporary tables as a prerequisite to any query.

Even when the use of temporary tables is justified, they should never be implemented as permanent tables masquerading as work tables if the number of rows to be stored in them is or can be large. One of the problems lies in the automated collection of statistics: when statistics are not collected in real time, they are typically gathered by the DBMS at a time of zero or low activity. The nature of work tables is that they will probably be empty at such slack times, thus giving a wholly erroneous indicator to the optimizer. The result of this incorrect, and biased, statistical data can be totally inappropriate execution plans that not surprisingly lead to dismal performance. If you *really* have to use temporary storage, use tables that the database can recognize as being temporary.

Temporary work tables mean more byte-pushing to less suitable storage.

Set Processing in SQL

SQL processes data in complete sets. For most `update` or `delete` operations against a database—and assuming one is not operating against the entire table contents—one has to define precisely the set of rows in that table that will be affected by the process. This defines the *granularity* of the impending process, which may be described as *coarse* if a large number of rows will be affected or as *fine* if only few rows will be involved.

Any attempt to process a large amount of data in small chunks is usually a very bad idea and can be massively inefficient. This approach can be defended only where very extensive changes will be made to the database which can, first, consume an enormous amount of space for storing prior values in case of a transaction `rollback`, and second, take a very long time to rollback if any attempted change should fail. Many people would argue that where very considerable changes are to be made, regular `commit` statements should be scattered throughout the data manipulation language (DML) code. However, regular commit statements may not help when resuming a file upload that has failed. From a strictly practical standpoint, it is often much easier, simpler, and faster to resume a process from the start rather than try to locate where and when the failure occurred and then to skip over what has already been committed.

Concerning the size of the log required to rollback transactions in case of failure, it can also be argued that the physical database layout has to accommodate processes, and not that processes have to make do with a given physical implementation. If the amount of undo storage that is required is really enormous, perhaps the question should be raised as to the frequency with which changes are applied. It may be that switching from massive monthly updates to not-so-massive weekly ones or even smaller daily ones may provide an effective solution.

Thousands of statements in a cursor loop for endless batch processing, multiple statements applied to the same data for users doomed to wait, one swoop statement to outperform them all.

Action-Packed SQL Statements

SQL is not a procedural language. Although procedural logic can be applied to SQL, such approaches should be used with caution. The confusion between procedural and declarative processing is most frequently seen when data is required to be extracted from the database, processed, and then re-inserted back into the database. When a program—or a function within a program—is provided with some input value, it is all too common to see that input value used to retrieve one or several other values from the database, followed by a loop or some conditional logic (usually *if...then...else*) being applied to yet other statements applied to the database. In most cases, this behavior is the result of deeply ingrained bad habits or a poor knowledge of SQL, combined with a slavish obsession with functional specifications. Many relatively complex operations can be accomplished in a single SQL statement. If the user provides some value, try to get the result set that is of interest without decomposing the process into multiple statements fetching intermediate results of only minimal relevance to the final output.

There are two main reasons for shunning procedural logic in SQL:

Any access to the database means crossing quite a number of software layers, some of which may include network accesses.

Even when no network is involved, there will be interprocess communications; more accesses mean more function calls, more bandwidth, and more time waiting for the answer. As soon as those calls are repeated a fair number of times, the impact on process performance can become distinctly perceptible.

Procedural means that performance and future maintenance burdens fall to your program.

Most database systems incorporate sophisticated algorithms for executing operations such as joins, and for transforming queries so as to execute them in a more efficient way. Cost-based optimizers (CBOs) are complex pieces of software that have sometimes grown from being totally unusable when originally introduced to becoming mature products, capable of giving excellent results in most cases. A good CBO can be extremely efficient in choosing the most suitable execution plan. However, the scope of operation of the CBO is the SQL statement, nothing more. By doing as much as possible in a single statement, you shift the burden of achieving the best possible performance from your program to the DBMS kernel. You enable your program to take advantage of any improvement to the DBMS code, and therefore you are indirectly shifting a large part of the future maintenance of your program to the DBMS vendor.

As ever, there will be exceptions to the general rule that you should shun procedural logic, where in some cases procedural logic may indeed help make things faster. The monstrous all-singing-and-dancing SQL statement is not always a model for efficiency. However, the procedural logic that glues together successive statements that work on the same data and hit the same rows can often be pushed into one SQL statement. The CBO can consider a single statement that stays close to the sound rules of the relational model as a whole and can execute it in the most efficient way.

Leave as much as you possibly can to the database optimizer to sort out.

Profitable Database Accesses

When you plan a visit to several shops, the first step is to decide what purchases have to be made at each shop. From this point, a trip is planned that will ensure minimum repetitive walking backward and forward between different shops. The first shop is then visited, the purchase completed, and then the next closest shop is visited. This is only common sense, and yet the principle underlying this obvious approach is not seen in the practical implementation of many database programs.

When several pieces of information are required from a single table—even if it appears as if they are "unrelated" (which in fact is unlikely to be the case)—it is highly inefficient to retrieve this data in several separate visits to the database. For example, do not fetch row values column by column if multiple columns are required: do the work in one operation.

Unfortunately, good object-oriented (OO) practice makes a virtue out of defining one method for returning each attribute. But do not confuse OO methods with relational database processing. It is a fatal mistake to mix relational and object-oriented concepts and to consider tables to be *classes* with columns as the *attributes*.

Maximize each visit to the database to complete as much work as can reasonably be achieved for every visit.

Closeness to the DBMS Kernel

The nearer to the DBMS kernel your code can execute, the faster it will run. This is where the true strength of the database lies. For example, several database management products allow you to extend them by adding new functions, which can sometimes be written in comparatively low-level languages such as C. The snag with a low-level language that manipulates pointers is that if you mishandle a pointer, you can end up corrupting memory. It would be bad enough if you were the only user affected. But the trouble with a database server is that, as the name implies, it can serve a large number of users: if you corrupt the server memory, you can corrupt the data handled by another, totally innocent program. As a consequence, responsible DBMS kernels run code in a kind of sandbox, where it can crash without taking everything with it in its downfall. For instance, Oracle implements a complicated communication mechanism between external functions and itself. In some ways, this process is similar to that which controls database links, by which communication between two (or more) database instances on separate servers is managed. If the overall gain achieved by running tightly tailored C functions rather than stored PL/SQL procedures is greater than the costs of setting up an external environment and context-switching, use external functions. But do not use them if you intend to call a function for every row of a very large table. It is a question of balance, of knowing the full implications of the alternative strategies available to solve any given problem.

If functions are to be used, try to always use those that are provided by the DBMS. It is not merely a matter of not reinventing the wheel: built-in functions always execute much closer to the database kernel than any code a third-party programmer can construct, and are accordingly far more efficient.

Here is a simple example using Oracle's SQL that will demonstrate the efficiencies to be gained by using Oracle functions. Let's assume we have some text data that has been manually input and that contains multiple instances of adjacent "space" characters. We require a function that will replace any sequence of two or more spaces by a single space.

Ignoring the regular expressions available since Oracle Database 10*g*, our function might be written as follows:

```
create or replace function squeeze1(p_string in varchar2)
return varchar2
is
  v_string varchar2(512) := '';
  c_char   char(1);
  n_len    number := length(p_string);
  i        binary_integer := 1;
  j        binary_integer;
begin
  while (i <= n_len)
  loop
    c_char := substr(p_string, i, 1);
    v_string := v_string || c_char;
    if (c_char = ' ')
    then
      j := i + 1;
      while (substr(p_string || 'X', j, 1) = ' ')
      loop
        j := j + 1;
      end loop;
      i := j;
    else
      i := i + 1;
    end if;
  end loop;
  return v_string;
end;
/
```

As a side note, 'X' is concatenated to the string in the inner loop to avoid testing j against the length of the string.

There are alternate ways of writing a function to eliminate multiple spaces, which can make use of some of the string functions provided by Oracle. Here's one alternative:

```
create or replace function squeeze2(p_string in varchar2)
return varchar2
is
  v_string varchar2(512) := p_string;
  i        binary_integer := 1;
begin
  i := instr(v_string, '  ');
  while (i > 0)
  loop
    v_string := substr(v_string, 1, i)
                || ltrim(substr(v_string, i + 1));
    i := instr(v_string, '  ');
  end loop;
  return v_string;
end;
/
```

And here's a third way to do it:

```
create or replace function squeeze3(p_string in varchar2)
return varchar2
is
  v_string varchar2(512) := p_string;
  len1     number;
  len2     number;
begin
  len1 := length(p_string);
  v_string := replace(p_string, '  ', ' ');
  len2 :=  length(v_string);
  while (len2 < len1)
  loop
    len1 := len2;
    v_string := replace(v_string, '  ', ' ');
    len2 :=  length(v_string);
  end loop;
  return v_string;
end;
/
```

When these three alternative methods are tested on a simple example, each behaves exactly as specified, and there is no visible performance difference:

```
SQL> select squeeze1('azeryt  hgfrdt   r')
  2  from dual
  3  /
azeryt hgfrdt r

Elapsed: 00:00:00.00
SQL> select squeeze2('azeryt  hgfrdt   r')
  2  from dual
  3  /
azeryt hgfrdt r

Elapsed: 00:00:00.01
SQL> select squeeze3('azeryt  hgfrdt   r')
  2  from dual
  3  /
azeryt hgfrdt r

Elapsed: 00:00:00.00
```

Assume now that this operation of stripping out multiple spaces is to be called many thousands of times each day. You can use the following code to create and populate a test table with random data, by which you can examine whether there are differences in performance among these three space-stripping functions under a more realistic load:

```
create table squeezable(random_text  varchar2(50))
/

declare
    i          binary_integer;
```

```
    j         binary_integer;
    k         binary_integer;
    v_string  varchar2(50);
begin
  for i in 1 .. 10000
  loop
    j := dbms_random.value(1, 100);
    v_string := dbms_random.string('U', 50);
    while (j < length(v_string))
    loop
      k := dbms_random.value(1, 3);
      v_string := substr(substr(v_string, 1, j) || rpad(' ', k)
                  || substr(v_string, j + 1), 1, 50);
      j := dbms_random.value(1, 100);
    end loop;
    insert into squeezable
    values(v_string);
  end loop;
  commit;
end;
/
```

This script creates a total of 10,000 rows in the test table (a fairly modest total when it is considered how many times some SQL statements are executed). The test can now be run as follows:

```
select squeeze_func(random_text)
from squeezable;
```

When I ran this test, headers and screen display were all switched off. Getting rid of output operations ensured that the results reflected the space-reduction algorithm and not the time needed to display the results. The statements were executed several times to ensure that there was no caching effect.

Table 2-2 shows the results on the test machine.

Function	Mechanism	Time
squeeze1	*PL/SQL loop on chars*	0.86 seconds
squeeze2	instr() + ltrim()	0.48 seconds
squeeze3	replace() called in a loop	0.39 seconds

TABLE 2-2. *Time to trim spaces from 10,000 rows*

Even though all functions can be called 10,000 times in under one second, squeeze3 is 1. 8 times as fast as squeeze1, and squeeze2 almost 2.2 times as fast. Why? Simply because PL/SQL is not "as close to the kernel" as is a SQL function. The performance difference may look like a tiny thing when functions are executed once in a while, but it can make quite a difference in a batch program—or on a heavily loaded OLTP server.

Code loves the SQL kernel—the closer they get, the hotter the code.

Doing Only What Is Required

Developers often use count(*) for no purpose other than to implement an existence test. This usually happens as a result of a specification such as:

```
If there are rows meeting a certain condition
Then do something to them
```

which immediately becomes:

```
select count(*)
into counter
from table_name
where <certain_condition>

if (counter > 0) then
```

Of course in 90% of the cases the count(*) is totally unnecessary and superfluous, as in the above example. If an action is required to operate on a number of rows, just do it. If no row is affected, so what? No harm is done. Moreover, if the process to be applied to those hypothetical rows is complex, the very first operation will tell you how many of them were affected, either in a system variable (@@ROWCOUNT with Transact-SQL, SQL%ROWCOUNT with PL/SQL, and so forth), in a special field of the SQL Communication Area (SQLCA) when using embedded SQL, or through special APIs such as mysql_affected_rows() in PHP. The number of processed rows is also sometimes directly returned by the function, which interacts with the database, such as the JDBC executeUpdate() method. Counting rows very often achieves nothing other than doubling your total search effort, because it applies a process twice to the same data.

Further, do not forget that if your purpose is to update or insert rows (a frequent case when rows are counted first to check whether the key already exists), some database systems provide dedicated statements (for instance, Oracle 9*i* Database's MERGE statement) that operate far more efficiently than you can ever achieve by executing redundant counts.

There is no need to code explicitly what the database performs implicitly.

SQL Statements Mirror Business Logic

Most database systems provide monitoring facilities that allow you to check statements currently being executed, as well as to monitor how many times they are executed. At the same time, you should have an idea of how many "business units" are being processed—activities such as orders or claims to be processed, customers to be billed, or anything else that makes sense to the business managers. You should review whether there is a reasonable (not absolutely precise) correlation between the two classes of activities. In other words, for a given number of customers, is the same number of activities being initiated against the database? If a query against the `customers` table is executed 20 times more than the number of customers being processed at the same time, it is a certainty that there is a problem somewhere. This situation would suggest that instead of going once to the table to find required information, repeated (and superfluous) visits are being made to the same rows in the same table.

Check that your database activity is reasonably consistent with the business requirements currently being addressed.

Program Logic into Queries

There are several ways to achieve procedural logic in a database application. It's possible to put some degree of procedurality inside an SQL statement (even if a *statement* should say *what*, and not *how*). Even when using a well-integrated host language within which SQL statements are embedded, it is still preferable to embed as much procedural logic as possible within an actual SQL statement, rather than in the host language. Of the two alternatives, embedding logic in the SQL statement will yield higher performance than embedding it in the application. Procedural languages are characterized by the ability to iterate (loops) and to perform conditional logic (*if...then...else* constructs). SQL doesn't need looping, since by essence it operates on sets; all it requires is the ability to test logically for some conditions.

Obtaining conditional logic breaks down into two components—IF and ELSE. Achieving IF is easy enough—the `where` condition provides the capability. What is difficult is to obtain the ELSE logic. For example, we may need to retrieve a set of rows, and then apply different transformations to different subsets. The case expression (Oracle has also long provided a functionally equivalent operator in `decode( )`*) makes it easy to simulate some logic: it allows us to change on the fly the values that are returned to the result set by testing on row values. In pseudocode, the case construct operates like this:†

* `decode( )` is a bit more rudimentary than case and may require the use of additional functions such as `sign( )` to obtain the same results.

† There are two variants of the case construct; the example shown is the most sophisticated variant.

```
CASE
WHEN condition THEN <return something to the result set>
   WHEN condition THEN <return something else>
...
   WHEN condition THEN <return still something else>
   ELSE <fall back on this value>
END
```

Comparing numerical values or dates is straightforward. With strings, functions such as Oracle's `greatest()` or `least()` or MySQL's `strcmp()` can be useful. It is also sometimes possible to add some logic to `insert` statements, through multiple table inserts and conditional inserts,* and by using the `merge` statement. Don't hesitate to use such statements if they are available with your DBMS. In other words, a lot of logic can be pushed into SQL statements; although the benefit may be small when executing only one of several statements, the gain can be much greater if you can manage to use `case` or `merge` or similar functionality to combine several statements into one.

Wherever possible, try to embed your conditional logic within your SQL statements rather than in an associated host language.

Multiple Updates at Once

My basic assertion here is that successive updates to a single table are acceptable if they affect disjoint sets of rows; otherwise they should be combined. For example, here is some code from an actual application:†

```
update tbo_invoice_extractor
set pga_status = 0
where pga_status in (1,3)
  and inv_type = 0;
update tbo_invoice_extractor
    set rd_status = 0
 where rd_status in (1,3)
   and inv_type = 0;
```

Two successive updates are being applied to the same table. Will the same rows be hit twice? There is no way to tell. The question is, how efficient are the search criteria? Any attribute with a name like `type` or `status` is typically a column with a totally skewed distribution. It is quite possible that both updates may result in two successive full scans of the same table. One update may use an index efficiently, and the second update may result in an unavoidable full table scan. Or, fortuitously, both may be able to make

* Available, for instance, in Oracle since release 9.2.

† Table names have been changed.

efficient use of an index. In any case, there is almost nothing to lose and everything to win by trying to combine both updates into a single statement:

```
update tbo_invoice_extractor
set pga_status = (case pga_status
                    when 1 then 0
                    when 3 then 0
                    else pga_status
                  end),
    rd_status = (case rd_status
                    when 1 then 0
                    when 3 then 0
                    else rd_status
                  end)
where (pga_status in (1,3)
       or rd_status in (1, 3))
  and inv_type = 0;
```

There is indeed the possibility of some slight overhead due to the update of some columns with exactly the same contents they already have. But in most cases, one update is a lot faster than several separate ones. Notice that in regard to the previous section on logic, how we have used implicit conditional logic, by virtue of the case statement, to process only those rows that meet the update criteria, irrespective of how many different update criteria there may be.

Apply updates in one fell swoop if possible; try to minimize repeated visits to the same table.

Careful Use of User-Written Functions

When a user-written function is embedded in a statement, the function may be called a large number of times. If the function appears within the select list, it is called for each returned row. If it appears within the where clause, it is called for each and every row that has successfully passed the filtering criteria previously evaluated. This may be a considerable number of times if the other criteria are not very selective.

Consider what happens if that same function executes a query. The query is executed each time the function is called; in practice, the result is exactly the same as a correlated subquery, except that the function is an excellent way to prevent the cost-based optimizer from executing the main query more intelligently! Precisely because the subquery is hidden within the function, the database optimizer cannot take any account of this query. Moreover, the stored procedure is not as close to the SQL execution engine as is a correlated subquery, and it will consequently be even less efficient.

Now I shall present an example demonstrating the dangers of hiding SQL code away inside a user-written function. Consider a table flights that describes commercial flights, with columns for flight number, departure time, arrival time, and the usual three-letter IATA* codes for airports. The translation of those codes (over 9,000 of them) is stored in a reference table that contains the name of the city (or of the particular airport when there are several located in one city), and of course the name of the country, and so on. Quite obviously any display of flight information should include the name of the destination city airport rather than the rather austere IATA code.

Here we come to one of the contradictions in modern software engineering. What is often regarded as "good practice" in programming is modularity, with many insulated software layers. That principle is fine in the general case, but in the context of database programming, in which code is a shared activity between the developer and the database engine itself, the desirability of code modularity is less clear. For example, we can follow the principle of modularity by building a small function to look up IATA codes and present the full airport name whenever the function is cited in a query:

```
create or replace function airport_city(iata_code in char)
return varchar2
is
  city_name  varchar2(50);
begin
  select city
  into city_name
  from iata_airport_codes
  where code = iata_code;
  return(city_name);
end;
/
```

For readers unfamiliar with Oracle syntax, trunc(sysdate) in the following query refers to today at 00:00 a.m., and date arithmetic is based on days; the condition on departure times therefore refers to times between 8:30 a.m. and 4:00 p.m. today. Queries using the airport_city function might be very simple. For example:

```
select flight_number,
       to_char(departure_time, 'HH24:MI') DEPARTURE,
       airport_city(arrival) "TO"
from flights
where departure_time between trunc(sysdate) + 17/48
                         and trunc(sysdate) + 16/24
order by departure_time
/
```

This query executes with satisfactory speed; on a random sample on my machine, 77 rows were returned in 0.18 seconds (the average of several runs), the kind of time that

* International Air Transport Association.

leaves users happy (statistics indicate that 303 database blocks were accessed, 53 read from disk—and there is one recursive call per row).

As an alternative to using a look-up function we could simply write a join, which of course looks slightly more complicated:

```
select f.flight_number,
       to_char(f.departure_time, 'HH24:MI') DEPARTURE,
       a.city "TO"
from flights f,
     iata_airport_codes a
where a.code = f.arrival
  and departure_time between trunc(sysdate) + 17/48
                         and trunc(sysdate) + 16/24
order by departure_time
```

This query runs in only 0.05 seconds (the same statistics, but there are no recursive calls). It may seem petty and futile to be more than three times as fast for a query that runs for less than a fifth of a second. However, it is quite common in large systems (particularly in the airline world) to have extremely fast queries running several hundred thousand times in one day. Let's say that a query such as the one above runs *only* 50,000 times per day. Using the query with the lookup function, the query time will amount to a total of 2:30 hours. Without the lookup function, it will be under 42 minutes. This maintains an improvement ratio of well over 300%, which in a high traffic environment represents real and tangible savings that may ultimately translate into a financial saving. Very often, the use of lookup functions makes the performance of batch programs dreadful. Moreover, they increase the "service time" of queries for no benefit—which means that fewer concurrent users can use the same box, as you shall see in Chapter 9.

The code of user-written functions is beyond the examination of the optimizer.

Succinct SQL

The skillful developer will attempt to do as much as possible with as few SQL statements as possible. By contrast, the ordinary developer tends to closely follow the different functional stages that have been specified; here is an actual example:

```
-- Get the start of the accounting period
select closure_date
into dtPerSta
from tperrslt
where fiscal_year=to_char(Param_dtAcc,'YYYY')
  and rslt_period='1' || to_char(Param_dtAcc,'MM');
```

```
-- Get the end of the period out of closure
select closure_date
into dtPerClosure
from tperrslt
where fiscal_year=to_char(Param_dtAcc,'YYYY')
  and rslt_period='9' || to_char(Param_dtAcc,'MM');
```

This is an example of very poor code, even if in terms of raw speed it is probably acceptable. Unfortunately, this quality of code is typical of much of the coding that performance specialists encounter. Two values are being collected from the very same table. Why are they being collected through two different, successive statements? This particular example uses Oracle, and a `bulk collect` of the two values into an array can easily be implemented. The key to doing that is to add an `order by` clause on `rslt_period`, as follows:

```
select closure_date
bulk collect into dtPerStaArray
from tperrslt
where fiscal_year=to_char(Param_dtAcc,'YYYY')
  and rslt_period in ('1' || to_char(Param_dtAcc,'MM'),
                      '9' || to_char(Param_dtAcc,'MM'))
order by rslt_period;
```

The two dates are stored respectively into the first and second positions of the array. `bulk collect` is specific to the PL/SQL language but the same reasoning applies to any language allowing an explicit or implicit array fetch.

Note that an array is not even required, and the two values can be retrieved into two distinct scalar variables using the following little trick:*

```
select max(decode(substr(rslt_period, 1, 1), -- Check the first character
                  '1', closure_date,
                       -- If it's '1' return the date we want
                      to_date('14/10/1066', 'DD/MM/YYYY'))),
                       -- Otherwise something old
       max(decode(substr(rslt_period, 1, 1),
                  '9', closure_date, -- The date we want
                      to_date('14/10/1066', 'DD/MM/YYYY'))),
into dtPerSta, dtPerClosure
from tperrslt
where fiscal_year=to_char(Param_dtAcc,'YYYY')
  and rslt_period in ('1' || to_char(Param_dtAcc,'MM'),
                      '9' || to_char(Param_dtAcc,'MM'));
```

In this example, since we expect two rows to be returned, the problem is to retrieve in one row and two columns what would naturally arrive as two rows of a single column each (as in the array fetch example). We do that by checking each time the column that allows

* The Oracle function `decode()` works like `case`. What is compared is the first argument. If it is equal to the second argument, then the third one is returned; if there is no fifth parameter, then the fourth one corresponds to else; otherwise, if the first argument is equal to the fourth one, the fifth one is returned and so on as long as we have pairs of values.

distinction between the two rows, `rslt_period`. If the row is the required one, the date of interest is returned. Otherwise, we return a date (here the arbitrary date is that of the battle of Hastings), which we know to be in all cases much older (*smaller* in terms of date comparison) than the one we want. By taking the maximum each time, we can be ensured that the correct date is obtained. This is a very practical trick that can be applied equally well to character or numerical data; we shall study it in more detail in Chapter 11.

SQL is a declarative language, so try to distance your code from the procedurality of business specifications.

Offensive Coding with SQL

Programmers are often advised to code defensively, checking the validity of all parameters before proceeding. In reality, when accessing a database, there is a real advantage in coding offensively, trying to do several things simultaneously.

A good example is a succession of various checks, designed to flag up an exception whenever the criterion required by any of these checks fails to be met. Let's assume that some kind of payment by a credit card has to be processed. There are a number of steps involved. It may be necessary to check that the customer id and card number that have been submitted are valid, and that they are correctly associated one with the other. The card expiration date must also be validated. Finally, the current purchase must not exceed the credit limit for the card. If everything is correct, the debit operation may proceed.

An unskilled developer may write as follows:

```
select count(*)
from customers
where customer_id = provided_id
```

and will check the result.

Then the next stage will be something like this:

```
select card_num, expiry_date, credit_limit
from accounts
where customer_id = provided_id
```

These returns will be checked against appropriate error codes.

The financial transaction will then proceed.

A skillful developer will do something more like the following (assuming that today( ) is the function that returns the current date):

```
update accounts
set balance = balance - purchased_amount
where balance >= purchased_amount
  and credit_limit >= purchased_amount
  and expiry_date > today( )
  and customer_id = provided_id
  and card_num = provided_cardnum
```

Then the number of rows updated will be checked. If the result is 0, the reason can be determined in a single operation, by executing:

```
select c.customer_id, a.card_num, a.expiry_date,
       a.credit_limit, a.balance
from customers c
     left outer join accounts a
          on a.customer_id = c.customer_id
          and a.card_num = provided_cardnum
where c.customer_id = provided_id
```

If the query returns no row, the inference is that the value of customer_id is wrong, if card_num is null the card number is wrong, and so on. But in most cases this query will not even be executed.

> **NOTE**
>
> **Did you notice the use of count(*) in the first piece of novice code? This is a perfect illustration of the misuse of count(*) to perform an existence test.**

The essential characteristic of "aggressive coding" is to proceed on the basis of reasonable probabilities. For example, there is little point in checking whether the customer exists—if they don't, they won't be in the database in the first place! Assume nothing will fail, and if it does, have mechanisms in place that will address the problem at that point and only that point. Interestingly, this approach is analogous to the "optimistic concurrency control" method adopted in some database systems. Here update conflicts are assumed not to occur, and it is only when they do that control strictures are brought into play. The result is much higher throughput than for systems using pessimistic methods.

Code on a probabilistic basis. Assume the most likely outcome and fall back on exception traps only when strictly necessary.

Discerning Use of Exceptions

There is a thin line between courage and rashness; when I recommend coding aggressively, my model is not the charge of the Light Brigade at Balaclava.* Programming by exception can also be the consequence of an almost foolhardy bravado, in which our proud developers determine to "go for it." They have an overriding confidence that testing and the ability to handle exceptions will see them through. Ah, the brave die young!

As their name implies, exceptions should be exceptional occurrences. In the particular case of database programming, all exceptions do not require the same computer resources—and this is probably the key point to understand if they are to be used intelligently. There are good exceptions, conditions that are raised before anything has been done, and bad exceptions, which are raised only when the full extent of the disaster has actually happened.

For instance, a query against a primary key that finds no row will take minimal resources—the situation is detected while searching the index. However, if the query cannot use an index, then you have to carry out a full table scan before being able to tell positively that no data has been found. For a very large table, a total sequential read can represent a disaster on a machine near maximum capacity.

Some exceptions are extremely costly, even in the best-case scenario; take the detection of duplicate keys. How is uniqueness enforced? Almost always by creating a unique index, and it is when a key is submitted for entry into that index that any constraint violation of that unique index will be revealed. However, when an index entry is created, the physical address of the row must be provided, which means that the insertion into the table takes place prior to the insertion into the index. The constraint violation requires that the partial insert must be undone, together with the identification of the exact constraint violated being returned as an error message. All of these activities carry some significant processing cost. But the greatest sin is trying to fight at the individual exception level. Here, one is forced to think about individual rows rather than data sets—the very antithesis of relational database processing. The consequence of repeated constraint violations can be a serious deterioration in performance.

Let's look at an Oracle example of the previous points. Assume that following the merger of two companies, email addresses are standardized on the *<Initial><Name>* pattern, on 12 characters at most, with all spaces or quotes replaced by an underscore character.

* During the Crimean War of 1854 that saw England, France, and Turkey fight against Russia, a poorly specified order and personal enmity between some of the commanders led more than 600 British cavalry men to charge down a valley in full line of fire of the Russian guns. Around 120 men and half the horses were killed, for no result. The bravery of the men, celebrated in a poem by Tennyson and (later) several Hollywood movies, helped turn a stupid military action into a myth.

Let's assume that a new employee table is created with the new email addresses obtained from a 3,000-row employee_old table. We want each employee to have a unique email address. We must therefore assign, for instance, *flopez* to Fernando Lopez, and *flopez2* to Francisco Lopez (no relation). In fact, in our test data, a total of 33 potential duplicate entries exist, which is the reason for the following result:

```
SQL> insert into employees(emp_num, emp_name,
                               emp_firstname, emp_email)
     select emp_num,
            emp_name,
            emp_firstname,
            substr(substr(EMP_FIRSTNAME, 1, 1)
                  ||translate(EMP_NAME, ' ''', '__'), 1, 12)
     from employees_old;

insert into employees(emp_num, emp_name, emp_firstname, emp_email)
*
ERROR at line 1:
ORA-00001: unique constraint (EMP_EMAIL_UQ) violated


Elapsed: 00:00:00.85
```

Thirty-three duplicates out of 3,000 is about 1%, so perhaps it would be possible to quietly process the conformant 99% and handle the rest through exceptions? After all, it would seem that a 1% load could be accommodated with some additional exception processing which should not be too significant. Following is the code for this optimistic approach:

```
SQL> declare
       v_counter    varchar2(12);
       b_ok         boolean;
       n_counter    number;
       cursor c is  select emp_num,
                           emp_name,
                           emp_firstname
                      from employees_old;
     begin
       for rec in c
       loop
         begin
           insert into employees(emp_num, emp_name,
                                 emp_firstname, emp_email)
           values (rec.emp_num,
                   rec.emp_name,
                   rec.emp_firstname,
                   substr(substr(rec.emp_firstname, 1, 1)
                   ||translate(rec.emp_name, ' ''', '__'), 1, 12));
         exception
          when dup_val_on_index then
            b_ok := FALSE;
            n_counter := 1;
            begin
              v_counter := ltrim(to_char(n_counter));
```

```
            insert into employees(emp_num, emp_name,
                                  emp_firstname, emp_email)
            values (rec.emp_num,
                    rec.emp_name,
                    rec.emp_firstname,
                    substr(substr(rec.emp_firstname, 1, 1)
                      ||translate(rec.emp_name, ' ''', '__'), 1,
                      12 - length(v_counter)) || v_counter);
            b_ok := TRUE;
          exception
           when dup_val_on_index then
             n_counter := n_counter + 1;
          end;
        end;
      end loop;
    end;
    /

PL/SQL procedure successfully completed.

Elapsed: 00:00:18.41
```

But what exactly is the cost of this exception handling? If the same exercise is attempted after removing the "problem" rows, the comparison between the loop with duplicates and the loop without duplicates shows that the cost of processing exceptions in the loop is fairly negligible—with duplicates the procedure also takes about 18 seconds to run. However, when we run the `insert...select` of our first attempt without duplicates it is considerably faster than the loop: we discover that the switch to the one-row-at-a-time logic adds close to 50% to processing time. But in such a case, is it possible to avoid the row-at-a-time process? Yes, but only by avoiding exceptions. It's the decision of dealing with problem rows through exception handling that forced our adoption of sequential row processing.

Alternatively, there might be value in attempting to identify those rows that contain email addresses subject to contention, and assigning those addresses some arbitrary number to achieve uniqueness.

It is easy to determine how many rows are involved in this contention by adding a `group by` clause to the SQL statement. However, assigning numbers might be a difficult thing to do without using the analytical functions available in the major database systems. (Oracle calls them *analytical* functions, DB2 knows them as *online analytical processing*, or OLAP, functions, SQL Server as *ranking* functions.) It is worthwhile to explore the solution to this problem in terms of pure SQL.

Each email address can be assigned a unique number: *1* for the oldest employee whose first name initial and surname result in the given email address, *2* to the second oldest and so on. By pushing this result into a subquery, it is possible to check and concatenate nothing to the first email address in each group, and the sequence numbers (not in the Oracle sense of the word) to the following ones. The following code shows how our logic can be applied:

```
SQL> insert into employees(emp_num, emp_firstname,
                          emp_name, emp_email)
     select emp_num,
            emp_firstname,
            emp_name,
            decode(rn, 1, emp_email,
                          substr(emp_email,
                          1, 12 - length(ltrim(to_char(rn))))
                           || ltrim(to_char(rn)))
     from (select emp_num,
                  emp_firstname,
                  emp_name,
                  substr(substr(emp_firstname, 1, 1)
                    ||translate(emp_name, ' ''', '__'), 1, 12)
                         emp_email,
                  row_number()
                     over (partition by
                            substr(substr(emp_firstname, 1, 1)
                             ||translate(emp_name,' ''','__'),1,12)
                            order by emp_num) rn
           from employees_old)
     /

3000 rows created.

Elapsed: 00:00:11.68
```

We avoid the costs of row-at-a-time processing, and this solution requires only 60% of the original time.

Exception handling forces the adoption of procedural logic. Always try to anticipate possible exceptions by remaining within declarative SQL.

CHAPTER THREE

Tactical Dispositions
Indexing

Chi vuole fare tutte queste cose, conviene che tenga lo stile e modo romano: il quale fu in prima di fare le guerre, come dicano i Franciosi, corte e grosse.

Whoever wants to do all these things must hold to the Roman conduct and method, which was first to make the war, as the French say, short and sharp.

—*Niccolò Machiavelli (1469–1527)*

Discorsi sopra la prima Deca di Tito Livio, II, 6

Once the layout of the battlefield is determined, the general should be able to precisely identify which are the key parts of the enemy possessions that must be captured. It is exactly the same with information systems. The crucial data to be retrieved will determine the most efficient access paths into the data system. Here, the fundamental tactic is indexing. It is a complex area, and one in which competing priorities must be resolved. In this chapter, we discuss various aspects of indexes and indexing strategy, which, taken together, provide general guidelines for database access strategies.

The Identification of "Entry Points"

Even before starting to write the very first SQL statement in a program, you should have an idea about the search criteria that will be of importance to users. Values that are fed into a program and the size of the data subset defined lay the foundations for indexing. Indexes are, above all, a technique for achieving the fastest possible access to specific data. Note that I say "specific data," as indexes must be carefully deployed. They are not a panacea: they will not enable fast access to all data. In fact, sometimes the very opposite is the result, if there is a serious mismatch between the original index strategy and the new data-retrieval requirements.

Indexes can be considered to be shortcuts to data, but they are not shortcuts in the same sense as a shortcut in a graphical desktop environment. Indexes come with some heavy costs, both in terms of disk space and, possibly more importantly, in terms of processing costs. For example, it is not uncommon to encounter tables in which the volume of index data is much larger than the volume of the actual data being indexed. I can say the same of index data as I said of redundant table data in Chapter 1: indexes are usually mirrored, backed up to other disks, and so on, and the very large volumes involved cost a lot, not only in terms of storage, but also in terms of downtime when you have to restore from a backup.

Figure 3-1 shows a real-life case, the main accounting table of a major bank; out of 33 GB total for all indexes and the table, indexes take more than 75%.

Let's forget about storage for a moment and consider processing. Whenever we insert or delete a row, all the indexes on the table have to be adjusted to reflect the new data. This adjustment, or "maintenance," also applies whenever we update an indexed column; for example, if we change the value of an attribute in a column that is either itself indexed, or is part of a compound index in which more than one column is indexed together. In practice this maintenance activity means a lot of CPU resources are used to scan data blocks in memory, I/O activity is needed to record the changes to logfiles, together with possibly more I/O work against the database files. Finally, recursive operations may be required on the database system to maintain storage allocations.

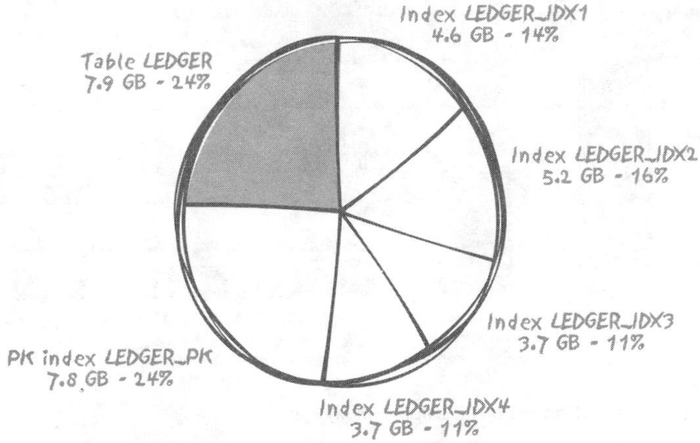

FIGURE 3-1. *A real-life case: Data versus Index out of a 33 GB total*

Tests have quantified the real cost of maintaining indexes on a table. For example, if the unit time required to insert data into a non-indexed table is 100 (seconds, minutes, or hours—it does not really matter for this illustration), each additional index on that table will add an additional unit time of anything from 100 to 250.

Maintenance costs for one index may exceed those for one table.

Although index implementation varies from DBMS to DBMS, the high cost of index maintenance is true for all products, as Figures 3-2 and 3-3 show with Oracle and MySQL.

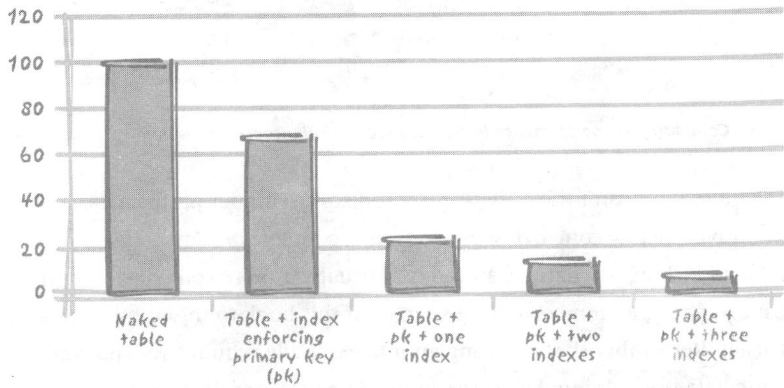

FIGURE 3-2. *The impact of indexes on insertion with Oracle*

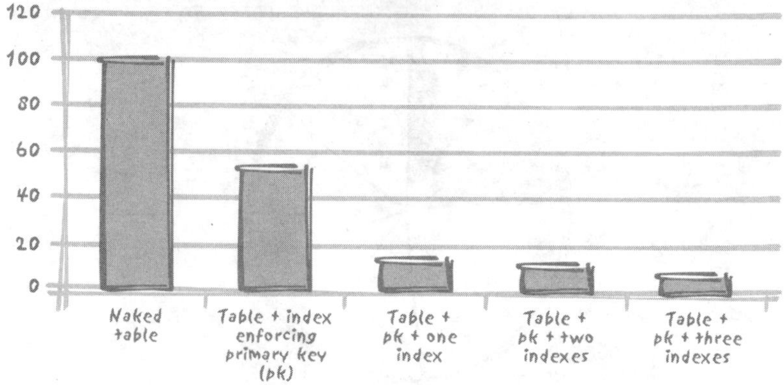

FIGURE 3-3. *The impact of indexes on insertion with MySQL*

Interestingly, this index maintenance overhead is of the same magnitude as a simple trigger. I have created a simple trigger to record into a *log* table the key of each row inserted together with the name of the user and a timestamp—a typical audit trail. As one might expect, performance suffers—but in the same order of magnitude as the addition of two indexes, as shown in Figure 3-4. Recall how often one is urged to avoid triggers for performance reasons! People are usually more reluctant to use triggers than they are to use indexes, yet the impact may well be very similar.

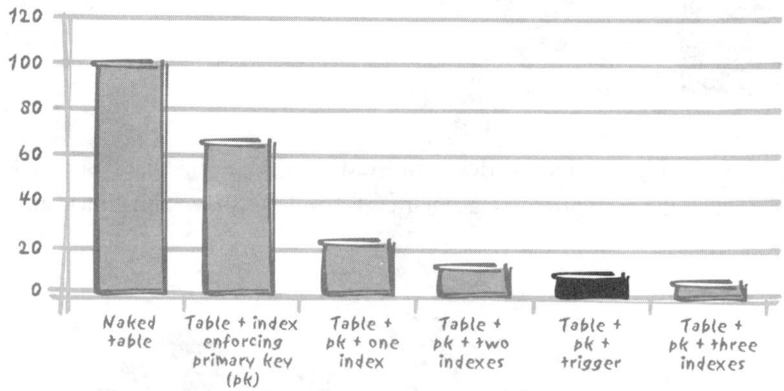

FIGURE 3-4. *Comparing the performance impact of indexes and triggers*

Generating more work isn't the only way for indexes to hinder performance. In an environment with heavy concurrent accesses, more indexes will mean aggrieved contention and locking. By nature, an index is usually a more compact structure than a table—just compare the number of index pages in this book to the number of pages in the book itself. Remember that updating an indexed table requires two data activities: updating the data itself and updating the index data. As a result, concurrent updates, which may affect relatively scattered areas of a huge table, and therefore not suffer from any serialization during the changes to the actual data, may easily find themselves with much less elbow room when updating the indexes. As explained above, these indexes are by definition much "tighter" data assemblages.

It must be stressed that, whatever the cost in terms of storage and processing power, indexes are vital components of databases. Their importance is nowhere greater, as I discuss in Chapter 6, than in transactional databases where most SQL statements must either return or operate on few rows in large tables. Chapter 10 shows that decision support systems are also heavily dependent for performance on indexing. However, if the data tables we are dealing with have been properly normalized (and once again I make no apologies for referring to the importance of design), those columns deserving some *a priori* indexing will be very few in a transactional database. They will of course include the primary key* (the tuple, or row, identifier). This column (or columns in the case of a compound key) will be automatically indexed simply by virtue of its declaration as the primary key. Unique columns are similar and will, in all probability, be indexed simply as a by-product of the implementation of integrity constraints. Consideration should also be given to indexing columns that, although not unique, approach uniqueness—in other words, columns with a high variability of values.

As a general rule, experience would suggest that very few indexes are required for most tables in a general purpose or transactional database, because many tables are searched with a very limited set of criteria. The rationale may be very different in decision support systems, as you shall see in Chapter 10. I tend to grow suspicious of tables with many indexes, especially when these tables are very large and much updated. A high number of indexes may exceptionally be justified, but one should revisit the original design to validate the case for heavily indexed tables.

In a transactional database, "too many indexes" is often the mark of an uncertain design.

Indexes and Content Lists

The book metaphor can be helpful in another respect—as a means of better understanding the role of the index in the DBMS. It is important to recognize the distinction between the two mechanisms of the table of contents and the book index. Both provide a means of fast access into the data, but at two very different levels of granularity. The *table of contents* provides a structured overview of the whole book. As such, it is regarded as complementary to the index device in books, which is often compared to the index of a database.

When you look for a very precise bit of information in a book, you turn to the index. You are ready to check 2 or 3 entries, but not 20—flipping pages between the index and the book itself to check so many entries would be both tedious and inefficient. Like a book index, a database index will direct you to specific values in one or more records (I overlook the use of indexes in range searching for the moment).

If you look for substantial information in a book, you either turn to the index, get the first index entry about the topic you want to study, and then read on, or you turn to the table of contents and identify the chapter that is most relevant to your topic. The distinction between the table of contents and the index is crucial: an entry in a table of contents directs the reader to a block of text, perhaps a chapter, or a section. Similarly, Chapter 5 shows mechanisms by which you can organize a table and enable data retrieval in a manner similar to a table of contents' access.

An index must primarily be regarded as a means of accessing data at an atomic level of granularity, as defined by the original data design, and not as a means of retrieving large quantities of undifferentiated data. When an indexing strategy is used to pull in large quantities of data, the role of indexes is being seriously misunderstood. Indexing is being used as a desperate measure to recover from an already untenable situation. The commander is beginning to panic and is sending off sorties in all directions, hoping that sheer numbers will compensate for the lack of a coherent strategy. It never does, of course.

Be very sure you understand what you are indexing, and why you are indexing it.

Making Indexes Work

To justify the use of an index, it must provide benefit. Just as in our metaphor of the book, you may use an index if you simply require very particular information on one item of data. But if you want to review an entire subject area, you will turn not to the index, but to the table of contents of the book.

There will always be times when the decision between using an index or a broader categorization is a difficult one. This is an area where the use of retrieval ratios makes its persuasive appearance. Such ratios have a hypnotic attraction to many IT and data practitioners because they are so neat, so easy, so very scientific!

The applicability of an index has long been judged on the percentage of the total data retrieved by a query that uses a key value as only search criterion, and conventionally that percentage has often been set at 10% (the percentage of rows that match, on average, an index key defines the *selectivity* of the index; the lower the percentage, the more selective the index). You will often find this kind of rule in the literature. This ratio, and others like it, is based on old assumptions regarding such things as the relative performance of disk access and memory access. Even if we forget that these performance ratios, which have been around since at least the mid-1980s, were based on what is today outdated technology (ideal percentages are grossly simplistic views), far more factors need to be taken into account.

When magical ratios such as our 10% ratio were designed, a 500,000-row table was considered a very big table; 10% of such a table usually meant a few tens of thousand rows. When you have tables with hundreds of millions or even billions of rows, the number of rows returned by using an index with a similar selectivity of about 10% may easily be greater than the number of rows in those mega-tables of yore against which the original ratios were estimated.

Consider the part played by modern hard disk systems, equipped as they are with large cache storage. What the DBMS sees as "physical I/O" may well be memory access; moreover, since the kernel usually shifts different amounts of data into memory depending on the type of access (table or index), you may be in for a surprise when comparing the relative performance of retrievals with and without using an index. But these are not the only factors to consider. You also need to watch the number of operations, which can truly be performed in parallel. Take note of whether the rows associated with an index key value are likely to be physically close. For instance, when you have an index on the insertion date, barring any quirk such as the special storage options I describe in Chapter 5, any query on a range of insertion dates will probably find the corresponding rows grouped together by construction. Any block or page pointed to by the very first key in the range will probably contain as well the rows pointed to by the immediately following key values. Therefore, any chunk of table we return through use of the index will be rich in data of interest to our query, and any data block found through the index will be of considerable value to the query's performance.

When the indexed rows associated with an index key are spread all over the table (for example, the references to an article in a table of orders), it is quite another matter. Even though the number of relevant rows is small as a proportion of the whole, because they are scattered all over the disk, the value of the index diminishes. This is illustrated by Figure 3-5: we can have two unique indexes that are strictly equivalent for fetching a single row, and yet one will perform significantly better than the other if we look for a range of values, a frequent occurrence when working with dates.

Factors such as these blur the picture, and make it difficult to give a prescriptive statement on the use of indexes.

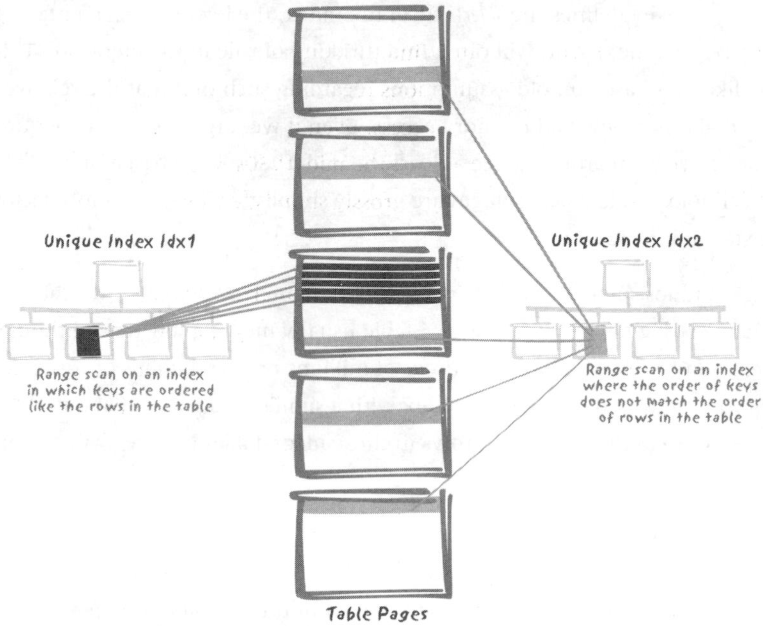

FIGURE 3-5. *When two highly selective indexes may perform differently*

Rows ordered as index keys lead to a faster range scan.

Indexes with Functions and Conversions

Indexes are usually implemented as tree structures—mostly complex trees—to avoid a fast decay of indexes on heavily inserted, updated, and deleted tables. To find the physical location of a row, the address of which is stored in the index, one must *compare* the key value to the value stored in the current node of the tree to be able to determine which sub-tree must be recursively searched. Let's now suppose that the value that drives our search doesn't exactly match an actual column value but can be compared to the result of a function f( ) applied to the column value. In that case we may be tempted to express a condition as follows:

```
where f(indexed_column) = 'some value'
```

This kind of condition will typically torpedo the index, making it useless. The problem is that nothing guarantees that the function f( ) will keep the same order as the index data; in fact, in most cases it will not. For instance, let's suppose that our tree-index looks like Figure 3-6.

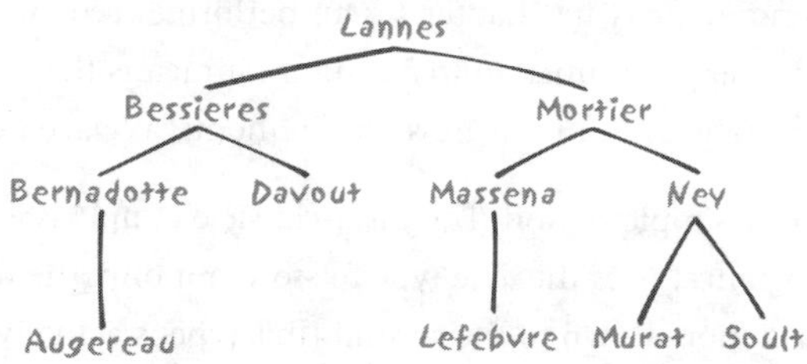

FIGURE 3-6. *A simplistic representation of how names might be stored in an index*

(If the names look familiar, it is because they are those of some of Napoleon's marshals.) Figure 3-6 is of course an outrageously simplified representation, just for the purpose of explaining a particular point; the actual indexes do not look exactly like the binary tree shown in Figure 3-6. If we look for the `MASSENA` key, with this search condition:

```
where name = 'MASSENA'
```

then the index search is simple enough. We hit `LANNES` at the root of the tree and compare `MASSENA` to `LANNES`. We find `MASSENA` to be greater, based on the alphabetical order. We therefore recursively search the right-hand sub-tree, the root of which is `MORTIER`. Our search key is smaller than `MORTIER`, so we search the left-hand sub-tree and immediately hit `MASSENA`. Bingo—success.

Now, let's say that we have a condition such as:

```
where substr(name, 3, 1) = 'R'
```

The third letter is an uppercase *R*—which should return `BERNADOTTE`, `MORTIER`, and `MURAT`. When we make the first visit to the index, we hit `LANNES`, which doesn't satisfy the condition. Not only that, the value that is associated with the current tree node gives us no indication whatsoever as to which branch we should continue our search into. We are at a loss : the fact that the third letter is *R* is of no help in deciding whether we should search the left sub-tree or the right sub-tree (in fact, we find elements belonging to our result set in both sub-trees), and we are unable to descend the tree in the usual way, by selecting a branch thanks to the comparison of the search key to the value stored in the current node.

Given the index represented in Figure 3-6, selecting names with an *R* in the third position is going to require a sequential data scan, but here another question arises. If the optimizer is sufficiently sophisticated, it may be able to judge whether the most efficient execution path is a scan of the actual data table or inspecting, in turn, each and every node in the index on the column in question. In the latter case, the search would lead to an index-based retrieval, but not as envisaged in the original model design since we would be using the index in a rather inefficient way.

Recall the discussion on atomicity in Chapter 1. Our performance issue stems from a very simple fact: if we need to apply a function to a column, it means that the atomicity of data in the table isn't suitable for our business requirements. We are not in 1NF!

Atomicity, though, isn't a simple notion. The ultra-classic example is a search condition on dates. Oracle, for instance, uses the `date` type to store not only the date information, but also the time information, down to the second (this type is actually known as `datetime` to most other database systems). However, to test the unwary, the default date format doesn't display the time information. If you enter something such as:

```
where date_entered = to_date('18-JUN-1815',
                             'DD-MON-YYYY')
```

then only the rows for which the date (and time!) happens to be *exactly* the 18th of June 1815 at 00:00 (i.e., at midnight) are returned. Everyone gets caught out by this issue the very first time that they query datetime data. Quite naturally, the first impulse is to suppress the time information from `date_entered`, which the junior practitioners usually do in the following way:

```
where trunc(date_entered) = to_date('18-JUN-1815',
                                    'DD-MON-YYYY')
```

Despite the joy of seeing the query "work," many people fail to realize (before the first performance issues begin to arise) that by writing their query in such a way they have waved goodbye to using the index on `date_entered`, assuming there was one. Does all this mean that you cannot be in 1NF if you are using `datetime` columns? Fortunately, no. In Chapter 1, I defined an atomic attribute as an attribute in which a `where` clause can always be referred to in full. You can refer in full to a date if you are using a range condition. An index on `date_entered` is usable if the preceding condition is written as:

```
where date_entered >= to_date('18-JUN-1815',
                              'DD-MON-YYYY')
  and date_entered < to_date('19-JUN-1815',
                             'DD-MON-YYYY')
```

Finding rows with a given date in this way makes an index on `date_entered` usable, because the very first condition allows us to descend the tree and reach a sorted list of all keys at the bottom of the index hierarchy (we may envision the index as a sorted list of keys and associated addresses, above which is plugged a tree allowing us to get direct access to every item in the list). Therefore, once the first condition has taken us to the bottom layer of the index and to the very first item of interest in the list, all we have to do is scan the list as long as the second condition is true. This type of access is known as an *index range scan*.

The trap of functions preventing the use of indexes is often even worse if the DBMS engine is able to perform *implicit* conversions when a column of a given type is equated or compared to a constant of another type in a `where` condition—a logical error and yet one that is allowed by SQL. Once again Oracle provides an excellent example of such behavior. For instance, dangers arise when a character column is compared to a number. Instead of immediately generating a run-time error, Oracle implicitly converts the column to a number to enable the comparison to take place. The conversion may indeed generate a run-time error if there is an alpha character in that numerical string, but in many cases when a string of digits without any true numerical meaning is stored as characters (social security numbers or a date of birth shown as *mmddyy*, or *ddmmyy*, both meaning the same, but having very different numerical values), the conversion and subsequent comparison will "work"—except that the conversion will have rendered any index on the character column almost useless.

In the light of the neutralization of indexes by functions, Oracle's design choice to apply the conversion to the column rather than to the constant may at first look surprising. However, that decision does make some sense. First of all, comparing potatoes to carrots is a logical error. By applying the conversion to the column, the DBMS is more likely (depending on the execution path) to encounter a value to which the conversion does not apply, and therefore the DBMS is more likely to generate a runtime error. An error at this stage of the process will prove a healthy reminder to the developer, doubtless prompting for a correction in the actual data field and raising agonizing questions about the quality of the data. Second, assuming that no error is generated, the very last thing we want is to return incorrect information. If we encounter:

```
where account_number = 12345
```

it is quite possible, and in fact most likely, that the person who wrote the query was expecting the account `0000012345` to be returned—which will be the case if `account_number` (the alpha string) is converted to number, but not if the query `12345` is converted to a string without any special format specification.

One may think that implicit conversions are a rare occurrence, akin to bugs. There is much truth in the latter point, but implicit conversions are in fact pretty common, especially when such things come into play as a `parameters` table holding in a column named `parameter_value` string representations of numbers and dates, as well as filenames or any other regular character string. Always make conversions explicit by using conversion functions.

It is sometimes possible to index the *result* of a function applied to one or more columns. This facility is available with most products under various names (*functional index*, *function-based index*, *index extension*, and so on, or, more simply, *index on a computed column*). In my view, one should be careful with this type of feature and use it only as a standby for those cases in which the code cannot be modified.

I have already mentioned the heavy overhead added to data modifications as a result of the presence of indexes. Calling a function in addition to the normal index load each time an index needs to be modified cannot improve the situation: indeed it only adds to the total index maintenance cost. As the `date_entered` example given earlier demonstrates, creating a function-based index may be the lazy solution to something that can easily be remedied by writing the query in a different way. Furthermore, nothing guarantees that a function applied to a column retains the same degree of precision that a query against the raw column will achieve. Suppose that we store five years of sales online and that the `sales_date` column is indexed. On the face of it, such an index looks like an efficient one. But indexing with a function that is the month part of the date is not necessarily very selective, especially if every year the bulk of sales occurs in the run up to Christmas. Evaluating whether the resulting functional index will really bring any benefit is not necessarily easy without very careful study.

From a purely design point of view, one can argue that a function is an implicit recognition that the column in question may be storing two or more discrete items of data. Use of a functional index is, in most cases, a way to extract some part of the data from a column. As pointed out earlier, we are violating the famous first normal form, which requires data to be "atomic." Not using strictly "atomic" data in the *select list* is a forgivable sin. Repeatedly using "subatomic" search criteria is a deadly one.

There are some cases, though, when a function-based index may be justified. Case-insensitive searches are probably the best example; indexing a column converted to upper- or lowercase will allow us to perform case-insensitive searches on that column efficiently. That said, forcing the case during `inserts` and `updates` is not a bad solution either. In any event, if data is stored in lowercase, then required in uppercase, one has to question the thoroughness with which the original data design was carried out.

Another tricky conundrum is the matter of duration in the absence of a dedicated `interval` data type. Given three time fields, a start date, a completion date, and a duration, one value can be determined from any existing two—but only by either building a functional index or by storing redundant data. Whichever solution is followed, redundancy will be the inevitable consequence: in the final analysis, you must weigh the benefits and disadvantages of the issues surrounding function-based indexes so that you can make informed decisions about using them.

Use of functional indexes is often implicit recognition that your data analysis has not even resolved basic data item atomicity.

Indexes and Foreign Keys

It is quite customary to systematically index the foreign keys of a table; and it is widely acknowledged to be common wisdom to do so. In fact, some design tools automatically generate indexes on these keys, and so do some DBMS. However, I urge caution in this respect. Given the overall cost of indexes, unnecessarily indexing foreign keys may prove a mistake, especially for a table that has many foreign keys.

NOTE

Of course, if your DBMS automatically indexes foreign keys, then you have no choice in the matter. You will have to resign yourself to potentially incurring unnecessary index overhead.

The rule of indexing the foreign keys comes from what happens when (for example) a foreign key in table A references the primary key in table B, and then both tables are concurrently modified. The simple model in Figure 3-7 illustrates this point.

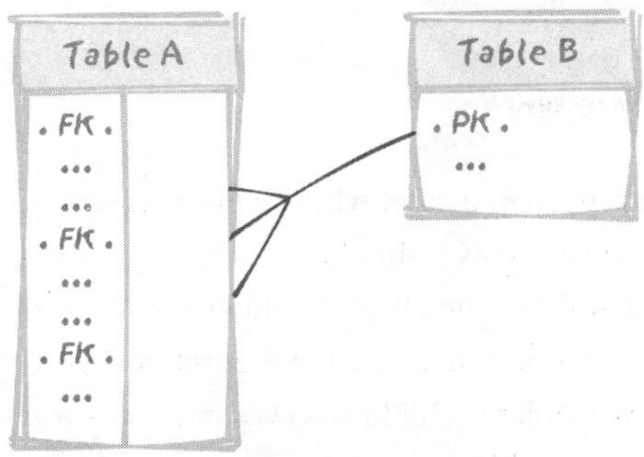

FIGURE 3-7. *The simple, Master-Detail example*

Imagine that table A is very large. If user U1 wants to remove a row from table B, since the primary key for B is referenced by a foreign key in A, the DBMS must check that removal of the row will not lead to inconsistencies in the intertable dependencies, and must therefore see whether there is any child row in A referencing the row about to be deleted from B. If there does happen to be a row in A that references our row in B, then the deletion must fail, because otherwise we would end up with an orphaned row and inconsistent data. If the foreign key in A is indexed, it can be checked very quickly. If it is not indexed, it will take a significant period of time since the session of user U1 will have to scan all of table A.

Another problem is that we are not supposed to be alone on this database, and lots of things can happen while we scan A. For instance, just after user U1 has started the hunt in table A for an hypothetical child row, somebody else, say user U2, may want to insert a new row into table A which references that very same row we want to delete from table B.

This situation is described in Figure 3-8, with user U1 first accessing table B to check the identifier of the row it wants to delete *(1)*, and then searching for a child in table A *(2)*. Meanwhile, U2 will have to check that the parent row exists in table B. But we have a primary key index on B, which means that unlike user U1, who is condemned to a slow sequential scan of the foreign key values of table A, user U2 will get the answer immediately from table B. If U2 quietly inserts the new row in table A *(3)*, U2 may commit the change at such a point that user U1 finishes checking and wrongly concludes, having found no row, that the path is clear for the `delete`.

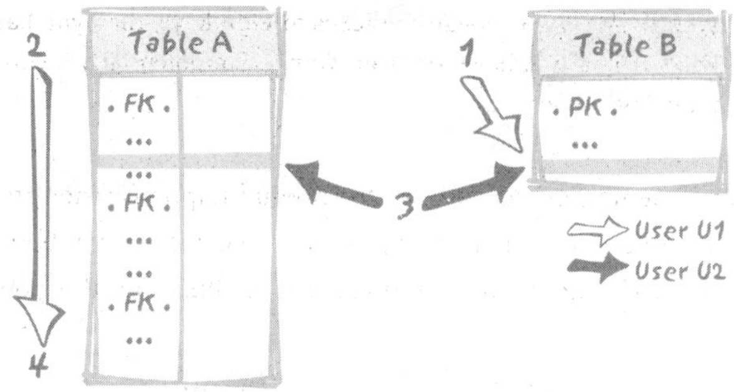

FIGURE 3-8. *Fight for the primary key*

Locking is required to prevent such a case, which would otherwise irremediably lead to inconsistent data. Data integrity is, as it should be, one of the prime concerns of an enterprise-grade DBMS. It will take no chance. Whenever we want to delete a row from table B, we must prevent insertion into any table that references B of a row referencing that particular one while we look for child rows. We have two ways to prevent insertions into referencing tables (there may be several ones) such as table A:

- We lock all referencing tables (the heavy-handed approach).
- We apply a lock to table B and make another process, such as U2, wait for this lock to be released before inserting a new row into a referencing table (the approach taken by most DBMS). The lock will apply to the table, a page, or the row, depending on the granularity allowed by the DBMS.

In any case, if foreign keys are not indexed, checking for child rows will be slow, and we will hold locks for a very long time, potentially blocking many changes. In the worst case of the heavy-handed approach we can even encounter deadlocks, with two processes holding locks and stubbornly refusing to release them as long as the other process doesn't release its lock first. In such a case, the DBMS usually solves the dispute by killing one of the processes (hasta la vista, baby...) to let the other one proceed.

The case of concurrent updates therefore truly requires indexing foreign keys to prevent sessions from locking objects much longer than necessary. Hence the oft heard rule that "foreign keys should always be indexed." The benefit of indexing the foreign key is that the elapsed time for each process can be drastically reduced, and in turn locking is reduced to the minimum level required for ensuring data integrity.

What people often forget is that "always index foreign keys" is a rule associated with a special case. Interestingly, that special case often arises from design quirks, such as the maintenance of summary or aggregate denormalized columns in the master table of a master/detail relationship. There may be excellent reasons for updating concurrently two tables linked by referential integrity constraints. But there are also many cases with transactional databases where the referenced table is a "true" reference table (e.g., a dictionary, or "look-up" table that is very rarely updated, or it's updated in the middle of the night when there is no other activity). In such a case, the only justification for the creation of an index on the foreign key columns should be whether such an index would be of any benefit from a strictly performance standpoint. We mustn't forget the heavy penalty performance imposed by index maintenance. There are many cases when an index on a foreign key is not required.

There must be a reason behind indexing; this is as true of foreign keys as of other columns.

Multiple Indexing of the Same Columns

The systematic indexing of foreign keys can often lead to situations in which columns belong to several indexes. Let's consider once again a classic example. This consists of an ordering system in which some `order_details` table contains, for each order (identified by an `order_id`, a foreign key referencing the `orders` table) articles (identified by `article_id`, a foreign key referencing the `articles` table) that have been purchased, and in what quantity. What we have here is an associative table (`order_details`) resolving a many-to-many relationship between the tables `orders` and `articles`. Figure 3-9 illustrates the relationships among the three tables.

FIGURE 3-9. *The Orders/Articles example*

Typically, the primary key of `order_details` will be a composite key, made of the two foreign keys. Order entry is the very case when the referenced table and the referencing table are likely to be concurrently modified, and therefore we *must* index the `order_id` foreign key. However, the column that is defined here as a foreign key is *already* indexed as part of the composite primary key, and (this is the important point) as the very first column in the primary key. Since this column is the first column of the composite primary key, it can for all intents and purposes provide all the benefits as if it were an indexed foreign key. A composite index is perfectly usable even if not all columns in the key are specified, as long as those *at the beginning of the key* are.

When descending an index tree such as the one described earlier in this chapter, it is quite sufficient to be able to compare the leading characters of the key to the index nodes to determine which branch of the index the search should continue down. There is therefore no reason to index `order_id` alone, since the DBMS will be able to use the index on `(order_id, article_id)` to check for child rows when somebody is working on the `orders` table. Locks will therefore not be required for both tables. Note, once again, that this reasoning applies only because `order_id` happens to be the very first column in the composite primary key. Had the primary key been defined as `(article_id, order_id)`, then we would have had to create an index on `order_id` alone, while not building an index on the other foreign key, `article_id`.

Indexing every foreign key may result in redundant indexing.

System-Generated Keys

System-generated keys (whether through a special number column defined as self-incrementing or through the use of system-generated counters such as Oracle's sequences) require special care. Some inexperienced designers just love system-generated keys even when they have perfectly valid natural identifiers at their disposal. System-generated sequential numbers are certainly a far better solution than looking for the greatest current value and incrementing it by one (a certain recipe for generating duplicates in an environment with some degree of concurrency), or storing a "next value" that has to be locked and updated into a dedicated table (a mechanism that serializes and dramatically slows down accesses). Nevertheless, when many concurrent insertions are running against the same table in which these automatic keys are being generated, some very serious contention can occur at the creation point of the primary key index level. The purpose of the primary key index is primarily to ensure the uniqueness of the primary key columns.

The problem is usually that if there is one unique generator (as opposed to as many generators as there are concurrent processes, hitting totally disjoint ranges of values) we are going to rapidly generate numbers that are in close proximity to each other. As a result, when trying to insert key values into the primary key index, all processes are going to converge on the same index page, and the DBMS engine will have to serialize—through locks, latches, semaphores, or whichever locking mechanism is at its disposal—the various processes so that each one does not try to overwrite the bytes that another one is writing to. This is a typical example of contention that leads to some severe underuse of the hardware. Processes that could and should work in parallel have to wait in order, one behind the other. This bottleneck can be particularly severe on multi-processor machines, the very environment in which parallelism should be operating.

Some database systems provide some means to reduce the impact of system-generated keys; for instance, Oracle allows you to define *reverse indexes,* indexes in which the sequence of bits making up the key is inversed before being stored into the index. To indicate a very approximate idea of what such an index looks like, let's simply take the same names of marshals as we did in Figure 3-5 and reverse the letters instead of bits. We get something looking like Figure 3-10.

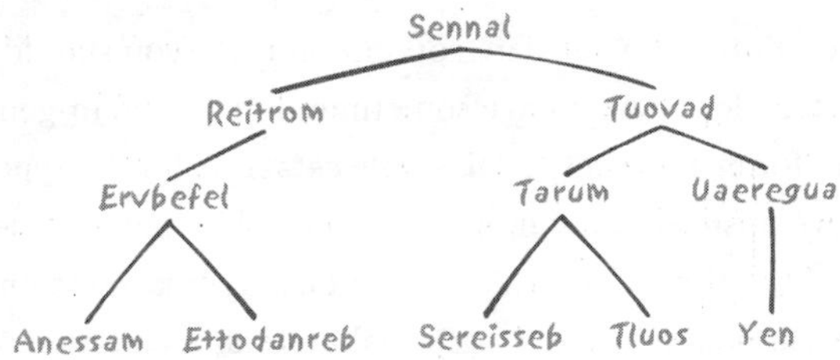

FIGURE 3-10. *A simplified representation of reverse indexing*

It is easy to understand that even when we insert names that are alphabetically very close to one another, they are spread all over the various branches of the index tree: look for instance at the respective positions of `MASSENA` (a.k.a. `ANESSAM`), `MORTIER` (`REITROM`) and `MURAT` (`TARUM`). Therefore, we hit different places in the index and have much less contention than with a normally organized index. Close grouping of the index values would lead to a very high write activity that is very localized within the index. Before searching, Oracle simply applies the same reversing to the value we want to search against, and then proceeds as usual to traverse the index tree.

Of course, every silver lining has its cloud: when our search condition attempts to use a leading string search like this:

```
where name like 'M%'
```

which is a typical range search, the reverse index is no help at all. By contrast, a regular index can be used to quickly identify the range of values beginning with a certain string that we are interested in. The inability of reverse indexes to be used for range searches is, of course, a very minor inconvenience with system-generated keys, which are often unknown to end users and therefore unlikely to be the object of range scans. But it becomes a major hindrance when rows contain timestamps. Timestamped rows might arrive in close succession, making the timestamp column a potentially good candidate for reverse indexing, but then a timestamp is also the type of column against which we are quite likely to be looking for ranges of values.

The hash index used in some database systems represents a different way to avoid bottlenecking index updates all on one index page. With hash indexing, the actual key is transformed into a meaningless, randomly distributed numeric key generated by the system, which is based on the column value being indexed. Although it is not impossible for two values to be transformed into similar, meaningless keys, two originally "close" keys will normally hash into two totally disconnected values. Once again, hash indexes represent a trick to avoid having a *hot spot* inside an index tree, but that benefit too, comes with certain restrictions. The use of a hash index is on an "equality or nothing" basis; in other words, range searching, or indeed any query against a part of the index key, is out of the question. Nevertheless, direct access based on one particular value of the key can be very fast.

Even when there are solutions to alleviate contention risks, you should not create too many system-generated identifiers. I have sometimes found system-generated keys in each and every table (for instance a special, single `detail_id` for the type of `order_details` table mentioned above, instead of the more natural combination of `order_id` and some sequential number within the order). This blunderbuss approach is something that, by any standard, simply cannot be justified—especially for tables that are referenced by no other table.

System-generated keys can provide benefit in the right circumstances, but beware of their indiscriminate use!

Variability of Index Accesses

It is very common to believe that if indexes are used in a query, then everything is fine. This is a gross misconception: there are many different characteristics of index access. Obviously, the most efficient type of index access is through a unique index, in which, at most, one row matches a given search value. Typically, such a search operation might be based on the primary key. However, as you saw in Chapter 2, accessing a table through its primary key may be very bad—if you are looping on all key values. Such an approach would be like using a teaspoon to move a big heap of sand instead of the big shovel of a full scan. So, at the tactical level, the most efficient index access is through a unique index, but the wider picture may reveal that this could be a costly mistake.

When several rows may match a single key value in a non-unique index (or when we search on a range of distinct values against a unique index), then we enter the world of range scanning. In this situation, we may retrieve a series of row addresses from the index, all containing the key values we are looking for. It may be a near-unique index, in which all key values match one row with the exception of a handful of values that match very few rows. Or it may be the other extreme of the non-unique indexed column for which all rows contain the same value. Indexed columns in which all rows contain the same value are in fact something you occasionally find with off-the-shelf software packages in which most columns are indexed, just in case. Never forget that finding the row in the index is all the work that is required only if:

1. You need no other information than data that is part of the index key.
2. The index is not compressed; otherwise, finding a match in the index is nothing more than a presumption that must be corroborated by the actual value found in the table.

In all other cases, we are only halfway to meeting the query requirement, and we must now access each data block (or page) by the address that is provided by the search of the index. Once again, all other things being equal, we may have widely different performance, depending on whether we shall find the rows matching our search value lumped together in the same area of the disk, or scattered all over the place.

The preceding description applies to the "regular" index accesses. However, a clever query optimizer may decide to use indexes in another way. It could operate on several indexes, combining them and doing some kind of pre-filtering before fetching the rows. It may decide to execute a full scan of a particular index, a strategy based on the judgment that this is the most efficient of all available methods for this particular query (we won't go into the subtleties of what "most efficient" means here). The query optimizer may decide to systematically collect row addresses from an index, without taking the trouble to descend the index tree.

So, any reference to an index in an execution plan is far from meaning that "all's well that runs well." Some index accesses may indeed be very fast—and some desperately slow. Even a fast access in a query is no guarantee that by combining the query with another one, we could have got the result even faster. In addition, if the optimizer is indeed smart enough to ignore a useless index in queries, that same useless index will nevertheless require to be maintained whenever the table contents are modified. This index maintenance is something that may be especially significant in the massive uploads or purges routinely performed by a batch program. Useful or useless, an index *has* to be maintained.

Indexing is not a panacea: effective deployment rests on your complete understanding of the data you are dealing with and making the appropriate judgments.

CHAPTER FOUR

Maneuvering

Thinking SQL Statements

There is only one principle of war, and that's this. Hit the other fellow, as quickly as you can, as hard as you can, where it hurts him most, when he ain't lookin'.

—Field Marshal Sir William Slim (1891–1970)

quoting an anonymous Sergeant-Major

In this chapter, we are going to take a close look at the SQL query and examine how its construct can vary according to the tactical demands of particular situations. This will involve examining complex queries and reviewing how they can be decomposed into a succession of smaller components, all interdependent, and all contributing to a final, complete query.

The Nature of SQL

Before we begin examining query constructs in detail, we need to review some of the general characteristics of SQL itself: how it relates to the database engine and the associated optimizer, and what may limit the efficiency of the optimizer.

SQL and Databases

Relational databases owe their existence to pioneering work by E.F. Codd on the relational theory. From the outset, Codd's work provided a very strong mathematical basis to what had so far been a mostly empirical discipline. To make an analogy, for thousands of years mankind has built bridges to span rivers, but frequently these structures were grossly overengineered simply because the master builders of the time didn't fully understand the true relationships between the materials they used to build their bridges, and the consequent strengths of these bridges. Once the science of civil engineering developed a solid theoretical knowledge of material strengths, bridges of a far greater sophistication and safety began to emerge, demonstrating the full exploitation of the various construction materials being used. Indeed, the extraordinary dimensions of some modern bridges reflect the similarly huge increase in the data volumes that modern DBMS software is able to address. Relational theory has done for databases what civil engineering has done for bridges.

It is very common to find confusion between the SQL language, databases, and the relational model. The function of a database is primarily to store data according to a model of the part of the real world from which that data has been obtained. Accordingly, a database must provide a solid infrastructure that will allow multiple users to make use of that same data, without, at any time, prejudicing the integrity of that data when they change it. This will require the database to handle contention between users and, in the extreme case, to keep the data consistent if the machine were to fail in mid-transaction. The database must also perform many other functions outside the scope of this book.

As its name says, Structured Query Language, or SQL for short, is nothing other than a language, though admittedly with a very tight coupling to databases. Equating the SQL language with relational databases—or even worse with the relational theory—is as misguided as assuming that familiarity with a spreadsheet program or a word processor is indicative of having mastered "information technology." In fact, some products that are not databases support SQL,* and before becoming a standard SQL had to compete against other languages such as RDO or QUEL, which were considered by many theorists to be superior to SQL.

Whenever you have to solve what I shall generically call an *SQL problem*, you must realize that there are two components in action: the SQL expression of the query and the database optimizer. These two components interact within three distinct zones, as shown in Figure 4-1. At the center lies the relational theory, where mathematicians freely roam. If we simplify excessively, we can say that (amongst other useful things) the theory informs us that we can retrieve data that satisfies some criteria by using a handful of relational operators, and that these operators will allow us to answer basically any question. Most importantly, because the relational theory is so firmly grounded in mathematics, we can be totally confident that relational expressions can be written in different ways and yet return the same result. In exactly the same way, arithmetic teaches us that 246/369 is exactly the same as 2/3.

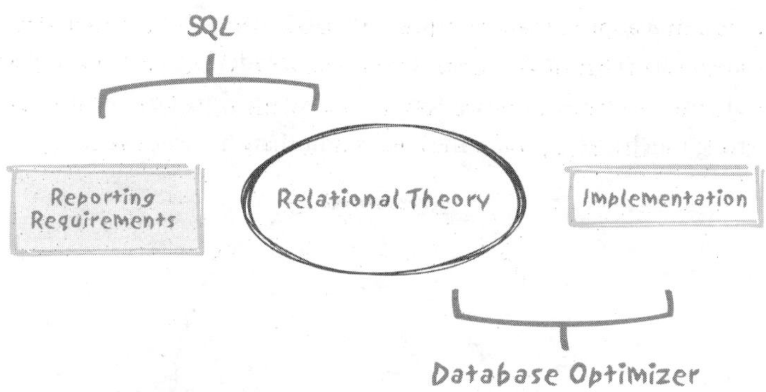

FIGURE 4-1. *DBMS Protagonists*

However, despite the crucial theoretical importance of relational theory, there are aspects of great practical relevance that the relational theory has nothing to say about. These fall into an area I call "reporting requirements." The most obvious example in this area is the ordering of result sets. Relational theory is concerned only with the retrieval of a correct data set, as defined by a query. As we are practitioners and not theorists, for us the relational phase consists in correctly identifying the rows that will belong to our final result set. The matter of how some attributes (columns) of one row relate to similar attributes in another row doesn't belong to this phase, and yet this is what ordering is all about. Further, relational theory has nothing to say about the numerous statistical functions (such as percentiles and the like) that often appear in various dialects of the

* A good example would be sqlite, a remarkable storage engine that allows the management of data inside a file using SQL, but that is not a database server.

SQL language. The relational theory operates on set, and knows nothing of the imposition of ordering on these sets. Despite the fact that there are many mathematical theories built around ordering, none have any relevance to the relational theory.

At this stage I must point out that what distinguishes relational operations from what I have called *reporting requirements* is that relational operations apply to mathematical sets of theoretically infinite extent. Irrespective of whether we are operating on tables of 10, one million, or one billion rows, we can apply any filtering criterion in an identical fashion. Once again, we are concerned only with identifying and returning the data that matches our criteria. Here, we are in the environment where the relational theory is fully applicable. Now, when we want to order rows (or perform an operation such as `group by` that most people would consider a relational operation) we are no longer working on a potentially infinite data set, but on a necessarily finite set. The consequent data set thus ceases to be a relation in the mathematical sense of the word. We are outside the bounds of the relational theory. Of course, this doesn't mean that we cannot still do clever and useful things against this data using SQL.

So we may, as a first approximation, represent an SQL query as a double-layered operation as shown in Figure 4-2; first, a relational core identifying the set of data we are going to operate on, second, a non-relational layer which works on this now finite set to give the polishing touch and produce the final result that the user expects.

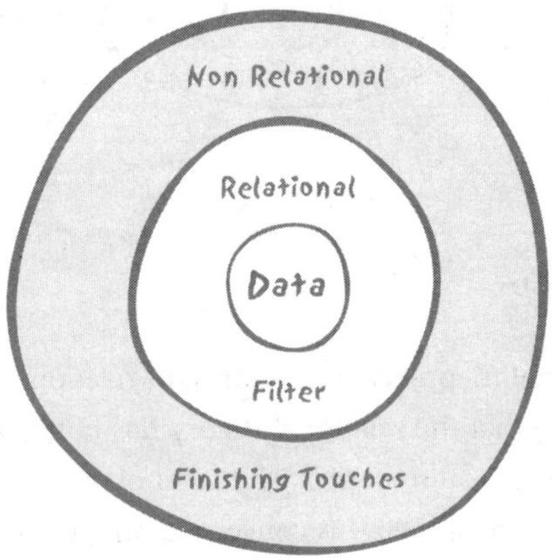

FIGURE 4-2. *The various layers of an SQL query*

Despite Figure 4-2's appealingly simple representation of the place of SQL within the data environment, an SQL query will in most cases be considerably more complex than Figure 4-2 may suggest; Figure 4-2 only represents the overall pattern. The relational filter may be a generic name for several independent filters combined, for instance, through a `union` construct or by the means of subqueries, and the complexity of some SQL constructs can be considerable. I shall come back to the topic of SQL code a little later. But first I must talk about the relationship between the physical implementation of data and the database optimizer.

Do not confuse the true relational functionality of the SQL query execution with the additional presentation layer.

SQL and the Optimizer

An SQL engine that receives a query to process will have to use the optimizer to find out how to execute that query in the most efficient way possible. Here the relational theory strikes again, because that theory informs the optimizer of transformations that are valid equivalents of the semantically correct query initially provided by the developer—even if that original query was clumsily written.

Optimization is when the physical implementation of data comes into play. Depending on the existence of indexes and their usability in relation to a query, some transformations may result in much faster execution than other semantically equivalent transformations. Various storage models that I introduce in Chapter 5 may also make one particular way to execute a query irresistibly attractive. The optimizer examines the disposition of the indexes that are available, the physical layout of data, how much memory is available, and how many processors are available to be applied to the task of executing the query. The optimizer will also take into account information concerning the volume of the various tables and indexes that may be involved, directly or indirectly, through views used by the query. By weighing the alternatives that theory says are valid equivalents against the possibilities allowed by the implementation of the database, the optimizer will generate what is, hopefully, the best execution plan for the query.

However, the key point to remember is that, although the optimizer may not always be totally weaponless in the non-relational layer of an SQL query, it is mainly in the relational core that it will be able to deploy its full power—precisely because of the mathematical underpinnings of the relational theory. The transformation from one SQL query to another raises an important point: it reminds us that SQL is supposed to be a declarative language. In other words, one should use SQL to express what is required, rather than how that requirement is to be met. Going from *what* to *how*, should, in theory, be the work of the optimizer.

You saw in Chapters 1 and 2 that SQL queries are only some of the variables in the equation; but even at the tactical query level, a poorly written query may prevent the optimizer from working efficiently. Remember, the mathematical basis of the relational theory provides an unassailable logic to the proceedings. Therefore, part of the art of SQL is to minimize the thickness, so to speak, of the non-relational layer—outside this layer, there is not much that the optimizer can safely do that guarantees returning exactly the same rows as the original query.

Another part of the art of SQL is that when performing non-relational operations—loosely defined as operations for which the whole (at least at this stage) resulting dataset is known—we must be extremely careful to operate on only the data that is strictly required to answer the original question, and nothing more. Somehow, a finite data set, as opposed to the *current row*, has to be stored somewhere, and storing anything in temporary storage (memory or disk) requires significant overhead due to byte-pushing. This overhead may dramatically increase as the result set data volumes themselves increase, particularly if main memory becomes unavailable. A shortage of main memory would initiate the high-resource activity of swapping to disk, with all its attendant overheads. Moreover, always remember that indexes refer to disk addresses, not temporary storage—as soon as the data is in temporary storage, we must wave farewell to most fast access methods (with the possible exception of hashing).

Some SQL dialects mislead users into believing that they are still in the relational world when they have long since left it. Take as a simple example the query "Who are the five top earners among employees who are not executives?"—a reasonable real-life question, although one that includes a distinctly non-relational twist. Identifying employees who are not executives is the relational part of the query, from which we obtain a finite set of employees that we can order. Several SQL dialects allow one to limit the number of rows returned by adding a special clause to the select statement. It is then fairly obvious that both the *ordering* and the *limitation* criteria are outside the relational layer. However, other dialects, the Oracle version figuring prominently here, use other mechanisms. What Oracle has is a dummy column named `rownum` that applies a sequential numbering to the rows in the order in which they are returned—which means the numbering is applied during the relational phase. If we write something such as:

```
select empname, salary
from employees
where status != 'EXECUTIVE'
  and rownum <= 5
order by salary desc
```

we get an incorrect result, at least in the sense that we are not getting the top five most highly paid nonexecutives, as the query might suggest at first glance. Instead, we get back the first five nonexecutives found—they could be the five lowest paid!—ordered in descending order of salary. (This query illustrates a well-known trap among Oracle practitioners, who have all been burnt at least once.)

Let's just be very clear about what is happening with the preceding query. The relational component of the query simply retrieves the first five rows (attributes `empname` and `salary` only) from the table `employees` where the employee is not an executive *in a totally unpredictable order*. Remember that relational theory tells us that a relation (and therefore the table that represents it) is not defined in any way by the order in which tuples (and therefore the rows in that table) are either stored or retrieved. As a consequence the nonexecutive employee with the highest salary may or may not be included in this result set—and there is no way we will ever know whether this result set actually meets our search criteria correctly.

What we really want is to get all nonexecutives, order them by decreasing salary, and only then get the top five in the set. We can achieve this objective as follows:

```
select *
from (select empname, salary
      from employees
      where status != 'EXECUTIVE'
      order by salary desc)
where rownum <= 5
```

So, how is our query *layered* in this case? Many would be tempted to say that by applying a filtering condition to an ordered result, we end up with something looking more or less like Figure 4-3.

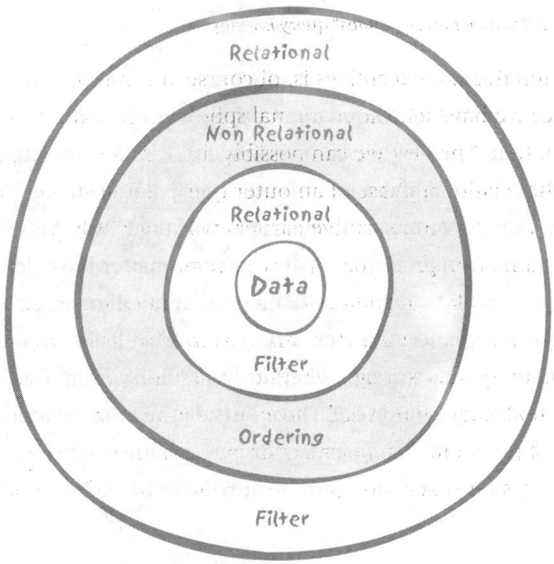

FIGURE 4-3. *A misleading view of what the "top five nonexecutives" query looks like*

The truth, however, is more like Figure 4-4.

Using constructs that look relational doesn't take us back to the relational world, because to be in the relational world we must apply relational operators to relations. Our subquery uses an `order by` to sort the results. Once we've imposed ordering, we no longer have, strictly speaking, a relation (a relation is a set, and a set has no order). We end up with an outer `select` that looks relational on the surface but is applied to the output of an inline view in which a significant component (the `order by` clause) is not a relational process.

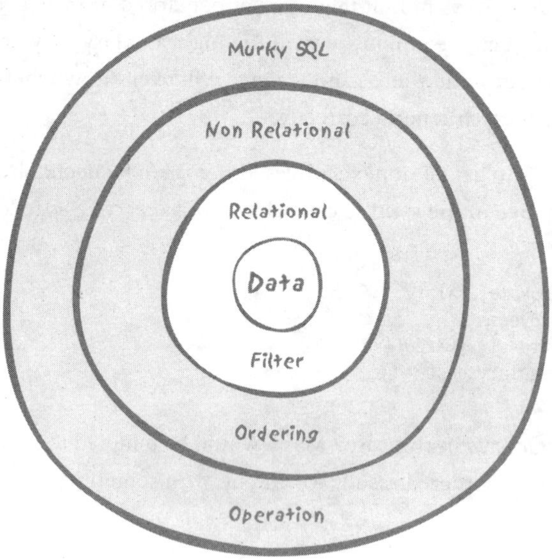

FIGURE 4-4. *What the "top five nonexecutives" query is really like*

My example of the top five nonexecutives is, of course, a simple example, but do understand that once we have left the relational sphere in the execution of a query, we can no longer return to it. The best we can possibly do is to use the output of such a query to feed into the relational phase of an outer query. For instance, "in which departments are our five top nonexecutive earners working?" What is extremely important to understand, though, is that at this stage no matter how clever the optimizer is, it will be absolutely unable to combine the queries, and will more or less have to execute them in a given sequence. Further, any resulting set from an intermediate query is likely to be held in temporary storage, whether in memory or on disk, where the choice of access methods may be reduced. Once outside the pure relational layer, the way we write a query is of paramount importance for performance because it will inevitably impose onto the query some execution path from which the SQL engine will not be able to stray.

To summarize, we can say that the safest approach we can adopt is to try to do as much of the job as possible inside the relational layer, where the optimizer can operate to maximum efficiency. When the situation is such that a given SQL task is no longer a purely relational problem, then we must be particularly careful about the construct, or the writing of the query itself. Understanding that SQL has, like Dr. Jekyll, a double nature is the key to mastering the language. If you see SQL as a single-edged sword, then you are condemned to remain in the world of tips and tricks for dummies, smarties, and mere mortals, possibly useful for impressing the opposite sex—although in my experience it doesn't work much—but an approach that will never provide you with a deep understanding of how to cope with a difficult SQL problem.

The optimizer rewards those who do the most work in the relational layer.

Limits of the Optimizer

Any decent SQL engine relies heavily on its query optimizer, which very often performs an excellent job. However, there are many aspects of the way optimizers work that you must keep in mind:

Optimizers rely on the information they find in the database.
: This information is of two types: general statistical data (which must be verified as being fitting), and the essential declarative information held in the data definitions. Where important semantic information relating to the data relations is embedded in triggers or, worse, in application program code, that vital information will be totally unavailable to the optimizer. Such circumstances will inevitably impact the potential performance of the optimizer.

Optimizers can perform to their best advantage where they can apply transformations that are mathematically proven to be equivalent.
: When they are required to assess components of a query that are non-relational in character, they are on less certain grounds and the execution path will stick more closely to what was voluntarily or involuntarily suggested by the original writing.

The work of the optimizer contributes to the overall response time.
: Comparing a large number of alternative execution paths may take time. The end user sees only the total elapsed time and is unaware of how much was spent on optimization and how much on execution. A clever optimizer might allow itself more time to try to improve a query that it expects to take a lot of time to run, but there is always a self-imposed limit on its work. The trouble is that when you have a 20-way join (which is by no means unusual in some applications), the number of combinations the optimizer could examine can become unmanageably large even when adequate indexing make some links obvious. Compound this with the inclusion of a combination of complex views and subqueries, and at some point, the optimizer will have to give in. It is quite possible to find a situation in which a query running in isolation of any others may be very well optimized, while the same query deeply nested inside a much more complex outer query may take a completely wrong path.

The optimizer improves individual queries.
: It is unable to relate independent queries one to another, however. Whatever its efforts, if the bulk of your program is fetching data inside procedural code just to feed into subsequent queries, the optimizer will not be able to do anything for you.

Feed the optimizer with little chunks, and it will optimize little pieces. Feed it with a big chunk, and it will optimize a task.

Five Factors Governing the Art of SQL

You have seen in the first part of this chapter exactly how SQL includes both relational and non-relational characteristics. You have also seen how this affects the efficient (and not-so-efficient) workings of the database optimizer. From this point forward, and bearing in mind the lessons of the first part of this chapter, we can concentrate on the key factors that must be considered when using SQL. In my view, there are five main factors:

- The total quantity of data from which a result set has to be obtained
- The criteria required to define the result set
- The size of the result set
- The number of tables to be processed in order to obtain the desired result set
- The number of other users also modifying this same data

Total Quantity of Data

The volume of data we need to read is probably the most important factor to take into account; an execution plan that is perfectly suitable for a fourteen-row `emp` table and a four-row `dept` table may be entirely inappropriate for dealing with a 15 million–row `financial_flows` table against which we have to join a 5 million–row `products` table. Note that even a 15 million–row table will not be considered particularly large by the standards of many companies. As a matter of consequence, it is hard to pronounce on the efficiency of a query before having run it against the target volume of data.

Criteria Defining the Result Set

When we write an SQL statement, in most cases it will involve filtering conditions located in `where` clauses, and we may have several `where` clauses—a major one as well as minor ones—in subqueries or views (regular views or in-line views). A filtering condition may be efficient or inefficient. However, the significance of *efficient* or *inefficient* is strongly affected by other factors, such as physical implementation (as discussed in Chapter 5) and once again, by how much data we have to wade through.

We need to approach the subject of defining the result in several parts, by considering filtering, the central SQL statements, and the impact of large data volumes on our queries. But this is a particularly complex area that needs to be treated in some depth, so I'll reserve this discussion until later in this chapter, in the major section entitled "Filtering."

Size of the Result Set

An important and often overlooked factor is how much data a query returns (or how much data a statement changes). This is often dependent on the size of the tables and the details of the filtering, but not in every case. Typically, the combination of several selection criteria which of themselves are of little value in selecting data may result in highly efficient filtering when used in combination with one another. For example, one could cite that retrieving students' names based on whether they received a science or an arts degree will give a large result set, but if both criteria are used (e.g., students who studied under both disciplines) the consequent result set will collapse to a tiny number.

In the case of queries in particular, the size of the result set matters not so much from a technical standpoint, but mostly because of the end user's perception. To a very large extent, end users adjust their patience to the number of rows they expect: when they ask for one needle, they pay little attention to the size of the haystack. The extreme case is a query that returns nothing, and a good developer should always try to write queries that return few or no rows as fast as possible. There are few experiences more frustrating than waiting for several minutes before finally seeing a "no data found" message. This is especially annoying if you have mistyped something, realized your error just after hitting Enter, and then have been unable to abort the query. End users are willing to wait to get a lot of data, but not to get an empty result. If we consider that each of our filtering criteria defines a particular result set and the final result set is either the intersection (when conditions are anded) or the union (when conditions are ored together) of all the intermediate result sets, a zero result is most likely to result from the intersection of small, intermediate result sets. In other words, the (relatively) most precise criteria are usually the primary reason for a zero result set. Whenever there is the slightest possibility that a query might return no data, the most likely condition that would result in a null return should be checked first—especially if it can be done quickly. Needless to say, the order of evaluation of criteria is extremely context-sensitive as you shall see later under "Filtering."

A skillful developer should aim for response times proportional to the number of rows returned.

Number of Tables

The number of tables involved in a query will naturally have some influence on performance. This is not because a DBMS engine performs joins badly—on the contrary, modern systems are able to join large numbers of tables very efficiently.

Joins

The perception of poor join performance is another enduring myth associated with relational databases. Folklore has it that one should not join too many tables, with five often suggested as the limit. In fact, you can quite easily have 15 table joins perform extremely well. But there are additional problems associated with joining a large number of tables, of which the following are examples:

- When you routinely need to join, say, 15 tables, you can legitimately question the correctness of the design; keep in mind what I said in Chapter 1—that a row in a table states some kind of truth and can be compared to a mathematical axiom. By joining tables, we derive other truths. But there is a point at which we must decide whether something is an obvious truth that we can call an axiom, or whether it is a less obvious truth that we must derive. If we spend much of our time deriving our truths, perhaps our axioms are poorly chosen in the first place.
- For the optimizer, the complexity increases exponentially as the number of tables increases. Once again, the excellent work usually performed by a statistical optimizer may comprise a significant part of the total response time for a query, particularly when the query is run for the first time. With large numbers of tables, it is quite impractical for the optimizer to explore all possible query paths. Unless a query is written in a way that eases the work of the optimizer, the more complex the query, the greater the chance that the optimizer will bet on the wrong horse.
- When we write a complex query involving many tables, and when joins can be written in several fairly distinct ways, the odds are high that we'll pick the wrong construct. If we join tables A to B to C to D, the optimizer may not have all the information present to know that A can be very efficiently joined directly to D, particularly if that join happens to be a special case. A sloppy developer trying to fix duplicate rows with a `distinct` can also easily overlook a missing join condition.

Complex queries and complex views

Be aware that the apparent number of tables involved in a query can be deceptive; some of the tables may actually be views, and sometimes pretty complex ones, too. Just as with queries, views can also have varying degrees of complexity. They can be used to mask columns, rows, or even a combination of rows and columns to all but a few privileged users. They can also be used as an alternate perspective on the data, building relations that are derived from the existing relations stored as tables. In cases such as these, a view can be considered shorthand for a query, and this is probably one of the most common usages of views. With increasingly complex queries, there is a temptation to break a query down into a succession of individual views, each representing a component of the greater query.

The simplicity of a given query may hide the complexity of participating views.

Like most extreme positions, it would be absurd to banish views altogether. Many of them are rather harmless animals. However, when a view is itself used in a rather complex query, in most cases we are only interested in a small fraction of the data returned by the view—possibly in a couple of columns, out of a score or more. The optimizer may attempt to recombine a simple view into a larger query statement. However, once a query reaches a relatively modest level of complexity, this approach may become too complex in itself to enable efficient processing.

In some cases a view may be written in a way that effectively prevents the optimizer from combining it into the larger statement. I have already mentioned `rownums`, those virtual columns used in Oracle to indicate the order in which rows are initially found. When `rownums` are used inside a view, a further level of complexity is introduced. Any attempt to combine a view that references a `rownum` into a larger statement would be almost guaranteed to change the subsequent `rownum` order, and therefore the optimizer doesn't permit a query rewrite in those circumstances. In a complicated query, such a view will necessarily be executed in isolation. In quite a number of cases then, the DBMS optimizer will push a view *as is* into a statement,* running it as a step in the statement execution, and using only those elements that are required from the result of the view execution.

Frequently, many of the operations executed in a view (typically joins to return a description associated with codes) will be irrelevant in the context of a larger query, or a query may have special search criteria that would have been particularly selective when applied to the tables underlying the view. For instance, a subsequent `union` may prove to be totally unnecessary because the view is the `union` of several tables representing subtypes, and the larger query filters on only one of the subtypes. There is also the danger of joining a view with a table that itself appears in the same view, thus forcing multiple passes over this table and probably hitting the same rows several times when one pass would have been quite sufficient.

When a view returns much more data than required in the context of a query that references that view, dramatic performance gains can often be obtained by eliminating the view (or using a simpler version of the view). Begin by replacing the view reference in the main query with the underlying SQL query used to define the view. With the components of the view in full sight, it becomes easy to remove everything that is not

* The optimizer may also sometimes push criteria down into the view.

strictly necessary. More often than not, it's precisely what isn't necessary that prevents the view from being merged by the optimizer, and a simpler, cut-down view may give excellent results. When the query is correctly reduced to its most basic components, it runs much faster.

Many developers may hesitate to push the code for a very complex view into an already complex query, not least because it can make a complex situation even more complicated. The exercise of developing and factoring a complex SQL expression may indeed appear to be daunting. It is, however, an exercise quite similar to the development of mathematical expressions, as practiced in high school. It is, in my view, a very formative exercise and well worth the effort of mastering. It is a discipline that provides a very sound understanding of the inner workings of a query for developers anxious to improve their skills, and in most cases the results can be highly rewarding.

Rather than embedding a view inside a query when that view returns unnecessary elements, try to decompose the view components into the main query body.

Number of Other Users

Finally, concurrency is a factor that you must carefully take into account when designing your SQL code. Concurrency is usually a concern while writing to the database where block-access contention, locking, latching (which means locking of internal DBMS resources), and others are the more obvious problem areas; even read consistency can in some cases lead to some degree of contention. Any server, no matter how impressive its specification, will always have a finite capacity. The ideal plan for a query running on a machine with little to no concurrency is not necessarily the same as the ideal plan for the same query running on the same machine with a high level of concurrency. Sorts may no longer find the memory they need and may instead resort to writing to disk, thus creating a new source of contention. Some CPU-intensive operations—for example, the computation of complicated functions, repetitive scanning of index blocks, and so forth—may cause the computer to overload. I have seen cases in which more physical I/Os resulted in a significantly better time to perform a given task. In those cases, there was a high level of concurrency for CPU-intensive operations, and when some processes had to wait for I/Os, the overworked CPUs were relieved and could run other processes, thus ensuring a better overlap. We must often think in terms of global throughput of one particular business task, rather than in terms of individual user response-time.

NOTE

Chapter 9 examines concurrency in greater detail.

Filtering

How you restrict your result set is one of the most critical factors that helps you determine which tactics to apply when writing an SQL statement. The collective criteria that filters the data are often seen as a motley assortment of conditions associated in the where clause. However, you should very closely examine the various where-clause (and having-clause, too) conditions when writing SQL code.

Meaning of Filtering Conditions

Given the syntax of the SQL language, it is quite natural to consider that all filtering conditions, as expressed in the where clause, are similar in nature. This is absolutely not the case. Some filtering conditions apply directly to the select operator of relational theory, where checking that a column in a row (purists would say an attribute in a relation variable) matches (or doesn't match) a given condition. However, historically the where clause also contains conditions that implement another operator—the join operator. There is, since the advent of the SQL92 join syntax, an attempt to differentiate join filtering conditions, located between the (main) from clause and the where clause, from the select filtering conditions listed in the where clause. Joining two (or more) tables logically creates a new relation.

Consider this general example of a join:

```
select .....
from t1
   inner join t2
      on t1.join1 = t2.joind2
where ...
```

Should a condition on column c2 belonging to t2 come as an additional condition on the inner join, expressing that in fact you join on a subset of t2? Or should a condition inside the where clause, along with conditions on columns of t1, express that the filtering applies to the result of joining t1 to t2? Wherever you choose to place your join condition ought not to make much of a difference; however, it has been known to lead to variations in performance with some optimizers.

We may also have conditions other than joins and the simple filtering of values. For instance, we may have conditions restricting the returned set of rows to some subtype; we may also have conditions that are just required to check the existence of something inside another table. All these conditions are not necessarily semantically identical, although the SQL syntax makes all of them look equivalent. In some cases, the order of evaluation of the conditions is of no consequence; in other cases, it is significant.

Here's an example that you can actually find in more than one commercial software package to illustrate the importance of the order of the evaluation of conditions. Suppose that we have a parameters table, which holds: parameter_name, parameter_type, and parameter_value, with parameter_value being the string representation of whatever type of parameter we have, as defined by the attribute parameter_type. (To the logical mind this is indeed a story of more woe than that of Juliet and her Romeo, since the domain type of attribute parameter_value is a variable feast and thus offends a primary rule of relational theory.) Say that we issue a query such as:

```
select * from parameters
where parameter_name like '%size'
  and parameter_type = 'NUMBER'
```

With this query, it does not matter whether the first condition is evaluated before or after the second one. However, if we add the following condition, where int( ) is a function to convert from char to integer value, then the order of evaluation becomes very significant:

```
and int(parameter_value) > 1000
```

Now, the condition on parameter_type *must* be evaluated before the condition on the value, because otherwise we risk a run-time error consequent upon attempting to convert a character string (if for example parameter_type for that row is defined as char) to an integer. The optimizer may not be able to figure out that the poor design demands that one condition should have higher priority—and you may have trouble specifying it to the database.

All search criteria are not equal; some are more equal than others.

Evaluation of Filtering Conditions

The very first questions to consider when writing a SQL statement are:

- What data is required, and from which tables?
- What input values will we pass to the DBMS engine?
- What are the filtering conditions that allow us to discard unwanted rows?

Be aware, however, that some data (principally data used for joining tables) may be stored redundantly in several tables. A requirement to return values known to be held in the primary key of a given table doesn't necessarily mean that this table must appear in the from clause, since this primary key may well appear as the foreign key of another table from which we also need the data.

Even before writing a query, we should rank the filtering conditions. The really efficient ones (of which there may be several, and which may apply to different tables) will drive the query, and the inefficient ones will come as icing on the cake. What is the criterion that defines an efficient filter? Primarily, one that allows us to cut down the volume of the data we have to deal with as fast as possible. And here we must pay a lot of attention to the way we write; the following subsections work through a simple example to illustrate my point.

Buyers of Batmobiles

Assume that we have four tables, namely customers, orders, orderdetail, and a table of articles, as shown in Figure 4-5. Please note that in the figure the sizes of the boxes representing each table are more or less proportional to the volume of data in each table, not simply to the number of columns. Primary key columns are underlined.

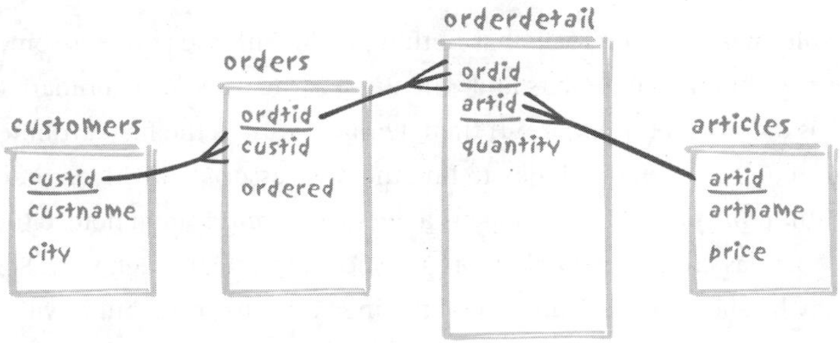

FIGURE 4-5. *A classical order schema*

Let's now suppose that our SQL problem is to find the names of all the customers living in the city named "Gotham" who have ordered the article called "Batmobile" during the last six months. We have, of course, several ways to formulate this query; the following is probably what an ANSI SQL fan would write:

```
select distinct c.custname
from customers c
     join orders o
       on o.custid = c.custid
     join orderdetail od
       on od.ordid = o.ordid
     join articles a
       on a.artid = od.artid
where c.city = 'GOTHAM'
  and a.artname = 'BATMOBILE'
  and o.ordered >= somefunc
```

somefunc is supposed to be a function that returns the date six months prior to the current date. Notice too, the presence of distinct, which may be required if one of our customers is an especially heavy consumer of Batmobiles and has recently ordered several of them.

Let's forget for a while that the optimizer may rewrite the query, and look at the execution plan such a statement suggests. First, we walk the customers table, keeping only rows for which the city happens to be Gotham. Then we search the orders table, which means that the custid column there had better be indexed, because otherwise the only hope the SQL engine has of executing the query reasonably fast is to perform some sorting and merging or to scan the orders table to build a hash table and then operate against that. We are going to apply another filter at this level, against the order date. A clever optimizer will not mind finding the filtering condition in the where clause and will understand that in order to minimize the amount of data to join it must filter on the date before performing the join. A not so clever optimizer might be tempted to join first, and then filter, and may therefore be grateful to you for specifying the filtering condition with the join condition, as follows:

```
join orders o
  on o.custid = c.custid
  and a.ordered >= somefunc
```

Even if the filtering condition really has nothing to do with the join, it is sometimes difficult for the optimizer to understand when that is the case. If the primary key of orderdetail is defined as (ordid, artid) then, because ordid is the first attribute of the index, we can make use of that index to find the rows associated with an order as in Chapter 3. But if the primary key happens to be (artid, ordid) (and note, either version is exactly the same as far as relational theory is concerned), then tough luck. Some products may be able to make some use of the index* in that case, but it will not provide the efficient access that (ordid, artid) would have allowed. Other products will be totally unable to use the index. The only circumstance that may save us is the existence of a separate index on ordid.

Once we have linked orderdetails to orders, we can proceed to articles—without any problem this time since we found artid, the primary key, in orderdetail. Finally, we can check whether the value in articles is or is not a Batmobile. Is this the end of the story? Not quite. As instructed by distinct, we must now sort the resulting set of customer names that have passed across all the filtering layers so as to eliminate duplicates.

It turns out that there are several alternative ways of expressing the query that I've just described. One example is to use the older join syntax, as follows:

```
select distinct c.custname
from customers c,
     orders o,
     orderdetail od,
     articles a
where c.city = 'GOTHAM'
  and c.custid = o.custid
  and o.ordid = od.ordid
  and od.artid = a.artid
  and a.artname = 'BATMOBILE'
  and o.ordered >= somefunc
```

* A feature known as *skip-scan* may allow for searching the index.

It may just be old habits dying hard, but I prefer this older way, if only for one simple reason: it makes it slightly more obvious that from a logical point of view the order in which we process data is arbitrary, because the same data will be returned irrespective of the order in which we inspect tables. Certainly the `customers table` is particularly important, since that is the source from which we obtain the data that is ultimately required, while in this very specific context, all the other tables are used purely to support the remaining selection processes. One really has to understand that there is no one recipe that works for all cases. The pattern of table joins will vary for each situation you encounter. The deciding factor is the nature of the data you are dealing with.

A given approach in SQL may solve one problem, but make another situation worse. The way queries are written is a bit like a drug that may heal one patient but kill another.

More Batmobile purchases

Let's explore alternative ways to list our buyers of Batmobiles. In my view, as a general rule, `distinct` at the top level should be avoided whenever possible. The reason is that if we have overlooked a join condition, a `distinct` will hide the problem. Admittedly this is a greater risk when building queries with the older syntax, but nevertheless still a risk when using the ANSI/SQL92 syntax if tables are joined through several columns. It is usually much easier to spot duplicate rows than it is to identify incorrect data.

It's easy to give a proof of the assertion that incorrect results may be difficult to spot: the two previous queries that use `distinct` to return the names of the customers may actually return a wrong result. If we happen to have several customers named "Wayne," we won't get that information because `distinct` will not only remove duplicates resulting from multiple orders by the same customer, but also remove duplicates resulting from homonyms. In fact, we should return both the unique customer id and the customer name to be certain that we have the full list of Batmobile buyers. We can only guess at how long it might take to identify such an issue in production.

How can we get rid of `distinct` then? By acknowledging that we are looking for customers in Gotham that satisfy an existence test, namely a purchase order for a Batmobile in the past six months. Note that most, but not all, SQL dialects support the following syntax:

```
select c.custname
from customers c
where c.city = 'GOTHAM'
  and exists (select null
              from orders o,
                   orderdetail od,
                   articles a
              where a.artname = 'BATMOBILE'
                and a.artid = od.artid
                and od.ordid = o.ordid
                and o.custid = c.custid
                and o.ordered >= somefunc)
```

If we use an existence test such as this query uses, a name may appear more than once if it is common to several customers, but each individual customer will appear only once, irrespective of the number of orders they placed. You might think that my criticism of the ANSI SQL syntax was a little harsh, since customers figure as prominently, if not more prominently than before. However, it now features as the source for the data we want the query to return. And another query, nested this time, appears as a major phase in the identification of the subset of customers.

The inner query in the preceding example is strongly linked to the outer select. As you can see on line 11 (in bold), the inner query refers to the current row of the outer query. Thus, the inner query is what is called a *correlated subquery*. The snag with this type of subquery is that we cannot execute it before we know the current customer. Once again, we are assuming that the optimizer doesn't rewrite the query. Therefore we must first find each customer and then check for each one whether the existence test is satisfied. Our query as a whole may perform excellently if we have very few customers in Gotham. It may be dreadful if Gotham is the place where most of our customers are located (a case in which a sophisticated optimizer might well try to execute the query in a different way).

We have still another way to write our query, which is as follows:

```
select custname
from customers
where city = 'GOTHAM'
  and custid in
             (select o.custid
              from orders o,
                   orderdetail od,
                   articles a
              where a.artname = 'BATMOBILE'
                and a.artid = od.artid
                and od.ordid = o.ordid
                and o.ordered >= somefunc)
```

In this case, the inner query no longer depends on the outer query: it has become an *uncorrelated subquery*. It needs to be executed only once. It should be obvious that we have now reverted the flow of execution. In the previous case, we had to search first for customers in the right location (e.g., *where city is Gotham*), and then check each order in turn. In this latest version of the query, the identifiers of customers who have ordered what we are looking for are obtained via a join that takes place in the inner query.

If you have a closer look, however, there are more subtle differences as well between the current and preceding examples. In the case of the correlated subquery, it is of paramount importance to have the orders table indexed on custid; in the second case, it no longer matters, since then the index (if any) that will be used is the index associated with the primary key of customers.

You might notice that the most recent version of the query performs an implicit distinct. Indeed, the subquery, because of its join, might return many rows for a single customer. That duplication doesn't matter, because the in condition checks only to see whether a value is in the list returned by the subquery, and in doesn't care whether a given value is in that list one time or a hundred times. Perhaps though, for the sake of consistency we should apply the same rules to the subquery that we have applied to the query as a whole, namely to acknowledge that we have an existence test within the subquery as well:

```
select custname
from customers
where city = 'GOTHAM'
  and custid in
           (select o.custid
            from orders o
            where o.ordered >= somefunc
              and exists (select null
                          from orderdetail od,
                               articles a
                          where a.artname = 'BATMOBILE'
                            and a.artid = od.artid
                            and od.ordid = o.ordid))
```

or:

```
select custname
from customers
where city = 'GOTHAM'
  and custid in
           (select custid
            from orders
            where ordered >= somefunc
              and ordid in (select od.ordid
                            from orderdetail od,
                                 articles a
                            where a.artname = 'BATMOBILE'
                              and a.artid = od.artid)
```

Irrespective of the fact that our nesting is getting deeper and becoming less legible, choosing which query is the best between the exists and the in follows the very same rule inside the subquery as before: the choice depends on the effectiveness of the condition on the date versus the condition on the article. Unless business has been very, very slow for the past six months, one might reasonably expect that the most efficient condition on which to filter the data will be the one on the article name. Therefore, in the particular case of the subquery, in is better than exists because it will be faster to find all the order lines that refer to a Batmobile and then to check whether the sale occurred in the last six months rather than the other way round. This approach will be faster assuming that the table orderdetail is indexed on artid; otherwise, our bright, tactical move will fail dismally.

NOTE

It may be a good idea to check in against exists whenever an existence test is applied to a significant number of rows.

Most SQL dialects allow you to rewrite uncorrelated subqueries as inline views in the from clause. However, you must always remember that an in performs an implicit removal of duplicate values, which must become explicit when the subquery is moved to become an in-line view in the from clause. For example:

```
select custname
from customers
where city = 'GOTHAM'
  and custid in
           (select o.custid
            from orders o,
                 (select distinct od.ordid
                  from orderdetail od,
                       articles a
                  where a.artname = 'BATMOBILE'
                    and a.artid = od.artid) x
            where o.ordered >= somefunc
              and x.ordid = o.ordid)
```

The different ways you have to write functionally equivalent queries (and variants other than those given in this section are possible) are comparable to words that are synonyms. In written and spoken language, synonyms have roughly the same meaning, but each one introduces a subtle difference that makes one particular word more suitable to a particular situation or expression (and in some cases another synonym is totally inappropriate). In the same way, both data and implementation details may dictate the choice of one query variant over others.

Lessons to be learned from the Batmobile trade

The various examples of SQL that you saw in the preceding section may look like an idle exercise in programming dexterity, but they are more than that. The key point is that there are many different ways in which we can attack the data, and that we don't necessarily have to go first through customers, then orders, then orderdetail, and then articles as some of the ways of writing the query might suggest.

If we represent the strength of our search criteria with arrows—the more discriminant the criterion, the larger the arrow—we can assume that we have very few customers in Gotham, but that we sell quite a number of Batmobiles and business has been brisk for the past six months, in which case our battle map may look like Figure 4-6. Although we have a condition on the article name, the medium arrow points to orderdetail because that is what truly matters. We may have very few articles for sale, which may represent similar percentages of our revenue, or we may have a huge number of articles, of which one of the best sellers is the Batmobile.

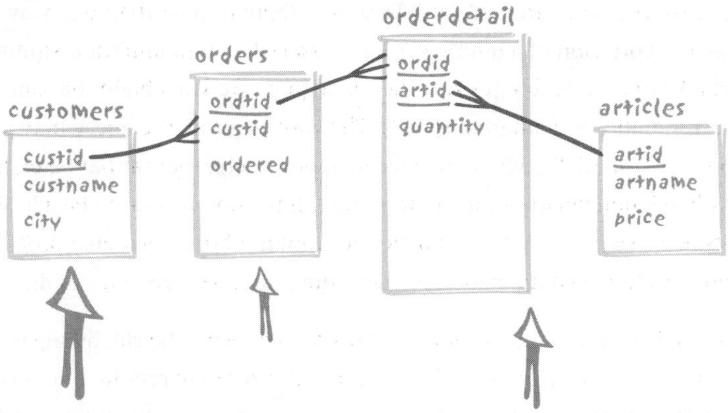

FIGURE 4-6. *When query discrimination is based on location*

Alternatively, we can assume that most of our customers are indeed based in Gotham, but that very few actually buy Batmobiles, in which case our battle plan will look more like Figure 4-7. It is quite obvious then, that we really have to cut to pieces the `orderdetail` table, which is the largest one. The faster we slash this table, the faster our query will run.

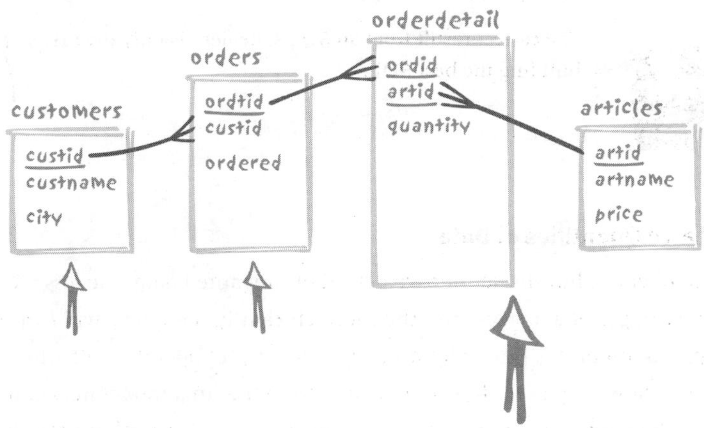

FIGURE 4-7. *When query discrimination is based on purchase*

Note also—and this is a very important point—that the criterion "during the last six months" is not a very precise one. But what if we change the criterion to specify the last two months and happen to have 10 years of sales history online? In that case, it may be more efficient to get to those recent orders first—which, thanks to some techniques described in Chapter 5, may be clustered together—and then start from there, selecting customers from Gotham, on the one hand, and orders for Batmobiles on the other. To put it another way, the best execution plan does not only depend on the data values, it may also evolve over time.

What then can we conclude from all this? First, that there is more than one way to skin a cat...and that an expression of a query is usually associated with implicit assumptions about the data. With each different expression of a query we will obtain the same result set, but it may be at significantly different speeds. The way we write the query may influence the execution path, especially when we have to apply criteria that cannot be expressed within the truly relational part of the environment. If the optimizer is to be allowed to function at its best, we must try to maximize the amount of true relational processing and ensure the non-relational component has minimum impact on the final result.

We have assumed all along in this chapter that statements will be run as suggested by the way they are written. Be aware though, that an optimizer may rewrite queries—sometimes pretty aggressively. You could argue that rewrites by the optimizer don't matter, because SQL is supposed to be a declarative language in which you state what you want and let the DBMS provide it. However, you have seen that each time we have rewritten a query in a different way, we have had to change assumptions about the distribution of data and about existing indexes. It is highly important, therefore, to anticipate the work of the optimizer to be certain that it will find what it needs, whether in terms of indexes or in terms of detailed-enough statistical information about the data.

The correct result from an SQL statement is only the first step in building the best SQL.

Querying Large Quantities of Data

It may sound obvious, but the sooner we get rid of unwanted data, the less we have to process at later stages of a query—and the more efficiently the query will run. An excellent application of this principle can be found with set operators, of which `union` is probably the most widely used. It is quite common to find in a moderately complex `union` a number of tables appearing in several of the queries "glued" together with the `union` operator. One often sees the `union` of fairly complex joins, with most of the joined tables occurring in both `select` statements of the `union`—for example, on both sides of the `union`, something like the following:

```
select ...
from A,
     B,
     C,
     D,
     E1
where (condition on E1)
  and (joins and other conditions)
```

```
union
select ...
from A,
     B,
     C,
     D,
     E2
where (condition on E2)
  and (joins and other conditions)
```

This type of query is typical of the cut-and-paste school of programming. In many cases it may be more efficient to use a union of those tables that are not common, complete with the screening conditions, and to then push that union into an inline view and join the result, writing something similar to:

```
select ...
from A,
     B,
     C,
     D,
     (select ...
      from E1
      where (condition on E1)
      union
      select ...
      from E2
      where (condition on E2)) E
where (joins and other conditions)
```

Another classic example of conditions applied at the wrong place is a danger associated with filtering when a statement contains a group by clause. You can filter on the columns that define the grouping, or the result of the aggregate (for instance when you want to check whether the result of a count( ) is smaller than a threshold) or both. SQL allows you to specify all such conditions inside the having clause that filters after the group by (in practice, a sort followed by an aggregation) has been completed. Any condition bearing on the result of an aggregate function must be inside the having clause, since the result of such a function is unknown before the group by. Any condition that is independent on the aggregate should go to the where clause and contribute to decrease the number of rows that we shall have to sort to perform the group by.

Let's return to our customers and orders example, admitting that the way we process orders is rather complicated. Before an order is considered complete, we have to go through several phases that are recorded in the table orderstatus, of which the main columns are ordid, the identifier of the order; status; and statusdate, which is a timestamp. The primary key is compound, consisting of ordid, and statusdate. Our requirement is to list, for all orders for which the status is not flagged as complete (assumed to be final), the identifier of the order, the customer name, the last known order status, and when this status was set. To that end, we might build the following query, filtering out completed orders and identifying the current status as the latest status assigned:

```
select c.custname, o.ordid, os.status, os.statusdate
from customers c,
     orders o,
     orderstatus os
where o.ordid = os.ordid
  and not exists (select null
                  from orderstatus os2
                  where os2.status = 'COMPLETE'
                    and os2.ordid = o.ordid)
  and os.statusdate = (select max(statusdate)
                       from orderstatus os3
                       where os3.ordid = o.ordid)
  and o.custid = c.custid
```

At first sight this query looks reasonable, but in fact it contains a number of deeply disturbing features. First, notice that we have two subqueries, and notice too that they are not nested as in the previous examples, but are only indirectly related to each other. Most worrying of all, both subqueries hit the very same table, already referenced at the outer level. What kind of filtering condition are we providing? Not a very precise one, as it only checks for the fact that orders are not yet complete.

How can such a query be executed? An obvious approach is to scan the `orders` table, for each row checking whether each order is or is not complete. (Note that we might have been happy to find this information in the orders table itself, but this is not the case.) Then, and only then, can we check the date of the most recent status, executing the subqueries in the order in which they are written.

The unpleasant fact is that both subqueries are correlated. Since we have to scan the `orders` table, it means that for every row from `orders` we shall have to check whether we encounter the status set to `COMPLETE` for that order. The subquery to check for that status will be fast to execute, but not so fast when repeated a large number of times. When there is no `COMPLETE` status to be found, then a second subquery must be executed. What about trying to un-correlate queries?

The easiest query to un-correlate happens to be the second one. In fact, we can write, at least with some SQL dialects:

```
  and (o.ordid, os.statusdate) = (select ordid, max(statusdate)
                                  from orderstatus
                                  group by ordid)
```

The subquery that we have now will require a full scan of orderstatus; but that's not necessarily bad, and we'll discuss our reasoning in a moment.

There is something quite awkward in the condition of the pair of columns on the left-hand side of the rewritten subquery condition. These columns come from different tables, and they need not do so. In fact, we want the order identifier to be the same in orders and orderstatus; will the optimizer understand the subtlety of this situation? That is rather uncertain. If the optimizer doesn't understand, then it will be able to execute the subquery first, but will have to join the two other tables together before being able to exploit the result of the subquery. If the query were written slightly differently, the optimizer would have greater freedom to decide whether it actually wants to do what I've just described or exploit the result of the subquery and then join orders to orderstatus:

```
and (os.ordid, os.statusdate) = (select ordid, max(statusdate)
                                 from orderstatus
                                 group by ordid)
```

The reference on the left side to two columns from the same table removes the dependence of identification of the most recent status for the order on a preliminary join between orderstatus and orders. A very clever optimizer might have performed the modification for us, but it is wiser to take no risk and specify both columns from the same table to begin with. It is always much better to leave the optimizer with as much freedom as we can.

You have seen previously that an uncorrelated subquery can become a join in an inline view without much effort. We can indeed rewrite the entire query to list pending orders as follows:

```
select c.custname, o.ordid, os.status, os.statusdate
from customers c,
     orders o,
     orderstatus os,
     (select ordid, max(statusdate) laststatusdate
      from orderstatus
      group by ordid) x
where o.ordid = os.ordid
  and not exists (select null
                  from orderstatus os2
                  where os2.status = 'COMPLETE'
                    and os2.ordid = o.ordid)
  and os.statusdate = x.laststatusdate
  and os.ordid = x.ordid
  and o.custid = c.custid
```

But then, if COMPLETE is indeed the final status, do we need the subquery to check the nonexistence of the last stage? The inline view helps us to identify which is the last status, whether it is COMPLETE or anything else. We can apply a perfectly satisfactory filter by checking the latest known status:

```
select c.custname, o.ordid, os.status, os.statusdate
from customers c,
     orders o,
     orderstatus os,
     (select ordid, max(statusdate) laststatusdate
      from orderstatus
      group by ordid) x
where o.ordid = os.ordid
  and os.statusdate = x.laststatusdate
  and os.ordid = x.ordid
  and os.status != 'COMPLETE'
  and o.custid = c.custid
```

The duplicate reference to orderstatus can be further avoided by using OLAP or analytical functions available with some SQL engines. But let's pause here and consider how we have modified the query and, more importantly, the execution path. Basically, our natural path was initially to scan the orders table, and then access through what may reasonably be expected to be an efficient index on the table orderstatus. In the last version of our query, we will attack through a full scan of orderstatus, to perform a group by. In terms of the number of rows, orderstatus will necessarily be several times bigger than orders. However, in terms of mere volume of data to scan, we can expect it to be smaller, possibly significantly smaller, depending on how much information is stored for each order.

We cannot say with certainty which approach will be better, it depends on the data. Let me add that seeing a full scan on a table that is expected to grow is not a good idea (restricting the search to the last month's, or last few months' worth of data can help). But there are significant chances that this last version of our query will perform better than the first attempt with the subquery in the where clause.

We cannot leave the subject of large data volumes without mentioning a slightly special case. When a query returns a very large amount of data, you have reasonable grounds for suspecting that it's not an individual sitting at a terminal that executed the query. The likelihood is that such a query is part of a batch process. Even if there is a longish "preparatory phase," nobody will complain so long as the whole process performs to a satisfactory standard. Do not, of course, forget that a phase, preparatory or not, requires resources—CPU, memory, and possibly temporary disk space. It helps to understand that the optimizer, when returning a lot of data, may choose a path which has nothing in common with the path it would adopt when returning few rows, even if the fundamental query is identical.

Filter out unneeded data as early as possible.

The Proportions of Retrieved Data

A typical and frequently quoted saying is the famous "don't use indexes when your query returns more than 10% of the rows of a table." This states implicitly that (regular) indexes are efficient when an index key points to 10% or less of the rows in a table. As I have already pointed out in Chapter 3, this rule of thumb dates back to a time when relational databases were still regarded with suspicion in many companies. In those days, their use was mostly confined to that of departmental databases. This was a time when a 100,000–row table was considered a really big one. Compared to 10% of a 500 million–row table, 10% of 100,000 rows is a trifle. Can we seriously hope that the best execution plan in one case will still be the best execution plan in the other case? Such is wishful thinking.

Independently from the evolution of table sizes since the time when the "10% of rows" rule of thumb was first coined, be aware that the number of rows returned means nothing in itself, except in terms of response time expectations by end users. If you compute an average value over 1 billion rows, you return a single row, and yet the DBMS performs a lot of work. Even without any aggregation, what matters is the number of data pages that the DBMS is going to hit when performing the query. Data page hits don't only depend on the existence of indexes: as you saw in Chapter 3, the relation of indexes to the physical order of rows in the table can make a significant difference in the number of pages to visit. Other implementation issues that I am going to discuss in Chapter 5 play an important part, too: depending on how data is physically stored, the same number of rows returned may mean that you have to visit massively different numbers of data pages. Furthermore, operations that would execute sequentially with one access path may be massively parallelized with another one. Don't fall into the row percentage trap.

When we want a lot of data, we don't necessarily want an index.

CHAPTER FIVE

Terrain

Understanding Physical Implementation

[...] haben Gegend und Boden eine sehr nahe [...] Beziehung zur kriegerischen Tätigkeit, nämlich einen sehr entscheidenden Einfluß auf das Gefecht.

[...] Country and ground bear a most intimate [...] relation to the business of war, which is their decisive influence on the battle.

—Carl von Clausewitz (1780–1831)
Vom Kriege, V, 17

What a program sees as a table is not always the plain table it may look like. Sometimes it's a view, and sometimes it really is a table, but with storage parameters that have been very carefully established to optimize certain types of operations. In this chapter, I explore different ways to arrange the data in a table and the operations that those arrangements facilitate.

I should emphasize from the start that the topic of this chapter is not disk layout, nor even the relative placement of journal and data files. These are the kinds of subjects that usually send system engineers and database administrators into mouth-watering paroxysms of delight—but no one else. There is much more to database organization than the physical dispersion of bytes on permanent storage. It is the actual nature of the data that dictates the most important choices.

Both system engineers and database administrators know how much storage is used, and they know the various possibilities available in terms of data containers, whether very low-level data containers such as disk stripes or high-level data containers such as tables. But frequently, even database administrators have only a scant knowledge of what lies inside those containers. It can sometimes be helpful to choose the terrain on which to fight. Just as a general may discuss tactics with the engineering corps, so the architect of an application can study with the database administrators how best to structure data at the physical level. Nevertheless, you may be required to fight your battle on terrain over which you have no control or, worse, to use structures that were optimized for totally different purposes.

Structural Types

Even though matters of physical database structure are not directly related to the SQL language, the underlying structures of your database will certainly influence your tactical use of SQL. The chances are that any well-established and working database will fall into one of the following structural types:

The fixed, inflexible model

There are times when you will have absolutely no choice in the matter. You will have to work with the existing database structures, no matter how obvious it may be to you that they are contributing to the performance difficulties, if they are not their actual cause. Whether you are developing new applications, or simply trying to improve existing ones, the underlying structures are going to control the choices you can make in the deployment of your SQL armory. You must try to understand the reasoning behind the system and work with it.

The evolutionary model

Everything is not always cast in stone, and altering the physical layout of data (without modifying the logical model) is sometimes an option. Be very aware that there are dangers here and that the reluctance of database administrators to make such modifications doesn't stem from laziness. In spite of the risks and potential for service interruption attached to such operations, many people cling to database reorganization as their last hope when facing performance issues. Physical reorganization is not in itself the panacea for correcting poor performance. It may be quite helpful in some cases, irrelevant elsewhere, and even harmful in other cases. It is important to know both what you can and cannot expect from such drastic action.

In a sense, if you have to work with a flawed design, neither scenario is a particularly attractive option. "Abandon hope, all ye that have an incorrect design" might just possibly be overstating the situation, but nevertheless I am stressing once again the crucial importance of getting the design right at the earliest opportunity.

In more than one way, implementation choices are comparable to the choice of tires in Formula One motor racing: you have to take a bet on the race conditions that you are expecting. The wrong tire choice may prove costly, the right one may help you win, but even the best choice will not, of itself, assure you of victory.

I won't discuss SQL constructs in this chapter, nor will I delve into the intricacies of specific implementations, which in any case are all very much product dependent. However, it is difficult in practice to design a reliable architecture without an understanding of all the various conditions, good and bad, with or against which the design will have to function. Understanding also means sensing how much a particular physical implementation can impact performance, for better or for worse. This is why I shall try to give you an idea, first of some of the practical problems DBMS implementers have had to face to help improve the speed of queries and changes to the database (of which more will be said in Chapter 9), and second of some of the answers they have found. From a practical point of view, though, be aware that some of the features presented in this chapter are not available with *all* database systems. Or, if they are available, they may require separate licensing.

One last word before we begin. I have tried to establish some points of comparison between various commercial products. To that end, this chapter presents a number of actual test results. However, it is by no means the purpose of this book to organize a beauty contest between various database products, especially as the balance may change between versions. Similarly, absolute values have no meaning, since they depend very strongly on your hardware and the design of the database. This is why I have chosen to present only relative values, and why I have also chosen (with one exception) to compare variations for only one particular DBMS.

The Conflicting Goals

There are often two conflicting goals when trying to optimize the physical layout of data for a system that expects a large number of active users, some of them reading and others writing data. One goal is to try to store the data in as compact a way as possible and to help queries find it as quickly as possible. The other goal is to try to spread the data, so that several processes writing concurrently do not impede one another and cause contention and competition for resources that cannot be shared.

Even when there is no concurrency involved, there is always some tension when designing the physical aspect of a database, between trying to make both queries and updates (in the general sense of "changes to the data") as fast as possible. Indexing is an obvious case in point: people often index in anticipation of queries using the indexed columns as selection criteria. However, as seen in Chapter 3, the cost of maintaining indexes is extremely high and inserting into an index is often much more expensive than inserting into the underlying table alone.

Contention issues affect any data that has to be stored, especially in change-heavy transactional applications (I am using the generic term *change* to mean any insert, delete, and update operation). Various storage units and some very low layers of the operating system can take care of some contention issues. The files that contain the database data may be sliced, mirrored, and spread all over the place to ensure data integrity in case of hardware failure, as well as to limit contention.

Unfortunately, relying on the operating system alone to deal with contention is not enough. The base units of data that a DBMS handles (known as pages or blocks depending on the product) are usually, even at the lowest layers, atomic from a database perspective, especially as they are ultimately all scanned in memory. Even when everything is perfect for the systems engineer, there may be pure DBMS performance issues.

To get the best possible response time, we must try to keep the number of data pages that have to be accessed by the database engine as low as possible. We have two principal means of decreasing the number of pages that will have to be accessed in the course of a query:

- Trying to ensure a high data density per page
- Grouping together those pieces of data most likely to be required during one retrieval process

However, trying to squeeze the data into as few pages as possible may not be the optimum approach where the same page is being written by several concurrent processes and perhaps also being read at the same time. Where that single data page is the subject of multiple read or write attempts, conflict resolution takes on an altogether more complex and serious dimension.

Many believe that the structure of a database is the exclusive responsibility of the database administrator. In reality, it is predominantly *but not exclusively* the responsibility of that very important person. The way in which you physically structure your data is extremely dependent on the nature of the data and its intended use. For example, partitioning can be a valuable aid in optimizing a physical design, but it should never be applied in a haphazard way. Because there is such an intimate relationship between process requirements and physical design, we often encounter profound conflicts between alternative designs for the same data when that data is shared between two or more business processes. This is just like the dilemma faced by the general on the battlefield, where the benefits of using alternative parts of his forces (infantry, cavalry, or artillery) have to be balanced against the suitability of the terrain across which he has to deploy them. The physical design of tables and indexes is one of those areas where database administrators and developers must work together, trying to match the available DBMS features in the best possible way against business requirements.

The sections to follow introduce some different strategies and show their impact on queries and updates from a single-process perspective, which, in practice, is usually the batch program perspective.

Reads and writes don't live in harmony: readers want data clustered; and concurrent writers want data scattered.

Considering Indexes as Data Repositories

Indexes allow us to find quickly the addresses (references to some particular storage in persistent memory, typically file identifiers and offsets within the files) of the rows that contain a key we are looking for. Once we have an address, then it can be translated into a low-level, operating system reference which, if we are lucky, will direct us to the true memory address where the data is located. Alternatively, the index search will result in some input/output operation taking place before we have the data at our disposal in memory.

As discussed previously in Chapter 3, when the value of a key we are looking for refers to a very large number of rows, it is often more efficient simply to scan the table from the beginning to the end and ignore the indexes. This is why, at least in a transactional database, it is useless to index columns with a low number of distinct values (i.e., a low *cardinality*) unless one value is highly selective and appears frequently in `where` clauses. Other indexes that we can dispose of are single-column indexes on columns that already participate in composite indexes as the leading column: there is no need whatsoever to index the same column twice in these circumstances. The very common tree-structured, or hierarchical, index can be efficiently searched even if we do not have the full key value, just as long as we have a sufficient number of leading bytes to ensure discrimination.

The use of leading bytes rather than the full index key for querying an index introduces an interesting type of optimization. If there is an index on (`c1, c2, c3`), this index is usable even if we only specify the value of `c1`. Furthermore, if the key values are not compressed, then the index contains all the data held in the (`c1, c2, c3`) triplets that are present in the table. If we specify `c1` to get the corresponding values of `c2`, or of `c2` to find the corresponding `c3`, we find within the index itself all the data we need, without requiring further access to the actual table. For example, to take a very simple analogy, it's exactly as though you were looking for William Shakespeare's year of birth. Submitting the string *William Shakespeare* to any web search engine will return information such as you see in Figure 5-1.

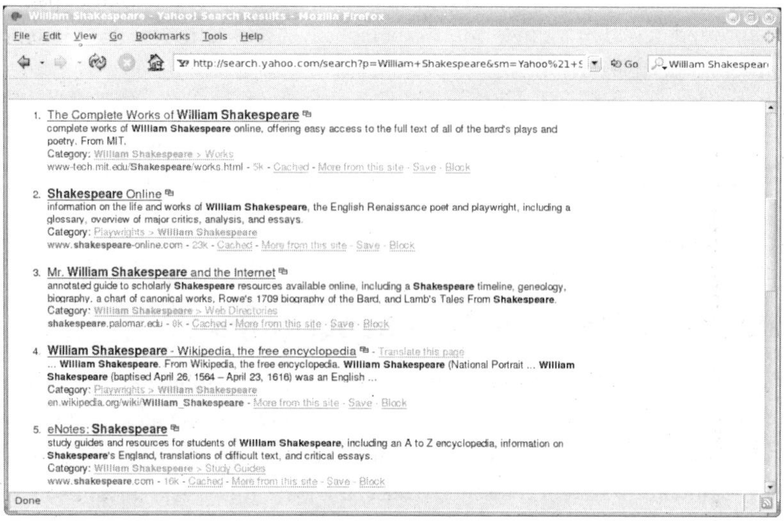

FIGURE 5-1. *Searching the Web for "William Shakespeare"*

There is no need to visit any of these sites (which may be a pity): we have found our answer in the data returned from the search engine index itself. The fourth entry tells us that Shakespeare was born in 1564.

When an index is sufficiently loaded with information, going to the place it points to becomes unnecessary. This very same reasoning is at the root of an often used optimization tactic. We can improve the speed of a frequently run query by stuffing into an index additional columns (one or more) which of themselves have no part to play in the actual search criteria, but which crucially hold the data we need to answer our query.

Thus the data that we require can be retrieved entirely from the index, cutting out completely the need to access the original source data. Some products such as DB2 are clever enough to let us specify that a unique index *includes* some other columns and check uniqueness of only a part of the composite key. The same result can be achieved with Oracle, in a somewhat more indirect fashion, by using a non-unique index to enforce a uniqueness or primary key constraint.

Conversely, there have been cases of batch programs suddenly taking much more time to run to completion than previously, following what appears to be the most insignificant modification to the query. This minor change was the addition of another column to the list of columns returned by a `select` statement. Unfortunately, prior to the modification, the entire query could be satisfied by reference to the data returned from an index. The addition of the new column forced the database to go back to the table, resulting in a hugely significant increase in processor activity.

Let's look in more detail at the contrast between "index only" and "index plus table" retrieval performance. Figure 5-2 illustrates the performance impact of fetching one additional column absent from the index that is used to answer the query for three of the major database systems. The table used for the test was the same in all cases, having 12 columns populated with 250,000 rows. The primary key was defined as a three-column composite key, consisting of first an integer column with random values uniformly spread between 1 and 5,000, then a string of 8 to 10 characters, and then finally a `datetime` column. There is no other index on the table other than the unique index that implements the primary key. The reference query is fetching the second and third columns in the primary key on the basis of a random value of between 1 and 5,000 in the first column. The test measures the performance impact of fetching one more column—numeric and therefore relatively small—that doesn't belong to the index. The results in Figure 5-2 are normalized such that the case of fetching two columns that are found in the index is always pegged at 100%. The case of having to go to the table and fetch an additional column absent from the index is then expressed as some percentage less than 100%.

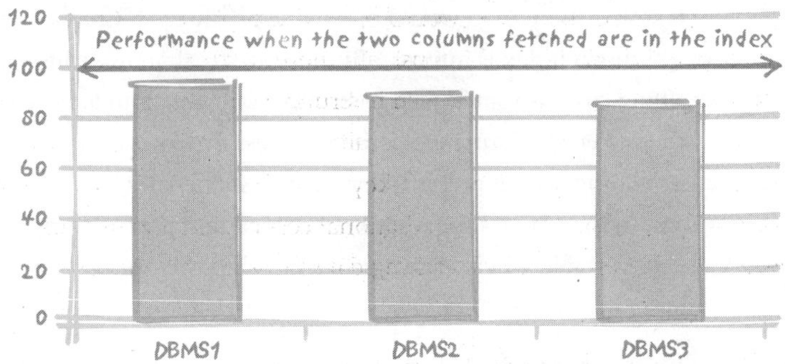

FIGURE 5-2. *Performance impact of fetching a third column that has to be retrieved from the table*

Figure 5-2 shows that the performance impact of having to go to the table as well as to the index isn't enormous (around 5 or 10%) but nevertheless it is noticeable, and it is much more so with some database products than with others. As always, the exact numbers may vary with circumstances, and the impact can be much more severe if the table access requires additional physical I/O operations, which isn't the case here.

Pushing to the extreme the principle of storing as much data as possible in the indexes, some database management systems, such as Oracle, allow you to store all of a table's data into an index built on the primary key, thus getting rid of the table structure altogether. This approach saves storage and may save time. The table *is* the index, and is known as an *index-organized table* (IOT) as opposed to the regular *heap* structure.

After the discussion in Chapter 3 about the cost penalty of index insertion, you might expect insertions into an index-organized table to be less costly than applying insertions to a table with no other index than the primary key enforcement index. In fact, in some circumstances the opposite is true, as you can see from Figure 5-3. It compares insertion rates for a regular table against those for an IOT. The tests used a total of four tables. Two table patterns with the same column definitions were created, once as a regular heap table, and once as an IOT. The first table pattern was a small table consisting of the primary key columns plus one additional column, and the second pattern a table consisting of the primary key columns plus nine other columns, all numeric. The (compound) primary key in every table was defined as a number column, a 10-character string, and a timestamp. For each case, two tests were performed. In the first test, the primary key was subjected to the insertion of randomly ordered primary key values. The second test involved the insertion into the leading primary key column of an increasing, ordered sequence of numbers.

Where the table holds few columns other than the ones that define the primary key, it is indeed faster to insert into an IOT. However, if the table has even a moderate number of columns, all those columns that don't pertain to the primary key also have to be stored in the index structure (sometimes to an overflow area). Since the table is the index, much more information is stored there than would otherwise be the case. Chapter 3 has also shown that inserting into an index is intrinsically more costly than inserting into a regular table. The byte-shuffling cost associated with inserting more data into a more complicated structure can lead to a severe performance penalty, unless the rows are inserted in the same or near-the-same order as the primary key index. The penalty is even worse with long character strings. In many cases the additional cost of insertion outweighs the benefit of not having to go to the table when fetching data through the primary key index.*

* A reviewer remarked that implementation reasons that are beyond the scope of this book also make *other* indexes than the primary key index less efficient on an IOT than they would be on a regular table.

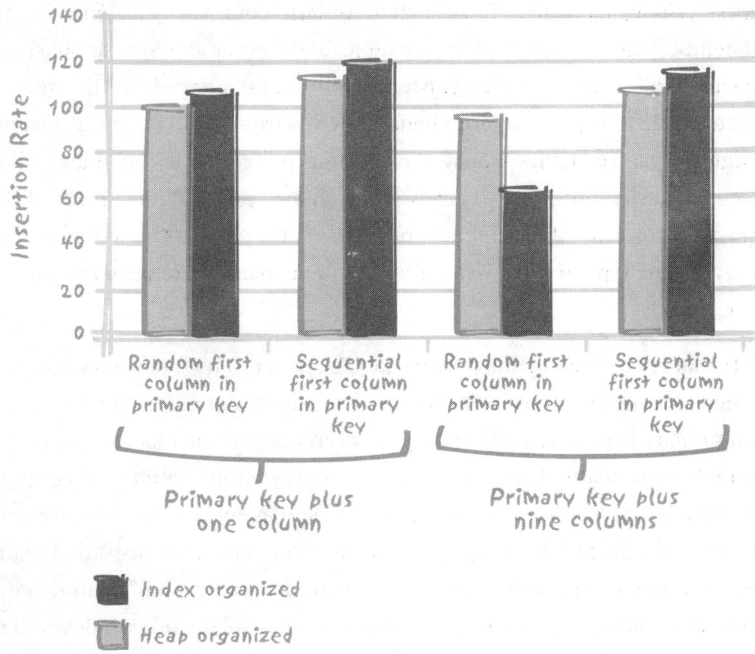

FIGURE 5-3. *Relative cost of inserting into an Oracle index-organized table compared to a regular (heap-organized) table*

There are, however, some other potential benefits linked to the strong internal ordering of indexes, as you shall see next.

Some queries can be answered by retrieving only the index data.

Forcing Row Ordering

There is another aspect to an index-organized table than just finding all required data in the index itself without requiring an additional access to the table. Because IOTs, being indexes, are, first and foremost, strongly ordered structures, their rows are internally ordered. Although the notion of order is totally foreign to the relational theory, from a practical point of view whenever a query refers to a range of values, it helps to find them together instead of having to gather data scattered all over the table. The most common example of this sort of application is range searching on time series data, when you are looking for events that occurred between two particular dates.

Most database systems manage to force such an ordering of rows by assigning to an index the role of defining the order of rows in the table. SQL Server and Sybase call such an index a clustered index. DB2 calls it a clustering index, and it has much the same effect in practice as an Oracle IOT. Some queries benefit greatly from this type of organization. But similar to index organized tables, updates to columns pertaining to the index that defines the order are obviously more costly because they entail a physical movement of the data to a new position corresponding to the "rank" of the new values. The ordering of rows inevitably favors one type of range-scan query at the expense of range scans on alternative criteria.

As with IOTs that are defined by the primary key, it is safer to use the primary key index as the clustering index, since primary keys are never updated (and if your application needs to update your primary key, there is something very seriously wrong indeed with your design, and it won't take long before there is something seriously wrong with the integrity of your data). In contrast to IOTs, an index other than the one that enforces the primary key constraint can be chosen as the clustering index. But remember that any ordering unduly favors some processes at the expense of others. The primary key, if it is a natural key, has a logical significance; the associated index is more equal than all the other indexes that may be defined on the table, even unique ones. If some columns must be given some particular prominence through the physical implementation, these are the ones.

Figure 5-4 illustrates the kind of differences you may expect between clustered and non-clustered index performance in practice. If we take the same table as was used for the index-organized table in Figure 5-3's example (a three-column primary key plus nine numeric columns), and if we insert rows in a totally random way, the cost of insertion into a table where the primary key index is clustered is quite high, since tests show that our insertion rate is about half the insertion rate obtained with a non-clustered primary key. But when we run a range scan test on about 50,000 rows, this clustered index provides really excellent performance. In this particular case, the clustered index allows us to outperform the non-clustered approach by a factor of 20. We should, of course, see no difference when fetching a single row.

A structural optimization, such as a clustered index or an IOT, necessarily has some drawbacks. For one thing, such structures apply some strong, tree-based, and therefore hierarchical ordering to tables. This approach resurrects many of the flaws that saw hierarchical databases replaced by relational databases in the corporate world. Any hierarchical structure favors one vision of the data and one access path over all the others. One particular access path will be better than anything you could get with a non-clustered table, but most other access paths are likely to be significantly worse. Updates may prove more costly. The initial tidy disposition of the data inside the database files may deteriorate faster at the physical level, due to chaining, overflow pages, and similar constructs, which take a heavy toll on performance. Clustered structures are excellent in

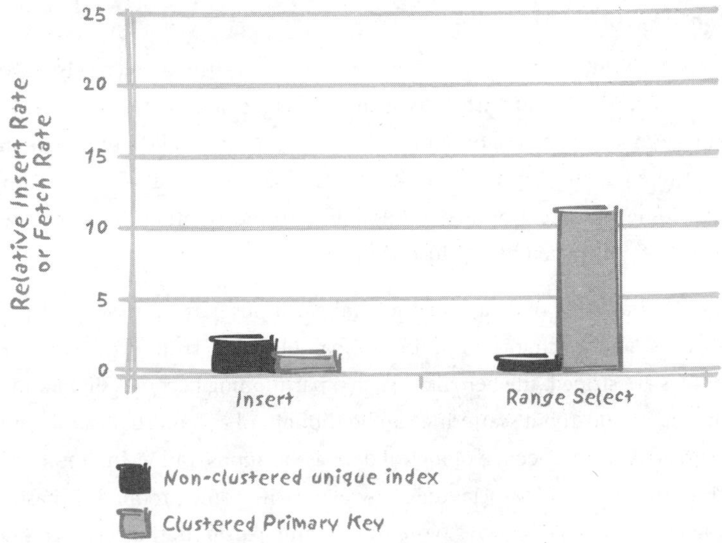

FIGURE 5-4. *How clustered indexes perform*

some cases, boosting performance by an impressive factor. But they always need to be carefully tested, because there is a high probability that they will make many other processes run slower. One must judge their suitability while looking at the global picture—and not on the basis of one particular query.

Range scanning on clustered data can give impressive performance, but other queries will suffer as a consequence.

Automatically Grouping Data

You have seen that finding all the rows together when doing a range scan can be highly beneficial to performance. There are, actually, other means to achieve a grouping of data than the somewhat constraining use of clustering indexes or index-organized tables. All database management systems let us *partition* tables and indexes—an application of the old principle of *divide and rule*. A large table may be split into more manageable chunks. Moreover, in terms of process architecture, partitioning allows an increased concurrency and parallelism, thus leading to more *scalable* architectures, as you shall see in Chapters 9 and 10.

First of all, beware that this very word, *partition*, has a different meaning depending on the DBMS under discussion, sometimes even depending on the version of the DBMS. There was a time, long ago, when what is now known as an Oracle *tablespace* used to be referred to as a *partition*.

Round-Robin Partitioning

In some cases, partitioning is a totally internal, non-data-driven mechanism. We arbitrarily define a number of partitions as distinct areas of disk storage, usually closely linked to the number of devices on which we want the data to be stored. One table may have one or more partitions assigned to it. When data is inserted, it is loaded to each partition according to some arbitrary method, in a round-robin fashion, so as to balance the load on disk I/O induced by the insertions.

Incidentally, the scattering of data across several partitions may very well assist subsequent random searches. This mechanism is quite comparable to file striping over disk arrays. In fact, if your files are striped, the benefit of such a partitioning becomes slight and sometimes quite negligible. Round-robin scattering can be thought of as a mechanism designed only to arbitrarily spread data irrespective of logical data associations, rather than to regroup data on the basis of those natural associations. However, with some products, Sybase being one of them, one transaction will always write to the same partition, thus achieving some business-process-related grouping of data.

Data-Driven Partitioning

There is, however, a much more interesting type of partitioning known as *data-driven partitioning*. With data-driven partitioning, it is the values, found in one or several columns, that defines the partition into which each row is inserted. As always, the more the DBMS knows about the data and how it is stored, the better.

Most really large tables are large because they contain historical data. However, our interest in a particular news event quickly wanes as new and fresher events crowd in to demand our attention, so it is a safe assumption to make that the most-often-queried subset of historical data is the most recent one. It is therefore quite natural to try to partition data by date, separating the wheat from the chaff, the active data from the dormant data.

For instance, a manual way to partition by date is to split a large `figures` table (containing data for the last twelve months) into twelve separate tables, one for each month, namely `jan_figures`, `feb_figures`...all the way to `dec_figures`. To ensure that a global vision of the year is still available for any queries that require it, we just have to define `figures` as the `union` of those twelve tables. Such a `union` is often given some kind of official endorsement at the database level as a *partitioned view*, or (in MySQL) a *merge table*. During the month of March, we'll insert into the table `mar_figures`. Then we'll switch to `apr_figures` for the following month. The use of a view as a blanket object over a set of similarly structured tables may appear an attractive idea, but it has drawbacks:

- The capital sin is that such a view builds in a fundamental design flaw. We know that the underlying tables are logically related, but we have no way to inform the DBMS of their relationships except, in some cases, via the rather weak definition of the partitioned view. Such a multi-table design prevents us from correctly defining integrity constraints. We have no easy way to enforce uniqueness properly across all the underlying tables, and as a matter of consequence, we would have to build multiple foreign keys referencing this "set" of tables, a situation that becomes utterly difficult and unnatural. All we can do in terms of integrity is to add a `check` constraint on the column that determines partitioning. For example, we could add a `check` constraint to `sales_date`, to ensure that `sales_date` in the `jun_sales` table cannot fall outside the June 1 to June 30 range.
- Without specific support for partitioned views in your DBMS, it is rather inconvenient to code around such a set of tables, because every month we must insert into a different underlying table. This means that `insert` statements must be dynamically built to accommodate varying table names. The effect of dynamic statements is usually to significantly increase the complexity of programs. In our case, for instance, a program would have to get the date, either the current one or some input value, check it, determine the name of the table corresponding to that date, and build up a suitable SQL statement. However, the situation is much better with partitioned views, because insertions can then usually be performed directly through the view, and the DBMS takes care of where to insert the rows.

  In all cases, however, as a direct consequence of our flawed design, it is quite likely that after some unfortunate and incoherent insertions we shall be asked to code referential integrity checks, thus further compounding a poor design with an increased development load—both for the developers and for the machine that runs the code. This will move the burden of integrity checking from the DBMS kernel to, in the best of cases, code in triggers and stored procedures and, in the worst of cases, to the application program.
- There is a performance impact on queries when using blanket views. If we are interested in the figures for a given month, we can query a single table. If we are interested in the figures from the past 30 days, we will most often need to query two tables. For queries, then, the simplest and more maintainable way to code is to query the view rather than the underlying tables. If we have a partitioned view and if the column that rules the placement of rows belongs to our set of criteria, the DBMS optimizer will be able to limit the scope of our query to the proper subset of tables. If not, our query will necessarily be more complicated than it would be against a regular table, especially if it is a complex query involving subqueries or aggregates. The complexity of the query will continue to increase as more tables become involved in the `union`. The overhead of querying a large `union` view over directly querying a single table will quickly show in repeatedly executed statements.

Historically, the first step taken by most database management systems towards partitioning has been the support of partitioned views. The next logical step has been support for true data-driven partitioning. With true partitioning, we have a single table at the logical level, with a true primary key able to be referenced by other tables. In addition, we have one or several columns that are defined as the *partition key*; their values are used to determine into which partition a row is inserted. We have all the advantages of partitioned views, transparency when operating on the table, *and* we can push back to the DBMS engine the task of protecting the integrity of the data, which is one of the primary functions of the DBMS. The kernel knows about partitioning, and the optimizer will know how to exploit such a physical structure, by either limiting operations to a small number of partitions (something known as *partition pruning*), or by operating on several partitions in parallel.

The exact way partitioning is implemented and the number of available options is product-dependent. There are several different ways to partition data, which may be more or less appropriate to particular situations:

Hash-partitioning

Spreads data by determining the partition as the result of a computation on the partition key. It's a totally arbitrary placement based entirely on an arithmetic computation, and it takes no account at all of the distribution of data values. Hash-partitioning does, however, ensure very fast access to rows for any specific value of the partition key. It is useless for range searching, because the hash function transforms consecutive key values into non-consecutive hash values, and it's these hash values that translate to physical address.

NOTE

DB2 provides an additional mechanism called *range-clustering*, which, although not the same as partitioning, nevertheless uses the data from the key to determine physical location. It does this through a mechanism that, in contrast to hashing, preserves the order of data items. We then gain on both counts, with efficient specific accesses as well as efficient range scans.

Range-partitioning

Seeks to gather data into discrete groups according to continuous data ranges. It's ideally suited for dealing with historical data. Range-partitioning is closest to the concept of partitioned views that we discussed earlier: a partition is defined as being dedicated to the storage of values falling within a certain range. An `else` partition is set up for catching everything that might slip through the net. Although the most common use of range partitioning is to partition by range of temporal values, whether it is hours or years or anything between, this type of partitioning is in no way restricted to a particular type of data. A multivolume encyclopedia in which the articles in each volume would indeed be within the alphabetical boundaries of the volume but otherwise in no particular order provides a good example of range partitioning.

List-partitioning

Is the most manual type of partitioning and may be suitable for tailor-made solutions. Its name says it all: you explicitly specify that rows containing a list of the possible values for the partition key (usually just one column) will be assigned to a particular partition. List-partitioning can be useful when the distribution of values is anything but uniform.

The partitioning process can sometimes be repeated with the creation of subpartitions. A subpartition is merely a partition within a partition, giving you the ability to partition against a second dimension by creating, for instance, hash-partitions within a range-partition.

Data partitioning is most valuable when it is based on the data values themselves.

The Double-Edged Sword of Partitioning

Despite the fact that partitioning spreads data from a table over multiple, somewhat independent partitions, data-driven partitioning is not a panacea for resolving concurrency problems. For example, we might partition a table by date, having one partition per week of activity. Doing so is an efficient way to spread data for one year over 52 logically distinct areas. The problem is that during any given week everybody will rush to the same partition to insert new rows. Worse, if our partitioning key is the current system date and time, all concurrent sessions will be directed towards the very same data block (unless some structural implementation tricks have been introduced, such as maintaining several lists of pages or blocks where we can insert). As a result, we may have some very awkward memory contention. Our large table will become a predominantly cold area, with a very hot spot corresponding to most current data. Such partitioning is obviously less than ideal when many processes are inserting concurrently.

NOTE

If all data is inserted through a single process, which is sometimes the case in data-warehousing environments, then we won't have a hot spot to contend with, and our 52-week partitioning scheme won't lead to concurrency problems.

On the other hand, let's assume that we choose to partition according to the geographical origin of a purchase order (we may have to carefully organize our partitioning if our products are more popular in some areas and suffer from heavier competition elsewhere).

At any given moment, since sales are likely to come from nowhere in particular, our inserts will be more or less randomly spread over all our partitions. The performance impact from our partitioning will be quite noticeable when we are running geographical reports. Of course, because we have partitioned on spatial criteria, time-based reports will be less efficiently generated than if we had partitioned on time. Nevertheless, even time-based queries may, to some extent, benefit from partitioning since it is quite likely that on a multiprocessor box the various partitions will be searched in parallel and the subsequent results merged.

There are therefore two sides to partitioning. On the one hand, it is an excellent way to cluster data according to the partitioning key so as to achieve faster data retrieval. On the other hand, it is a no-less-excellent way to spread data during concurrent inserts so as to avoid hot spots in the table. These two objectives can work in opposition to one another, so the very first thing to consider when partitioning is to identify the major problem, and partition against that. But it is important to check that the gain on one side is not offset by the loss on the other. The ideal case is when the clustering of data for `selects` goes hand in hand with suitably spread `inserts`, but this is unfortunately not the most common situation.

Data partitioning can be used to scatter or cluster your data: it all depends on your requirements.

Partitioning and Data Distribution

You may be tempted to believe that if we have a very large table and want to avoid contention when many sessions are simultaneously writing to the database, then we are necessarily better off partitioning the data in one way or another. This is not always true.

Suppose that we have a large table storing the details of orders passed by our customers. If, as sometimes happens, a single customer represents the bulk of our activity, partitioning on the customer identifier is not going to help us very much. We can very roughly divide our queries into two families: queries relating to our big customer and queries relating to the other, smaller customers. When we query the data relating to one small customer, an index on the customer identifier will be very selective and therefore efficient, without any compelling need for partitioning. A clever optimizer fed with suitable statistics about the distribution of keys will be able to detect the skewness and use the index. There will be little benefit to having those small customers stored into smallish partitions next to the big partition holding our main customer.

Conversely, when querying the data attached to our major customer, the very same clever optimizer will understand that scanning the table is by far the most efficient way of proceeding. In that case, fully scanning a partition that comprises, for example, 80% of the total volume will not be much faster than doing a full table scan. The end users will hardly notice the performance advantage, whereas the purchasing department will most certainly notice the extra cost of the separately priced partitioning option.

The biggest benefits to queries of table partitioning are obtained when data is uniformly spread in respect to the partitioning key.

The Best Way to Partition Data

Never forget that what dictates the choice of a nonstandard storage option such as partitioning is the global improvement of business operations. It may mean improving a business process that is perceived as being of paramount importance to the detriment of some other processes. For instance, it makes sense to optimize transactional processing that takes place during business hours at the expense of a nightly batch job that has ample time to complete. The opposite may also be true, and we may decide that we can afford to have very slightly less responsive transactions if it allows us to minimize a critical upload time during which data is unavailable to users. It's a matter of balance.

In general, you should avoid unduly favoring one process over another that needs to be run under similar conditions. In this regard, any type of storage that positions data at different locations based on the data value (for example both clustering indexes as well as partitioning) are very costly when that value is updated. What would have previously been an *in situ* update in a regular table, requiring hardly more than perhaps changing and shifting a few bytes in the table at an invariant physical address, becomes a `delete` on one part of the disk, followed by an `insert` somewhere else, with all the maintenance operations usually associated with indexes for this type of operation.

Having to move data when we update partition keys seems, on the surface, to be a situation best avoided. Strangely, however, partitioning on a key that is updated may sometimes be preferable to partitioning on a key that is immutable once it has been inserted. For example, suppose that we have a table being used as a service queue. Some process inserts service requests into this table that are of different types (say type T_1 to type T_n). New service requests are initially set to status *W*, meaning "waiting to be processed." Server processes S_1 to S_p regularly poll the table for requests with the *W* status, change the status of those requests to *P* (meaning "being processed"), and then, as each request is completed its status is set to *D* for "done."

Let's further suppose that we have as many server processes as we have request types, and that each server process is dedicated to handling a particular type of request. Figure 5-5 shows the service queue as well as the processes. Of course, since we cannot let the table fill with "done" requests, there must be some garbage-collecting process, not shown, that removes processed requests after a suitable delay.

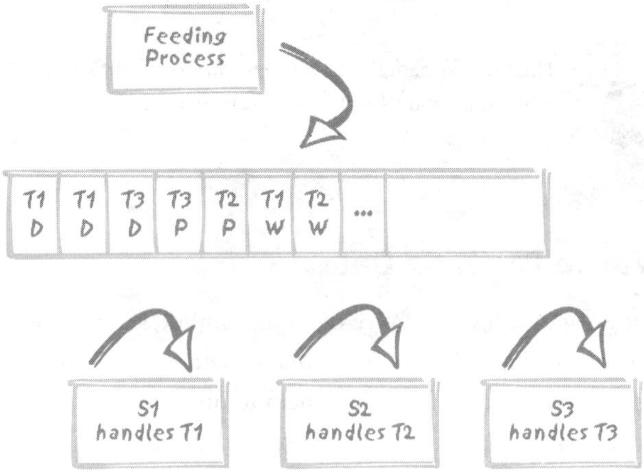

FIGURE 5-5. *A service queue*

Each server process regularly executes a `select` (actually, a `select ... for update`) query with two criteria, the type, which depends on the server, and a condition:

```
and status = 'W'
```

Let's consider alternative ways of partitioning the service queue table. One way to partition the table, and possibly the most obvious, is to partition by request type. There is a big advantage here should any server process crash or fall behind in one way or another. The queue will lengthen for that process until it finally catches up, but the interruption to the processing of that queue will have no influence on the other processes.

Another advantage of partitioning by request type is that we avoid having requests of any one type swamp the system. Without partitioning, the polling processes scan a queue that under normal circumstances contains very few rows of interest. If we have a common waiting line and all of a sudden we have a large number of requests of one type and status, *all* the processes will have more requests to inspect and therefore each will be slowed down. If we partition by type, we establish a watertight wall between the processing of different types.

But there is another possible way to partition our service queue table, and that is by status. The downside is obvious: any status change will make a request migrate from one partition to the next. Can there be any advantage to such migration? Actually, there may indeed be benefit in this approach. Everything in partition *W* is ready and waiting to be processed. So there is no need to scan over requests being processed by another server or requests that have already been processed. Therefore, the cost of polling may be significantly reduced. Another advantage is that garbage collection will operate on a separate partition, and will not disturb the servers.

We cannot say definitively that "partitioning must be by type" or "partitioning must be by status." It depends on how many servers we have, their polling frequency, the relative rate at which data arrives, the processing time for each type of request, and how often we remove processed requests, and so on. We must carefully test various hypotheses and consider the overall picture. But it is sometimes more efficient for the overall system to sacrifice outright performance for one particular operation, if by doing so other, more frequently running processes are able to obtain a net advantage, thus benefiting the global business operations.

There may be several ways to partition tables, and the most obvious is not always the most efficient. Always consider the global picture.

Pre-Joining Tables

We have seen that physically grouping rows together is of most benefit when performing range scans, where we are obviously interested in a succession of logically adjacent rows. But our discussion so far has been with regard to retrieving data from only one table. Unless the database design is very, very, very bad, most queries will involve far more than one table. It may therefore seem somewhat questionable if we group all the data from one table into one physical location, only to have to complete the retrieval by visiting several randomly scattered locations for data from a second and subsequent tables. We need some method to group data from at least two tables into the same physical location on disk.

The answer lies in pre-joined tables, a technique that is supported by some database systems. Pre-joining is not the same as *summary tables* or *materialized views*, which are themselves nothing other than redundant data, pre-digested results that are updated more or less automatically.

Pre-joined tables are tables that are physically stored together, based on some criterion that will usually be the join condition. (Oracle calls such a set of pre-joined tables a *cluster*, which has nothing to do with either index clustering, as defined earlier in this chapter, nor with the MySQL clusters of databases, which are multiple servers accessing the same set of tables.)

When tables are pre-joined, the basic unit of storage (a page or a block), normally devoted to the data from a single table, holds data from two or more tables, brought together on the basis of a common join key. This arrangement may be very efficient for one specific join. But it often proves to be a disaster for everything else. Here's a review of some of the disadvantages of pre-joining tables:

- Once the data from two or more tables starts to be shared within one page (or block), the amount of data from one table that can be held in one database page obviously falls, as the page is now sharing its fixed space between two or more tables. Consequently, there is a net increase in the number of pages needed to hold all the data from that one table. More I/O is required than previously if a full table scan has to be performed.
- Not only is data being shared across additional pages, but the effective size of those pages has been reduced from what was obviously judged to be the optimum at database creation time, and so overflow and chaining start to become significant problems. When this happens, the number of successive accesses required to reach the actual data also increases.
- Moreover, as anybody who has ever shared an apartment will know, one person often expands space occupancy at the expense of the other. Database tables are just the same! If you want to address this problem by allocating strictly identical storage to each table per page in the cluster, the result is frequently storage waste and the use of even more pages.

This particular type of storage should be used extremely sparingly to solve very specific issues, and then only by database administrators. Developers should forget about this technique.

Pre-joining tables is a very specialized tactic to facilitate queries, but is often done to the detriment of just about every other database activity.

Holy Simplicity

It is reasonable and safe to assume that any storage option that is not the default one, however attractive it may look, can introduce a degree of complexity out of all proportion to the possible gains that may (or may not) be achieved. In the worst case, a poorly chosen storage option can dramatically degrade performance. Military history is full of impregnable fortresses built in completely the wrong places that failed to fill any useful purpose, and of many a Great Wall that never prevented any invasion because the enemy, a bad sport, failed to behave as planned. All organizations undergo changes, such as divisions and mergers. Business plans and processes may change, too. Careful plans may have to be scrapped and rebuilt from scratch.

The trouble with structuring data in a particular way is that it is often done with a particular type of process in mind. One of the beauties of the relational model is its flexibility. By strongly structuring your data at the physical level, you may sacrifice, in a somewhat hidden way, some of this flexibility. Of course, some structures are less constraining than others, and data partitioning is almost unavoidable with enormous databases. But always test very carefully and keep in mind that changing the physical structure of a big database because it was poorly done initially can take days, if not weeks, to complete.

The physical storage organization that works for us today may work against us tomorrow.

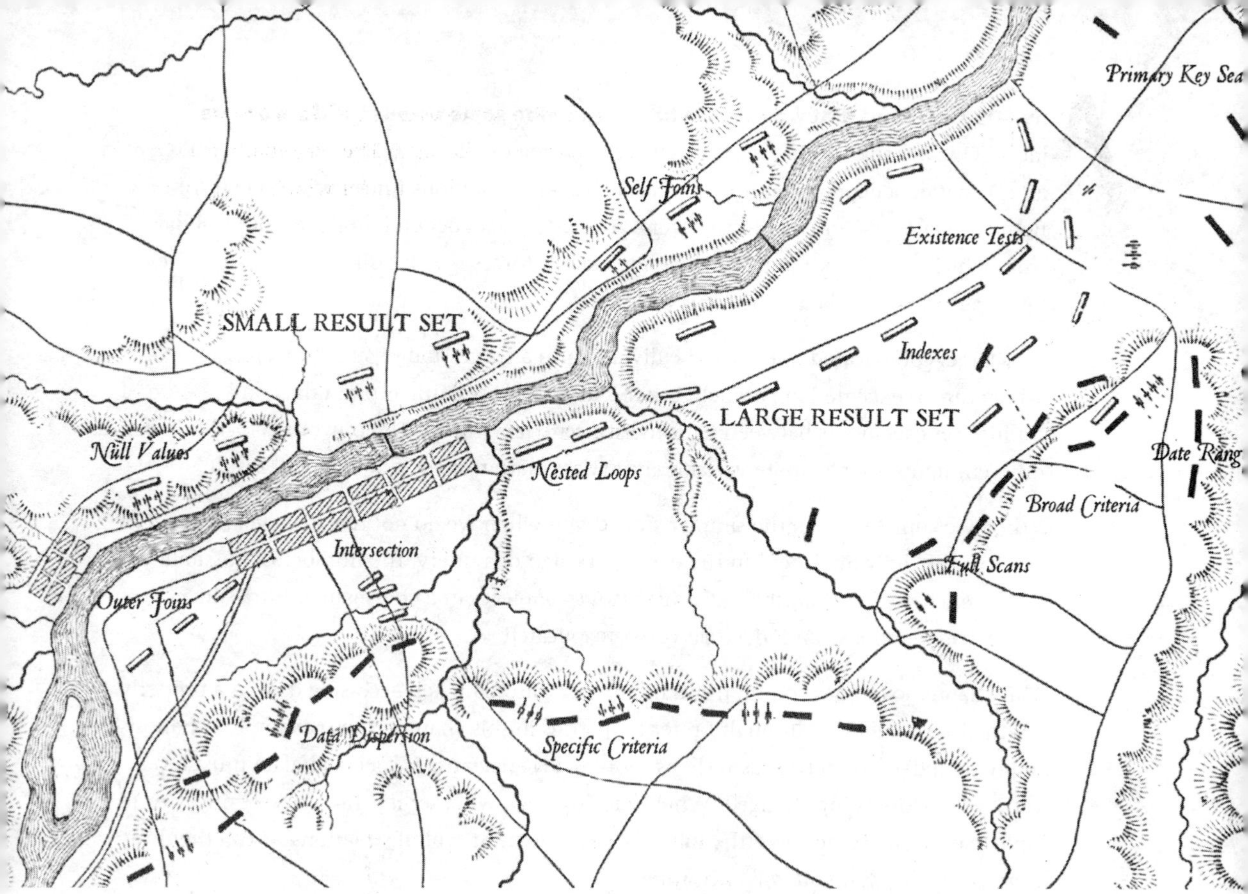

CHAPTER SIX

The Nine Situations

Recognizing Classic SQL Patterns

Je pense que pour conserver la clarté dans le récit d'une action de guerre, il faut se borner à...ne raconter que les faits principaux et décisifs du combat.

To preserve clarity in relating a military action, I think one ought to be content with... reporting only the facts that affected the decision.

—*Général Baron de Marbot (1782–1854)*

Mémoires, Book I, xxvi

Any SQL statement that we execute has to examine some amount of data before identifying a result set that must be either returned or changed. The way that we have to attack that data depends on the circumstances and conditions under which we have to fight the battle. As I discuss in Chapter 4, our attack will depend on the amount of data from which we retrieve our result set and on our forces (the filtering criteria), together with the volume of data to be retrieved.

Any large, complicated query can be divided into a succession of simpler steps, some of which can be executed in parallel, rather like a complex battle is often the combination of multiple engagements between various distinct enemy units. The outcome of these different fights may be quite variable. But what matters is the final, overall result.

When we come down to the simpler steps, even when we do not reach a level of detail as small as the individual steps in the execution plan of a query, the number of possibilities is not much greater than the individual moves of pieces in a chess game. But as in a chess game, combinations can indeed be very complicated.

This chapter examines common situations encountered when accessing data in a properly normalized database. Although I refer to queries in this chapter, these example situations apply to updates or deletes as well, as soon as a `where` clause is specified; data must be retrieved before being changed. When filtering data, whether it is for a simple query or to update or delete some rows, the following are the most typical situations—I call them the *nine situations*—that you will encounter:

- Small result set from a few tables with specific criteria applied to those tables
- Small result set based on criteria applied to tables other than the data source tables
- Small result set based on the intersection of several broad criteria
- Small result set from one table, determined by broad selection criteria applied to two or more additional tables
- Large result set
- Result set obtained by self-joining on one table
- Result set obtained on the basis of aggregate function(s)
- Result set obtained by simple searching or by range searching on dates
- Result set predicated on the absence of other data

This chapter deals with each of these situations in turn and illustrates them with either simple, specific examples or with more complex real-life examples collected from different programs. Real-life examples are not always basic, textbook, one- or two-table affairs. But the overall pattern is usually fairly recognizable.

As a general rule, what we require when executing a query is the filtering out of any data that does not belong in our final result set as soon as possible; this means that we must apply the most efficient of our search criteria as soon as possible. Deciding which criterion to apply first is normally the job of the optimizer. But, as I discuss in Chapter 4, the optimizer must take into account a number of variable conditions, from the physical implementation of tables to the manner in which we have written a query. Optimizers do not always "get it right," and there are things we can do to facilitate performance in each of our nine situations.

Small Result Set, Direct Specific Criteria

The typical online transaction-processing query is a query returning a small result set from a few tables and with very specific criteria applied to those tables. When we are looking for a few rows that match a selective combination of conditions, our first priority is to pay attention to indexes.

The trivial case of a single table or even a join between two tables that returns few rows presents no more difficulty than ensuring that the query uses the proper index. However, when many tables are joined together, and we have input criteria referring to, for instance, two distinct tables TA and TB, then we can either work our way from TA to TB or from TB to TA. The choice depends on how fast we can get rid of the rows we do not want. If statistics reflect the contents of tables with enough accuracy, the optimizer should, hopefully, be able to make the proper decision as to the join order.

When writing a query to return few rows, and with direct, specific criteria, we must identify the criteria that are most efficient at filtering the rows; if some criteria are highly critical, before anything else, we must make sure that the columns corresponding to those criteria are indexed and that the indexes can be used by the query.

Index Usability

You've already seen in Chapter 3 that whenever a function is applied to an indexed column, a regular index cannot be used. Instead, you would have to create a functional index, which means that you index the result of the function applied to the column instead of indexing the column.

Remember too that you don't have to explicitly invoke a function to see a function applied; if you compare a column of a given type to a column or literal value of a different type, the DBMS may perform an implicit type conversion (an implicit call to a conversion function), with the performance hit that one can expect.

Once we are certain that there are indexes on our critical search criteria and that our query is written in such a way that it can take full advantage of them, we must distinguish between unique index fetches of a single row, and other fetches—non-unique index or a range scan of a unique index.

Query Efficiency and Index Usage

Unique indexes are excellent when joining tables. However, when the input to a query is a primary key and the value of the primary key is not a primitive input to the program, then you may have a poorly designed program on your hands.

What I call *primitive input* is data that has been fed into the program, either typed in by a user or read from a file. If the primary key value has been derived from some primitive input and is itself the result of a query, the odds are very high that there is a massive design flaw in the program. Because this situation often means that the output of one query is used as the input to another one, you should check whether the two queries can be combined.

Excellent queries don't necessarily come from excellent programs.

Data Dispersion

When indexes are not unique, or when a condition on a unique index is expressed as a range, for instance:

```
where customer_id between ... and ...
```

or:

```
where supplier_name like 'SOMENAME%'
```

the DBMS must perform a range scan. Rows associated with a given key may be spread all over the table being queried, and this is something that a cost-based optimizer often understands. There are therefore cases when an index range scan would require the DBMS kernel to fetch, one by one, a large number of table data pages, each with very few rows of relevance to the query, and when the optimizer decides that the DBMS kernel is better off scanning the table and ignoring the index.

You saw in Chapter 5 that many database systems offer facilities such as table partitions or clustered indexes to direct the storage of data that we would like to retrieve together. But the mere nature of data insertion processes may well lead to clumping of data. When we associate a timestamp with each row and do mostly inserts into a table, the chances are that most rows will be inserted next to one another (unless we have taken special measures to limit contention, as I discuss in Chapter 9). The physical proximity of the inserted rows is not an absolute necessity and, in fact, the notion of order as such is totally foreign to relational algebra. But, in practice, it is what may happen. Therefore, when we perform a range scan on the index on the timestamp column to look for index entries close together in time, the chances are that the rows in question will be close together too. Of course, this will be even truer if we have tweaked the storage so as to get such a result.

Now, if the value of a key bears no relation to any peculiar circumstance of insertion nor to any hidden storage trick, the various rows associated with a key value or with a range of key values can be physically placed anywhere on disk. The keys in the index are always, by construction, held in sorted order. But the associated rows will be randomly located in the table. In practice, we shall have to visit many more blocks to answer a query involving such an index than would be the case were the table partitioned or the index clustered. We can have, therefore, two indexes on the same table, with strictly identical degrees of selectivity, one of which gives excellent results, and the other one, significantly worse results, a situation that was mentioned in Chapter 3 and that it is now time to prove.

To illustrate this case I have created a 1,000,000–row table with three columns `c1`, `c2`, and `c3`, `c1` being filled with a sequence number (1 to 1,000,000), `c2` with all different random numbers in the range 1 to 2,000,000, and `c3` with random values that can be, and usually are, duplicated. On face value, and from a logical point of view, `c1` and `c2` are both unique and therefore have identical selectivity. In the case of the index on column `c1`, the order of the rows in the table matches the order in the index. In a real case, some activity against the table might lead to "holes" left by deletions and subsequently filled with out-of-order records due to new insertions. By contrast, the order of the rows in the table bears no relation to the ordering of the keys in the index on `c2`.

When we fetch `c3`, based on a range condition of the type:

```
where column_name between some_value and some_value + 10
```

it makes a significant difference whether we use `c1` and its associated index (the *ordered* index, where keys are ordered as the rows in the table) or `c2` and its associated index (the *random* index), as you can see in Figure 6-1. Don't forget that we have such a difference because additional accesses to the table are required in order to fetch the value of `c3`; there would be no difference if we had two composite indexes, on `(c1, c3)` and `(c2, c3)`, because then we could return everything from an index in which the keys are ordered.

The type of difference illustrated in Figure 6-1 also explains why sometimes performance can degrade over time, especially when a new system is put into production with a considerable amount of data coming from a legacy system. It may happen that the initial data loading imposes some physical ordering that favors particular queries. If a few months of regular activity subsequently destroys this order, we may suffer over this period a mysterious 30–40% degradation of performance.

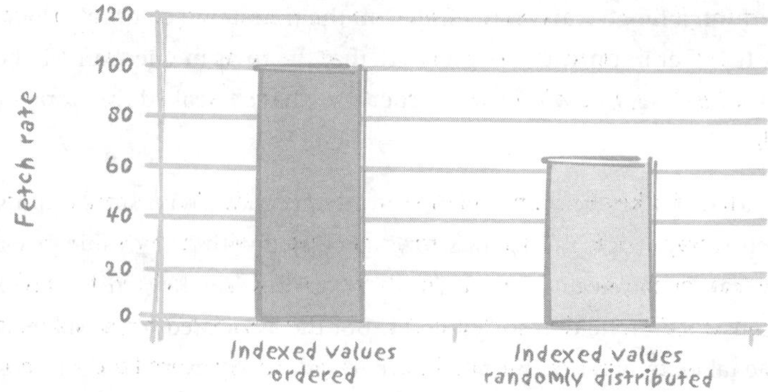

FIGURE 6-1. *Difference of performance when the order in the index matches the order of the rows in the table*

It should be clear by now that the solution "can't the DBAs reorganize the database from time to time?" is indeed a fudge, not a solution. Database reorganizations were once quite in vogue. Ever-increasing volumes, 99.9999% uptime requirements and the like have made them, for the most part, an administrative task of the past. If the physical implementation of rows really is crucial for a critical process, then consider one of the self-organizing structures discussed Chapter 5, such as clustered indexes or index-organized tables. But keep in mind that what favors one type of query sometimes disadvantages another type of query and that we cannot win on all fronts.

Performance variation between comparable indexes may be due to physical data dispersion.

Criterion Indexability

Understand that the proper indexing of specific criteria is an essential component of the "small set, direct specific criteria" situation. We can have cases when the result set is small and some criteria may indeed be quite selective, but are of a nature that isn't suitable for indexing: the following real-life example of a search for differences among different amounts in an accounting program is particularly illustrative of a very selective criterion, yet unfit for indexing.

In the example to follow, a table named `glreport` contains a column named `amount_diff` that ought to contain zeroes. The purpose of the query is to track accounting errors, and identify where `amount_diff` isn't zero. Directly mapping ledgers to tables and applying a logic that dates back to a time when these ledgers where inked with a quill is rather questionable when using a modern DBMS, but unfortunately one encounters questionable databases on a routine basis. Irrespective of the quality of the design, a column such as `amount_diff` is typical of a column that should not be indexed: ideally `amount_diff` should contain nothing but zeroes, and furthermore, it is obviously the result of a denormalization and the object of numerous computations. Maintaining an index on a column that is subjected to computations is even costlier than maintaining an index on a static column, since a modified key will "move" inside the index, causing the index to undergo far more updates than from the simple insertion or deletion of nodes.

All specific criteria are not equally suitable for indexing. In particular, columns that are frequently updated increase maintenance costs.

Returning to the example, a developer came to me one day saying that he had to optimize the following Oracle query, and he asked for some expert advice about the execution plan:

```
select
    total.deptnum,
    total.accounting_period,
    total.ledger,
    total.cnt,
    error.err_cnt,
    cpt_error.bad_acct_count
from
 -- First in-line view
 (select
      deptnum,
      accounting_period,
      ledger,
      count(account) cnt
 from
      glreport
 group by
      deptnum,
      ledger,
      accounting_period) total,
 -- Second in-line view
 (select
     deptnum,
     accounting_period,
     ledger,
     count(account) err_cnt
 from
     glreport
 where
     amount_diff <> 0
```

```
    group by
        deptnum,
        ledger,
        accounting_period) error,
    -- Third in-line view
    (select
        deptnum,
        accounting_period,
        ledger,
        count(distinct account) bad_acct_count
    from
        glreport
    where
        amount_diff <> 0
    group by
        deptnum,
        ledger,
        accounting_period
    ) cpt_error
  where
     total.deptnum = error.deptnum(+) and
     total.accounting_period = error.accounting_period(+) and
     total.ledger = error.ledger(+) and
     total.deptnum = cpt_error.deptnum(+) and
     total.accounting_period = cpt_error.accounting_period(+) and
     total.ledger = cpt_error.ledger(+)
  order by
     total.deptnum,
     total.accounting_period,
     total.ledger
```

For readers unfamiliar with Oracle-specific syntax, the several occurrences of (+) in the outer query's where clause indicate outer joins. In other words:

```
select whatever
from ta,
     tb
where ta.id = tb.id (+)
```

is equivalent to:

```
select whatever
from ta
     outer join tb
             on tb.id = ta.id
```

The following SQL*Plus output shows the execution plan for the query:

```
10:16:57 SQL> set autotrace traceonly
10:17:02 SQL> /

37 rows selected.

Elapsed: 00:30:00.06
```

```
Execution Plan
----------------------------------------------------------
   0      SELECT STATEMENT Optimizer=CHOOSE
                    (Cost=1779554 Card=154 Bytes=16170)
   1    0   MERGE JOIN (OUTER) (Cost=1779554 Card=154 Bytes=16170)
   2    1     MERGE JOIN (OUTER) (Cost=1185645 Card=154 Bytes=10780)
   3    2       VIEW (Cost=591736 Card=154 Bytes=5390)
   4    3         SORT (GROUP BY) (Cost=591736 Card=154 Bytes=3388)
   5    4           TABLE ACCESS (FULL) OF 'GLREPORT'
                            (Cost=582346 Card=4370894 Bytes=96159668)
   6    2       SORT (JOIN) (Cost=593910 Card=154 Bytes=5390)
   7    6         VIEW (Cost=593908 Card=154 Bytes=5390)
   8    7           SORT (GROUP BY) (Cost=593908 Card=154 Bytes=4004)
   9    8             TABLE ACCESS (FULL) OF 'GLREPORT'
                              (Cost=584519 Card=4370885 Bytes=113643010)
  10    1     SORT (JOIN) (Cost=593910 Card=154 Bytes=5390)
  11   10       VIEW (Cost=593908 Card=154 Bytes=5390)
  12   11         SORT (GROUP BY) (Cost=593908 Card=154 Bytes=5698)
  13   12           TABLE ACCESS (FULL) OF 'GLREPORT'
                            (Cost=584519 Card=4370885 Bytes=161722745)


Statistics
----------------------------------------------------------
        193  recursive calls
          0  db block gets
    3803355  consistent gets
    3794172  physical reads
       1620  redo size
       2219  bytes sent via SQL*Net to client
        677  bytes received via SQL*Net from client
          4  SQL*Net roundtrips to/from client
         17  sorts (memory)
          0  sorts (disk)
         37  rows processed
```

I must confess that I didn't waste too much time on the execution plan, since its most striking feature was fairly apparent from the text of the query itself: it shows that the table `glreport`, a tiny 4 to 5 million–row table, is accessed three times, once per subquery, and each time through a full scan.

Nested queries are often useful when writing complex queries, especially when you mentally divide each step, and try to match a subquery to every step. But nested queries are not silver bullets, and the preceding example provides a striking illustration of how easily they may be abused.

The very first inline view in the query computes the number of accounts for each department, accounting period, and ledger, and represents a full table scan that we cannot avoid. We need to face realities; we have to fully scan the table, because we are including all rows when we check how many accounts we have. We need to scan the table once, but do we absolutely need to access it a second or third time?

If a full table scan is required, indexes on the table become irrelevant.

What matters is to be able to not only have a very analytic view of processing, but also to be able to stand back and consider what we are doing in its entirety. The second inline view counts exactly the same things as the first one—except that there is a condition on the value of `amount_diff`. Instead of counting with the `count()` function, we can, at the same time as we compute the total count, add 1 if `amount_diff` is not 0, and 0 otherwise. This is very easy to write with the Oracle-specific `decode(u, v, w, x)` function or using the more standard `case when u = v then w else x end` construct.

The third inline view filters the same rows as the second one; however, here we want to count distinct account numbers. This counting is a little trickier to merge into the first subquery; the idea is to replace the account numbers (which, by the way, are defined as `varchar2`* in the table) by a value which is totally unlikely to occur when `amount_diff` is 0; `chr(1)` (Oracle-speak to mean *the character corresponding to the ASCII value 1*) seems to be an excellent choice (I always feel a slight unease at using `chr(0)` with something written in C like Oracle, since C terminates all character strings with a `chr(0)`). We can then count how many distinct accounts we have and, of course, subtract one to avoid counting the dummy `chr(1)` account.

So this is the suggestion that I returned to the developer:

```
select  deptnum,
        accounting_period,
        ledger,
        count(account) nb,
        sum(decode(amount_diff, 0, 0, 1)) err_cnt,
        count(distinct decode(amount_diff, 0, chr(1), account)) - 1
                                             bad_acct_count
 from
      glreport
 group by
       deptnum,
       ledger,
       accounting_period
```

My suggestion was reported to be four times as fast as the initial query, which came as no real surprise since the three full scans had been replaced by a single one.

Note that there is no longer any `where` clause in the query: we could say that the condition on `amount_diff` has "migrated" to both the logic performed by the `decode()` function inside the select list and the aggregation performed by the `group by` clause. The

* To non-Oracle users, the `varchar2` type is, for all practical purposes, the same as the `varchar` type.

replacement of a filtering condition that *looked* specific with an aggregate demonstrates that we are here in another situation, namely a result set obtained on the basis of an aggregate function.

In-line queries can simplify a query, but can result in excessive and duplicated processing if used without care.

Small Result Set, Indirect Criteria

A situation that is superficially similar to the previous one is when you have a small result set that is based on criteria applied to tables *other than* the data source tables. We want data from one table, and yet our conditions apply to other, related tables from which we don't want any data to be returned. A typical example is the question of "which customers have ordered a particular item" that we amply discussed earlier in Chapter 4. As you saw in Chapter 4, this type of query can be expressed in either of two ways:

- As a regular join with a `distinct` to remove duplicate rows that are the result, for instance, of customers having ordered the same item several times
- By way of either a correlated or uncorrelated subquery

If there is some particularly selective criterion to apply to the table (or tables) from which we obtain the result set, there is no need to say much more than what has been said in the previous situation "Small Result Set, Direct Specific Criteria": the query will be driven by the selective criterion. and the same reasoning applies. But if there is no such criterion, then we have to be much more careful.

To take a simplified version of the example in Chapter 4, identifying the customers who have ordered a Batmobile, our typical case will be something like the following:

```
select distinct orders.custid
from orders
     join orderdetail
        on (orderdetail.ordid = orders.ordid)
     join articles
        on (articles.artid = orderdetail.artid)
where articles.artname = 'BATMOBILE'
```

In my view it is much better, because it is more understandable, to make explicit the test on the presence of the article in a customer's orders by using a subquery. But should that subquery be correlated or uncorrelated? Since we have no other criterion, the answer should be clear: uncorrelated. If not, one would have to scan the `orders` table and fire the subquery for each row—the type of big mistake that passes unnoticed when we start with a small `orders` table but becomes increasingly painful as the business gathers momentum.

The uncorrelated subquery can either be written in the classic style as:

```
select distinct orders.custid
from orders
where ordid in (select orderdetails.ordid
                from orderdetail
                     join articles
                       on (articles.artid = orderdetail.artid)
                where articles.artname = 'BATMOBILE')
```

or as a subquery in the from clause:

```
select distinct orders.custid
from orders,
     (select orderdetails.ordid
      from orderdetail
           join articles
             on (articles.artid = orderdetail.artid)
      where articles.artname = 'BATMOBILE') as sub_q
where sub_q.ordid = orders.ordid
```

I find the first query more legible, but it is really a matter of personal taste. Don't forget that an in() condition on the result of the subquery implies a distinct and therefore a sort, which takes us to the fringe of the relational model.

Where using subqueries, think carefully before choosing either a correlated or uncorrelated subquery.

Small Intersection of Broad Criteria

The situation we talk about in this section is that of a small result set based on the intersection of several broad criteria. Each criterion individually would produce a large result set, yet the intersection of those individual, large sets is a very small, final result set returned by the query.

Continuing on with our query example from the preceding section, if the existence test on the article that was ordered is not selective, we must necessarily apply some other criteria elsewhere (otherwise the result set would no longer be a small result set). In this case, the question of whether to use a regular join, a correlated subquery, or an uncorrelated subquery usually receives a different answer depending on both the relative "strength" of the different criteria and the existing indexes.

Let's suppose that instead of checking people who have ordered a Batmobile, admittedly not our best-selling article, we look for customers who have ordered something that I hope is much less unusual, in this case some soap, but purchased last Saturday. Our query then becomes something like this:

```
select distinct orders.custid
from orders
     join orderdetail
        on (orderdetail.ordid = orders.ordid)
     join articles
        on (articles.artid = orderdetail.artid)
where articles.artname = 'SOAP'
  and <selective criterion on the date in the orders table>
```

Quite logically, the processing flow will be the reverse of what we had with a selective article: get the article, then the order lines that contained the article, and finally the orders. In the case we're currently discussing, that of orders for soap, we should first get the small number of orders placed during the relatively short interval of time, and then check which ones refer to the article soap. From a practical point of view, we are going to use a totally different set of indexes. In the first case, ideally, we would like to see one index on the article name and one on the article identifier in the orderdetail table, and then we would have used the index on the primary key ordid in the orders table. In the case of orders for soap, what we want to find is an index on the date in orders and then one on orderid in orderdetail, from which we can use the index on the primary key of articles—assuming, of course, that in both cases using the indexes is the best course to take.

The obvious natural choice to get customers who bought soap last Saturday would appear to be a correlated subquery:

```
select distinct orders.custid
from orders
where <selective criterion on the date in the orders table>
  and exists (select 1
              from orderdetail
                  join articles
                    on (articles.artid = orderdetail.artid)
                where articles.artname = 'SOAP'
                  and orderdetails.ordid = orders.ordid)
```

In this approach, we take for granted that the correlated subquery executes very quickly. Our assumption will prove true only if orderdetail is indexed on ordid (we shall then get the article through its primary key artid; therefore, there is no other issue).

You've seen in Chapter 3 that indexes are something of a luxury in transactional databases, due to their high cost of maintenance in an environment of frequent inserts, updates, and deletes. This cost may lead us to opt for a "second-best" solution. The absence of the vital index on orderdetail and good reason for not creating further indexes might prompt us to consider the following:

```
select distinct orders.custid
from orders,
     (select orderdetails.ordid
      from orderdetail,
           articles
```

```
      where articles.artid = orderdetail.artid
        and articles.artname = 'SOAP') as sub_q
where sub_q.ordid = orders.ordid
  and <selective criterion on the date in the orders table>
```

In this second approach, the index requirements are different: if we don't sell millions of articles, it is likely that the condition on the article name will perform quite satisfactorily even in the absence of any index on `artname`. We shall probably not need any index on the column `artid` of `orderdetail` either: if the article is popular and appears in many orders, the join between `orderdetail` and `articles` is probably performed in a more efficient manner by hash or merge join, rather than by a nested loop that would need such an index on `artid`. Compared to the first approach, we have here a solution that we could call a *low index* solution. Because we cannot afford to create indexes on each and every column in a table, and because we usually have in every application a set of "secondary" queries that are not absolutely critical but only require a decent response time, the *low index* approach may perform in a perfectly acceptable manner.

Adding one extra search criterion to an existing query can completely change a previous construct: *a modified query is a new query.*

Small Intersection, Indirect Broad Criteria

An *indirect criterion* is one that applies to a column in a table that you are joining only for the purpose of evaluating the criterion. The retrieval of a small result set through the intersection of two or more broad criteria, as in the previous situation "Small Intersection of Broad Criteria," is often a formidable assignment. Obtaining the intersection of the large intermediary result sets by joining from a central table, or even through a chain of joins, makes a difficult situation even more daunting. This situation is particularly typical of the "star schema" that I discuss in some detail in Chapter 10, but you'll also encounter it fairly frequently in operational databases. When you are looking for that rare combination of multiple nonselective conditions on the columns of the row, you must expect to perform full scans at some point. The case becomes particularly interesting when several tables are involved.

The DBMS engine needs to start from somewhere. Even if it can process data in parallel, at some point it has to start with one table, index, or partition. Even if the resulting set defined by the intersection of several huge sets of data is very small, a boot-strapping full table scan, and possibly two scans, will be required—with a nested loop, hash join, or merge join performed on the result. The difficulty will then be to identify which combination of tables (not necessarily the smallest ones) will result in the least number of rows from which the final result set will be extracted. In other words, we must find the weakest point in the line of defense, and once we have eliminated it, we must concentrate on obtaining the final result set.

Let me illustrate such a case with a real-life Oracle example. The original query is a pretty complicated query, with two tables each appearing twice in the `from` clause. Although none of the tables is really enormous (the biggest one contains about 700,000 rows), the problem is that none of the nine parameters that are passed to the query is really selective:

```
select (data from ttex_a,
                  ttex_b,
                  ttraoma,
                  topeoma,
                  ttypobj,
                  ttrcap_a,
                  ttrcap_b,
                  trgppdt,
                  tstg_a)
from ttrcapp ttrcap_a,
     ttrcapp ttrcap_b,
     tstg tstg_a,
     topeoma,
     ttraoma,
     ttex ttex_a,
     ttex ttex_b,
     tbooks,
     tpdt,
     trgppdt,
     ttypobj
where ( ttraoma.txnum = topeoma.txnum )
  and ( ttraoma.bkcod = tbooks.trscod )
  and ( ttex_b.trscod = tbooks.permor )
  and ( ttraoma.trscod = ttrcap_a.valnumcod )
  and ( ttex_a.nttcod = ttrcap_b.valnumcod )
  and ( ttypobj.objtyp = ttraoma.objtyp )
  and ( ttraoma.trscod = ttex_a.trscod )
  and ( ttrcap_a.colcod = :0 ) -- not selective
  and ( ttrcap_b.colcod = :1 ) -- not selective
  and ( ttraoma.pdtcod = tpdt.pdtcod )
  and ( tpdt.risktyp = trgppdt.risktyp )
  and ( tpdt.riskflg = trgppdt.riskflg )
  and ( tpdt.pdtcod = trgppdt.pdtcod )
  and ( trgppdt.risktyp = :2 ) -- not selective
  and ( trgppdt.riskflg = :3 ) -- not selective
  and ( ttraoma.txnum = tstg_a.txnum )
  and ( ttrcap_a.refcod = :5 ) -- not selective
  and ( ttrcap_b.refcod = :6 ) -- not selective
  and ( tstg_a.risktyp = :4 ) -- not selective
  and ( tstg_a.chncod = :7) -- not selective
  and ( tstg_a.stgnum = :8 ) -- not selective
```

When run with suitable parameters (here indicated as :0 to :8), the query takes more than 25 seconds to return fewer than 20 rows, doing about 3,000 physical I/Os and hitting data blocks 3,000,000 times. Statistics correctly represent the actual contents of tables (one of the very first things to check), and a query against the data dictionary gives the number of rows of the tables involved:

```
TABLE_NAME                     NUM_ROWS
---------------------------- ----------
ttypobj                             186
trgppdt                             366
tpdt                               5370
topeoma                           12118
ttraoma                           12118
tbooks                            12268
ttex                             102554
ttrcapp                          187759
tstg                             702403
```

A careful study of the tables and of their relationships allows us to draw the enemy position of Figure 6-2, showing our weak criteria represented as small arrows, and tables as boxes the size of which approximately indicates the number of rows. One thing is especially remarkable: the central position of the ttraoma table that is linked to almost every other table. Unfortunately, all of our criteria apply elsewhere. By the way, an interesting fact to notice is that we are providing two values to match columns risktyp and riskflg of trgppdt—which is joined to tpdt on those very two columns, plus pdtcod. In such a case, it can be worth contemplating reversing the flow—for example, comparing the columns of tpdt to the constants provided, and only then pulling the data from trgppdt.

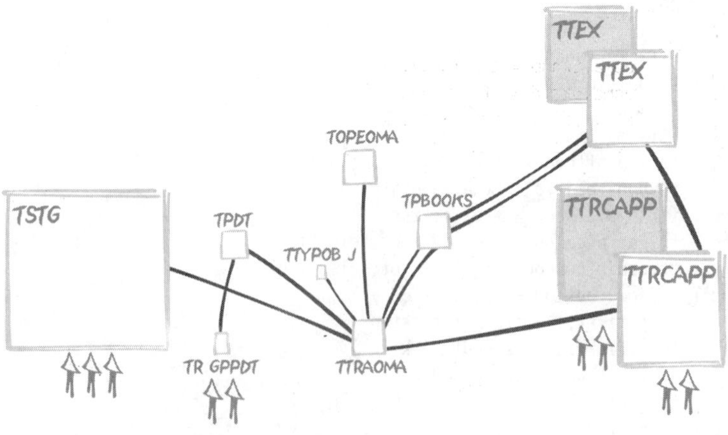

FIGURE 6-2. *The enemy position*

Most DBMS allow you to check the execution plan chosen by the optimizer, either through the explain command or sometimes by directly checking in memory how something has been executed. When this query took 25 seconds, the plan, although not especially atrocious, was mostly a full scan of ttraoma followed by a series of nested loops, using the various indexes available rather efficiently (it would be tedious to detail the numerous indexes, but suffice to say that all columns we are joining on are correctly indexed). Is this full scan the reason for slowness? Definitely not. A simple test, fetching all the rows of `ttraoma` (without displaying them to avoid the time associated with displaying characters on a screen) proves that it takes just a tiny fraction, hardly measurable, of the elapsed time for the overall query.

When we consider the weak criteria we have, our forces are too feeble for a frontal attack against `tstg`, the bulk of the enemy troops, and even `ttrcap` won't lead us very far, because we have poor criteria against each instance of this table, which intervenes twice in the query. However, it should be obvious that the key position of `ttraoma`, which is relatively small, makes an attack against it, as a first step, quite sensible—precisely the decision that the optimizer makes without any prompting.

If the full scan is not to blame, then where did the optimizer go wrong? Have a look at Figure 6-3, which represents the query as it was executed.

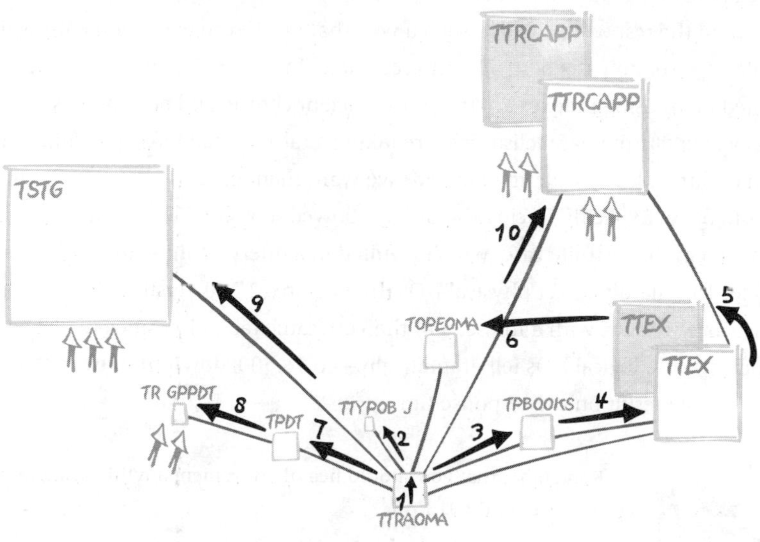

FIGURE 6-3. *What the optimizer chose to do*

When we check the order of operations, it all becomes obvious: our criteria are so bad, on face value, that the optimizer chose to ignore them altogether. Starting with a pretty reasonable full scan of `ttraoma`, it then chose to visit all the smallish tables gravitating around `ttraoma` before ending with the tables to which our filtering criteria apply. This approach is the mistake. It is likely that the indexes of the tables we first visit look much more efficient to the optimizer, perhaps because of a lower average number of table rows per key or because the indexes more closely match the order of the rows in the tables. But postponing the application of our criteria is not how we cut down on the number of rows we have to process and check.

Once we have taken ttraoma and hold the key position, why not go on with the tables against which we have criteria instead? The join between those tables and ttraoma will help us eliminate unwanted rows from ttraoma before proceeding to apply joins with the other tables. This is a tactic that is likely to pay dividends since—and this is information we have but that is unknown to the optimizer—we know we should have, in all cases, very few resulting rows, which means that our combined criteria should, through the joins, inflict heavy casualties among the rows of ttraoma. Even when the number of rows to be returned is larger, the execution path I suggest should still remain relatively efficient.

How then can we force the DBMS to execute the query as we want it to? It depends on the SQL dialect. As you'll see in Chapter 11, most SQL dialects allow directives, or hints, to the optimizer, although each dialect uses different syntax for such hints—telling the optimizer, for instance, to take on the tables in the same order as they are listed in the from clause. The trouble with hints is that they are more imperative than their name suggests, and every hint is a gamble on the future—a bet that circumstances, volumes, database algorithms, hardware, and the rest will evolve in such a way that our forced execution path will forever remain, if not absolutely the best, at least acceptable. In the particular case of our example, since nested loops using indexes are the most efficient choice, and because nested loops don't really benefit from parallelism, we are taking a rather small risk concerning the future evolution of our tables by ordering tables as we want them processed and instructing the optimizer to obey. Explicitly forcing the order followed to visit tables was the approach actually taken in this real-life case, which resulted in a query running in a little less than one second, with hardly fewer physical I/Os than before (2,340 versus 3,000—not too surprising since we start with a full scan of the very same table) but since we "suggested" a more efficient path, logical I/Os fell dramatically—to 16,500, down from over 3,000,000—with a noticeable result on the response time.

Remember that you should heavily document anything that forces the hand of the DBMS.

Explicitly forcing the order in which to visit tables by using optimizer directives is a heavy-handed approach. A more gentle way to obtain the same result from the optimizer, provided that it doesn't savagely edit our SQL clauses, may be to nest queries in the from clause, thus suggesting associations like parentheses would in a numerical expression:

```
select (select list)
from (select ttraoma.txnum,
             ttraoma.bkcod,
             ttraoma.trscod,
             ttraoma.pdtcod,
             ttraoma.objtyp,
             ...
      from ttraoma,
           tstg tstg_a,
           ttrcapp ttrcap_a
     where tstg_a.chncod = :7
       and tstg_a.stgnum = :8
       and tstg_a.risktyp = :4
       and ttraoma.txnum = tstg_a.txnum
       and ttrcap_a.colcod = :0
       and ttrcap_a.refcod = :5
       and ttraoma.trscod = ttrcap_a.valnumcod) a,
     ttex ttex_a,
     ttrcapp ttrcap_b,
     tbooks,
     topeoma,
     ttex ttex_b,
     ttypobj,
     tpdt,
     trgppdt
where ( a.txnum = topeoma.txnum )
  and ( a.bkcod = tbooks.trscod )
  and ( ttex_b.trscod = tbooks.permor )
  and ( ttex_a.nttcod = ttrcap_b.valnumcod )
  and ( ttypobj.objtyp = a.objtyp )
  and ( a.trscod = ttex_a.trscod )
  and ( ttrcap_b.colcod = :1 )
  and ( a.pdtcod = tpdt.pdtcod )
  and ( tpdt.risktyp = trgppdt.risktyp )
  and ( tpdt.riskflg = trgppdt.riskflg )
  and ( tpdt.pdtcod = trgppdt.pdtcod )
  and ( tpdt.risktyp = :2 )
  and ( tpdt.riskflg = :3 )
  and ( ttrcap_b.refcod = :6 )
```

It is often unnecessary to be very specific about the way we want a query to be executed and to multiply esoteric hints; the right initial guidance is usually enough to put an optimizer on the right track. Nested queries making explicit some table associations have the further advantage of being quite understandable to a qualified human reader.

A confused query can make the optimizer confused. Clarity and suggested joins are often enough to help the optimizer provide good performance.

Large Result Set

The situation of a large result set includes any result, irrespective of how it is obtained (with the exception of the explicit cases discussed here) that might be described as "large" or, in other words, a result set which it would be sensible to generate in a batch environment. When you are looking for a very large number of rows, even if this number looks like a fraction of the total number of rows stored in the tables involved in the query, conditions are probably not very selective and the DBMS engine must perform full scans, except perhaps in some very special cases of data warehousing, which are discussed in Chapter 10.

When a query returns tens of thousand of rows, whether as the final result or an intermediate step in a complex query, it is usually fairly pointless to look for a subtle use of indexes and fast jumps from an index to the table rows of interest. Rather, it's time to hammer the data remorselessly through full scans, usually associated with hash or merge joins. There must, however, be intelligence behind the brute force. We always must try to scan the objects, whether they are tables, indexes, or partitions of either tables or indexes, for which the ratio of data returned to data scanned is highest. We must scan objects for which filtering is the most coarse, because the best justification for the "effort" of scanning is to make it pay by a rich data harvest. A situation when a scan is unavoidable is the major exception to the rule of trying to get rid of unnecessary data as soon as possible; but we must fall back to the usual rule as soon as we are done with the unavoidable scans.

As ever, if we consider scanning rows of no interest to us as useless work, we must minimize the number of blocks we access. An approach often taken is to minimize accesses by hitting indexes rather than tables—even if the total volume of indexes is often bigger than the volume of data, each individual index is usually much smaller than its underlying table. Assuming that an index contains all the required information, scanning the index rather than the table makes a lot of sense. Implementation techniques such as adding columns to an index to avoid visiting the table can also show their worth.

Processing very large numbers of rows, whether you need to return them or simply have to check them, requires being very careful about what you do when you process each row. Calling a suboptimal, user-defined function, for instance, is not extremely important when you do it in the select list of a query that returns a small result set or when it comes as an additional criterion in a very selective `where` clause. But when you call such a function hundreds of thousands of times, the DBMS is no longer forgiving, and a slight awkwardness in the code can bring your server to its knees. This is a time for lean and mean code.

One key point to watch is the use of subqueries. Correlated subqueries are the death toll of performance when we are processing massive amounts of rows. When we can identify several subqueries within a query, we must let each of them operate on a distinct and "self-sufficient" subset, removing any dependence of one subquery on the result set of another. Dependencies between the various datasets separately obtained must be solved at the latest stage of query execution through hash joins or set operators.

Relying on parallelism may also be a good idea, but only when there are very few concurrently active sessions—typically in a batch job. Parallelism as it is implemented by a DBMS consists in splitting, when possible, one query into multiple subtasks, which are run in parallel and coordinated by a dedicated task. With a very high number of users, parallelism comes naturally with many similar tasks being executed concurrently, and adding DBMS parallelism to de facto parallelism often makes throughput worse rather than better. Generally speaking, processing very large volumes of information with a very high number of concurrent sessions qualifies as a situation in which the best you can aim for is an honorable fight and in which the solution is often to throw more hardware into the ring.

Response times are, lest we forget about the various waits for the availability of a resource in the course of processing, mostly dependent on the amount of data we have to browse through. But don't forget that, as you saw in Chapter 4, the subjective vision of an end user may be utterly different from a cold analysis of the size of the haystack: the only interest to the end user is the needle.

Self-Joins on One Table

In a correctly designed relational database (third normal form or above), all non-key columns are about the key, the whole key, and nothing but the key, to use an excellent and frequently quoted formula.* Each row is both logically consistent and distinct from all other rows in the same table. It is this design characteristic that enables join relationships to be established within the same table. You can therefore select in the same query different (not necessarily disjoint) sets of rows from the same table and join them as if those rows came from several different tables. In this section, I'll discuss the simple self-join and exclude the more complex examples of nested hierarchies that I discuss later in Chapter 7.

Self-joins—tables joined to themselves—are much more common than hierarchies. In some cases, it is simply because the data is seen in an identical way, but from two

* I have seen this elegant formula credited only once—to a 1983 paper by William Kent, available at *http://www.bkent.net*.

different angles; for instance, we can imagine that a query listing air flights would refer to the airports table twice, once to find the name of the departure airport, and once to find the name of the arrival airport. For example:

```
select f.flight_number,
       a.airport_name departure_airport,
       b.airport_name arrival_airport
from flights f,
     airports a,
     airports b
where f.dep_iata_code = a.iata_code
  and f.arr_iata_code = b.iata_code
```

In such a case, the usual rules apply: what matters is to ensure that highly efficient index access takes place. But what if the criteria are such that efficient access is not possible? The last thing we want is to do a first pass on the table, then a second one to pick up rows that were discarded during the first pass. In that case, what we should do is a single pass, collect all the rows of interest, and then use a construct such as the case statement to display separately rows from the two sets; I show examples of this "single-pass" approach in Chapter 11.

There are subtle cases that only superficially look like the airport case. Imagine that we store in some table cumulative values taken at regular intervals* and we want to display by how much the counter increased between two successive snapshots. In such a case, we have a relationship between two different rows in the same table, but instead of having a strong relationship coming from another table, such as the flights table that links the two instances of airports together, we have a weak, internal relationship: we define that two rows are related not because their keys are associated in another table, but because the timestamp of one row happens to be the timestamp which immediately follows the timestamp of another row.

For instance, if we assume that snapshots are taken every five minutes, with a timestamp expressed in seconds elapsed since a reference date, we might issue the following query:

```
select a.timestamp,
       a.statistic_id,
      (b.counter - a.counter)/5 hits_per_minute
from hit_counter a,
     hit_counter b
where b.timestamp = a.timestamp + 300
  and b.statistic_id = a.statistic_id
order by a.timestamp, a.statistic_id
```

* This is exactly what happens when you collect values from the V$ views in Oracle, which contain monitoring information.

There is a significant flaw in this script: if the second snapshot has not been taken *exactly* five minutes after the first one, down to the second, we may be unable to join the two rows. We may therefore choose to express the join condition as a range condition. For example:

```
select a.timestamp,
       a.statistic_id,
       (b.counter - a.counter) * 60 /
           (b.timestamp - a.timestamp) hits_per_minute
from  hit_counter a,
      hit_counter b
where b.timestamp between a.timestamp + 200
                     and a.timestamp + 400
  and b.statistic_id = a.statistic_id
order by a.timestamp, a.statistic_id
```

One side effect of this approach is the risk of having bigger data gaps than needed when, for one reason or another (such as a change in the sampling frequency), two successive records are no longer collected between 200 and 400 seconds of each other.

We may play it even safer and use an OLAP function that operates on windows of rows. It is indeed difficult to imagine something less relational in nature, but such a function can come in handy as the final shine on a query, and it can even make a noticeable difference in performance. Basically, OLAP functions allow the consideration of different subsets of the final result set, through the use of the `partition` clause. Sorts, sums, and other similar functions can be applied separately to these individual result subsets. We can use the `row_number( )` OLAP function to create one subset by `statistic_id`, and then assign to each different statistic successive integer numbers that increase as timestamps do. When these numbers are generated by the OLAP function, we can join on both `statistic_id` and two sequential numbers, as in the following example:

```
select a.timestamp,
       a.statistic_id,
       (b.counter - a.counter) * 60 /
             (b.timestamp - a.timestamp)
from (select timestamp,
             statistic_id,
             counter,
             row_number( ) over (partition by statistic_id
                                 order by timestamp) rn
      from hit_counter) a,
      (select timestamp,
              statistic_id,
              counter,
              row_number( ) over (partition by statistic_id
                                  order by timestamp) rn
      from hit_counter) b
where b.rn = a.rn + 1
  and a.statistic_id = b.statistic_id
order by a.timestamp, a.statistic_id
```

We may even do better—about 25% faster than the previous query—if our DBMS implements, as Oracle does, a lag(*column_name*, *n*) OLAP function that returns the *n*th previous value for column_name, on the basis of the specified partitioning and ordering:

```
select timestamp,
       statistic_id,
       (counter - prev_counter) * 60 /
       (timestamp - prev_timestamp)
from (select timestamp,
             statistic_id,
             counter,
             lag(counter, 1) over (partition by statistic_id
                                   order by timestamp) prev_counter,
             lag(timestamp, 1) over (partition by statistic_id
                                     order by timestamp) prev_timestamp
      from hit_counter) a
order by a.timestamp, a.statistic_id
```

In many cases we don't have such symmetry in our data, as is shown by the flight example. Typically, a query looking for all the data associated with the smallest, or the largest, or the oldest, or the most recent value of a specific column, first needs to find the actual smallest, largest, oldest, or most recent value in the column used for filtering (this is the first pass, which compares rows), and then search the table again in a second pass, using as a search criterion the value identified in the first pass. The two passes can be made (at least superficially) into one through the use of OLAP functions that operate on sliding windows. Queries applied to data values associated to timestamps or dates are a special case of sufficient importance to deserve further discussion later in this chapter as the situation "Simple or Range Searching on Dates."

When multiple selection criteria are applied to different rows in the same table, functions that operate on sliding windows may be of assistance.

Result Set Obtained by Aggregation

An extremely common situation is the case in which the result set is a dynamically computed summary of the detailed data from one or more main tables. In other words, we are facing an *aggregation* of data. When data is aggregated, the size of the result set isn't dependent on the precision of the criteria that are provided, but merely on the cardinality of the columns that we group by. As in the first situation of the small result set obtained through precise criteria (and as you'll see again in Chapter 11), aggregate functions (or *aggregates*) are also often quite useful for obtaining in a single pass on the table results that are not truly aggregated but that would otherwise require self-joins and multiple passes. In fact, the most interesting SQL uses of aggregates are not the cases in which sums or averages are an obvious part of the requirements, but situations in which a clever use of aggregates provides a pure SQL alternative to a procedural processing.

I stress in Chapter 2 that one of the keys to efficient SQL coding is a swashbuckling approach to code execution, testing for success after the deed rather than executing preliminary queries to check if, by chance, the really useful query we want to execute may fail: you cannot win a swimming race by tiptoeing carefully into the water. The other key point is to try to pack as much "action" as possible into an SQL query, and it is in respect to this second key point that aggregate functions can be particularly useful.

Much of the difficulty of good SQL programming lies in seeing how a problem can translate, not into a succession of queries to a database, but into very few queries. When, in a program, you need a lot of intermediate variables to hold values you get from the database before reinjecting them into the database as input to other queries, and if you perform against those variables nothing but very simple tests, you can bet that you have the algorithm wrong. And it is a striking feature of poorly written SQL programs to see the high number of lines of code outside of SQL queries that are simply devoted to summing up, multiplying, dividing, and subtracting inside loops what is painfully returned from the database. This is a totally useless and utterly inefficient job: we have SQL aggregate functions for that sort of work.

> **NOTE**
>
> Aggregate functions are very useful tools for solving SQL problems (and we will revisit them in Chapter 11, when I talk about stratagems); however, it often appears to me that developers use only the least interesting aggregate function of all, namely `count()`, the real usefulness of which is often, at best, dubious in most programs.

Chapter 2 shows that using `count(*)` to decide whether to update an existing row or insert a new one is wasteful. You can misuse `count(*)` in reports as well. A test for existence is sometimes implemented as a mock-Boolean value such as:

```
case count(*)
when 0 then 'N'
else 'Y'
end
```

Such an implementation gets, when rows are found, all the rows that match the condition in order to obtain a precise count, whereas finding only one is enough to decide whether `Y` or `N` must be displayed. You can usually write a much more effective statement by using a construct that either limits the number of rows returned or tests for existence, effectively stopping processing as soon as a row that matches the condition is found.

But when the question at hand is about the most, the least, the greatest, or even the first or the last, it is likely that aggregate functions (possibly used as OLAP functions) will provide the best answer. If you believe that aggregate functions should be used only when counts, sums, maxima, minima, or averages are explicitly required, then you risk seriously underusing them.

Interestingly, aggregate functions are extremely narrow in scope. If you exclude the computation of maximum and minimum values, the only thing they can really do is simple arithmetic; a `count( )` is nothing more than adding 1s for each row encountered. Similarly, the computation of `avg( )` is just, on one hand, adding up the values in the column it is applied to and, on the other hand, adding 1s, and then dividing.

But it is sometimes wonderful what you can do with simple sums. If you're mathematically inclined, you'll remember how easily you can switch between sums and products by the magic of logarithms and power functions. And if you're logically inclined, you know well how much `OR` owes to sums and `AND` to products.

I'll show the power of aggregation with a simple example. Assume that we have a number of shipments to make and that each shipment is made of a number of different orders, each of which has to be separately prepared; it is only when each order in a shipment is complete that the shipment itself is ready. The problem is how to detect when all the orders comprising a shipment are complete.

As is so often the case, there are several ways to determine the shipments that are complete. The worst approach would probably be to loop on all shipments, inside a second loop on each shipment count how many orders have `N` as value for the `order_complete` column, and return shipment IDs for which the count is `0`. A much better solution would be to recognize the test on the nonexistence of an `N` value for what it is, and use a subquery, correlated or uncorrelated; for instance:

```
select shipment_id
from shipments
where not exists (select null from orders
                  where order_complete = 'N'
                    and orders.shipment_id = shipments.shipment_id)
```

This approach is pretty bad if we have no other condition on the `shipments` table. Following is a query that may be much more efficient if we have a large `shipments` table and few uncompleted orders:

```
select shipment_id
from shipments
where shipment_id not in (select shipment_id
                          from orders
                          where order_complete = 'N')
```

This query can also be expressed as follows, as a variant that an optimizer may like better but that wants an index on the column shipment_id of the table orders:

```
select shipments.shipment_id
from shipments
    left outer join orders
          on orders.shipment_id = shipments.shipment_id
          and orders.order_complete = 'N'
where orders.shipment_id is null
```

Another alternative is a massive set operation that will operate on the primary key index of shipments on one hand, and that will perform a full table scan of orders on the other hand:

```
select shipment_id
from shipments
except
select shipment_id
from orders
where order_complete = 'N'
```

Be aware that not all DBMS implement the except operator, sometimes known as minus.

But there is still another way to express our query. What we are doing, basically, is to return the identifiers of all shipments for which a logical AND operation on all orders which have been completed returns TRUE. This kind of operation happens to be quite common in the real world. As hinted previously, there is a very strong link between AND and multiplication, and between OR and addition. The key is to convert flags such as Y and N to 0s and 1s. This conversion is a trivial operation with the case construct. To get just order_complete as a 0 or 1 value, we can write:

```
select shipment_id,
       case when order_complete = 'Y' then 1
                                      else 0
       end flag
from orders
```

So far, so good. If we always had a fixed number of orders per shipment, it would be easy to sum the calculated column and check if the result is the number of orders we expect. However, what we want here is to multiply the flag values per shipment and check whether the result is 0 or 1. That approach works, because even one incomplete order, represented by a 0, will cause the final result of all the multiplication to also be 0. The multiplication can be done with the help of logarithms (although 0s are not the easiest values to handle with logarithms). But in this particular case, our task is even easier.

What we want are the shipments for which the first order is completed and the second order is completed and...the *n*th order is completed. Logic and the laws of de Morgan* tell us that this is exactly the same as stating that we *do not* have (first order not completed or second order not completed...or *n*th order not completed). Since their kinship to sums makes ORs much easier to process with aggregates than ANDs, checking that a list of conditions linked by OR is false is much easier than checking that a list of conditions linked by AND is true. What we must consider as our true predicate is "the order is not completed" rather than the reverse, and convert the order_complete flag to 1 if it is N, and 0 if it is Y. In that way, we can easily check that we have 0s (or yeses) everywhere by summing up values—if the sum is 0, then all orders are completed; otherwise, we are at various stages of incompletion.

Therefore we can also express our query as:

```
select shipment_id
from (select shipment_id,
             case when order_complete = 'N' then 1
                                                 else 0
             end flag
       from orders) s
group by shipment_id
having sum(flag) =0
```

And it can be expressed in an even more concise way as:

```
select shipment_id
from orders
group by shipment_id
having sum(case when order_complete = 'N' then 1
                                              else 0
           end) =0
```

There is another way to write this query that is even simpler, using another aggregate function, and without any need to convert flag values. Noticing that Y is, from an alphabetical point of view, greater than N, it is not too difficult to infer that if all values are Y then the minimum will necessarily be Y too. Hence:

```
select shipment_id
from orders
group by shipment_id
having min(order_complete) = 'Y'
```

* The India-born Augustus de Morgan (1806–1871) was a British mathematician who contributed to many areas of mathematics, but most significantly to the field of logic. The de Morgan laws state that the complement of the intersection of any number of sets equals the union of their complements and that the complement of the union of any number of sets equals the intersection of their complements. If you remember that SQL is about sets, and that negating a condition returns the complement of the result set returned by the initial condition (if you have no null values), you'll understand why these laws are particularly useful to the SQL practitioner.

This approach of depending on Y to be greater than N may not be as well grounded mathematically as the flag-to-number conversion, but it is just as efficient.

Of course we must see how the query that uses a group by and a condition on the minimum value for order_complete compares to the other versions that use subqueries or except instead of an aggregate function. What we can say is that it has to fully sort the orders table to aggregate the values and check whether the sum is or is not 0. As I've specified the problem, this solution involving a non-trivial use of an aggregate function is likely to be faster than the other queries, which hit two tables (shipments and orders), and usually less efficiently.

I have made an extensive use of the having clause in the previous examples. As already mentioned in Chapter 4, a common example of careless SQL statements involves the use of the having clause in aggregate statements. Such an example is illustrated in the following (Oracle) query, which attempts to obtain the sales per product per week during the past month:

```
select product_id,
       trunc(sale_date, 'WEEK'),
       sum(sold_qty)
from sales_history
group by product_id, trunc(sale_date, 'WEEK')
having trunc(sale_date, 'WEEK') >= add_month(sysdate, -1)
```

The mistake here is that the condition expressed in the having clause doesn't depend on the aggregate. As a result, the DBMS has to process all of the data in sales_history, sorting it and aggregating against each row, before filtering out ancient figures as the last step before returning the required rows. This is the kind of mistake that can go unnoticed until sales_history grows really big. The proper approach is, of course, to put the condition in a where clause, ensuring that the filtering occurs at an early stage and that we are working afterwards on a much reduced set of data.

I should note that when we apply criteria to views, which are aggregated results, we may encounter exactly the same problem if the optimizer is not smart enough to reinject our filter *before* aggregation.

You can have slightly more subtle variants of a filter applied later than it should be. For instance:

```
select customer_id
from orders
where order_date < add_months(sysdate, -1)
group by customer_id
having sum(amount) > 0
```

In this query, the following condition looks at first glance like a reasonable use of having:

```
having sum(amount) > 0
```

However, this use of having does not really make sense if amount is always a positive quantity or zero. In that event, we might be better using the following condition:

```
where amount > 0
```

We have two possibilities here. Either we keep the group by:

```
select customer_id
from orders
where order_date < add_months(sysdate, -1)
  and amount > 0
group by customer_id
```

or we notice that group by is no longer required to compute any aggregate and replace it with a distinct that in this case performs the same task of sorting and eliminating duplicates:

```
select distinct customer_id
from orders
where order_date < add_months(sysdate, -1)
  and amount > 0
```

Placing the condition in the where clause allows unwanted rows to be filtered at an earlier stage, and therefore more effectively.

Aggregate as little data as you can.

Simple or Range Searching on Dates

Among search criteria, dates (and times) hold a particular place that is all their own. Dates are extremely common, and more likely than other types of data to be subjected to range conditions, whether they are bounded ("between this date and that date") or only partially bounded ("before this date"). Very often, and what this situation describes, the result set is derived from searches against date values referenced to the current date (e.g., "six months earlier than the current date," etc.).

The example in the previous section, "Result Set Obtained by Aggregation," refers to a sales_history table; our condition was on an amount, but it is much more common with this type of table to have conditions on date, especially to get a snapshot of the data either at a given date or between two dates. When you are looking for a value on a given date in a table containing historical data, you must pay particular attention to the way you identify current data. The way you handle current data may happen to be a special case of data predicated on an aggregate condition.

I have already pointed out in Chapter 1 that the design of a table destined to store historical data is a tricky affair and that there is no easy, ready-made solution. Much depends on what you plan to do with your data, whether you are primarily interested in current values or in values as of a particular date. The best solution also depends on how fast data becomes outdated. If you are a retailer and wish to keep track of the wares you sell, it is likely that, unless your country suffers severe hyper-inflation, the rate of change of your prices will be pretty slow. The rate of change will be higher, possibly much higher, if you are recording the price of financial instruments or monitoring network traffic.

To a large extent, what matters most with history tables is how much historical data you keep on average per item: you may store a lot of historical information for very few items, or have few historical records for a very large number of items, or anything in between. The point here is that the selectivity of any item depends on the number of items being tracked, the frequency of sampling (e.g., either once per day or every change during the day), and the total time period over which the tracking takes place (infinite, purely annual, etc.). We shall therefore first consider the case when we have many items with few historical values, then the opposite case of few items with a rich history, and then, finally, the problem of how to represent the current value.

Many Items, Few Historical Values

If we don't keep an enormous amount of historical data per item, the identification of an item is quite selective by itself. Specifying the item under study restricts our "working set" to just a few historical rows, and it then becomes fairly easy to identify the value at a given reference date (the current or a previous date) as the value recorded at the closest date prior to the reference date. In this case, we are dealing once again with aggregate values.

Unless some artificial, surrogate key has been created (and this is a case where there is no real need for a surrogate key), the primary key will generally be a composite key on the identifier of items (`item_id`) and the date associated with the historical value (`record_date`). We mostly have two ways of identifying the rows that store values that were current as of a given reference date: subqueries and OLAP functions.

Using subqueries

If we are looking for the value of one particular item as of a given date, then the situation is relatively simple. In fact, the situation is deceptively simple, and you'll often encounter a reference to the value that was current for a given item at a given date coded as:

```
select whatever
from hist_data as outer
where outer.item_id = somevalue
  and outer.record_date = (select max(inner.record_date)
                           from hist_data as inner
                           where inner.item_id = outer.item_id
                             and inner.record_date <= reference_date)
```

It is interesting to see what the consequences of this type of construct suggest in terms of the execution path. First of all, the inner query is correlated to the outer one, since the inner query references the `item_id` of the current row returned by the outer query. Our starting point is therefore the outer query.

Logically, from a theoretical point of view, the order of the columns in a composite primary key shouldn't matter much. In practice, it is critical. If we have made the mistake of defining the primary key as `(record_date, item_id)` instead of `(item_id, record_date)`, we desperately need an additional index on `item_id` for the inner query; otherwise, we will be unable to efficiently descend the tree-structured index. And we know how costly each additional index can be.

Starting with our outer query and finding the various rows that store the history of `item_id`, we will then use the current value of `item_id` to execute the subquery each time. Wait! This inner query depends only on `item_id`, which is, by definition, the same for all the rows we check! The logical conclusion: we are going to execute exactly the same query, returning exactly the same result for each historical row for `item_id`. Will the optimizer notice that the query always returns the same value? The answer may vary. It is better not to take the chance.

There is no point in using a correlated subquery if it always returns the same value for all the rows for which it is evaluated. We can easily uncorrelate it:

```
select whatever
from hist_data as outer
where outer.item_id = somevalue
  and outer.record_date = (select max(inner.record_date)
                           from hist_data as inner
                           where inner.item_id = somevalue
                             and inner.record_date <= reference_date)
```

Now the subquery can be executed without accessing the table: it finds everything it requires inside the primary key index.

It may be a matter of personal taste, but a construct that emphasizes the primary key is arguably preferable to the preceding approach, if the DBMS allows comparing several columns to the output of a subquery (a feature that isn't supported by all products):

```
select whatever
from hist_data as outer
where (outer.item_id, outer.record_date) in
                          (select inner.item_id, max(inner.record_date)
                           from hist_data as inner
                           where inner.item_id = somevalue
                             and inner.record_date <= reference_date
                           group by inner.item_id)
```

The choice of a subquery that precisely returns the columns matching a composite primary key is not totally gratuitous. If we now need to return values for a list of items, possibly the result of another subquery, this version of the query naturally suggests a good execution path. Replace *somevalue* in the inner query by an `in()` list or a subquery, and the overall query will go on performing efficiently under the very same assumptions that each item has a relatively short history. We have also replaced the equality condition by an `in` clause: in most cases the behavior will be exactly the same. As usual, it is at the fringes that you encounter differences. What happens if, for instance, the user mistyped the identification of the item? The `in()` will return that no data was found, while the equality may return a different error.

Using OLAP functions

With databases, OLAP functions such as `row_number()` that we have already used in the *self-joins* situation can provide a satisfactory and sometimes even a more efficient way to answer the same question "what was the current value for one particular item at a given date?" (remember that OLAP functionality does, however, introduce a distinctly non-relational aspect to the proceedings*).

> **NOTE**
>
> **OLAP functions belong to the non-relational layer of SQL. They represent the final, or almost final, step in query execution, since they have to operate on the post-retrieval result set after the filtering has completed.**

With a function such as `row_number()` we can assign a degree of freshness (one meaning most recent) to the data by ranking on date:

```
select row_number() over (partition by item_id
                          order by record_date desc) as freshness,
       whatever
from hist_data
where item_id = somevalue
  and record_date <= reference_date
```

Selecting the freshest data is then simply a matter of only retaining the rows with a value of one for `freshness`:

```
select x.<suitable_columns>
from (select row_number() over (partition by item_id
                                 order by record_date desc) as freshness,
             whatever
      from hist_data
      where item_id = somevalue
        and record_date <= reference_date) as x
where x.freshness = 1
```

* ...even if the term OLAP was coined by Dr. E.F. Codd himself in a 1993 paper.

In theory, there should be hardly any difference between the OLAP function approach and the use of subqueries. In practice, an OLAP function hits the table only once, even if the usual sorting happens behind the scene. There is no need for additional access to the table, even a fast one that uses the primary key. The OLAP function approach may therefore be faster (albeit only slightly so).

Many Historical Values Per Item

The picture may be different when we have a very large number of historical values—for instance, a monitoring system in which metrics are collected at a rather high frequency. The difficulty here lies in the fact that all the intermediate sorting required for identifying the value at or nearest a given date may have to operate on a really large amount of data.

Sorting is a costly operation. If we apply the principles of Chapter 4, the only way we have to reduce the thickness of the non-relational layer is by doing a bit more work at the relational level—by increasing the amount of filtering. In such a case, it is very important to *narrow* our scope by bracketing the date (or time) more precisely for which we want the data. If we only provide an upper boundary, then we shall have to scan and sort the full history since the beginning of ages. If data is collected at a high frequency, it is then reasonable to give a lower limit. If we succeed in restraining the "working set" of rows to a manageable size, we are back to the case in which we have relatively few historical values per item. If specifying both an upper boundary (such as the current date) *and* a lower boundary isn't an option, our only hope is in partitioning per item; operating on a single partition will take us closer to the "large result set" situation.

Current Values

When we are predominantly interested in the most recent or current values, it is very tempting to design a way to avoid either the nested subquery or the OLAP function (which both entail a sort), and hit the proper values directly. We mentioned in Chapter 1 that one solution to this problem is to associate each value with some "end date"—the kind of "best before" you find on your cereal boxes—and to say that for current values that end date is far, far away into the future (let's say December 31, 2999). We also mentioned that there were some practical issues associated with such a design and the time has now come to explore these issues.

With a fixed date, it certainly becomes extremely easy to find the current value. Our query simply becomes:

```
select whatever
from hist_data
where item_id = somevalue
  and record_date = fixed_date_in_the_future
```

We then hit the right row, spot on, through the primary key. And of course, nothing prevents us from using either subqueries or OLAP functions whenever we need to refer to a date other than the current one. There are, however, two main drawbacks to this approach—an obvious one and a more subtle one:

- The obvious drawback is that each insertion of a new historical value will first require updating what used to be the current value with, for example, today's date, to mean that it used to be the current value until today. Then the new value can be inserted with the later date, to mean that it is now the current value until further notice. This process leads to double the amount of work, which is bad enough. Moreover, since in the relational theory the primary key is what identifies a row, the combination (`item_id, record_date`) can be unique but cannot be the primary key since we have to partially update it. We therefore need a surrogate key to be referenced by foreign keys (identity column or sequence), which further complicates programs. The trouble with big historical tables is that usually, to grow that big, they also undergo a high rate of insertion. Does the benefit of faster querying offset the disadvantage of inserting more slowly? It's difficult to say, but definitely a question worth asking.
- The subtle drawback has to do with the optimizer. The optimizer relies on statistics that may be of variable detail, with the result that it is not unusual for it to check the lowest and highest value in a column to try to assess the spread of values. Let us say that our historical table contains values since January 1, 2000. Our data will therefore consist of perhaps 99.9% historical data, spread over several, but relatively few, years, and 0.1% of current data, officially as of December 31, 2999. The view of the optimizer will be of data spread over one millennium. This skewness on the part of the optimizer view of the data range is because it is being misled by the upper boundary date in the query ("`and record_date =` *`fixed_date_in_the future`*"). The problem is then that when you search for something other than current values (for instance if you want to collect variations over time for statistical purposes), the optimizer may well incorrectly decide that since you are accessing such a tiny fraction of the millennium, then using indexes is the thing to do, but what you really need is to scan the data. Skewness can lead to totally wrong execution plans, which are not easy to correct.

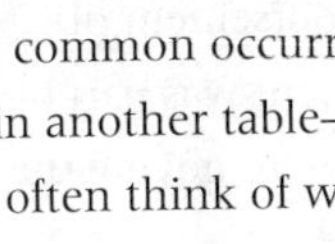

You must understand your data and your data distributions if you are to understand how the optimizer views your system.

Result Set Predicated on Absence of Data

It is a common occurrence to look for rows in one table for which there is no matching data in another table—usually for identifying exceptions. There are two solutions people most often think of when having to deal with this type of problem: using either `not in ()`

with an uncorrelated subquery or `not exists ()` with a correlated subquery. Popular wisdom says that you should use `not exists`. Since a correlated subquery is efficient when used to mop up after the bulk of irrelevant data has been cleared out by efficient filtering, popular wisdom has it right when the subquery comes after the strong forces of efficient search criteria, and totally wrong when the subquery happens to be the only criterion.

One sometimes encounters more exotic solutions to the problem of finding rows in one table for which there is no matching data in another. The following example is a real-life case that monitoring revealed to be one of the costliest queries performed against a database (note that question marks are placeholders, or *bind variables*, for constant values that are passed to the query on successive executions):

```
insert into ttmpout(custcode,
                    suistrcod,
                    cempdtcod,
                    bkgareacod,
                    mgtareacod,
                    risktyp,
                    riskflg,
                    usr,
                    seq,
                    country,
                    rating,
                    sigsecsui)
select distinct custcode,
                ?,
                ?,
                ?,
                mgtareacod,
                ?,
                ?,
                usr,
                seq,
               country,
               rating,
               sigsecsui
from ttmpout a
where a.seq = ?
  and 0 = (select count(*)
           from ttmpout b
           where b.suistrcod = ?
             and b.cempdtcod = ?
             and b.bkgareacod = ?
             and b.risktyp = ?
             and b.riskflg = ?
             and b.seq = ?)
```

This example must not be understood as an implicit unconditional endorsement of temporary tables! As a passing remark, I suspect that the `insert` statement was part of a loop. Proper performance improvement would probably be achieved by removing the loop.

An insertion into a table based on a select on the very same table as in the current example is a particular and yet not uncommon case of self-reference, an insertion derived from existing rows and conditional on the absence of the row to be created.

Using count(*) to test whether something exists or doesn't exist is a bad idea: to count, the DBMS must search and find all rows that match. We should use exists in such a case, which stops as soon as the first match is encountered. Arguably, it does not make much difference if the filtering criterion happens to be the primary key. But it may make a very significant difference in other cases—and anyway from a semantic point of view there is no reason to say this:

```
and 0 = (select count(*) ...)
```

when we mean this:

```
and not exists (select 1 ...)
```

If we use count(*) as a test for existence, we may be lucky enough to benefit from the "invisible hand" of a smart optimizer, which will turn our query into something more suitable. But this will not necessarily be the case, and it will never be the case if the rows are counted into some variable as an independent step, because then even the smartest of optimizers cannot guess for which purpose we are counting: the result of the count() could be a critical value that absolutely has to be displayed to the end user!

In such a case when we want to create new, unique rows derived from rows already present in the table, however, the right construct to use is probably a set operator such as except (sometimes known as minus).

```
insert into ttmpout(custcode,
                    suistrcod,
                    cempdtcod,
                    bkgareacod,
                    mgtareacod,
                    risktyp,
                    riskflg,
                    usr,
                    seq,
                    country,
                    rating,
                    sigsecsui)
(select custcode,
        ?,
        ?,
        ?,
        mgtareacod,
        ?,
        ?,
        usr,
        seq,
```

```
                country,
                rating,
                sigsecsui
         from ttmpout
         where seq = ?
         except
         select custcode,
                ?,
                ?,
                ?,
                mgtareacod,
                ?,
                ?,
                usr,
                seq,
                country,
                rating,
                sigsecsui
         from ttmpout
         where suistrcod = ?
           and cempdtcod = ?
           and bkgareacod = ?
           and risktyp = ?
           and riskflg = ?
           and seq = ?)
```

The big advantage of set operators is that they totally break the time frame imposed by subqueries, whether they are correlated or uncorrelated. What does *breaking the time frame* mean? When you have correlated subqueries, you must run the outer query, and then you must execute the inner query for each row that passes through all other filtering criteria. Both queries are extremely dependent on each other, since the outer query feeds the inner one.

The picture is slightly brighter with uncorrelated subqueries, but not yet totally rosy: the inner query must be executed, and in fact completed, before the outer query can step in and gather steam (something similar occurs even if the optimizer chooses to execute the global query as a hash join, which is the smart thing for it to do, because to execute a hash join, the SQL engine first has to scan one of the tables involved to build a hash array).

With set operators, on the contrary, whether they are `union`, `intersect` or `except`, none of the components in the query depends on any other. As a result, the different parts of the query can run in parallel. Of course, parallelism is of hardly any benefit if one of the steps is very slow while all the others are very fast; and it will be of no benefit at all if much of the work in one part is strictly identical to the work in another part, because then you are duplicating, rather than sharing, the work between processes. But in a favorable case, it is much more efficient to have all parts run in parallel before the final step, which combines the partial result sets—divide and rule.

There is an additional snag with using set operators: they require each part of the query to return compatible columns—an identical number of columns of identical types. A case such as the following (another real-life case, coming from a billing program) is typically unsuited to set operators:

```
select whatever, sum(d.tax)
from invoice_detail d,
     invoice_extractor e
where (e.pga_status = 0
       or e.rd_status = 0)
 and suitable_join_condition
 and (d.type_code in (3, 7, 2)
      or (d.type_code = 4
          and d.subtype_code not in
               (select trans_code
                from trans_description
                where trans_category in (6, 7))))
group by what_is_required
having sum(d.tax) != 0
```

I am always fascinated by the final condition:

```
sum(d.tax) != 0
```

and the way it evokes yellow brick roads and fantasy worlds where taxes are negative. A condition such as:

```
and d.tax > 0
```

might have been more appropriate in the `where` clause, as already demonstrated.

In such a case a set operator would be rather awkward, since we would have to hit the `invoice_detail` table—as we can guess, not a lightweight table—several times. However, depending on the selectivity of the various criteria provided, typically if `type_code=4` is a rare and therefore selective attribute condition, an `exists` might be more appropriate than a `not in ()`. If, however, `trans_description` happens to be, at least relatively, a small table, then there is no doubt that trying to improve the query by playing on the existence test alone is a dead end.

Another interesting way to express nonexistence—and often quite an efficient one—is to use outer joins. The purpose of outer joins is basically to return, in a join, all information from one table, including rows for which no match is found in the joined table. As it happens, when we are looking for data that has no match in another table, it is precisely these rows that are of interest to us. How can we identify them? By checking the joined table columns: when there is no match, they are replaced with null values.

Something such as:

```
select whatever
from invoice_detail
where type_code = 4
```

```
    and subtype_code not in
                 (select trans_code
                  from trans_description
                  where trans_category in (6, 7))
```

can therefore be rewritten:

```
select whatever
from invoice_detail
     outer join trans_description
            on trans_description.trans_category in (6, 7)
           and trans_description.trans_code = invoice_detail.subtype_code
where trans_description.trans_code is null
```

I have purposely included the condition on trans_category in the join clause. Whether it should rightly appear in this clause or in the where clause is debatable but, in fact, filtering before the join or after the join is result-neutral (of course, from a performance point of view, it can make a difference, depending on the relative selectivity of this condition and of the join condition itself). However, we have no such latitude with the condition on the null value, since this is something that can only be checked *after* the join.

Apart from the fact that the outer join may in some cases require a distinct, in practice there should be very little difference between checking the absence of data through an outer join or a not in () uncorrelated subquery, since the column which is used for the join happens to be the very same column that is compared to the result set of the subquery. But SQL is famous for being a language in which the manner of the query expression often has a very real effect on the pattern of execution, even if the theory says otherwise. It all depends on the degree of sophistication of the optimizer, and whether it processes both types of queries in a similar way or not. In other words, SQL is not a truly declarative language, even if the enhancement of optimizers with each new version slowly improves its reliability.

Before closing this topic, watch out for the perennial SQL party-poopers—null values. Although in an in () subquery a null value joining the flow of non-null values does not bother the outer query, with a not in () subquery, any null value returned by the inner query causes the not in () condition to be evaluated as false. It does not cost much to ensure that a subquery returns no null value—and doing so will save you a lot of grief.

Data sets can be compared using various techniques, but outer joins and set operators are likely to be efficient.

CHAPTER SEVEN

Variations in Tactics

Dealing with Hierarchical Data

The golden rule is that there are no golden rules.

—George Bernard Shaw (1856–1950)

Man and Superman/Maxims for Revolutionists

You have seen in the previous chapter that queries sometimes refer to the same table several times and that results can be obtained by joining a row from one table to another row in the same table. But there is a very important case in which a row is not only related to another row, but is dependent upon it. That latter row is itself dependent on another one—and so forth. I am talking here of the representation of hierarchies.

Tree Structures

Relational theory struck the final blow to hierarchical databases as the main repositories for structured data. Hierarchical databases were historically the first attempt at structuring data that had so far been stored as records in files. Instead of having linear sequences of identical records, various records were logically nested. Hierarchical databases were excellent for some queries, but their strong structure made one feel as if in a straitjacket, and navigating them was painful. They first bore the brunt of the assault by network, or CODASYL, databases, in which navigation was still difficult but that were more flexible, until the relational theory proved that database design was a science and not a craft. However, hierarchies, or at least hierarchical representations, are extremely common—which probably accounts for the resilience of the hierarchical model, still alive today under various names such as Lightweight Directory Access Protocol (LDAP) and XML.

The handling of hierarchical data, also widely known as the *Bill of Materials* (BOM) problem, is not the simplest of problems to understand. Hierarchies are complicated not so much because of the representation of relationships between different components, but mostly because of the way you *walk* a tree. Walking a tree simply means visiting all or some of the nodes and usually returning them in a given order. Walking a tree is often implemented, when implemented at all, by DBMS engines in a procedural way—and that procedurality is a cardinal relational sin.

Tree Structures Versus Master/Detail Relationships

Many designers tend, not unnaturally, to consider that a parent/child link is in itself not very different from a master/detail relationship—the classical `orders/order_detail` relationship, in which the `order_detail` table stores (as part of its own key) the reference of the order it relates to. There are, however, at least four major differences between the parent/child link and the master/detail relationship:

Single table

The first difference is that when we have a tree representing a hierarchy, all the nodes are of the very same nature. The leaf nodes, in other words the nodes that have no child node, are sometimes different, as happens in file management systems with folders—regular nodes and files—leaf nodes, but I'll set that case apart for the time being. Since all nodes are of the same nature, we describe them in the same way, and they will be represented by rows in the same table. Putting it another way, we have a kind of master/detail relationship, not between two different tables holding rows of different nature, but between a table and itself.

Depth

The second difference is that in the case of a hierarchy, how far you are from the top is often significant information. In a master/detail relationship, you are always either the master or the detail.

Ownership

The third difference is that in a master/detail relationship you can have a clean foreign key integrity constraint; for instance, every order identifier in the `order_detail` table must correspond to an existing identifier in the `orders` table, plain and simple. Such is not the case with hierarchical data. You can decide to say that, for instance, the manager number must refer to an existing employee number. Except that you then have a problem with the top manager, who in truth reports to the representatives of shareholders—the board, not an employee. This leaves us with that endless source of difficulties, a null value. And you may have several such "special case" rows, since we may need to describe in the same table several independent trees, each with its own root—something that is called a *forest*.

Multiple parents

Associating a "child" with the identifier of a "parent" assumes that a child can have only one parent. In fact, there are many real-life situations when this is not the case, whether it is investments, ingredients in formulae, or screws in mechanical parts. A case when a child has multiple parents is arguably not a tree in the mathematical sense; unfortunately, many real-life trees, including genealogical trees, are more complex than simple parent-child relationships, and may even require the handling of special cases (outside the scope of this book) such as cycles in a line of links.

In his excellent book, *Practical Issues in Database Management* (Addison Wesley), Fabian Pascal explains that the proper relational view of a tree is to understand that we have two distinct entity types, the nodes (for which we may have a special subtype of leaf nodes, bearing more information) and the links between the nodes. I should point out that this design approach solves the question of integrity constraints, since one only describes links that actually exist. Pascal's approach also solves the case of the "child" that appears in the descent of numerous "parents." This case is quite common in the industry and yet so rare in textbooks, which usually stick to the employee/manager example.

Pascal, following ideas of Chris Date, suggests that there should be an `explode()` operator to flatten, on the fly, a hierarchy, by providing a view which would make explicit the implicit links between nodes. The only snag is that this operator has never been implemented. DBMS vendors have quite often implemented specialized processes such as the handling of spatial data or full-text indexing, but the proper implementation of hierarchical data has oscillated between the nonexistent and the feeble, thus leaving most of the burden of implementation just where it doesn't belong: with the developer.

As I have already hinted, the main difficulty when dealing with hierarchical data lies in walking the tree. Of course, if your aim is just to display a tree structure in a graphical user interface, each time the user clicks on a node to expand it, you have no particular problem: issuing a query that returns all the children of the node for which you pass the identifier as argument is a straightforward task.

Practical Examples of Hierarchies

In real life, you meet hierarchies very often, but the tasks applied to them are rarely simple. Here are just three examples of real-life problems involving hierarchies, from different industries:

Risk exposure
: When you attempt to compute your exposure to risk in a financial structure such as a hedge fund, the matter becomes hierarchically complex. These financial structures invest in funds that themselves may hold shares in other funds.

Archive location
: If you are a big retail bank, you are likely to face a nontrivial task if you want to retrieve from your archives the file of a loan signed by John Doe seven years ago, because files are stored in folders, which are in boxes, which are on shelves, which are in cabinets in an alley in some room of some floor of some building. The nested "containers" (folders, boxes, shelves, etc.) form a hierarchy.

Use of ingredients
: If you work for the pharmaceutical industry, identifying all of the drugs you manufacture that contain an ingredient for which a much cheaper equivalent has just been approved and can now be used presents the very same type of SQL challenge in a totally unrelated area.

It is important to understand that these hierarchical problems are indeed quite distinct in their fundamental characteristics. A task such as finding the location of a file in an archive means walking a tree from the bottom to the top (that is, from a position of high granularity to one of increasing aggregation), because you start from some single file reference, that will point you to the folder in which it is stored, where you will find the identification of a box, and so forth on up to the room in a building, and so on, thus determining the exact location of the file. Finding all the products that contain a given ingredient also happens to be a bottom-up walk, although in that case our number of starting points may be very high—and we have to repeat the walk each time. By contrast, risk exposure analysis means, first, a top-down walk to find all investments, followed by computations on the way back up to the top. It is a kind of aggregation, only more complicated.

In general, the number of levels in trees tends to be rather small. This is, in fact, the main beauty of trees and the reason why they can be efficiently searched. If the number of levels is *fixed*, the only thing we have to do is to join the table containing a tree with itself as many times as we have levels. Let's take the case of archives and say that the inventory table shows us in which folder our loan file is located. This folder identifier will take us to a location table, that points us the identifier of the box which contains the folder, the shelf upon which the box is laid, the cabinet to which the shelf belongs, the alley where we can find this cabinet, the room which contains the alley, the floor on which the room is located, and, finally, the building. If the location table treats folders, boxes, shelves, and the like as generic "locations," a query returning all the components in the physical location of a file might look like this:

```
select building.name building,
       floor.name floor,
       room.name room,
       alley.name alley,
       cabinet.name cabinet,
       shelf.name shelf,
       box.name box,
       folder.name folder
from inventory,
     location folder,
     location box,
     location shelf,
     location cabinet,
     location alley,
     location room,
     location floor,
     location building
where inventory.id = 'AZE087564609'
  and inventory.folder = folder.id
  and folder.located_in = box.id
  and box.located_in = shelf.id
  and shelf.located_in = cabinet.id
  and cabinet.located_in = alley.id
  and alley.located_in = room.id
  and room.located_in = floor.id
  and floor.located_in = building.id
```

This type of query, in spite of an impressive number of joins, should run fast since each successive join will use the unique index on location (that is, the index on id), presumably the primary key. But yes, there is a catch: the number of levels in a hierarchy is rarely constant. Even in the rather sedate world of archives, the contents of boxes are often moved after the passage of time to new containers (which may be more compact and, therefore, provide cheaper storage). Such activity may well replace two levels in a hierarchy with just one, as containers will replace both boxes and shelves. What should we do when we don't know the number of levels? How best do we query such a hierarchy? Do we use a union? An outer-join?

Links between objects of the same nature should be modeled as trees as soon as the number of levels between two objects is no longer a constant.

Representing Trees in an SQL Database

Trees are generally represented in the SQL world by one of three models:

Adjacency model

The adjacency model is thus called because the identifier of the closest ancestor up in the hierarchy (the parent row) is given as an attribute of the child row. Two adjacent nodes in the tree are therefore clearly associated. The adjacency model is often illustrated by the employee number of the manager being specified as an attribute of each employee managed. (The direct association of the manager to the employee is in truth a poor design, because the manager identification should be an attribute of the *structure* that is managed. There is no reason that, when the head of a department is changed, one should update the records of all the people who work in the department to indicate the new manager). Some products implement special operators for dealing with this type of model, such as Oracle's `connect by` (introduced as early as Oracle version 4 around the mid 1980s) or the more recent recursive `with` statement of DB2 and SQL Server. Without any such operator, the adjacency model is very hard to manage.

Materialized path model

The idea here is to associate with each node in the tree a representation of its position within the tree. This representation takes the form of a concatenated list of the identifiers of all the node's ancestors, from the root of the tree down to its immediate parent, or as a list of numbers indicating the rank within siblings of a given ancestor at one generation (a method frequently used by genealogists). These lists are usually stored as delimited strings. For instance, `'1.2.3.2'` means (right to left) that the node is the second child of its parent (the path of which is `'1.2.3'`), which itself is the third child of the grandparent (`'1.2'`), and so forth.

Nested set model

In this model, devised by Joe Celko,* a pair of numbers (defined as a *left number* and a *right number*) is associated to each node in such a fashion that they define an interval which always contains the interval associated with any of the descendents. The upcoming subsection "Nested Sets Model (After Celko)" under "Practical Implementation of Trees" gives a practical example of this intricate scheme.

* First introduced in articles in *DBMS Magazine* (circa 1996), and much later developed in *Trees and Hierarchies in SQL for Smarties* (Morgan-Kauffman).

There is a fourth, less well-known model, presented by its author, Vadim Tropashko, who calls it the *nested interval model,* in a very interesting series of papers.* The idea behind this model is, to put it very simply, to encode the path of a given node with two numbers, which are interpreted as the numerator and the denominator of a rational number (a *fraction* to those uncomfortable with the vocabulary of mathematics) instead of an interval. Unfortunately, this model is heavy on computations and stored procedures and, while it looks promising for a future implementation of good tree-handling functions (perhaps the `explode( )` operator) in a DBMS, it is in practice somewhat difficult to implement and not the fastest you can do, which is why I shall focus on the three aforementioned models.

To keep in tone with our general theme, and to generate a reasonable amount of data, I have created a test database of the organizations of the various armies that were opposed in 1815 at the famous battle of Waterloo in Belgium, near Brussels† (known as *orders of battle*), which describe the structure of the Anglo-Dutch, Prussian, and French armies involved—corps, divisions, and brigades down to the level of the regiments. I use this data, and mostly the descriptions of the various units and the names of their commanders, as the basis for many of the examples that you'll see in this chapter.

I must hasten to say that the point of what follows in this chapter is to demonstrate various ways to walk hierarchies and that the design of my tables is, to say the least, pretty slack. Typically, a proper primary key for a fighting unit should be an understandable and standardized code, not a description that may suffer from data entry errors. Please understand that any reference to a surrogate `id` is indeed shorthand for an implicit, sound primary key.

The main difficulty with hierarchies is that there is no "best representation." When our interest is mostly confined to the ancestors of a few elements (a bottom-up walk), either `connect by` or the recursive `with` is, at least functionally and in terms of performance, sufficiently satisfactory. However, if we scratch the surface, `connect by` in particular is of course a somewhat ugly, non-relational, procedural implementation, in the sense that we can only move gradually from one row to the next one. It is much less satisfactory when we want to return either a bottom-up hierarchy for a very large number of items, or when we need to return a very large number of descendants in a top-down walk. As is so often the case with SQL, the ugliness that you can hide with a 14–row table becomes painfully obvious when you are dealing with millions, not to say billions, of rows, and that nice little SQL trick now shows its limits in terms of performance.

* Initially published on *http://www.dbazine.com*.

† Using, with his permission, the data compiled by Peter Kessler, at *http://www.kessler-web.co.uk*.

My example table, which contains a little more than 800 rows, is a bit larger than the usual examples, although it is in no way comparable to what you can regularly find in the industry. However, it is big enough to point out the strengths and weaknesses of the various models.

The SQL implementation of trees is DBMS dependent; use what your DBMS has to offer.

Practical Implementation of Trees

The following subsections provide examples of each of the three hierarchy models. In each case, rows have been inserted into the example tables in the same order (ordered by `commander`) in an attempt to divorce the physical order of the rows from the expected result. Remember that the design is questionable, and that the purpose is to show in as simple a way as possible how to handle trees according to the model under discussion.

Adjacency Model

The following table describes the hierarchical organization of an army using the adjacency model. The table name I've chosen to use is, appropriately enough, `ADJACENCY_MODEL`. Each row in the table describes a military unit. The `parent_id` points upward in the tree to the enclosing unit:

```
Name                           Null?    Type
------------------------------ -------- --------------
ID                             NOT NULL NUMBER
PARENT_ID                               NUMBER
DESCRIPTION                    NOT NULL VARCHAR2(120)
COMMANDER                               VARCHAR2(120)
```

Table `ADJACENCY_MODEL` has three indexes: a unique index on `id` (the primary key), an index on `parent_id`, and an index on `commander`. Here are a few sample lines from `ADJACENCY_MODEL`:

```
ID  PARENT_ID DESCRIPTION                  COMMANDER
--- --------- ---------------------------- ----------------------------
435         0 French Armée du Nord of 1815 Emperor Napoleon Bonaparte
619       435 III Corps                    Général de Division Dominique
                                           Vandamme
620       619 8th Infantry Division        Général de Division Baron
                                           Etienne-Nicolas Lefol
621       620 1st Brigade                  Général de Brigade Billard
                                           (d.15th)
622       621 15th Rgmt Léger              Colonel Brice
623       621 23rd Rgmt de Ligne           Colonel Baron Vernier
```

```
624        620 2nd Brigade              Général de Brigade Baron
                                        Corsin
625        624 37th Rgmt de Ligne       Colonel Cornebise
626        620 Division Artillery
627        626 7/6th Foot Artillery     Captain Chauveau
```

Materialized Path Model

Table MATERIALIZED_PATH_MODEL stores the same hierarchy as ADJACENCY_MODEL but with a different representation. The (id, parent_id) pair of columns associating adjacent nodes is replaced with a single materialized_path column that records the full "ancestry" of the current row:

```
Name                                      Null?    Type
----------------------------------------- -------- ----------------
MATERIALIZED_PATH                         NOT NULL VARCHAR2(25)
DESCRIPTION                               NOT NULL VARCHAR2(120)
COMMANDER                                          VARCHAR2(120)
```

Table MATERIALIZED_PATH_MODEL has two indexes, a unique index on materialized_path (the primary key), and an index on commander. In a real case, the choice of the path as the primary key is, of course, a very poor one, since people or objects rarely have as a defining characteristic their position in a hierarchy. In a proper design, there should be at least some kind of id, as in table ADJACENCY_MODEL. I have suppressed it simply because I had no use for it in my limited tests.

However, my questionable choice of materialized_path as the key was also made with the idea of checking in that particular case the benefit of the special implementations discussed in Chapter 5, in particular, what happens when the table that describes a tree happens to map the tree structure of an index? In fact, in this particular example such mapping makes no difference.

Here are the same sample lines as in the adjacency model, but with the materialized path:

```
MATERIALIZED_PATH DESCRIPTION                    COMMANDER
----------------- ------------------------------ --------------------------
F                 French Armée du Nord of 1815 Emperor Napoleon Bonaparte
F.3               III Corps                      Général de Division
                                                 Dominique Vandamme
F.3.1             8th Infantry Division          Général de Division Baron
                                                 Etienne-Nicolas Lefol
F.3.1.1           1st Brigade                    Général de Brigade Billard
                                                 (d.15th)
F.3.1.1.1         15th Rgmt Léger                Colonel Brice
F.3.1.1.2         23rd Rgmt de Ligne             Colonel Baron Vernier
F.3.1.2           2nd Brigade                    Général de Brigade Baron
                                                 Corsin
F.3.1.2.1         37th Rgmt de Ligne             Colonel Cornebise
F.3.1.3           Division Artillery
F.3.1.3.1         7/6th Foot Artillery           Captain Chauveau
```

Nested Sets Model (After Celko)

With the nested set model, we have two columns, `left_num` and `right_num`, which describe how each row relates to other rows in the hierarchy. I'll show shortly how those two numbers are used to specify a hierarchical position:

```
Name                                  Null?    Type
------------------------------------- -------- -------------
DESCRIPTION                                    VARCHAR2(120)
COMMANDER                                      VARCHAR2(120)
LEFT_NUM                              NOT NULL NUMBER
RIGHT_NUM                             NOT NULL NUMBER
```

Table `NESTED_SETS_MODEL` has a composite primary key, `(left_num, right_num)` plus an index on `commander`. As with the materialized path model, this is a poor choice but it is adequate for our present tests.

It is probably time now to explain how the mysterious numbers, `left_num` and `right_num`, are obtained. Basically, one starts from the root of the tree, assigning `1` to `left_num` for the root node. Then all child nodes are recursively visited, as shown in Figure 7-1, and a counter increases at each *call*. You can see the counter on the line in the figure. It begins with `1` for the root node and increases by one as each node is visited.

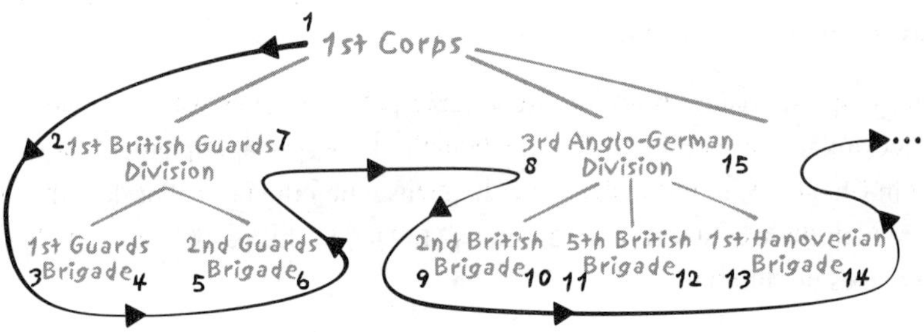

FIGURE 7-1. *How nested sets numbers are assigned*

Say that we visit a node for the very first time. For instance, in the example of Figure 7-1, after having assigned the integer `1` to the `left_num` value of the *1st Corps* node, we encounter (for the first time) the node *1st British Guards Division*. We increase our counter and assign `2` to `left_num`. Then we visit the node's children, encountering for the first time *1st Guards Brigade* and assigning the value of our counter, `3` at this stage, to `left_num`. But this node, on this example, has no child. Because there is no child, we increment our counter and assign its value to `right_num`, which in this case takes the value `4`. Then we move on to the node's sibling, *2nd Guards Brigade*. It is the same story with this sibling. Finally, we return—our second visit—to the parent node *1st British Guards Division* and can assign the new value of our counter, which has now reached `7`, to its `right_num`. We then proceed to the next sibling, *3rd Anglo-German Division*, and so on.

As mentioned earlier, you can see that the `[left_num, right_num]` pair of any node is enclosed within the `[left_num, right_num]` pair of any of its ascendants—hence the name of *nested sets*. Since, however, we have three independent trees (the Anglo-Dutch, Prussian, and French armies), which is called in technical terms a *forest*, I have had to create an artificial top level that I have called `Armies of 1815`. Such an artificial top level is not required by the other models.

Here is what we get from our example after having computed all numbers:

```
DESCRIPTION                  COMMANDER                    LEFT_NUM RIGHT_NUM
---------------------------- ---------------------------- -------- ---------
Armies of 1815                                                   1      1622
French Armée du Nord of 1815 Emperor Napoleon Bonaparte        870      1621
III Corps                    Général de Division              1237      1316
                             Dominique Vandamme
8th Infantry Division        Général de Division Baron        1238      1253
                             Etienne-Nicolas Lefol
1st Brigade                  Général de Brigade Billard       1239      1244
                             (d.15th)
15th Rgmt Léger              Colonel Brice                    1240      1241
23rd Rgmt de Ligne           Colonel Baron Vernier            1242      1243
2nd Brigade                  Général de Brigade Baron         1245      1248
                             Corsin
37th Rgmt de Ligne           Colonel Cornebise                1246      1247
Division Artillery                                            1249      1252
7/6th Foot Artillery         Captain Chauveau                 1250      1251
```

The rows in our sample that are at the bottom level in the hierarchy can be spotted by noticing that `right_num` is equal to `left_num + 1`.

The author of this clever method claims that it is much better than the adjacency model because it operates on sets and that is what SQL is all about. This is perfectly true, except that SQL is all about unbounded sets, whereas his method relies on finite sets, in that you must count all nodes before being able to assign the `right_num` value of the root. And of course, whenever you insert a node somewhere, you must renumber both the `left_num` and `right_num` values of all the nodes that should be visited after the new node, as well as the `right_num` value of all its ascendants. The necessity to modify many other items when you insert a new item is exactly what happens when you store an ordered list into an array: as soon as you insert a new value, you have to shift, on average, half the array. The nested set model is imaginative, no doubt, but a relational nightmare, and it is difficult to imagine worse in terms of denormalization. In fact, the nested sets model is a pointer-based solution, the very quagmire from which the relational approach was designed to escape.

Walking a Tree with SQL

In order to check efficiency and performance, I have compared how each model performed with respect to the following two problems:

1. To find all the units under the command of the French general Dominique Vandamme (a top-down query), if possible as an indented report (which requires keeping track of

the depth within the tree) or as a simple list. Note that in all cases we have an index on the commander's name. I refer to this problem as the *Vandamme query*.

2. To find, for all regiments of Scottish Highlanders, the various units they belong to, once again with and without proper indentation (a bottom-up query). We have no index on the names of units (column description in the tables), and our only way to spot Scottish Highlanders is to look for the Highland string in the name of the unit, which of course means a full scan in the absence of any full-text indexing. I refer to this problem as the *Highlanders query*.

To ensure that the only variation from test to test was in the model used, my comparisons are all done using the same DBMS, namely Oracle.

Top-Down Walk: The Vandamme Query

In the Vandamme query, we start with the commander of the French Third Corps, General Vandamme, and want to display in an orderly fashion all units under his command. We don't want a simple list: the structure of the army corps must be clear, as the corps is made of divisions that are themselves made of brigades that are themselves usually composed of two regiments.

Adjacency model

Writing the Vandamme query with the adjacency model is fairly easy when using Oracle's connect by operator. All you have to specify is the node you wish to start from (start with) and how each two successive rows returned relate to each other (connect by *<a column of the current row>* = prior *<a column of the previous row>*, or connect by *<a column of the previous row>* = prior *<a column of the current row>*, depending on whether you are walking down or up the tree). For indentation, Oracle maintains a pseudo-column named level that tells you how many levels away from the starting point you are. I am using this pseudo-column and left-padding the description with as many spaces as the current value of level. My query is:

```
select lpad(description, length(description) + level) description,
       commander
from adjacency_model
connect by parent_id = prior id
start with commander = 'Général de Division Dominique Vandamme'
```

And the results are:

```
DESCRIPTION                     COMMANDER
------------------------------- ---------------------------------------------
 III Corps                      Général de Division Dominique Vandamme
  8th Infantry Division         Général de Division Baron Etienne-Nicolas Lefol
   2nd Brigade                  Général de Brigade Baron Corsin
    37th Rgmt de Ligne          Colonel Cornebise
   1st Brigade                  Général de Brigade Billard (d.15th)
    23rd Rgmt de Ligne          Colonel Baron Vernier
    15th Rgmt Léger             Colonel Brice
       ...
```

```
10th Infantry Division           Général de Division Baron Pierre-Joseph Habert
 2nd Brigade                     Général de Brigade Baron Dupeyroux
  70th Rgmt de Ligne             Colonel Baron Maury
  22nd Rgmt de Ligne             Colonel Fantin des Odoards
  2nd (Swiss) Infantry Rgmt      Colonel Stoffel
 1st Brigade                     Général de Brigade Baron Gengoult
  88th Rgmt de Ligne             Colonel Baillon
  34th Rgmt de Ligne             Colonel Mouton
 Division Artillery
  18/2nd Foot Artillery          Captain Guérin

40 rows selected.
```

Now, what about the other member in the adjacency family, the recursive `with` statement?* With this model, a recursive-factorized statement is defined, which is made of the `union` (the `union all`, to be precise) of two `select` statements:

- The `select` that defines our starting point, which in this particular case is:

  ```
  select 1 level,
         id,
         description,
         commander
  from adjacency_model
  where commander = 'Général de Division Dominique Vandamme'
  ```

  What is this solitary `1` for? It represents, as the alias indicates, the depth in the tree. In contrast to the Oracle `connect by` implementation, this DB2 implementation has no system pseudo-variable to tell us where we are in the tree. We can compute our level, however, and I'll explain more about that in just a moment.

- The `select` which defines how each child row relates to its parent row, as it is returned by this very same query that we can call, with a touch of originality, `recursive_query`:

  ```
  select parent.level + 1,
         child.id,
         child.description,
         child.comander
  from recursive_query parent,
       adjacency_model child
  where parent.id = child.parent_id
  ```

  Notice in this query that we add `1` to `parent.level`. Each execution of this query represents a step down the tree. For each step down the tree, we increment our level, thus keeping track of our depth.

All that's left is to fool around with functions to nicely indent the description, and here is our final query:

```
with recursive_query(level, id, description, commander)
as (select 1 level,
           id,
           description,
```

* Using this time the first product that implemented it, namely DB2.

```
              commander
       from adjacency_model
       where commander = 'Général de Division Dominique Vandamme'
       union all
       select parent.level + 1,
              child.id,
              child.description,
              child.commander
       from recursive_query parent,
            adjacency_model child
       where parent.id = child.parent_id)
   select char(concat(repeat(' ', level), description), 60) description,
          commander
   from recursive_query
```

Of course, you have to be a real fan of the recursive `with` to be able to state without blushing that the syntax here is natural and obvious. However, it is not too difficult to understand once written; and it's even rather satisfactory, except that the query first returns General Vandamme as expected, but then all the officers directly reporting to him, and then all the officers reporting to the first one at the previous level, followed by all officers reporting to the second one at the previous level, and so on. The result is not quite the nice top-to-bottom walk of the `connect by`, showing exactly who reports to whom. I'll hasten to say that since ordering doesn't belong to the relational theory, there is nothing wrong with the ordering that you get from `with`, but that ordering does raise an important question: in practice, how can we order the rows from a hierarchical query?

Ordering the rows from a hierarchical query using recursive `with` is indeed possible if, for instance, we make the not unreasonable assumption that one parent node never has more than 99 children and that the tree is not monstrously deep. Given these caveats, what we can do is associate with each node a number that indicates where it is located in the hierarchy—say `1.030801`—to mean the first child (the two rightmost digits) of the eighth child (next two digits, from right to left) of the third child of the root node. This assumes, of course, that we are able to order siblings, and we may not always be able to assign any natural ordering to them. Sometimes it is necessary to arbitrarily assign an order to each sibling using, possibly, an OLAP function such as `row_number()`.

We can therefore slightly modify our previous query to arbitrarily assign an order to siblings and to use the just-described technique for ordering the result rows:

```
   with recursive_query(level, id, rank, description, commander)
   as (select 1,
              id,
              cast(1 as double),
              description,
              commander
        from adjacency_model
        where commander = 'Général de Division Dominique Vandamme'
        union all
```

```
        select parent.level + 1,
               child.id,
               parent.rank + ranking.sn / power(100.0, parent.level),
               child.description,
               child.commander
        from recursive_query parent,
             (select id,
                     row_number( ) over (partition by parent_id
                                         order by description) sn
              from adjacency_model) ranking,
             adjacency_model child
        where parent.id =child.parent_id
          and child.id = ranking.id)
select char(concat(repeat(' ', level), description), 60) description,
       commander
from recursive_query
order by rank
```

We might fear that the ranking query that appears as a recursive component of the query would be executed for each node in the tree that we visit, returning the same result set each time. This isn't the case. Fortunately, the optimizer is smart enough not to execute the ranking query more than is necessary, and we get:

```
DESCRIPTION                     COMMANDER
------------------------------  ---------------------------------------------
 III Corps                      Général de Division Dominique Vandamme
  10th Infantry Division        Général de Division Baron Pierre-Joseph Habert
   1st Brigade                  Général de Brigade Baron Gengoult
    34th Rgmt de Ligne          Colonel Mouton
    88th Rgmt de Ligne          Colonel Baillon
   2nd Brigade                  Général de Brigade Baron Dupeyroux
    22nd Rgmt de Ligne          Colonel Fantin des Odoards
    2nd (Swiss) Infantry Rgmt   Colonel Stoffel
    70th Rgmt de Ligne          Colonel Baron Maury
   Division Artillery
    18/2nd Foot Artillery       Captain Guérin
  11th Infantry Division        Général de Division Baron Pierre Berthézène
   ...
    23rd Rgmt de Ligne          Colonel Baron Vernier
   2nd Brigade                  Général de Brigade Baron Corsin
    37th Rgmt de Ligne          Colonel Cornebise
   Division Artillery
    7/6th Foot Artillery        Captain Chauveau
  Reserve Artillery             Général de Division Baron Jérôme Doguereau
   1/2nd Foot Artillery         Captain Vollée
   2/2nd Rgmt du Génie
```

The result is not strictly identical to the connect by case, simply because we have ordered siblings by alphabetical order on the description column, while we didn't order siblings at all with connect by (we could have ordered them by adding a special clause). But otherwise, the very same hierarchy is displayed.

While the result of the with query is logically equivalent to that of the connect by query, the with query is a splendid example of nightmarish, obfuscated SQL, which in comparison makes the five-line connect by query look like a model of elegant simplicity. And even if on this particular example performance is more than acceptable, one can but wonder with some anguish at what it might be on very large tables. Must we disregard the recursive with as a poor, substandard implementation of the superior connect by? Let's postpone conclusions until the end of this chapter.

The ranking number we built in the recursive query is nothing more than a numerical representation of the materialized path. It is therefore time to check how we can display the troops under the command of General Vandamme using a simple materialized path implementation.

Materialized path model

Our query is hardly more difficult to write under the materialized path model—but for the level, which is derived from the path itself. Let's assume just for an instant that we have at hand a function named mp_depth( ) that returns the number of hierarchical levels between the current node and the top of the tree. We can write a query as:

```
select lpad(a.description, length(a.description)
        + mp_depth(...)) description,
       a.commander
from materialized_path_model a,
     materialized_path_model b
where a.materialized_path like b.materialized_path || '%'
  and b.commander = 'Général de Division Dominique Vandamme')
order by a.materialized_path
```

Before dealing with the mp_depth( ) function, I'll note a few traps. In my example, I have chosen to start the materialized path with *A* for the Anglo-Dutch army, *P* for the Prussian one, and *F* for the French one. That first letter is then followed by dot-separated digits. Thus, the 12th Dutch line battalion, under the command of Colonel Bagelaar, is A.1.4.2.3, while the 11th Régiment of Cuirassiers of Colonel Courtier is F.9.1.2.2. Ordering by materialized path can lead to the usual problems of alphabetical sorts of strings of digits, namely that 10.2 will be returned before 2.3; however, I should stress that, since the separator has a lower code (in ASCII at least) than 0, then the order of levels will be respected. The sort may not, however respect the order of siblings implied by the path. Does that matter? I don't believe that it does because sibling order is usually information that can be derived from something other than the materialized path itself (for instance, brothers and sisters can be ordered by their birth dates, rather than by the path). Be careful with the approach to sorting that I've used here. The character encoding used by your database might throw off the results.

What about our mysterious mp_depth( ) function now? The hierarchical difference between any commander under General Vandamme and General Vandamme himself can be defined as the difference between the absolute levels (i.e., counting down from the root of the tree) of the unit commanded by General Vandamme and any of the underlying units. How then can we determine the absolute level? Well, by counting the dots.

To count the dots, the easiest thing to do is probably to start with *suppressing* them, with the help of the replace( ) function that you find in the SQL dialect of all major products. All you have to do next is subtract the length of the string *without* the dots from the length of the string *with* the dots, and you get exactly what you want, the dot-count:

```
length((materialized_path) - length(replace(materialized_path, '.', ''))
```

If we check the result of our dot-counting algorithm for the author of the epigraph that adorns Chapter 6 (a cavalry colonel at the time), here is what we get:

```
SQL> select materialized_path,
            length(materialized_path) len_w_dots,
            length(replace(materialized_path, '.', '')) len_wo_dots,
            length(materialized_path) -
                 length(replace(materialized_path, '.', '')) depth,
            commander
     from materialized_path_model
     where commander = 'Colonel de Marbot'
     /

MATERIALIZED_PATH LEN_W_DOTS LEN_WO_DOTS      DEPTH COMMANDER
----------------- ---------- ----------- ---------- ------------------
F.1.5.1.1                  9           5          4 Colonel de Marbot
```

Et voilà.

Nested sets model

Finding all the units under the command of General Vandamme is very easy under the nested sets model, since the model requires us to have numbered our nodes in such a way that the left_num and right_num of a node bracket are the left_num and right_num of all descendants. All we have to write is:

```
select a.description,
       a.commander
from nested_sets_model a,
     nested_sets_model b
where a.left_num between b.left_num and b.right_num
  and b.commander = 'Général de Division Dominique Vandamme'
```

All? Not quite. We have no indentation here. How do we get the level? Unfortunately, the only way we have to get the depth of a node (from which indentation is derived) is by counting how many nodes we have between that node and the root. There is no way to derive depth from left_num and right_num (in contrast to the materialized path model).

If we want to display an indented list under the nested sets model, then we must join a third time with our nested_sets_model table, for the sole purpose of computing the depth:

```
select lpad(description, length(description) + depth) description,
       commander
from (select count(c.left_num) depth,
             a.description,
             a.commander,
             a.left_num
      from nested_sets_model a,
           nested_sets_model b,
           nested_sets_model c
      where a.left_num between c.left_num and c.right_num
        and c.left_num between b.left_num and b.right_num
        and b.commander = 'Général de Division Dominique Vandamme'
      group by a.description,
               a.commander,
               a.left_num)
order by left_num
```

The simple addition of the indentation requirement makes the query, as with (sic) the recursive with( ), somewhat illegible.

Comparing the Vandamme query under the various models

After having checked that all queries were returning the same 40 rows properly indented, I then ran each of the queries 5,000 times in a loop (thus returning a total of 200,000 rows). I have compared the number of rows returned per second, taking the adjacency model as our 100-mark reference. You see the results in Figure 7-2.

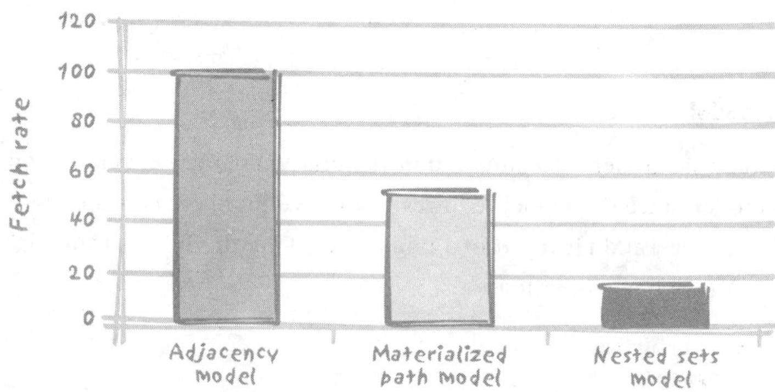

FIGURE 7-2. *Performance comparison for the Vandamme query*

As Figure 7-2 shows, for the Vandamme query, the adjacency model, in which the tree is walked using connect by, outperforms the competition despite the procedural nature of connect by. The materialized path makes a decent show, but probably suffers from the function calls to compute the depth and therefore the indentation. The cost of a nicely indented output is even more apparent with the nested sets model, where the obvious performance killer is the computation of the depth through an additional join and a group by. One might cynically suggest that, since this model is totally hard-wired, static, and non-relational, we might as well go whole hog in ignoring relational design tenets and store the depth of each node relative to the root. Doing so would certainly improve our query's performance, but at a horrendous cost in terms of maintenance.

Bottom-Up Walk: The Highlanders Query

As I said earlier, looking for the Highland string within the description attributes will necessarily lead to a full scan of the table. But let's write our query with each of the models in turn, and then we'll consider the resulting performance implications.

Adjacency model

The Highlanders query is very straightforward to write using connect by, and once again we use the dynamically computed level pseudo-column to indent our result properly. Note that level was previously giving the depth, and now it returns the height since it is always computed from our starting point, and that we now return the parent after the child:

```
select lpad(description, length(description) + level) description,
       commander
from adjacency_model
connect by id = prior parent_id
start with description like '%Highland%'
```

And here is the result that we get:

```
DESCRIPTION                         COMMANDER
----------------------------------- ---------------------------------------
 2/73rd (Highland) Rgmt of Foot     Lt-Colonel William George Harris
  5th British Brigade               Major-General Sir Colin Halkett
   3rd Anglo-German Division        Lt-General Count Charles von Alten
    I Corps                         Prince William of Orange
     The Anglo-Allied Army of 1815  Field Marshal Arthur Wellesley, Duke of
                                    Wellington
 1/71st (Highland) Rgmt of Foot     Lt-Colonel Thomas Reynell
  British Light Brigade             Major-General Frederick Adam
   2nd Anglo-German Division        Lt-General Sir Henry Clinton
    II Corps                        Lieutenant-General Lord Rowland Hill
     The Anglo-Allied Army of 1815  Field Marshal Arthur Wellesley, Duke of
                                    Wellington
 1/79th (Highland) Rgmt of Foot     Lt-Colonel Neil Douglas
  8th British Brigade               Lt-General Sir James Kempt
   5th Anglo-German Division        Lt-General Sir Thomas Picton (d.18th)
    General Reserve                 Duke of Wellington
     The Anglo-Allied Army of 1815  Field Marshal Arthur Wellesley, Duke of
                                    Wellington
 1/42nd (Highland) Rgmt of Foot     Colonel Sir Robert Macara (d.16th)
  9th British Brigade               Major-General Sir Denis Pack
   5th Anglo-German Division        Lt-General Sir Thomas Picton (d.18th)
    General Reserve                 Duke of Wellington
```

```
    The Anglo-Allied Army of 1815 Field Marshal Arthur Wellesley, Duke of
                                  Wellington
1/92nd (Highland) Rgmt of Foot    Lt-Colonel John Cameron
 9th British Brigade              Major-General Sir Denis Pack
  5th Anglo-German Division       Lt-General Sir Thomas Picton (d.18th)
   General Reserve                Duke of Wellington
    The Anglo-Allied Army of 1815 Field Marshal Arthur Wellesley, Duke of
                                  Wellington

25 rows selected.
```

The non-relational nature of connect by appears plainly enough: our result is not a relation, since we have duplicates. The name of the Duke of Wellington appears eight times, but in two different capacities, five times (as many times as we have Highland regiments) as commander-in-chief, and three as commander of the General Reserve. Twice—once as commander of the General Reserve and once as commander-in-chief—would have been amply sufficient. Can we easily remove the duplicates? No we cannot, at least not easily. If we apply a distinct, the DBMS will sort our result to get rid of the duplicate rows and will break the hierarchical order. We get a result that somehow answers the question. But you can take it or leave it according to the details of your requirements.

Materialized path model

The Highlanders query is slightly more difficult to write under the materialized path model. Identifying the proper rows and indenting them correctly is easy:

```
select lpad(a.description, length(a.description)
                       + mp_depth(b.materialized_path)
                         - mp_depth(a.materialized_path)) description,
       a.commander
from materialized_path_model a,
     materialized_path_model b
where b.materialized_path like a.materialized_path || '%'
  and b.description like '%Highland%')
```

However, we have two issues to solve:

- We have duplicates, as with the adjacency model.
- The order of rows is not the one we want.

Paradoxically, the second issue is the reason why we can solve the first one easily; since we shall have to find a means of correctly ordering anyway, adding a distinct will break nothing in this case. How can we order correctly? As usual, by using the materialized path as our sort key. By adding these two elements and pushing the query into the from clause so as to be able to sort by materialized_path without displaying the column, we get:

```
select description, commander
from (select distinct lpad(a.description, length(a.description)
                        + mp_depth(b.materialized_path)
                          - mp_depth(a.materialized_path)) description,
                        a.commander,
                        a.materialized_path
      from materialized_path_model a,
           materialized_path_model b
      where b.materialized_path like a.materialized_path || '%'
        and b.description like '%Highland%')
order by materialized_path desc
```

which displays:

```
DESCRIPTION                          COMMANDER
------------------------------------ ----------------------------------------
1/92nd (Highland) Rgmt of Foot       Lt-Colonel John Cameron
1/42nd (Highland) Rgmt of Foot       Colonel Sir Robert Macara (d.16th)
 9th British Brigade                 Major-General Sir Denis Pack
1/79th (Highland) Rgmt of Foot       Lt-Colonel Neil Douglas
 8th British Brigade                 Lt-General Sir James Kempt
  5th Anglo-German Division          Lt-General Sir Thomas Picton (d.18th)
   General Reserve                   Duke of Wellington
1/71st (Highland) Rgmt of Foot       Lt-Colonel Thomas Reynell
 British Light Brigade               Major-General Frederick Adam
  2nd Anglo-German Division          Lt-General Sir Henry Clinton
   II Corps                          Lieutenant-General Lord Rowland Hill
2/73rd (Highland) Rgmt of Foot       Lt-Colonel William George Harris
 5th British Brigade                 Major-General Sir Colin Halkett
  3rd Anglo-German Division          Lt-General Count Charles von Alten
   I Corps                           Prince William of Orange
    The Anglo-Allied Army of 1815    Field Marshal Arthur Wellesley, Duke of
                                     Wellington

16 rows selected.
```

This is a much nicer and more compact result than is achieved with the adjacency model. However, I should point out that a condition such as:

```
where b.materialized_path like a.materialized_path || '%'
```

where we are looking for a row in the table aliased by `a`, knowing the rows in the table aliased by `b`, is something that, generally speaking, may be slow because we can't make efficient use of the index on the column. What we would like to do, to make efficient use of the index, is the opposite, looking for `b.materialized_path` knowing `a.materialized_path`. There are ways to decompose a materialized path into the list of the materialized paths of the ancestors of the node (see Chapter 11), but that operation is not without cost. On our sample data, the query we have here was giving far better results than decomposing the material path so as to perform a more efficient join with the materialized path of each ancestor. However, this might not be true against several million rows.

Nested sets model

Once again, what hurts this model is that the depth must be dynamically computed, and that computation is a rather heavy operation. Since the Highlanders query is a bottom-up query, we must take care not to display the artificial root node (easily identified by `left_num = 1`) that we have had to introduce. Moreover, I have had to hard-code the maximum depth (6) to be able to indent properly. In our display, top levels are more indented than bottom levels, which means that padding is inversely proportional to depth. Since the depth is difficult to get, defining the indentation as `6 - depth` was the simplest way to achieve the required result.

As with the materialized path model, we have to reorder anyway, so we have no scruple about applying a `distinct` to get rid of duplicate rows. Here's the query:

```
select lpad(description, length(description) + 6 - depth) description,
       commander
from (select distinct b.description,
                      b.commander,
                      b.left_num,
                      (select count(c.left_num)
                       from nested_sets_model c
                       where b.left_num between c.left_num
                                          and c.right_num) depth
      from nested_sets_model a,
           nested_sets_model b
      where a.description like '%Highland%'
        and a.left_num between b.left_num and b.right_num
        and b.left_num > 1)
order by left_num desc
```

This query displays exactly the same result as does the materialized path query in the preceding section.

Comparing the various models for the Highlanders query

I have applied the same test to the Highlanders query as to the Vandamme query earlier, running each of the queries 5,000 times, with a minor twist: the adjacency model, as we have seen, returns duplicate rows that we cannot get rid of. My test returns 5,000 times 25 rows for the adjacency model, and 5,000 times 16 rows with the other models, because they are the only rows of interest. If we measure performance as a simple number of rows returned by unit of time, with the adjacency model we are also counting many rows that we are not interested in. I have therefore added an adjusted adjacency model, for which performance is measured as the number of rows of interest—the rows returned by the other two models—per unit of time. The result is given in Figure 7-3.

It is quite obvious from Figure 7-3 that the adjacency model outperforms the two other models by a very wide margin before adjustment, and still by a very comfortable margin after adjustment. Also notice that the materialized path model is still faster than the nested sets model, but only marginally so.

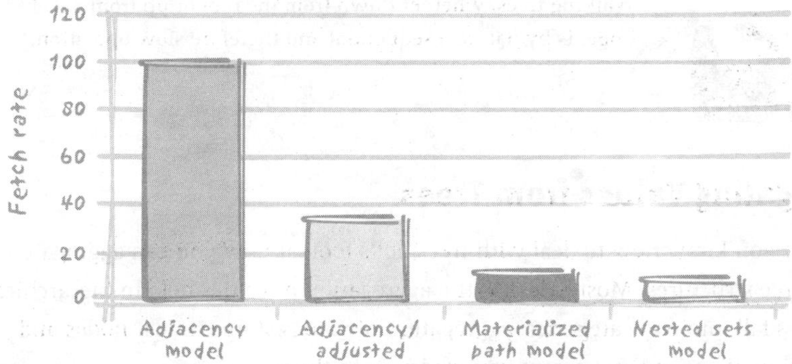

FIGURE 7-3. *Performance comparison for the Highlanders query*

We therefore see that, in spite of its procedural nature, the implementation of the `connect by` works rather well, both for top-down and bottom-up queries, provided of course that columns are suitably indexed. However, the return of duplicate rows in bottom-up queries when there are several starting points can prove to be a practical nuisance.

When `connect by` or a recursive `with` is not available, the materialized path model makes a good substitute. It is interesting to see that it performs better than the totally hard-wired nested sets model.

When designing tables to store hierarchical data, there are a number of mistakes to avoid, some of which are made in our example:

The materialized path should in no way be the key, even if it is unique.

It is true that strong hierarchies are not usually associated with dynamic environments, but you are not defined by your place in a hierarchy.

The materialized path should not imply any ordering of siblings.

Ordering does not belong to a relational model; it is simply concerned with the presentation of data. You must not have to change anything in other rows when you insert a new node or delete an existing one (which is probably the biggest practical reason, forgetting about all theoretical reasons, for not using the nested sets model). It is always easy to insert a node as the parents' last child. You can order everything first by sorting on the materialized path of the parent, and then on whichever attribute looks suitable for ordering the siblings.

The choice of the encoding is not totally neutral.

The choice is not neutral because whether you must sort by the materialized path or by the parent's materialized path, you must use that path as a sort key. The safest approach is probably to use numbers left padded with zeroes, for instance `001.003.004.005` (note that if we always use three positions for each number, the separator can go). You might be afraid of the materialized path's length; but if we assume that each parent never has more than 100 children numbered from 0 to 99, 20 characters allow us to store a materialized path for up to 10 levels, or trees containing up to 100^{10} nodes—probably more than needed.

Walking trees, whether down from the root or up from a leaf node, is by nature a sequential and therefore slow operation.

Aggregating Values from Trees

Now that you know how to deal with trees, let's look at how you can aggregate values held in tree structures. Most cases for the aggregation of values held in hierarchical structures fall into two categories: aggregation of values stored in leaf nodes and propagation of percentages across various levels in the tree.

Aggregation of Values Stored in Leaf Nodes

In a more realistic example than the one used to illustrate the Vandamme and Highlanders queries, nodes carry information—especially the leaf nodes. For instance, regiments should hold the number of their soldiers, from which we can derive the strength of every fighting unit.

Modeling head counts

If we take the same example we used previously, restricting it to a subset of the French Third Corps of General Vandamme and only descending to the level of brigades, a reasonably correct representation (as far as we can be correct) would be the tables described in the following subsections.

UNITS. Each row in the `units` table describes the various levels of aggregation (army corps, division, brigade) as in tables `adjacency_model`, `materialized_path_models`, or `nested_sets_model`, but without any attribute to specify how each unit relates to a larger unit:

```
ID NAME                       COMMANDER
-- -------------------------- ----------------------------------------------
 1 III Corps                  Général de Division Dominique Vandamme
 2 8th Infantry Division      Général de Division Baron Etienne-Nicolas Lefol
 3 1st Brigade                Général de Brigade Billard
 4 2nd Brigade                Général de Brigade Baron Corsin
 5 10th Infantry Division     Général de Division Baron Pierre-Joseph Habert
 6 1st Brigade                Général de Brigade Baron Gengoult
 7 2nd Brigade                Général de Brigade Baron Dupeyroux
 8 11th Infantry Division     Général de Division Baron Pierre Berthézène
 9 1st Brigade                Général de Brigade Baron Dufour
10 2nd Brigade                Général de Brigade Baron Logarde
11 3rd Light Cavalry Division Général de Division Baron Jean-Simon Domont
12 1st Brigade                Général de Brigade Baron Dommanget
13 2nd Brigade                Général de Brigade Baron Vinot
14 Reserve Artillery          Général de Division Baron Jérôme Doguereau
```

Since the link between units is no longer stored in this table, we need an additional table to describe how the different nodes in the hierarchy relate to each other.

UNIT_LINKS_ADJACENCY. We may use the adjacency model once more, but this time links between the various units are stored separately from other attributes, in an *adjacency list*, in other words a list that associates to the (technical) identifier of each row, `id`, the identifier of the parent row. Such a list isolates the structural information. Our `unit_links_adjacency` table looks like this:

```
        ID  PARENT_ID
---------- ----------
         2          1
         3          2
         4          2
         5          1
         6          5
         7          5
         8          1
         9          8
        10          8
        11          1
        12         11
        13         11
        14          1
```

UNIT_LINKS_PATH. But you have seen that an adjacency list wasn't the only way to describe the links between the various nodes in a tree. Alternatively, we may as well store the materialized path, and we can put that into the `unit_links_path` table:

```
        ID PATH
---------- -----------------
         1 1
         2 1.1
         3 1.1.1
         4 1.1.2
         5 1.2
         6 1.2.1
         7 1.2.2
         8 1.3
         9 1.3.1
        10 1.3.2
        11 1.4
        12 1.4.1
        13 1.4.2
        14 1.5
```

UNIT_STRENGTH. Finally, our historical source has provided us with the number of men in each of the brigades—the lowest unit level in our sample. We'll put that information into our `unit_strength` table:

```
        ID        MEN
--------- ----------
         3       2952
         4       2107
         6       2761
```

```
        7          2823
        9          2488
       10          2050
       12           699
       13           318
       14           152
```

Computing head counts at every level

With the adjacency model, it is typically quite easy to retrieve the number of men we have recorded for the third corps; all we have to write is a simple query such as:

```
select sum(men)
from unit_strength
where id in (select id
             from unit_links_adjacency
             connect by prior id = parent_id
             start with parent_id = 1)
```

Can we, however, easily get the head count at each level, for example, for each division (the battle unit composed of two brigades) as well? Certainly, in the very same way, just by changing the starting point—using the identifier of each division each time instead of the identifier of the French Third Corps.

We are now facing a choice: either we have to code procedurally in our application, looping on all fighting units and summing up what needs to be summed up, or we have to go for the full SQL solution, calling the query that computes the head count for each and every row returned. We need to slightly modify the query so as to return the actual head count each time the value is directly known, for example, for our lowest level, the brigade. For instance:

```
select u.name,
       u.commander,
       (select sum(men)
        from unit_strength
        where id in (select id
                     from unit_links_adjacency
                     connect by parent_id = prior id
                     start with parent_id = u.id)
           or id = u.id) men
from units u
```

It is not very difficult to realize that we shall be hitting again and again the very same rows, descending the very same tree from different places. Understandably, on large volumes, this approach will kill performance. This is where the procedural nature of `connect by`, which leaves us without a key to operate on (something I pointed out when I could not get rid of duplicates without destroying the order I wanted), leaves us no other choice than to adopt procedural processing when performance becomes a critical issue; "for all they that take the procedure shall perish with the procedure."

We are in a slightly better position with the materialized path here, if we are ready to allow a touch of black magic that I shall explain in Chapter 11. I have already referred to the *explosion* of links; it is actually possible, even if it is not a pretty sight, to write a query that *explodes* unit_links_path. I have called this view exploded_links_path and here is what it displays when it is queried:

```
SQL> select * from exploded_links_path;

        ID   ANCESTOR      DEPTH
---------- ---------- ----------
        14          1          1
        13          1          2
        12          1          2
        11          1          1
        10          1          2
         9          1          2
         8          1          1
         7          1          2
         6          1          2
         5          1          1
         4          1          2
         3          1          2
         2          1          1
         4          2          1
         3          2          1
         7          5          1
         6          5          1
        10          8          1
         9          8          1
        13         11          1
        12         11          1
```

depth gives the generation gap between id and ancestor.

When you have this view, it becomes a trivial matter to sum up over all levels (bar the bottom one in this case) in the hierarchy:

```
select u.name, u.commander, sum(s.men) men
from units u,
     exploded_links_path el,
     unit_strength s
where u.id = el.ancestor
  and el.id = s.id
group by u.name, u.commander
```

which returns:

```
NAME                       COMMANDER                                MEN
-------------------------- ---------------------------------------- -----
III Corps                  Général de Division Dominique Vandamme   16350
8th Infantry Division      Général de Division Baron Etienne-        5059
                           Nicolas Lefol
10th Infantry Division     Général de Division Baron Pierre          5584
                           Joseph Habert
```

```
11th Infantry Division      Général de Division Baron Pierre        4538
                            Berthézène
3rd Light Cavalry Division  Général de Division Baron Jean-Simon    1017
                            Domont
```

(We can add, through a `union`, a join between `units` and `unit_strength` to see units displayed for which nothing needs to be computed.)

I ran the query 5,000 times to determine the numerical strength for all units, and then I compared the number of rows returned per unit time. As might be expected, the result shows that the adjacency model, which had so far performed rather well, bites the dust, as is illustrated in Figure 7-4.

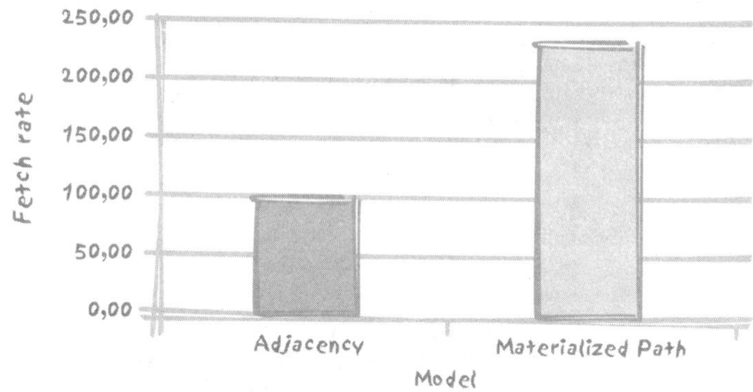

FIGURE 7-4. *Performance comparison when computing the head count of each unit*

Simpler tree implementation sometimes performs quite well when computing aggregates.

Propagation of Percentages Across Different Levels

Must we conclude that with a materialized path and a pinch of adjacency where available we can solve anything more or less elegantly and efficiently? Unfortunately not, and our last example will really demonstrate the limits of some SQL implementations when it comes to handling trees.

For this case, let's take a totally different example, and we will assume that we are in the business of potions, philters, and charms. Each of them is composed of a number of ingredients—and our recipes just list the ingredients and their percentage composition. Where is the hierarchy? Some of our recipes share a kind of "base philter" that appears as a kind of compound ingredient, as in Figure 7-5.

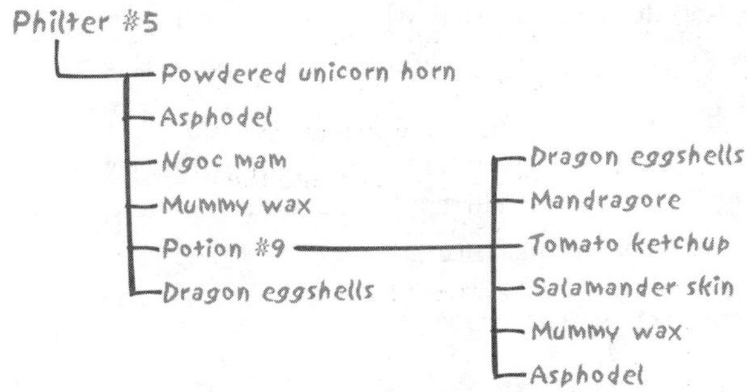

FIGURE 7-5. *Don't try this at home*

Our aim is, in order to satisfy current regulations, to display on the package of Philter #5 the names and proportions of all the basic ingredients. First, let's consider how we can model such a hierarchy. In such a case, a materialized path would be rather inappropriate. Contrarily to fighting units that have a single, well-defined place in the army hierarchy, any ingredient, including compound ones such as Potion #9, can contribute to many preparations. A path cannot be an attribute of an ingredient. If we decide to "flatten" compositions and create a new table to associate a materialized path to each basic ingredient in a composition, any change brought to Potion #9 would have to ripple through potentially hundreds of formulae, with the unacceptable risk in this line of business of one change going wrong.

The most natural way to represent such a structure is therefore to say that our philter contains so much of powdered unicorn horn, so much of asphodel, and so much of Potion #9 and so forth, and to include the composition of Potion #9.

Figure 7-6 illustrates one way we can model our database. We have a generic `components` table with two subtypes, `recipes` and `basic_ingredients`, and a `composition` table storing the quantity of a component (a recipe or a basic ingredient) that appears in each recipe.

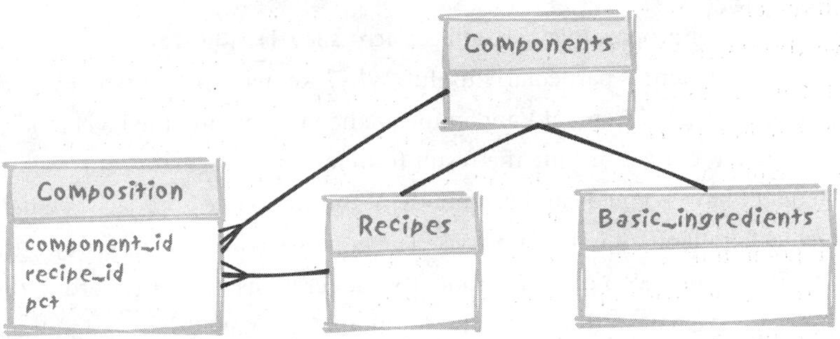

FIGURE 7-6. *The model for recipes*

However, Figure 7-6's design is precisely where an approach such as connect by becomes especially clunky. Because of the procedural nature of the connect by operator, we can include only two levels, which could be enough for the case of Figure 7-5, but not in a general case. What do I mean by including two levels? With connect by we have the visibility of two levels at once, the current level and the parent level, with the possible exception of the root level. For instance:

```
SQL> select connect_by_root recipe_id root_recipe,
            recipe_id,
            prior pct,
            pct
            component_id
     from composition
     connect by recipe_id = prior component_id
     /

ROOT_RECIPE  RECIPE_ID  PRIORPCT         PCT COMPONENT_ID
----------- ---------- ---------- ----------- ------------
         14         14                      5            3
         14         14                     20            7
         14         14                     15            8
         14         14                     30            9
         14         14                     20           10
         14         14                     10            2
         15         15                     30           14
         15         14         30           5            3
         15         14         30          20            7
         15         14         30          15            8
         15         14         30          30            9
 ...
```

In this example, root_recipe refers to the root of the tree. We can handle simultaneously the percentage of the current row and the percentage of the prior row, in tree-walking order, but we have no easy way to sum up, or in this precise case, to multiply values across a hierarchy, from top to bottom.

The requirement for propagating percentages across levels is, however, a case where a recursive with statement is particularly useful. Why? Remember that when we tried to display the underlings of General Vandamme we had to compute the level to know how deep we were in the tree, carrying the result from level to level across our walk. That approach might have seemed cumbersome then. But that same approach is what will now allow us to pull off an important trick. The great weakness of connect by is that at one given point in time you can only know two generations: the current row (the child) and its parent. If we have only two levels, if Potion #9 contains 15% of Mandragore and Philter #5 contains 30% of Potion #9, by accessing simultaneously the child (Potion #9) and the parent (Philter #5) we can easily say that we actually have 15% of 30%—in other words, 4.5% of Mandragore in Philter #5. But what if we have more than two levels? We may find a way to compute how much of each individual ingredient is contained in the final products with procedures, either in the program that accesses the database, or by invoking user-defined functions to store temporary results. But we have no way to make such a computation through plain SQL.

"What percentage of each ingredient does a formula contain?" is a complicated question. The recursive `with` makes answering it a breeze. Instead of computing the current level as being the parent level plus 1, all we have to do is compute the actual percentage as being the current percentage (how much Mandragore we have in Potion #9) multiplied by the parent percentage (how much Potion #9 we have in Philter #5). If we assume that the names of the components are held in the `components` table, we can write our recursive query as follows:

```
with recursive_composition(actual_pct, component_id)
as (select a.pct,
           a.component_id
    from composition a,
         components b
    where b.component_id = a.recipe_id
      and b.component_name = 'Philter #5'
    union all
    select parent.pct * child.pct,
           child.component_id
    from recursive_composition parent,
         composition child
    where child.recipe_id = parent.component_id)
```

Let's say that the `components` table has a `component_type` column that contains `I` for a basic ingredient and `R` for a recipe. All we have to do in our final query is filter (with an *f*) recipes out, and, since the same basic ingredient can appear at various different levels in the hierarchy, aggregate per ingredient:

```
select x.component_name, sum(y.actual_pct)
from recursive_composition y,
     components x
where x.component_id = y.component_id
  and x.component_type = 'I'
group by x.component_name
```

As it happens, even if the adjacency model looks like a fairly natural way to represent hierarchies, its two implementations are in no way equivalent, but rather complementary. While `connect by` may superficially look easier (once you have understood where `prior` goes) and is convenient for displaying nicely indented hierarchies, the somewhat tougher recursive `with` allows you to process much more complex questions relatively easily—and those complex questions are the type more likely to be encountered in real life. You only have to check the small print on a cereal box or a toothpaste tube to notice some similarities with the previous example of composition analysis.

In all other cases, including that of a DBMS that implements a `connect by`, our only hope of generating the result from a "single SQL statement" is by writing a user-defined function, which has to be recursive if the DBMS cannot walk the tree.

A more complex tree walking syntax may make a more complex question easier to answer in pure SQL.

While the methods described in this chapter can give reasonably satisfactory results against very small amounts of data, queries using the same techniques against very large volumes of data may execute "as slow as molasses." In such a case, you might consider a denormalization of the model and a trigger-based "flattening" of the data. Many, including myself, frown upon denormalization. However, I am not recommending that you consider denormalizing for the oft-cited inherent slowness of the relational model, so convenient for covering up incompetent programming, but because SQL still lacks a truly adequate, scaleable processing of tree structures.

CHAPTER EIGHT

Weaknesses and Strengths

Recognizing and Handling Difficult Cases

No one can guarantee success in war, but only deserve it.

—Sir Winston Churchill (1874–1965)

There are a number of cases when one has either to fight on unfavorable ground, or to attack a formidable amount of data with feeble weapons. In this chapter, I am going to try to describe a number of these difficult cases; first to try to sketch some tactics to disentangle oneself with honor from a perilous situation, and, perhaps more importantly, to be able to recognize as soon as possible those options that may just lead us into a trap. In mechanics, the larger the number of moving parts, the greater the odds that something will break. This is an observation that applies to complex architectures as well. Unfortunately, snappy, exciting new techniques—or indeed revamped, dull old ones—often make us forget this important principle: keep things simple. Simpler often means faster and always means more robust. But simpler for the database doesn't always mean simpler for the developer, and simplicity often requires more skills than complexity.

In this chapter, we shall first consider a case when a criterion that looks efficient proves rather weak but can be reinvigorated, and then we shall consider the dangers of abstract "persistency" layers and distributed systems. We shall finally look in some detail at a PHP/MySQL example showing the subtleties of combining flexibility with efficiency when a degree of freedom is left to the program user for the choice of search criteria.

Deceiving Criteria

I already mentioned in Chapter 6 that in some queries we have a very selective combination of criteria that individually are not very selective. I noted that this was a rather difficult situation from which to achieve good performance.

Another interesting case, but one in which we are not totally helpless, is a criterion that at first sight looks efficient, that has the potential for becoming an efficient criterion, but that requires some attention to fulfill its potential. Credit card validation procedures provide a good example of such a criterion. As you may know, a credit card number encodes several pieces of information, including credit card type, issuer, and so on. By way of example, let's look at the problem of achieving a first level of control for payments made at a toll road in one of the most visited Western European countries. This means checking a very large number of credit cards, supplied by a large number of international issuers, each with its own unique method of encoding.

Credit card numbers can have a maximum of 19 digits, with some exceptions, such as the cards issued by MasterCard (16 digits), Visa (16 or 13), and American Express (15 digits), to mention just three well-known issuers. The first six digits in all cases indicate who the issuer is, and the last digit is a kind of checksum to spot any mistyping. A first, coarse level of control could be to check that the issuer is known, and that the checksum is correct. However the checksum algorithm is public knowledge (it can be found on the

Internet) and can easily be faked. A more refined level of control also checks that the prefix of the card number belongs, for one given issuer, to a valid range of values for this issuer, together with an additional control on the number of digits in the card. In our case, we are provided with a list of about 200,000 valid prefixes of varying lengths.

How do we write the query to test a given card number against the valid ranges of values for the card's issuer? The following is easy enough:

```
select count(*)
from credit_card_check
where ? like prefix + '%'
```

The `where ?` indicates the card number to check and here + denotes string concatenation, often done via `||` or `concat()`. We just have to index the `prefix` column, and we will get a full table scan each time.

Why is a full table scan happening? Haven't we seen that an index was usable when we were addressing only the leftmost part of the key? True enough, but saying that the value we want to check is the leftmost part of the full key is not the same as saying, as here, that the *full* key is the leftmost part of the value we want to check. The difference may seem subtle, but the two cases are mirror images of each other.

Suppose that the credit card number to verify is 4000 0012 3456 7899*. Now imagine that our `credit_card_checks` table holds values such as `312345`, `3456` and `40001`. We can see those three values as prefixes and, more or less implicitly, we see them as being in sorted order. First of all, they are in ascending order if they are stored as strings of characters, but not if they are stored as numbers. But there is yet more to worry about.

When we descend a tree (our index), we have a value to compare to the keys stored in the tree. If the value is equal to the key stored into the current node, we are done. Otherwise, we have to search a subtree that depends on whether our value is smaller or greater than that key. If we had a prefix of fixed length, we would have no difficulty: we should only take the suitable number of digits from our card number (the current prefix), and compare it to the prefixes stored in the index. But when the length of the prefix varies, which is our case, we must compare a different number of characters each time. This is not a task that a regular SQL index search knows how to perform.

Is there any way out? Fortunately, there is one. An operator such as `like` actually selects a range of values. If we want to check, say, that a 16-digit Visa card number is *like* `4000%`, it actually means that we expect to find it between **4000**000000000000 and **4000**999999999999. If we had a composite index on these lower and upper boundary

* An invalid card number, in case you were wondering....

numbers, then we could very easily check the card number by checking the index. That is, if all card numbers had 16 digits. But a varying number of digits is a problem that is easy to solve. All cards have a maximum number of 19 digits. If we right-pad our Visa card number with three more 0s, thus bringing its total number of digits to 19, we can as validly check whether 4000001234567899*000* is between 4000000000000000*000* and 4000999999999999*999*.

Instead of storing prefixes, we need to have two columns: `lower_bound` and `upper_bound`. The first one, the `lower_bound`, is obtained by right-padding our prefix to the maximum length of 19 with 0s, and `upper_bound` is obtained by right-padding with 9s. Granted, this is denormalization of a sort. However, this is a real read-only reference table, which makes our sin slightly more forgivable. We just have to index (`lower_bound`, `upper_bound`) and write our condition as the following to see our query fly:

```
where substring(? + '0000000000000000000', 1, 19) between lower_bound
                                                      and upper_bound
```

Many products directly implement an `rpad( )` function for right-padding. When we have a variable-length prefix to check, the solution is to get back to a common access case—the index range scan.

Try to express unusual conditions such as comparisons on a prefix or a part of a key in known terms of range condition; whenever possible, try to ensure that there is a lower *and* an upper bound.

Abstract Layers

It is a common practice to create a succession of abstract layers over a suite of software primitives, ostensibly for maintenance reasons and software reuse. This is a worthy practice and provides superb material for exciting management presentations. Unfortunately, this approach can very easily be abused, especially when the software primitives consist of database accesses. Of course, such an industrial aspect of software engineering is usually associated with modern, object-oriented languages.

I am going to illustrate how *not* to encapsulate database accesses with some lines from a real-life program. Interestingly for a book entitled *The Art of SQL*, the following fragment of C# code (of questionable sharpness...) contains only bits of an SQL statement. It is nevertheless extremely relevant to our topic, for deplorable reasons.

```
public string Info_ReturnValueUS(DataTable dt,
                                 string    codeForm,
                                 string    infoTxt)
{
  string returnValue = String.Empty ;
```

```
6        try
7        {
8          infoTxt = infoTxt.Replace("'","''");
9          string expression = ComparisonDataSet.FRM_CD
10                             + " = '" + codeForm
11                             + "' and " + ComparisonDataSet.TXT_US
12                             + " = '" + infoTxt + "'" ;
13         DataRow[] drsAttr = dt.Select(expression);
14
15         foreach (DataRow dr in drsAttr)
16         {
17          if (dr[ComparisonDataSet.VALUE_US].ToString().ToUpper().Trim()
18                               != String.Empty)
19            {
20             returnValue = dr[ComparisonDataSet.VALUE_US].ToString() ;
21             break;
22            }
23         }
24       }
25       catch (MyException myex)
26       {
27         throw myex ;
28       }
29       catch (Exception ex)
30       {
31         throw new MyException("Info_ReturnValueUS " + ex.Message) ;
32       }
33       return returnValue ;
34     }
```

There is no need to be a C# expert to grasp the purpose of the above method, at least in general terms. The objective is to return the text associated with a message code. That text is to be returned in a given language (in this case American English, as `US` suggests). This code is from a multilingual system, and there is a second, identical function, in which two other letters replace the letters `U` and `S`. No doubt when other languages will be required, the same lines of code will be copied as many times as we have different languages, and the suitable ISO code substituted for `US` each time. Will it ease maintenance, when each change to the program has to be replicated to umpteen identical functions (...but for the ISO code)? I may be forgiven for doubting it, in spite of my legendary faith in what exciting management presentations promise modern languages to deliver.

But let's study the program a little more closely. The `string expression` in lines 9–12 is an example of shameless hardcoding, before being passed in line 13 to a `Select( )` method that can reasonably be expected to perform a query. In fact, it would seem that two different types of elements are hardcoded: column names (stored in attributes `ComparisonDataSet.FRM_CD` and `ComparisonDataSet.TXT_US`—and here, apparently, there is one column per supported language, which is a somewhat dubious design) and actual values passed to the query (`codeForm` and `infoTxt`). Column names can only be hardcoded, but there should not be a very great number of different combinations of column names, so that the number of different queries that can be generated will necessarily be small and we will have no reason to worry about this. The same cannot be said of actual values: we may query as many different values as we have rows in the table; in fact we may even query more, generating queries that may return nothing. The mistake of hard-coding values from `codeForm` and `infoTxt` into the SQL statement is serious because this type of "give me the associated label" query is likely to be called a very high number of times. As it is written, each call will trigger the full mechanism of parsing, determining the best execution plan, and so on—for no advantage. The values should be passed to the query as *bind variables*—just like arguments are passed to a function.

The loop of lines 15–23 is no less interesting. The program is looking for the first value that is not empty in the dataset just returned—dare we say the first value that is `not null`? Why code into an external application something that the SQL language can do perfectly well? Why return from the server possibly many more rows than are required, just to discard them afterwards? This is too much work. The database server will do more work, because even if we exit the loop at the first iteration, it is quite common to pre-fetch rows in order to optimize network traffic. The server may well have already returned tens or hundreds of rows before our application program begins its first loop. The application server does more work too, because it has to filter out most of what the database server painstakingly returned. Needless to say, the developer has written more code than is required. It is perfectly easy to add a suitable condition to `expression`, so that unneeded rows are not returned. As the C# code generates the query, the server has no idea that we are interested only in the first non-null value and will simply do as instructed. If we were to try and check on the database side for a clue indicating wrongly written code, the only thing that may possibly hint at a problem in the code will be the multitude of nearly identical hardcoded statements. This anomaly is, however, only a part of the larger problem.

One can write very poor code in any language, from plain old COBOL down to the coolest object-oriented language. But the greater the degree of independence between each layer of software, the better written those layers must each be. The problem here is that a succession of software layers may be called. No matter how skilled the developer who assembles these layers into the overall module, the final performance will be constrained by the weakest layer.

The problem of the weakest layer is all the more perverse when you inherit bad libraries—as with inheriting bad genes, there is not much you can do about it. Rewriting inefficient low-level layers is rarely allowed by schedules or budgets. I once learned about a case in which a basic operator in a programming language had been "overloaded" (redefined) and was performing a database access each time it was used by unsuspecting developers! It is all the more complicated to correct such a situation, because it is quite likely that individual queries, as seen from the database server, will look like conspicuously plain queries, not like the bad sort of SQL query that scans millions of rows and attracts immediate attention.

Cool database access libraries are not necessarily efficient libraries.

Distributed Systems

Whether you refer to federated systems, a linked server, or a database link, the principle is the same: in distributed queries, you are querying data that is not physically managed inside the server (or database to the Oracle crowd) you are connected to. Distributed queries are executed through complex mechanisms, especially for remote updates, in which transaction integrity has to be preserved. Such complexity comes at a very heavy cost, of which many people are not fully aware.

By way of example, I have run a series of tests against an Oracle database, performing massive inserts and selects against a very simple local table, and then creating database links and timing the very same operations with each database link. I have created three different database links:

Inter-process
: A link made by connecting through inter-process communications—typically what one might do to query data located in another database* on the same host. No network was involved.

Loop-back
: A link connecting through TCP, but specifying the loop-back address (127.0.0.1) to limit our foray into the network layers.

IP address
: A link specifying the actual IP address of the machine—but once again without really using a network, so there is no network latency involved.

The result of my tests, as it appears in Figure 8-1, is revealing. In my case, there is indeed a small difference linked to my using inter-process communications or TCP in loop-back or regular mode. But the big performance penalty comes from using a database link in the very first place. With inserts, the database link divides the number of rows inserted per second by five, and with selects it divides the number of rows returned per second by a factor of 2.5 (operating in each case on a row-by-row basis).

* Remember that what Oracle calls a *database* is what is known in most other database systems as a *server*.

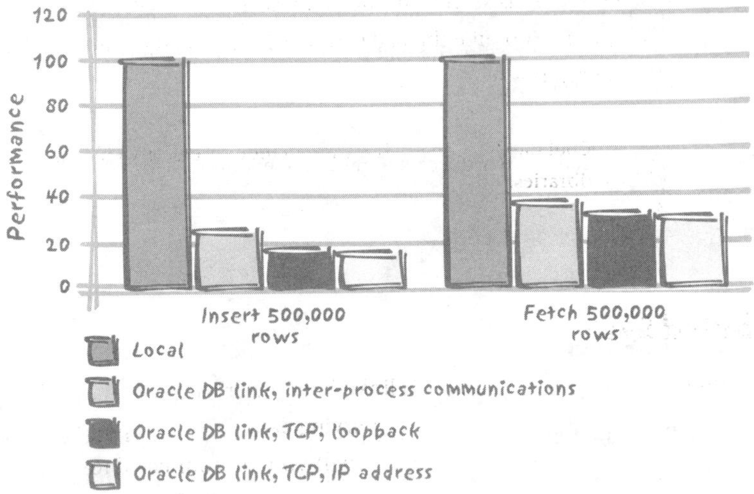

FIGURE 8-1. *The cost of faking being far away*

When we have to execute transactions across heterogeneous systems, we have no other choice than to use database links or their equivalent. If we want data integrity, then we need to use mechanisms that preserve data integrity, whatever the cost. There are, however, many cases when having a dedicated server is an architectural choice, typically for some reference data. The performance penalty is quite acceptable for the odd remote reference. It is quite likely that if at connection time some particular credentials are checked against a remote server, nobody will really notice, as long as the remote server is up. If, however, we are massively loading data into a local database and performing some validation check against a remote server for each row loaded locally, then you can be sure to experience extremely slow performance. Validating rows one by one is in itself a bad idea (in a properly designed database, all validation should be performed through integrity constraints): remote checks will be perhaps two or three times slower than the same checks being carried out on the same local server.

Distributed queries, involving data from several distinct servers, are also usually painful. First of all, when you send a query to a DBMS kernel, whatever that query is, the master of the game is the optimizer on that kernel. The optimizer will decide how to split the query, to distribute the various parts, to coordinate remote and local activity, and finally to put all the different pieces together. Finding the appropriate path is already a complicated-enough business when everything happens on the local server. We should take note that the notion of "distribution" is more logical than physical: part of the performance penalty comes from the unavailability of remote dictionary information in the local cache. The cost penalty will be considerably higher with two unrelated databases hosted by the same machine than with two databases hosted by two different servers but participating in a common federated database and sharing data dictionary information.

There is much in common between distributed and parallelized queries (when a query is split into a number of independent chunks that can be run in parallel) with, as you have seen, the additional difficulties of the network layers slowing down significantly some of the operations, and of the unavailability at one place of all dictionary information making the splitting slightly more hazardous. There is also an additional twist here: when sources are heterogeneous—for example when a query involves data coming from an Oracle database as well as data queried from an SQL Server database, all the information the optimizer usually relies on may not be available. Certainly, most products gather the same type of information in order to optimize queries. But for several reasons, they don't work in a mutually cooperative fashion. First, the precise way each vendor's optimizer works is a jealously guarded secret. Second, each optimizer evolves from version to version. Finally, the Oracle optimizer will never be able to take full advantage of SQL Server specifics and vice versa. Ultimately, only the greatest common denominator can be meaningfully shared between different product optimizers.

Even with homogeneous data sources, the course of action is narrowly limited. As we have seen, fetching one row across a network costs considerably more than when all processes are done locally. The logical inference for the optimizer is that it should not take a path which involves some kind of to and fro switching between two servers, but rather move as much filtering as close to the data as it can. The SQL engine should then either pull or push the resulting data set for the next step of processing. You have already seen in Chapters 4 and 6 that a correlated subquery was a dreadfully bad way to test for existence when there is no other search criterion, as in for instance, the following example:

```
select customer_name
from customers
where exists (select null
              from orders,
                   orderdetails
              where orders.customer_id = customers.customer_id
                and orderdetails.order_id = orders.order_id
                and orderdetails.article_id = 'ANVIL023')
```

Every row we scan from `customers` fires a subquery against `orders` and `orderdetails`.

It is of course even worse when `customers` happens to be hosted by one machine and `orders` and `orderdetails` by another. In such a case, given the high cost of fetching a single row, the reasonable solution looks like a transformation (in the ideal case, by the optimizer) of the above correlated subquery into an uncorrelated one, to produce the following instead:

```
select customer_name
from customers
where customer_id in (select orders.customer_id
```

```
                from orders,
                     orderdetails
                where orderdetails.article_id = 'ANVIL023'
                  and orderdetails.order_id = orders.order_id)
```

Furthermore, the subquery should be run at the remote site. Note that this is also what should be performed even if you write the query as like this:

```
select distinct customer_name
from customers,
     orders,
     orderdetails
where orders.customer_id = customers.customer_id
  and orderdetails.article_id = 'ANVIL023'
  and orders.order_id = orderdetails.order_id
```

Now will the optimizer choose to do it properly? This is another question, and it is better not to take the chance. But obviously the introduction of remote data sources narrows the options we have in trying to find the most efficient query. Also, remember that the subquery must be fully executed and all the data returned before the outer query can kick in. Execution times will, so to speak, add up, since no operation can be executed concurrently with another one.

The safest way to ensure that joins of two remote tables actually take place at the remote site is probably to create, at this remote site, a view defined as this join and to query the view. For instance, in the previous case, it would be a good idea to define a view vorders as:

```
select orders.customer_id, orderdetails.article_id
from orders,
     orderdetails
where orderdetails.order_id = orders.order_id
```

By querying vorders we limit the risks of seeing the DBMS separately fetching data from all the remote tables involved in the query, and then joining everything locally. Needless to say, if in the previous case, customers and orderdetails were located on the same server and orders were located elsewhere, we would indeed be in a very perilous position.

The optimizer works well with what it knows well: local data. Extensive interaction with remote data sinks performance.

Dynamically Defined Search Criteria

One of the most common causes for awful visible performance (as opposed to the common dismal performance of batch programs, which can often be hidden for a while) is the use of dynamically defined search criteria. In practice, such criteria are a consequence of the dreaded requirement to "let the user enter the search criteria as well as the sort order via a screen interface."

The usual symptoms displayed by this type of application is that many queries perform reasonably well, but that unfortunately from time to time a query that seems to be almost the same as a well-performing query happens to be very, very slow. And of course the problem is difficult to fix, since everything is so dynamic.

Dynamic-search applications are often designed as a two-step drill-down query, as in Figure 8-2. Basically, a first screen is displayed to the user with a large choice of criteria and an array of possible conditions such as `exclude` or `date between ... and ...`. These criteria are used to dynamically build a query that returns a list with some identifier and description, from which you can view all the associated details by selecting one particular item in the list.

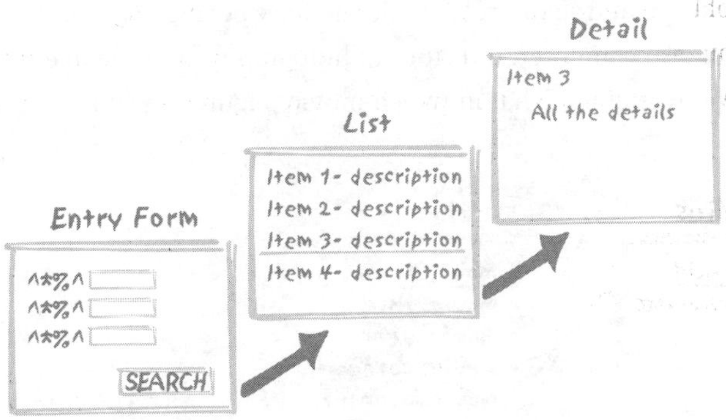

FIGURE 8-2. *A typical multi-criteria search*

When the same columns from the same tables are queried with varying search criteria, the key to success usually lays in a clever generation of SQL queries by the program that accesses the database. I am going to illustrate my point in detail with a very simple example, a movie database, and we shall only be concerned with returning a list of movie titles that satisfy a number of criteria. The environment used in this example is a widely popular combination, namely PHP and MySQL. Needless to say, the techniques shown in this chapter are in no way specific to PHP or to MySQL—or to movie databases.

Designing a Simple Movie Database and the Main Query

Our central table will be something such as the following:

```
Table MOVIES
   movie_id        int(10) (auto-increment)
   movie_title     varchar(50)
   movie_country   char(2)
   movie_year      year(4)
   movie_category  int(10)
   movie_summary   varchar(250)
```

We certainly need a `categories` table (referenced by a foreign key on `movie_category`) to hold the different genres, such as *Action, Drama, Comedy, Musical,* and so forth. It can be argued that some movies sometimes span several categories, and a better design would involve an additional table representing a many-to-many relationship (meaning that one genre can be associated with several movies and that each movie can be associated with several genres as well), but for the sake of simplicity we shall admit that a single, main genrc is enough for our needs in this example.

Do we need one table for actors and another for directors? Creating two tables would be a design mistake, because it is quite common to see actors-turned-directors, and there is no need to duplicate personal information. From time to time one even finds a movie directed by one of the lead actors.

We therefore need three more tables: `people` to store information such as name, first name, sex, year of birth, and so on; `roles` to define how people may contribute to a movie (actor, director, but also composer, director of photography, and the like); and `movie_credits` to state who was doing what in which movie. Figure 8-3 shows our complete movie schema.

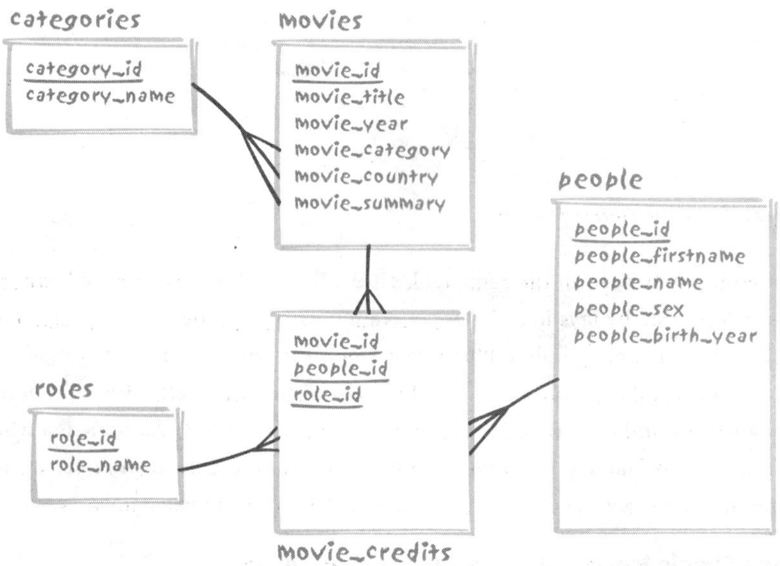

FIGURE 8-3. *The movie database schema*

Let's suppose now that we want to let people search movies in our database by specifying either: words from the title, the name of the director, or up to three names of any of the actors. Following is the source of our prototype page, which I have built in HTML to act as our screen display:

```
<html>
<head>
  <title>Movie Database</title>
```

```
</head>
<body>
<CENTER>
    <HR>
    <BR>
    Please fill the form to query our database and click on <b>Search</b> when you
are done...
    <BR>
    <HR>
    <BR>
<form action="display_query.php" method="post">
    <TABLE WIDTH="75%">
    <TR>
      <TD>Movie Title :</TD>
      <TD><input type="text" name="title"></TD>
    </TR>
    <TR>
      <TD>Director    :</TD>
      <TD><input type="text" name="director"></TD>
    </TR>
    <TR>
      <TD>Actor       :</TD>
      <TD><input type="text" name="actor1"></TD>
    </TR>
    <TR>
      <TD>Actor       :</TD>
      <TD><input type="text" name="actor2"></TD>
    </TR>
    <TR>
      <TD>Actor       :</TD>
      <TD><input type="text" name="actor3"></TD>
    </TR>
    <TR>
      <TD COLSPAN="2" ALIGN="CENTER">
      <HR>
      <input type="Submit" value="Search">
      <HR>
      </TD>
    </TR>
    </TABLE>
</form>
</CENTER>
</body>
</html>
```

This prototype page shows on screen as in Figure 8-4.

First, let me make a few remarks:

- Although we want to store the first and last names separately in our database (definitely more convenient if we want to generate a listing ordered by last name), we don't want our entry form to look like a passport renewal form: we just want a single entry field for each individual.
- We want our query input values to be case-insensitive.

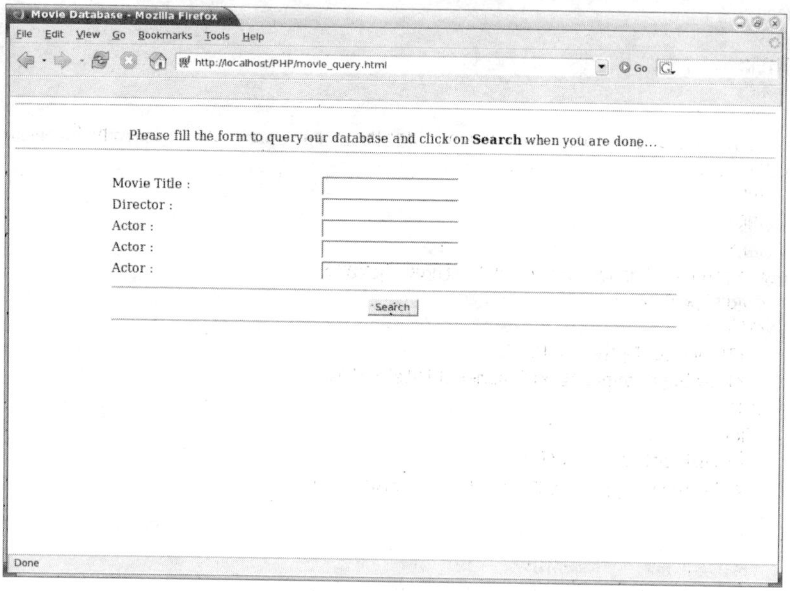

FIGURE 8-4. *The movie database search screen*

Certainly the thing *not* to do is to generate a query containing a criterion such as:

```
and upper(<value entered for actor1>) =
         concat(upper(people_firstname), ' ', upper(people_name))
```

As shown in Chapter 3, the right part of the equality in such a criterion would prevent us from using any regular index we might have logically created on the name. Several products allow the creation of functional indexes and index the result of expressions, but the simplest and therefore best solution is probably as follows:

1. Systematically store in uppercase any character column that is likely to be queried (we can always write a function to beautify it before output).
2. Split the entry field into first name and (last) name before passing it to the query.

The first point simply means inserting `upper(`*string*`)` instead of *string*, which is easy enough. Keep the second point in mind for the time being: I'll come back to it in just a bit.

If users were to fill *all* entry fields, all the time, then our resulting main query could be something such as:

```
select movie_title, movie_year
from movies
     inner join movie_credits mc1
       on mc1.movie_id = movies.movie_id
     inner join people actor1
       on  mc1.people_id = actor1.people_id
     inner join roles actor_role
       on  mc1.role_id = actor_role.role_id
       and mc2.role_id = actor_role.role_id
       and mc3.role_id = actor_role.role_id
```

```
        inner join movie_credits mc2
          on mc2.movie_id = movies.movie_id
        inner join people actor2
          on  mc2.people_id = actor2.people_id
        inner join movie_credits mc3
          on mc3.movie_id = movies.movie_id
        inner join people actor3
          on  mc3.people_id = actor3.people_id
        inner join movie_credits mc4
          on mc4.movie_id = movies.movie_id
        inner join people director
          on  mc4.people_id = director.people_id
        inner join roles director_role
          on mc4.role_id = director_role.role_id
    where actor_role.role_name = 'ACTOR'
      and director_role.role_name = 'DIRECTOR'
      and movies.movie_title like 'CHARULATA%'
      and actor1.people_firstname = 'SOUMITRA'
      and actor1.people_name = 'CHATTERJEE'
      and actor2.people_firstname = 'MADHABI'
      and actor2.people_name = 'MUKHERJEE'
      and actor3.people_firstname = 'SAILEN'
      and actor3.people_name = 'MUKHERJEE'
      and director.people_name = 'RAY'
      and director.people_firstname = 'SATYAJIT'
```

Unfortunately, will somebody who can name the title, director and the three main actors of a film (most typically a movie buff) really need to use our database? This is very unlikely. The most likely search will probably be when a single field or possibly two, at most, will be populated. We must therefore anticipate blank fields, asking the question: what will we do when no value is passed?

A common way of coding one's way out of a problematic situation like this is to keep the select list unchanged; then to join together all the tables that may intervene in one way or another, using suitable join conditions; and then to replace the straightforward conditions from the preceding example with a long series of:

```
and column_name = coalesce(?, column_name)
```

where ? will be associated with the value from an entry field, and `coalesce()` is the function that returns the first one of its arguments that is non null. If a value is provided, then a filter is applied; otherwise, all values in the column pass the test.

All values? Not really; if a column contains a `NULL`, the condition for that column will evaluate to false. We cannot say that something we don't know is equal to something we don't know, even if it is the same something (nothing?). If one condition in our long series of conditions linked by `and` evaluates to `false`, the query will return nothing, which is certainly not what we want. There is a solution though, which is to write:

```
and coalesce(column_name, constant) = coalesce(?, column_name, constant)
```

This solution would be absolutely perfect if only it did not mean forfeiting the use of any index on *column_name* when a parameter is specified. Must we sacrifice the correctness of results to performance, or performance to the correctness of results? The latter solution is probably preferable, but unfortunately both of them might also mean sacrificing our job, a rather unpleasant prospect.

A query that works in all cases, whatever happens, is quite difficult to write. The commonly adopted solution is to build such a query dynamically. What we can do in this example scenario is to store in a string everything up to the `where` and the fixed conditions on role names, and then to concatenate to this string the conditions which have been input by our program user—and only those conditions.

A variable number of search criteria calls for dynamically built queries.

Assuming that a user searched our database for movies starring Amitabh Bachchan, the resulting, dynamically written query might be something like the following:

```
select distinct movie_title, movie_year
from movies
     inner join movie_credits mc1
       on mc1.movie_id = movies.movie_id
     inner join people actor1
       on  mc1.people_id = actor1.people_id
     inner join roles actor_role
       on  mc1.role_id = actor_role.role_id
       and mc2.role_id = actor_role.role_id
       and mc3.role_id = actor_role.role_id
     inner join movie_credits mc2
       on mc2.movie_id = movies.movie_id
     inner join people actor2
       on  mc2.people_id = actor2.people_id
     inner join movie_credits mc3
       on mc3.movie_id = movies.movie_id
     inner join people actor3
       on  mc3.people_id = actor3.people_id
     inner join movie_credits mc4
       on mc4.movie_id = movies.movie_id
     inner join people director
       on  mc4.people_id = director.people_id
     inner join roles director_role
       on mc4.role_id = director_role.role_id
where actor_role.role_name = 'ACTOR'
  and director_role.role_name = 'DIRECTOR'
  and actor1.people_firstname = 'AMITABH'
  and actor1.people_name = 'BACHCHAN'
order by movie_title, movie_year
```

First, let me make two remarks:

- We have to make our `select` a `select distinct`. We do this because we keep the joins without any additional condition. Otherwise, as many rows would be returned for each movie as we have actors and directors recorded for the movie.
- It is very tempting when building the query to concatenate the values that we receive to the SQL text under construction proper, thus obtaining a query exactly as above. This is not, in fact, what we should do. I have already mentioned the subject of bind variables; it is now time to explain how they work. The proper course is indeed to build the query with placeholders such as ? (it depends on the language), and then to call a special function to *bind* the actual values to the placeholders. It may seem more work for the developer, but in fact it will mean less work for the DBMS engine. Even if we rebuild the query each time, the DBMS usually caches the statements it executes as a part of its standard optimization routines. If the SQL engine is given a query to process that it finds in its cache, the DBMS has already parsed the SQL text and the optimizer has already determined the best execution path. If we use placeholders, all queries that are built on the same pattern (such as searches for movies starring one particular actor) will use the same SQL text, irrespective of the actor's name. All the setup is done, the query can be run immediately, and the end user gets the response faster.

Besides performance, there is also a very serious concern associated with dynamically built hardcoded queries, a security concern: such queries present a wide-open door to the technique known as *SQL injection*. What is SQL injection? Let's say that we run a commercial operation, and that only subscribers are allowed to query the full database while access to movies older than 1960 is free to everybody. Suppose that a malicious non-subscriber enters into the `movie_title` field something such as:

```
X' or 1=1 or 'X' like 'X
```

When we simply concatenate entry fields to our query text we shall end up with a condition such as:

```
where movie_title like 'X' or 1=1 or 'X' like 'X%'
  and movie_year < 1960
```

which is always true and will obviously filter nothing at all! Concatenating the entry field to the SQL statement means that in practice anybody will be able to download our full database without any subscription. And of course some information is more sensitive than movie databases. Binding variables protects from SQL injection. SQL injection is a very real security matter for anyone running an on-line database, and great care should be taken to protect against its malicious use.

When using dynamically built queries, use parameter markers and pass values as bind variables, for both performance and security (SQL injection) reasons.

A query with prepared joins and dynamically concatenated filtering conditions executes very quickly when the tables are properly indexed. But there is nevertheless something that is worrisome. The preceding example query is a very complicated query, particularly when we consider the simplicity of both the output result and of what we provided as input.

Right-Sizing Queries

In fact, the complexity of the query is just one part of the issue. What happens, in the case of the final query in the preceding section, if we have not recorded the name of the director in our database, or if we know only the names of the two lead actors? The query will return no rows. All right, can we not use outer joins then, which return matching values when there is one and NULL when there is none?

Using outer joins might be a solution, except that we don't know what exactly will be queried. What if we only have the name of the director in our database? In fact, we would need outer joins everywhere—and putting them everywhere is often, logically, impossible. We therefore have an interesting case, in which we are annoyed by missing information even if all of our attributes are defined as mandatory and we have absolutely no NULL values in the database, simply because our query so far assumes joins that may be impossible to satisfy.

In fact, in the particular case when only one actor name is provided, we need a query no more complicated than the following:

```
select movie_title, movie_year
from movies
     inner join movie_credits mc1
       on mc1.movie_id = movies.movie_id
     inner join people actor1
       on  mc1.people_id = actor1.people_id
     inner join roles actor_role
       on  mc1.role_id = actor_role.role_id
where actor_role.role_name = 'ACTOR'
  and actor1.people_firstname = 'AMITABH'
  and actor1.people_name = 'BACHCHAN'
order by movie_title, movie_year
```

This "tight-fit" query assumes nothing about our also knowing the name of the director, nor of a sufficient number of other actors, and hence there is no need for outer joins. Since we have already begun building our query dynamically, why not try to inject a little more intelligence in our building exercise, so as to obtain a query really built to order, exactly tailored to our needs? Our code will no doubt be more complicated. Is the complication worth it? The simple fact that we are now certain to return all the information available when given an actor's name, even when we don't know who directed a film, should be reason enough for an unqualified "yes." But performance reasons also justify taking this step.

Nothing is as convincing as running a query in a loop a sufficient number of times to show the difference between two approaches: our "tight-fit" query is five times faster than the "one-size-fits-all" query. All other things aside, does it matter if our query executes in 0.001 second instead of 0.005 second? Not much, if our database is only queried now and then. But there may be a day when queries arrive at a rate higher than we can service and keep up with, and then we'll have a problem. Queries will have to be queued, and the queue length will increase very quickly—as fast as the number of complaints about poor database performance. Simply put, going five times faster enables five times as many queries to be processed on the same hardware. (We will consider these issues in more detail in Chapter 9.)

Matching criteria with dynamically built queries improves performance by minimizing joins, and eliminates the issue of missing values.

Wrapping SQL in PHP

Let's first start our PHP page with a smattering of regular HTML before the real PHP code:

```
<html>
  <head>
     <title>Query result</title>
</head>
<body>
<CENTER>
  <table width="80%">
    <TR><TH>Title</TH><TH>Year</TH><TR>


<?php
 ...
```

(Our page would probably be nicer with a stylesheet....)

Once we have our handle that represents the connection to the database, the very first thing to do is to get the values that were submitted to the entry screen. Since everything is stored in uppercase in our database we can convert the user-entered values directly to uppercase too. This is of course something that can be done in the SQL code, but it costs nothing to do it in the PHP code:

```
$title=strtoupper($_POST['title']);
$director=strtoupper($_POST['director']);
$actor1=strtoupper($_POST['actor1']);
$actor2=strtoupper($_POST['actor2']);
$actor3=strtoupper($_POST['actor3']);
```

We now have a technical problem linked to the implementation of PHP binding. Following is the process for binding variables in PHP:

1. We first write ? in the place of every parameter we want to pass to the query.
2. Then we call the `bind_param()` method that takes as its first argument a string containing as many characters as we have values to bind, each character telling the type of the parameter we pass (in this case it will always be s for string), then a variable number of parameters—one per each value we want to bind.

All parameters are identified by position (the same is true with JDBC, but not with all database systems and languages; for instance, you will refer to bind variables by name in an SQLJ program). But our main problem is the single call to `bind_param()`, which is very convenient when we know exactly how many parameters we have to bind, but is not so in our case here, in which we do not know in advance how many values a user will enter. It would be much more convenient in our case to have a method allowing us to loop and bind values one by one.

One way to bind a variable number of values, which is not necessarily the most elegant, is to loop on all the variables we have received from the form, check which ones actually contain something, and store each value in the subsequent positions of an array. We have no problem doing this with our example since all the values we may get are character strings. If we were expecting something else—for instance the year when a movie was first shown—the most sensible approach would probably be to treat such a value as a string inside the PHP code and to convert it to a number or date in the SQL code.

We can use a `$paramcnt` variable to count how many parameters were provided by the user of the form, and store the values into a `$params` array:

```
$paramcnt=0;

if ($title != "") {
   $params[$paramcnt] = $title;
   $paramcnt++;
  }
```

Things get a little more complicated with people names. Remember that we have decided that having a single field to enter a name was more user-friendly than having to enter the first and last names into two separate fields. However, comparing the string entered by the user to the concatenation of first name and last name in our `people` table would prevent the query from using the index on the last name and might, moreover, yield wrong results: if the user has mistakenly typed two spaces instead of one between first name and last name, for instance, we shall not find the person.

What we are therefore going to do is to split the entry field into first name and last name, assuming that the last name is the last word, and that the first name, which may be composed of 0, 1, or several words, is what precedes the last name. In PHP, we can easily write such a function which sets two parameters that are passed by reference:

```
function split_name($string, &$firstname, &$lastname)
{
/*
 *   We assume that the last name is the last element of the string,
 *   and that we may have several first names
 */
 $pieces = explode(" ", $string);
 $parts = count($pieces);
 $firstnames = array_slice($pieces, 0, $parts - 1);
 $firstname = implode(" ", $firstnames);
 $lastname = $pieces[$parts - 1];
}
```

This function will allow us to split `$director` into `$dfn` and `$dn`, `$actor1` into `$a1fn` and `$a1n` and so on, everything being coded on the same model:

```
if ($director != "") {
   /* Split firstname / name */
       split_name($director, $dfn, $dln);
   if ($dfn != "")
      {
       $params[$paramcnt] = $dfn;
       $paramcnt++;
      }
   $params[$paramcnt] = $dln;
   $paramcnt++;
  }
```

Once we have inspected our parameters, all we have to do is to build our query, being very careful to insert the parameter markers for the bind variables in exactly the same order as they will appear in the `$params` array:

```
$query = "select movie_title, movie_year "
          . "from movies";
/* Director was specified ? */
if ($director != "")
   {
    $query = $query . " inner join movie_credits mcd"
                    . "  on mcd.movie_id = movies.movie_id"
                    . " inner join people director"
                    . "  on  mcd.people_id = director.people_id"
                    . " inner join roles director_role"
                    . "  on mcd.role_id = director_role.role_id";
   }
/* Any actor was specified ? */
if ($actor1 . $actor2 . $actor3 != "")
   {
   /*
    *   First the join on the ROLES table
    */
    $query = $query . " inner join roles actor_role";
```

```
  /*
   *  Even if only one actor was specified, we may
   *  not necessarily find the name in $actor1 so careful
   */
   $actcnt = 0;
   if ($actor1 != "")
      {
       if ($actcnt == 0)
          {
           $query = $query . "  on";
          }
        else
          {
           $query = $query . "  and";
          }
       $query = $query . " mc1.role_id = actor_role.role_id";
      }
   if ($actor2 != "")
      {
       ...
      }
   if ($actor3 != "")
      {
       ...
      }
  /*
   *   Then join on MOVIE_CREDITS and PEOPLE
   */
   if ($actor1 != "")
      {
       $query = $query . " inner join movie_credits mc1"
                       . "  on mc1.movie_id = movies.movie_id"
                       . " inner join people actor1"
                       . "  on actor1.people_id = mc1.people_id";
      }
   if ($actor2 != "")
      {
       ...
      }
   if ($actor3 != "")
      {
       ...
      }
  }
/*
 *   We are done with the FROM clause; we are using the old 1=1
 *   trick to avoid checking each time whether it is the very
 *   first condition or not - the latter case requires an 'and'.
 */
$query = $query . " where 1=1";
/*
 * Be VERY careful to add parameters in the same order they were
 * stored into the $params array
 */
if ($title != "")
```

```
      {
       $query = $query . " and movies.movie_title like concat(?, '%')";
      }
    /* Director was specified ? */
    if ($director != "")
      {
       $query = $query . "  and director_role.role_name = 'DIRECTOR'";
       if ($dfn != "")
         {
         /*
          * Use like instead of regular equality for the first name, it will
          * work with some abbreviations or initials.
          */
          $query = $query
                  . " and director.people_firstname like concat(?, '%')";
         }
       $query = $query . " and director.people_name = ?";
      }
    if ($actor1 . $actor2 . $actor3 != "")
      {
       $query = $query . "  and actor_role.role_name = 'ACTOR'";
       if ($actor1 != "")
         {
          ...
         }
       if ($actor2 != "")
         {
          ...
         }
       if ($actor3 != "")
         {
          ...
         }
      }
```

Once our query is ready, we call the prepare( ) method, then bind our variables; this is where our code is not very pretty, since we can have between 1 and 9 variables to bind and handle, and each variable must be handled separately:

```
    /* create a prepared statement */
    if ($stmt = $mysqli->prepare($query)) {
       /*
        *  Bind parameters for markers
        *
        *  This is the messiest part.
        *  We can have anything between 1 and 9 parameters in all (all strings)
        */
       switch ($paramcnt)
          {
           case 1 :
                $stmt->bind_param("s", $params[0]);
                break;
           case ...
                ...
                break;
```

```
            case 9 :
                 $stmt->bind_param("sssssssss", $params[0],
                                                $params[1],
                                                $params[2],
                                                $params[3],
                                                $params[4],
                                                $params[5],
                                                $params[6],
                                                $params[7],
                                                $params[8]);
                 break;
            default :
                 break;
          }
```

Et voilà! We are done and just have to execute the query and display the result:

```
        /* execute query */
        $stmt->execute();
        /* fetch values */
        $stmt->bind_result($mt, $my);
        while ($row = $stmt->fetch())
           {
             printf ("<tr><TD>%s</TD><TD>%d</TD></TR>\n", $mt, $my);
           }
        /* close statement */
        $stmt->close();
       }
     else
       {
        printf("Error: %s\n", $mysqli->sqlstate);
       }
   ?>
   </TABLE>
   </CENTER>
```

Obviously, the code here is significantly more complicated than if we had tried to have one single query.

It may seem surprising, after I have advocated pushing as much work as possible onto the DBMS side, to now find me defending the use of complicated code to build as simple a SQL statement as possible. Doing as much work on the SQL side as possible makes sense when it is work that *has* to be performed. But joining three times as many tables as are needed in the average query, with some of these useless joins not necessarily being very efficient (especially when they happen to be against complex views) makes no sense at all.

By intelligently building the query, we tightly control what is executed in terms of security, correctness of the result, and performance. Any simpler solution bears risks of sacrificing at least one of these aspects.

To summarize, there are at least three mistakes that are very commonly made in queries that take a variable number of search criteria:

- First of all, it is quite common to see the *values* against which the columns of the tables are compared being concatenated with the statement-in-making, thus resulting in a magnificent, totally hardcoded statement. Even where queries are supposed to be absolutely unpredictable, you usually find a few queries that are issued again and again by the users, with only the constants varying. Some constants are susceptible to a high degree of variability (such as entity identifiers, as opposed to date formats or even status codes). It isn't much work to replace these constants by a parameter marker, the syntax of which depends on the language (for instance `'?'`) and then to *bind* the actual value to this parameter marker. This will result in much less work for the server, which will not need to re-analyze the statement each time it is issued, and in particular will not need to determine each time a *best execution plan*, that will always be the same. And no user will be able to bypass any additional restriction you may want to add to the query, which means that by binding variables you will plug a serious security issue at the same time.
- A second mistake is usually to try to include in the query everything that *may* matter. It is not because a search criterion *may* refer to data stored in one table that this table *must* appear in the `from` clause. I have already alluded to this issue in the previous chapters, but the `from` clause should only contain the tables from which we return data, as well as the tables enabling us to join them together. As we have seen in Chapter 6, existence tests should be solved by subqueries—which are no more difficult to generate dynamically than a regular condition in a `where` clause.
- The most important mistake is the one-size-fits-all philosophy. Behind every generic query are usually hidden three or four families of queries. Typically, input data is made up of identifiers, status values, or some ranges of dates. The input values may be strong, efficient criteria, or weak ones, or indeed anything in between (sometimes an additional criterion may reinforce a weak one by narrowing the scope). From here, trying to build several alternate queries in an intelligent fashion, as in the various cases of Chapter 6, is the only sound way out, even if it looks more complicated.

More intelligence in the dynamic construction of an SQL statement makes for a more efficient SQL statement.

CHAPTER NINE

Multiple Fronts
Tackling Concurrency

Yet to their General's Voice they soon obey'd
Innumerable.
—*John Milton (1608–1674)*

Paradise Lost, Book I

When we have a lot of sessions running concurrently, all accessing one database, we may encounter difficulties that can remain hidden when running single-user tests. Contention occurs, and locks may be held for unpredictable periods of time. This chapter discusses how to face the situation when users advance in overwhelming numbers.

There are several different issues associated with a large number of concurrent users. One of the most obvious is contention when updating (sometimes reading) data and the consequent requirement for locks at one level or another. But users are not only fighting for the right to modify bytes at one place in the system without any interference from others; they are also competing for processing power, access to disks, workspace in memory, and network bandwidth. Very often difficulties that are latent with a few users become blatant with many. Increases in the number of users are not always as smooth as one might expect them to be. Sudden increases can come through the meteoritic success of your company, but fast-paced increases more often happen through the gradual deployment of applications—or sometimes as a result of mergers or buyouts.

The Database Engine as a Service Provider

You might be tempted to consider the DBMS as an intelligent and dedicated servant that rushes to forestall your slightest desire and bring data at the exact time when you need it. Reality is slightly less exalted than the intelligent servant model, and at times a DBMS looks closer to a waiter in a very busy restaurant. If you take your time to choose from the menu, chances are that the waiter will tell you "I'll let you choose, and I'll come back later to take your order" before disappearing for a long time. A DBMS is a service provider or, perhaps more precisely, a collection of service providers. The service is simply to execute some operation against the data, fetching it or updating it—and the service may be requested by many concurrent sessions at the same time. It is only when *each* session queries efficiently that the DBMS can perform efficiently.

The Virtues of Indexes

Let's execute some fairly basic tests against a very simple table with three columns. The first two are integer columns (each populated with distinct values from 1 to 50,000), one being declared as the primary key and the second without an index. The third column (named `label`) is a text column consisting of random strings thirty to fifty characters long. If we generate random numbers between 1 and 50,000 and use these random numbers as query identifiers to return the label column, you might be surprised to discover that on any reasonably powerful machine, the following query:

```
select label
from test_table
where indexed_column = random value
```

as well as this one:

```
select label
from test_table
where unindexed_column = random value
```

provide virtually instant results. How is this possible? A query using an unindexed column should be much slower, surely? Actually, a 50,000–row table is rather small, and if it has as few columns as is the case in our example, the number of bytes to scan is not that enormous, and a modern machine can perform the full scan very rapidly. We indeed have, on one hand, a primary key index search, and on the other hand, a full-table scan. What's happening is that the difference between indexed and unindexed access is too small for a human to perceive.

To really test the benefit of an index, I have run our queries continuously for one minute, and then I have checked on how many queries I was able to process by unit of time. The result is reassuringly familiar: on the machine on which I ran the test, the query using the indexed column can be performed 5,000 times per second, while the query using the unindexed column can only be performed 25 times per second. A developer running single user tests may not really notice a difference, but there is one, and it is truly massive.

Even sub-second response times sometimes hide major performance issues. Don't trust unitary tests.

A Just-So Story

Continuing with the example from the preceding section, let's have a look at what may very well happen in practice. Suppose that instead of being a number, the key of our table happens to be a string of characters. During development, somebody notices that a query has unexpectedly returned the wrong result. A quick investigation shows that the key column contains both uppercase and lowercase characters. Under pressure to make a quick fix, a developer modifies the `where` clause in the query and applies an `upper()` function to the key column—thus forfeiting the index. The developer runs the query, the correct result set is returned, and anyone other than a native of the planet Krypton cannot possibly notice any significant difference in response time. All appears to be for the best, and we can ship the code to production.

Now we have hordes of users, all running our query again, again and again. Chapter 2 makes the point that in our programs we should not execute queries inside loops, whether they are cursor loops or the more traditional *for* or *while* constructs. Sadly, we very often find queries nested inside loops on the result set of other queries, and as a result, our query can be run at a pretty high rate, even without having tens of thousands of concurrent users. Let's see now what happens to our test table when we run the query at a high rate, with a set number of executions per unit of time, occurring at random intervals. When we execute our query at the relatively low rate of 500 per minute, everything appears normal whether we use the index or not, as you can see in Figure 9-1. All our queries complete in under 0.2 seconds, and nobody will complain.

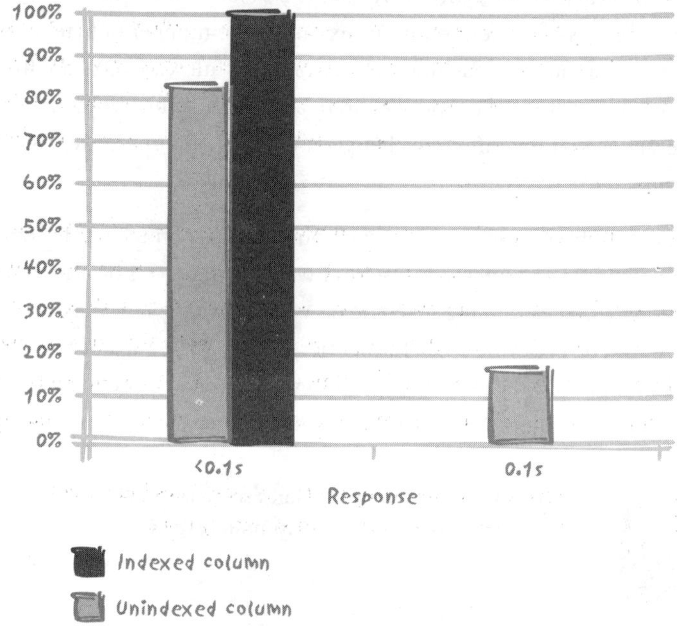

FIGURE 9-1. *Response time of a simple query against a 50,000–row table, low query rate*

We actually have to increase our execution rate 10 times, to a relatively high rate of 5,000 executions per minute, to notice in Figure 9-2 that we may occasionally have a slow response when we use the unindexed column as key. This, however, affects only a very low percentage of our queries. In fact, 97% of them perform in 0.3 seconds or less.

But at 5,000 queries per minute, we are unaware that we are tottering on the brink of catastrophe. If we push the rate up to a very high 10,000 executions per minute, you can see in Figure 9-3 that a very significant proportion of the queries will execute noticeably more slowly, some taking as long as 4 seconds to complete. If in another test we run the queries that use the index at the same high rate, all queries execute imperturbably in 0.1 seconds or less.

Of course, when some queries that used to run fast start to take much longer, users are going to complain; and other users who, unprompted, would otherwise have noticed nothing will probably grumble as well, out of sympathy. The database is slow—can't it be tuned? Database administrators and system engineers will tweak parameters, gaining a few weeks of relief, until the evidence will finally impose itself, in all its glorious simplicity: we need a more powerful server.

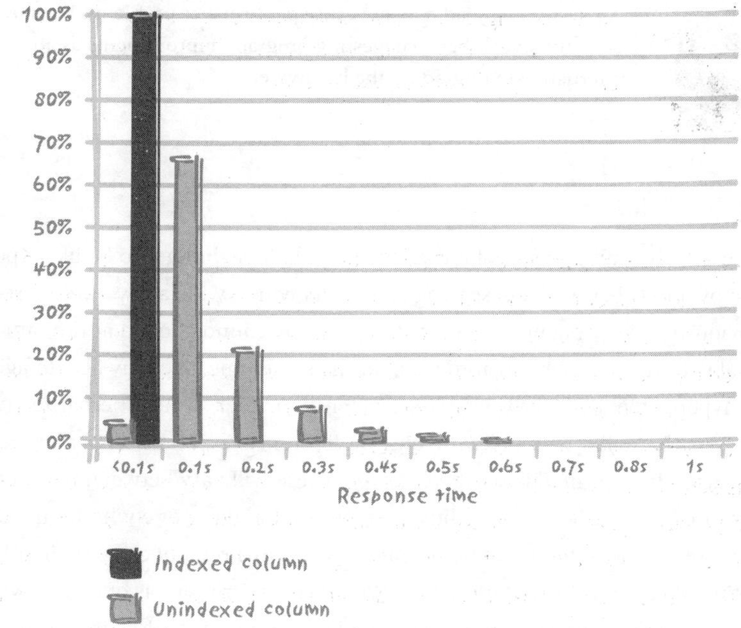

FIGURE 9-2. *Response time of a simple query against a 50,000–row table, high query rate*

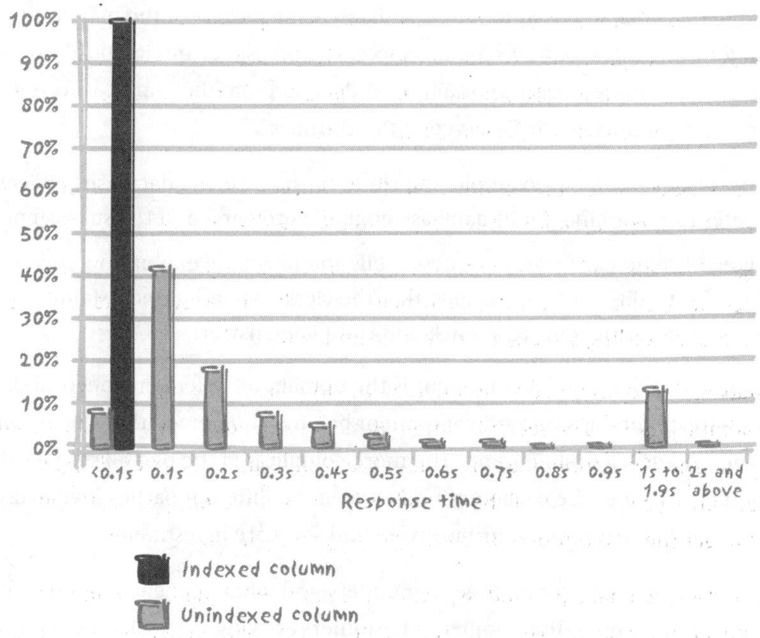

FIGURE 9-3. *Response time of a simple query against a 50,000–row table, very high query rate*

An increasing load may not cause performance problems, but may actually reveal them, suggesting program improvements as an alternative to upgrading the hardware.

Get in Line

One can take a fairly realistic view of a DBMS engine by imagining it to be like a post office staffed by a number of clerks serving customers with a wide array of requests—our queries. Obviously, a very big post office will have many counters open at the same time and will be able to serve several customers all at the same time. We may also imagine that young hypercaffeinated clerks will work faster than older, sedate, herbal-tea types. But we all know that what will make the biggest difference, especially at peak hours, is the requests actually presented by each customer. These will vary between the individual who has prepared the exact change to buy a stamp book and the one who inquires at length about the various rates at which to send a parcel to a remote country, involving the completion of customs forms, and so on. What is most irritating is of course when someone with a mildly complicated request spends several minutes looking for a purse when the moment for payment arrives. But fortunately, in post offices, you never encounter the case that is so frequent in real database applications: the man with 20 letters who joins the queue on 20 separate successive occasions, buying only one stamp in each visit to the counter. It is important to understand that there are two components that determine how quickly one is served at the counter:

- The performance of, in our example, the clerk. In the case of a database application, this equates to a combination of database engine, hardware, and I/O subsystems.
- The degree of complexity of the request itself, and to a large extent how the request is presented, its lucidity and clarity, such that the clerk can easily understand the request, and accordingly make a quick and complete answer.

In the database world, the first component is the domain of system engineers and database administrators. The second component belongs squarely within the business requirements and development arena. The more complicated the overall system, the more important becomes the collaboration between the different parties involved when you want to get the best out of your hardware and software investment.

With the post-office image in mind, we can understand what happened in our query test. What matters is the ratio of the number of customers arriving (e.g., the rate of execution of queries), to the average time required to answer the query. As long as the rate of arrival is low enough to enable everyone to find a free counter, nobody will complain. However, as soon as customers arrive faster than they can be serviced, queues will start to lengthen, just as much for the fast queries as for the slow ones.

There is a threshold effect, very similar to what one of Charles Dickens's characters says in *David Copperfield*:

> Annual income twenty pounds, annual expenditure nineteen six, result happiness. Annual income twenty pounds, annual expenditure twenty pounds ought and six, result misery.

This can easily be demonstrated by running our two queries simultaneously, the one using the indexed column and the other using the unindexed column, at a rate of 5,000 times per second. The compound result of Figure 9-4 is noticeably different from Figure 9-2, in which results were shown for the two queries running separately, not concurrently. As appears clearly from Figure 9-4, the performance of the fast query has deteriorated because of the simultaneous presence of slow queries.

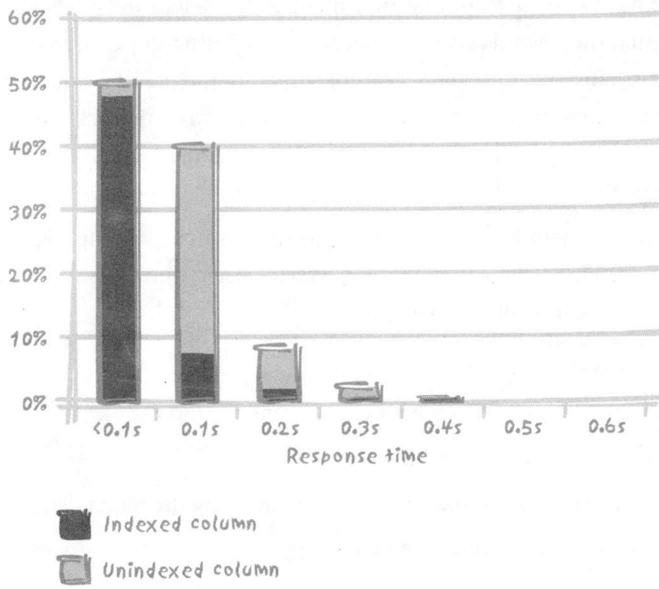

FIGURE 9-4. *Fast and slower queries running together, both at a high query rate*

System performance crashes when statements arrive faster than they can be serviced; all queries are affected, not only slow ones.

Concurrent Data Changes

When you change data, the task of maintaining a good level of performance becomes even more difficult as the level of activity increases. For one thing, any change is by essence a more costly operation than a mere query, since it involves both getting the data and then writing it back to the database. In the case of inserts, only the latter operation applies. Therefore, data modification, whether updates, deletes, or inserts, intrinsically requires a longer service time than the equivalent query-only task. This longer service time is made worse by one mechanism and one situation that are often confused. The mechanism is locking, and the situation is contention.

Locking

When several users want to modify the same data at once—for instance to book the very last seat on a flight—the only solution available to the DBMS is to block all but one user, who is usually the first person to present the request. The necessity of sequentializing access to critical resources is a problem that is as old as multiuser systems themselves. It existed with files and records long before database systems began to be adopted. One user acquires a lock over a resource, and the other users who also want to lock the same resource either have to queue up, waiting patiently for the lock to be released, or handle the error code that they will receive. In many ways, the situation is entirely analogous to our fictitious post office when several customers require the use of a single photocopier—people must wait patiently for their turn (or turn away and come back later).

Locking granularity

One of the most important practical questions to address when attempting to change the contents of the database will be to determine exactly where the locks will be applied. Locks can impact any or all of the following:

- The entire database
- The physical subset of the database where the table is stored
- The table identified for modification
- The particular block or page (unit of storage) containing the target data
- The table row containing the affected data
- The column(s) in the row

As you can see, how much users interfere with each other is a question that relates to the granularity of the locking procedures. The type of locking that can be applied varies with the DBMS. Locking granularity is an area where "big products," designed for large information systems, are significantly different from "small products" that have more limited ambitions.

When locks apply to a restricted amount of data, several concurrent processes can happily change data in the very same table at the same time without much affecting each other. Instead of having to wait until another process has finished with its transaction to get ahold of a lock, there can be some overlap between the various processes—which means that from a hardware point of view you can have more processors working, thus making better use of your hardware resources. The benefit of a finer granularity can be seen quite clearly in Figure 9-5, which shows the contrast in the total throughput of a number of concurrent sessions updating a table, first in table-locking mode and then second in row-locking mode. In each case the DBMS server is the same one.

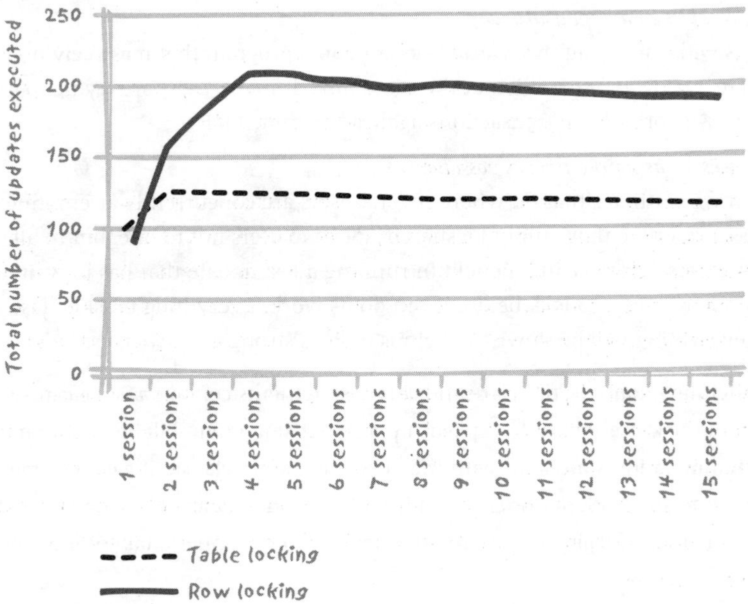

FIGURE 9-5. *Update performance for table versus row locking*

In the table-locking case, throughput increases slightly with two sessions, because the server, in the sense of service provider, is not saturated. But two sessions generate the maximum number of updates we can sequentially execute per unit of time, and from then on the curve is flat—actually, very slowly decreasing because system resources are required to handle more sessions, and this is detrimental to the system resources required to perform the updates. The situation of table locking can be contrasted with the situation of row locking, where changes applied to the same table can occur simultaneously as long as they do not affect identical rows. As in the case of table locking we will eventually reach a point where we saturate the server, but this point is reached both later and for a much higher number of concurrent updates.

If your DBMS is rather heavy-handed when locking resources, your only hope to cope with a sudden increase of activity, optimistically assuming that everything else has been tried, is to buy better hardware. "Better hardware" must of course be qualified. If locking is the bottleneck, more processors will not help, because the critical resource is access to the data. However, faster processors may speed up execution, reduce the time locks are actually held, and therefore allow the processing of more changes per unit of time. Processing still remains strictly sequential, of course, and the same number of locks is still applied.

Lock handling

Locking mechanisms are an integral part of the implementation of a DBMS and there is not much that we can do about them. We are limited to just two directions in dealing with locks:

Try not to lock tables in a haphazard way.
: It goes without saying that we should not run a program that massively updates rows in a table by the million at the same time as many users are trying to execute very short update transactions against the same table.

Try to hold locks for as short a time as possible.
: When we are in a situation where several users are concurrently attempting to access a resource that cannot be shared, speed matters not to one, but to all transactions. There is little benefit in running a fast update that has to wait for a slow one to release a lock before it can do its work. Everything must be fast, or else everything will be slow: "A chain is only as strong as its weakest link."

The overwhelming majority of `update` and `delete` statements contain a `where` clause, and so any rewrite of the `where` clause that speeds up a `select` statement will have the same effect on a data manipulation statement with the very same `where` clause. If a `delete` statement has no `where` clause (in other words the entire table is being deleted!), then it is likely that we would be better off using a `truncate` statement, which empties a table (or a partition) much more efficiently.

We mustn't forget, though, that indexes also have to be maintained, and that updating an indexed column is costly; we may have to arbitrate between the speed of fetches and the speed of changes. The index that might be helpful in the `where` clause may prove to be a nuisance when rows are changed. Concerning `insert` statements, a number of them may actually be `insert...select` constructs in which the link between `select` performance and `insert` performance is naturally obvious.

You've seen in Chapter 2 that impeccable statement performance doesn't necessarily rhyme with good program performance. When changing data, we have a particular scope to consider: the *transaction* or, in other words, the duration of a logical unit of work. We shall have to retain locks on a particular part of the database for most if not all of the transaction. Everything that need not be done within the transaction, especially if it is a slow activity, should be excluded from that transaction. The start of a transaction may sometimes be implicit with the first data manipulation language (DML) statement issued. The end of a transaction is always obvious, as it is marked by a `commit` or `rollback` statement. With this background, some practices are just common sense. Inside a transaction:

- Avoid looping on SQL statements as much as possible.
- Keep round-trips between the program and the database, whether running as an application server or as a mere client, to a minimum, since these add network latency to the overall elapsed time.
- Exploit to the full whatever mechanisms the DBMS offers to minimize the number of round-trips (e.g., take advantage of stored procedures or array fetching).
- Keep any nonessential SQL statements that are not strictly necessary within the logical unit of work outside of it. For instance, it is quite common to fetch error messages from a table, especially in localized applications. If we encounter an error, we should end our transaction with a `rollback` first, and then query the error message table, not the reverse: doing so will release locks earlier, and therefore help to maximize throughput.

As simple a transaction as one that inserts a new row in both a master table and a slave table provides ample ground for mistakes. An example for this type of transaction is typically the creation of a new customer order (in the master table) and of the first item in our shopping basket (held in an `order_detail` table). The difficulty usually comes as a result of using system-generated identifiers for the orders.

The primary mistake to avoid is to store into a table the "next value to use." Such a table is mercilessly locked by all concurrent processes updating it, thus becoming the major bottleneck in the whole application. Depending on the DBMS you are using, a system-generated identifier is either the value of an auto-incremented column, which will take for each new row inserted the value of the previous row plus one, or the next value of a database object such as a sequence, which is in essence very similar to an auto-incremented column but without the explicit reference to a column in an existing table. We have nothing to do to generate a new identifier for each new order other than to grab the value generated by the system. The snag is that we must know this value to be able to link the items in the basket to a particular order. In other words, we have to insert this value into table `order_detail` as well as the master table.

Some DBMS products that use auto-incremented columns provide either a system variable (as `@@IDENTITY` with Transact-SQL), or a function (such as MySQL's `last_insert_id()`) to retrieve the value that was last generated by the session. Fail to use facilities provided by your DBMS, and you are condemned to run useless queries to perform the same task in the middle of a transaction, thus wasting resources and slowing down your transaction. Using functions or variables referring implicitly to the last generated value requires a little discipline in executing statements in the proper order, particularly if one is juggling several auto-incremented columns simultaneously.

For some unknown reason, there is a marked tendency among developers who are using sequences to first issue a *<sequence name>*.nextval call to the database to get a new value, and then to store it in a program variable for future reference. There is actually a *<sequence name>*.currval call (or previous value for *<sequence name>* with DB2), and as its name implies its purpose is to return the last value that was generated for the given sequence. In most cases, there is no need to use a program variable to store the current value, and even less to precede true action with a special *get a new sequence value* call. In the worst case, some DBMS extensions can prove useful. For instance, Oracle (and PL/SQL) users can use the returning ... into ... clause of insert and update statements to return system-generated values without requiring a new round-trip to the server. Running one special statement to get the next sequence value and adding one more round-trip to the database generates overhead that can globally amount to a very significant percentage for simple and often executed transactions.

Where transactional activity is high, it is vital that locks are never held for operations that don't require them.

Locking and committing

If we try and hold locks for the minimum possible time, we are bound to have to make frequent commits. Committing is a very costly process, since it means writing to persistent memory (journal files), and therefore initiating physical I/O operations. If we commit changes after absolutely every logical unit of work, we add a lot of overhead as can be seen in Figure 9-6. The figure shows the performance impact of committing every 1, 2, 3...12 rows in the case of a very fast update executed by a single user process running on an empty test machine. Depending on the statement and the number of rows affected, figures may of course vary but the trend is always the same. If a batch update program commits every transaction, it can easily take two to three times as long to complete as when it commits less frequently.

In the case of batch programs in which concurrency control is not an issue, it is advisable to avoid committing changes too often. The snag with not committing zillions of changes, besides the impact of holding the inevitable locks, is that the system has to record the pre-change data image for a hypothetical undo operation, which will put some serious strain on resources. If the process fails for any reason, rolling back the changes may take a considerable amount of time. There are two schools of thought on this topic. One favors committing changes at regular intervals so as to moderate demands on the system in terms of resources, as well as reduce the amount of work which might have to be done in case of a database change failure. The other school is frankly more gung ho and argues,

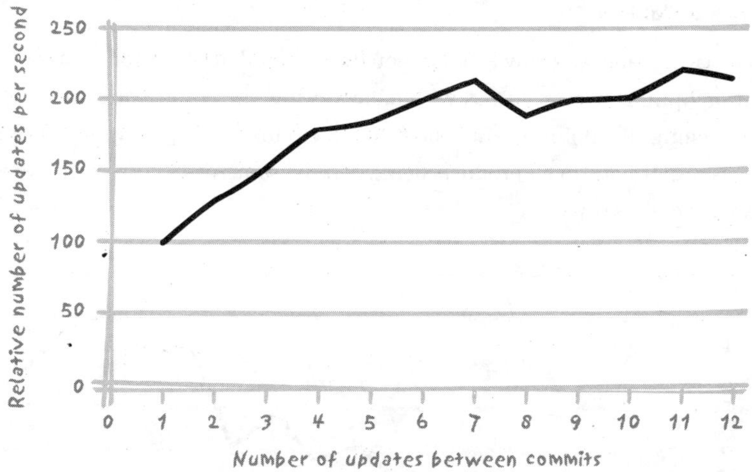

FIGURE 9-6. *Impact of committing on performance*

not without some reason, that system resources are here to sustain business processes, not the other way around. For the disciples of this school, if higher throughput can be achieved by less frequent commits—and if they can afford the occasional failure and still have processes completed properly and faster—then there is benefit in less frequent commits. Their case is further strengthened if the DBMS features some "pass or break" mode that shuns the generation of undo data. The commit-once-when-we're-done approach implicitly assumes that redoing everything from scratch when something has totally failed is often simpler than trying to fix something that only partially worked. Both schemes have advantages and disadvantages, and the final choice may often be linked to operational constraints—or perhaps even to politics.

In any case, a batch program committing once in a while may block interactive users. Likewise, it is possible for interactive users to block batch programs. Even when the locking granularity is at the row level, a mechanism such as *lock escalation* that is applied by some database systems (in which many fine-grain locks are automatically replaced by a coarser-grain lock) may lead to a hung system. Even without lock escalation, a single uncommitted change may block a massive update. One thing is clear: concurrency and batch programs are not a happy match, and we must think about our transactions in a different way according to whether they are interactive or batch.

The greater the number of concurrent users, the shorter should be the commit intervals.

Locking and scalability

When comparing table and row locking, you have seen that the latter facilitates a much better throughput. However, just as with table locking, the performance curve quickly reaches its ceiling (the point at which performance refuses to improve), and from then on the curve is rather flat. Do all products behave in the same way? As a matter of fact, they don't, as Figure 9-7 shows.

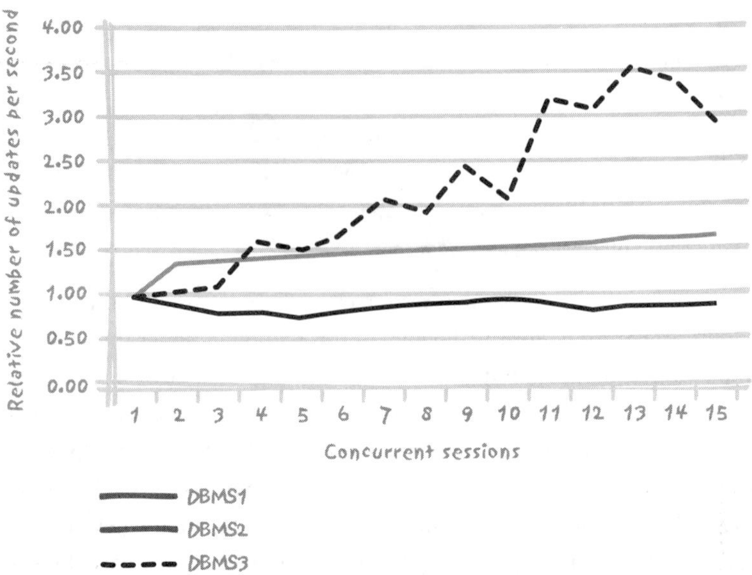

FIGURE 9-7. *Row locking and concurrency with three database systems*

To really compare how the various systems were behaving under increased concurrency, irrespective of speed on a particular example, I performed two series of updates against a large table: first, fast updates with a condition on the primary key, and second, slow updates with a condition on an unindexed column. These updates were repeated with a varying number of sessions, and the total number of updates performed was recorded each time.

None of the products displays a strong dependency of throughput on the number of sessions with fast updates, probably because of a saturation of hardware resources. What is interesting, though, is checking whether there is a benefit attached to running a larger number of sessions in parallel. Can increased concurrency somewhat compensate for speed? This is exactly the same type of question as asking "is it better to have a server machine with few fast processors or a higher number of slower processors?"

Figure 9-7 shows how the ratio of the number of slow updates to the number of fast updates evolves as we increase the number of sessions. The DBMS1 product stands out for two reasons:

- Slow updates are not that slow relatively to fast ones (hence a higher ratio than the other products).
- As the steep decrease between 1 and 3 concurrent sessions shows, slow updates also suffer relatively more of increased concurrency.

The product to watch, though, is not DBMS1. Even if row locking were in use in all systems, we see that one of the products, DBMS3 on the figure, will *scale* much better than the others, because the ratio slowly but significantly improves as more and more concurrent sessions enter the fray. This observation may have a significant impact on hardware choices and architectures; products such as DBMS1 and DBMS2 would probably get the most benefit from faster processors, not more numerous ones. From a software point of view, they would also benefit from query pooling on a small number of sessions. On the other hand, a product such as DBMS3 would better profit from additional processors at the same speed and, to some extent, from a higher number of concurrent sessions.

How can I explain such differences between DBMS3 and the other products? Mostly by two factors:

Saturation of hardware resources

This probably partly explains what occurs in the case of DBMS1, which achieves excellent overall results in terms of global throughput, but that simply cannot do better on this particular hardware.

Contention

Remember that we have the same locking granularity in all three cases (row-level locks). Exactly the same statements where executed and committed. There is in fact more than data locking that limits the amount of work that several sessions can perform in parallel. To take a mechanical analogy, we could say that there is more friction in the case of DBMS1 and DBMS2 than in the case of DBMS3. This friction can also be called *contention*.

Concurrency depends on integrity protection mechanisms that include locking as well as other controls that vary from product to product.

Contention

Rows in tables are not the only resources that cannot be shared. For instance, when one updates a value, the prior or original value (undo data) must be saved somewhere in case the user decides to roll back the change. On a loaded system, there may actually be some kind of competition between two or more processes trying to write undo data into the same physical location, even if these processes are operating on totally unrelated rows in different tables. Such a situation requires some kind of serialization to control events. Likewise, when changes are committed and written to transaction logfiles or in-memory buffers before being flushed to a file, there must be some means of preventing processes from overwriting each other's bytes.

The examples I've just given are examples of contention. More than contention, locking is a mechanism that tends to be a defining characteristic of particular DBMS architectures, leaving us little choice other than to try and keep to an absolute minimum the time that the lock is held. Contention, however, is linked to low-level implementation, and there are several actions that can be undertaken to tune contention. Some of these actions can be performed by systems engineers, for example by carefully locating transaction log files on disks. Database administrators can also help to improve the situation by playing with database parameters and storage options. Finally we can, as developers, address these problems in the way we build our applications. To show how we can try to code so as to limit contention, I shall walk you through a case in which contention is usually at its most visible: during multiple, concurrent inserts.

Insertion and contention

Let's take as an example a 14–column table with two unique indexes. The primary key constraint is defined on a system-generated number (a surrogate key), and a unique constraint (enforced by a unique index of course) is applied to a "natural" compound key, the combination of some short string of characters and a datetime value. We can now proceed to run a series of insert operations for an increasing number of simultaneous sessions.

As Figure 9-8 shows, although we are operating in row-locking mode, adding more processes inserting in parallel doesn't do much to improve the number of rows inserted by unit time. The figure displays the median and the minimum and maximum values for 10 one-minute runs for each of the different numbers of concurrent processes. As you can see, there is much variability in the results—but the best result is obtained for four concurrent processes (which, by some happy coincidence, is not totally unrelated to the number of processors on the machine).

Must we conclude that we are saturating the hardware resources? The answer of course is yes, but the real question is "can't we make *better* use of these resources?" There is, in a

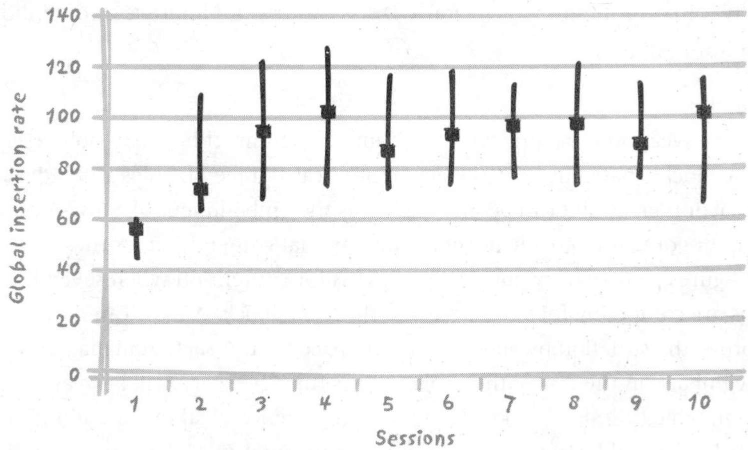

FIGURE 9-8. *Concurrent sessions inserting into a regular table*

case like this, not much we can do about locking, because we never have two processes trying to access the same row. However, we do have contention when trying to access the data *containers*. In this situation contention can occur at two places within the database: in the table and in the index. There may be other contention issues at the system level, but these often derive from choices made at the database level. Contention consumes CPU, because there is the execution of code that is required for handling that very same contention issue, with possibly some active waits involved or idle loops while waiting for a resource held by a process running on another processor to be released. Can we try to lower contention and divert some of the CPU cycles to our `inserts` proper?

I have run my example to generate Figure 9-8 on Oracle, one of the database systems that provides the widest range of possible options to try to limit contention. Basically, database-centric solutions to a contention issue will fall into one or more of the following three categories:

- DBA solutions
- Architectural solutions
- Development solutions

The following sections review each of these categories.

DBA solutions

A database administrator often has scant knowledge of business processes. What we call *DBA solutions* are changes that are applied to the containers themselves. They are application-neutral (as it is near impossible to be absolutely application-neutral, it would probably be more exact to say that the impact is minimal on processes other than the insertion process we are trying to improve).

There are two main zones in which Oracle DBAs can try and improve a contention issue with a minimum of fuss:

Transaction space

The first weapon is playing with the number of transaction entry slots reserved in the blocks that constitute the actual physical storage of tables and indexes. A transaction entry slot can be understood as the embodiment of a low-level lock. Without going into arcane detail, let me say that competition for these slots usually figures prominently among the reasons for contention when several sessions are competing for write access to the same block. A DBA can try to improve the situation by allocating more space for transaction management. The only impact on the rest of the application is that less space will be available for data in table or index blocks; the direct consequence of such a situation is that more blocks will be required to store the same amount of data, and operations such as full scans and, to a much lesser degree, index searches will have to access more blocks.

Free lists

The second weapon is trying to force insertions to be directed to different blocks, something that can be done if some degree of control is retained on storage management. For each table, Oracle maintains one or several lists of blocks where new rows can be inserted. By default, there is only one list, but if there are several such lists, then insertions are assigned in a round-robin fashion to blocks coming from the various lists. This solution is not as neutral as allocating more space to transaction management; remember that the clustering of data has a significant impact on the performance of queries, and therefore while we may improve insertion performance, we may degrade some other queries.

Architectural solutions

Architectural solutions are those based on a modification of the physical disposition of data using the facilities of the DBMS. They may have a much more profound impact, to the disadvantage of our other processes. The three most obvious architectural solutions are:

Partitioning

Range partitioning will of course defeat our purpose if our goal is to spread update activity over the table—unless, for instance, each process is inserting data for one particular month, and we could assign one process to one partition, but this is not the situation in our current example. Hash partitioning, however, might help. If we compute a hash value from our system-generated (sequence) value, successive values will be arbitrarily assigned to different partitions. Unfortunately, there are limitations to what we can do to an index used to enforce a constraint, and therefore it's only contention at the table level that we can hope to improve. Moreover, this is a solution that unclusters data, which may impact on the performance of other queries.

Reverse index

Chapter 3 shows that reversing the bytes in index keys can disperse the entries of keys that would otherwise have been in close proximity to one another, into unrelated leaves of the index, and that is a good way to minimize index contention (although it will do nothing for table contention). The disadvantage is that using a reverse index will prevent us from performing range scans on the index, which can be a very serious hindrance.

Index organized table

Organizing our table as an index will allow us to get rid of one of the sources of contention. It will do nothing for the second one by itself, but instead of stumbling from one point of contention—the table block—to a second point of contention—the index block—we will have everybody fighting in one place.

Development solutions

Development solutions are in the sole hands of the developer and require no change to the physical structure of the database. Here are two examples where the developer can influence matters:

Adjusting parallelization

The attempt at varying the number of concurrent processes shows clearly that there is a peak at 4 concurrent sessions and that adding more sessions doesn't help. There is no benefit in assigning 10 people to a task that 4 people can handle perfectly well; it makes coordination more complicated, and some simple subtasks are sooner performed than assigned. Figure 9-8 showed that the effect of adding extra sessions beyond a hardware-dependent number is, in the best of cases, worthless. Removing them would put less strain on the system.

Not using system-generated values

Do we really need sequential values for a surrogate key? This is not always the case. Sequential values are of interest if we want to process ranges of values, because they allow us to use operators such as > or `between`. But if all we need is a unique identifier that can be used as a foreign key value in some other tables, why should it belong to a particular range? Let's consider a possible alternative—namely to simply use a random number—and regenerate a new one if we hit a value we have already used.

Results

Figure 9-9 shows the insertion rates we obtained with 10 concurrent sessions, using each of the methods just described.

Once again there is a significant variability of results (each test was run 10 times, as before). We cannot conclude that a technique that works well in this case will behave as well in any other one, nor, conversely, that a technique which gives disappointing results here will not one day surpass all expectations. But the result is nevertheless interesting.

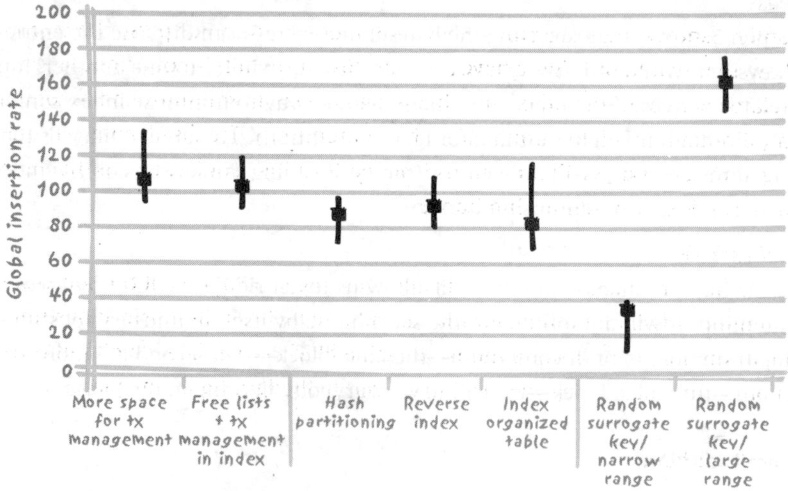

FIGURE 9-9. *Tactics for limiting insert contention*

First, the DBA techniques gave results that were positive, but not particularly remarkable. Architectural choices are, in this example, rather inefficient. It is worth mentioning that our two indexes are enforcing constraints, a situation that limits the number of options applicable to them. Therefore, some of the techniques may improve contention at the table level when most of the contention occurs within indexes. This is typically the case with the index organized table, in which table contention is eliminated by the simple expedient of removing the table; unfortunately, because we now have more data to store inside the index, index contention increases and offsets the benefit of no longer having the table. This is also a situation in which we find that the system resource most in demand happens to be the CPU. This situation puts at a disadvantage all the techniques that use extra CPU—such as computing hash values or reversing index keys.

Finally, random values provided both the worst and the best results. In the worst case, the (integer) random value was generated between 1 and a number equal to about twice the number of rows we were expecting to insert during the test. As a result, a significant number of values were generated more than once, causing primary key constraint violation and the necessity to generate a new random number. This was of course a waste of time, resulting in excessive consumption of resources—plus, since violation is detected when inserting the primary key index, and since this index stores the physical address, violation is detected *after* the row has been inserted into the table, so an operation must then be undone, again at additional cost.

In the best case, the random number was generated out of an interval 100 times greater than in the worst case. The improvement is striking. But since having 10 concurrent sessions is no more efficient than having 4 concurrent sessions, what would have been the result with only 4 sessions? Figure 9-10 provides the answer.

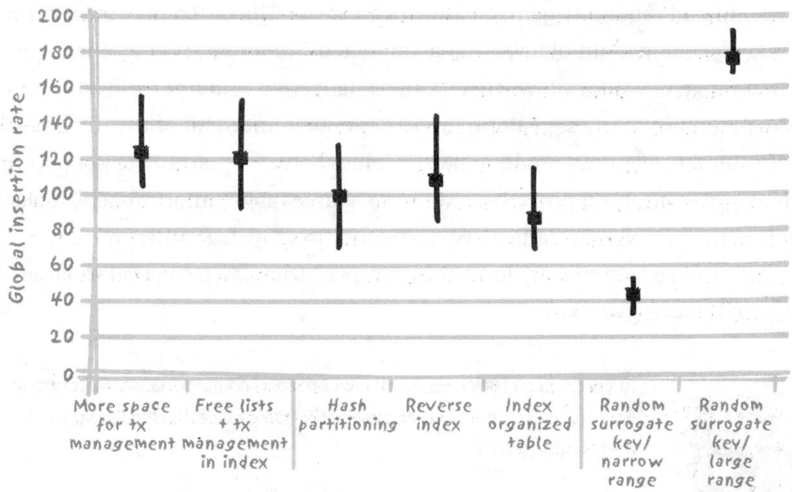

FIGURE 9-10. *The impact of contention limiting techniques with fewer sessions*

Very interestingly, all techniques give significantly better results, even if they rank identically in terms of improved throughput (e.g., their relative performances remain largely similar). The comparison of the results between Figures 9-9 and 9-10 teaches some interesting lessons:

- In our case study, the bottleneck is the primary key index. Techniques that should strongly limit contention at the table level (hash partitioning, IOT) bring no benefit; actually, the IOT provides worse performance on this example than does the combination of a regular table and a primary key index. On the contrary, techniques that reduce contention on both table and index (such as allowing more room for transaction management) or only improve the situation at the index level (reverse index, random surrogate key) all bring benefits.
- The comparison of 10 sessions with 4 sessions shows that some of the techniques require additional (and scarce) CPU resources from a machine already running flat out and consequentially show no improvement.
- The best way to avoid contention is not to use a sequentially generated surrogate key! Instead of considering how much performance we can gain by adopting various measures, let's consider how much performance loss is (inadvertently?) introduced by the use of a sequential key with the resulting contention on the primary key index. Solely because of contention on the primary key index, our insertion rate drops from a rate of 180 to 100 insertions per unit of time; in other words, it is divided by a factor of almost 2! The lesson is clear: we are better off without auto-incremented columns where they are not required, such as for tables that are not referenced by other tables or that do not have a very long natural primary key.

Can we recommend randomly generated surrogate keys? The difference in performance between a key generated out of a very large interval of values and a key generated out of too narrow a range of values shows that it can be dangerous and not really efficient if we expect a final number of rows greater than perhaps one hundredth of the total possible number of values. Generating random integer values between 1 and 2 billion (a common range for integer values) can prove hazardous for a large table; unfortunately, tables that are subject to heavy insertion traffic have a tendency to grow big rather quickly. However, if your system supports "long long integers," they can be a good solution—if you really need a surrogate key.

In contrast to locking, database contention can be improved upon. Architects, developers, and administrators can all design so as to limit contention.

CHAPTER TEN

Assembly of Forces

Coping with Large Volumes of Data

Thenne entryd in to the bataylle Iubance a geaunt
and fought and slewe doune ryght and distressyd many of our knyghtes.

—Sir Thomas Malory (d.1471)

Le Morte D'Arthur, V, 11

This chapter deals with the particular challenges that are facing us when data volumes swell. Those challenges include searching gigantic tables effectively, but also avoiding the sometimes distressing performance impact of even a moderate volume increase. We'll first look at the impact of data growth and a very large number of rows on SQL queries in the general case. Then we'll examine what happens in the particular environments of data warehousing and decision-support systems.

Increasing Volumes

Some applications see the volume of data they handle increase in considerable proportion over time. In particular, any application that requires keeping online, for regulatory or business analysis purposes, several months or even years of mostly inactive data, often passes through phases of crisis when (mostly) batch programs tend to overshoot the time allocated to them and interfere with regular, human activity.

When you start a new project, the volume of data usually changes, as shown in Figure 10-1. Initially, hardly anything other than a relatively small amount of reference data is loaded into the database. As a new system replaces an older one, data inherited from the legacy system is painfully loaded into the new one. First, because of the radical rethink of the application, conversion from the old system to the new system is fraught with difficulties. When deadlines have to be met and some noncritical tasks have to be postponed, the recovery of legacy data is a prime candidate for slipping behind schedule. As a result, this recovery goes on for some time after the system has become operational and teething problems have been solved. Second, the old system is usually much poorer from a functional perspective than the new one (otherwise, the cost of the new project would have made for difficult acceptance up the food chain). All this means that the volume of prehistoric data will be rather small compared to the data handled by the new system, and several months' worth of old data will probably be equivalent to a few weeks of new data at most.

Meanwhile, operational data accumulates.

Usually, one encounters the first serious performance issues about midway before the volume that the database is expected to hold at cruising speed. Bad queries and bad algorithms are almost invisible, from an end-user perspective, when volumes are low or moderate. The raw power of hardware often hides gigantic mistakes and may give comfortable sub-second response times for full scans of tables that contain several hundreds of thousands of rows. You may be seriously misusing the hardware, balancing gross programming mistakes with power—but nobody will see that until your volume becomes respectable.

At the first crisis point of the project, "expert tuning" is usually required to add a couple of indexes that should have been there from the start. The system then wobbles until it

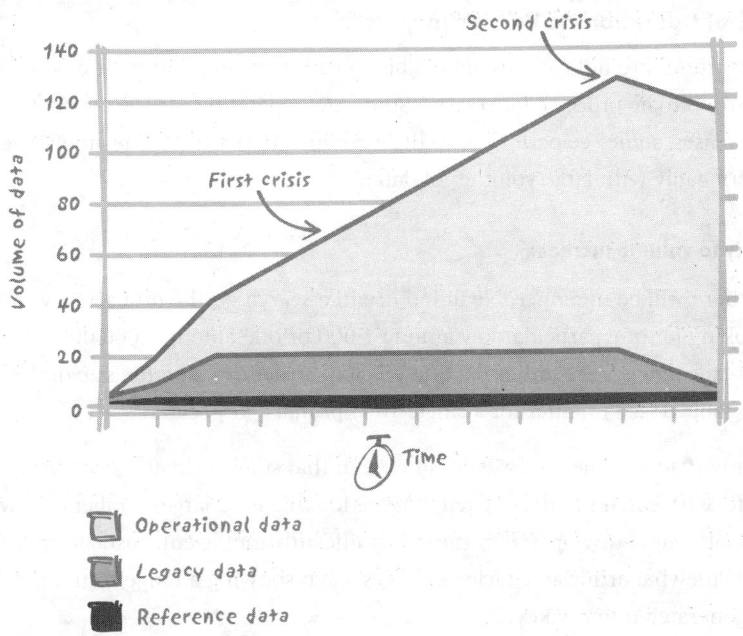

FIGURE 10-1. *The evolution of data in a new application*

reaches the target volume. There are usually two target volumes: a nominal one (which has been grossly overestimated and which is the volume the system has officially been designed to manage) and the real target volume (which the system just manages to handle and which is often exceeded at some point because archiving of older data has been relegated to the very last lot in the project). The second and more serious crisis often comes in the wake of reaching that point. When archival has finally been put into production, architectural weaknesses reviewed, and some critical processes vigorously rewritten, the system finally reaches cruising speed, with an increase of data related to the natural growth of business—a growth that can lie anywhere between flatness and exponential exuberance.

This presentation of the early months in the life of a new database application is partly caricature; but it probably bears more resemblance to reality than it often should, because the simple mistakes that lead to this caricature are not often avoided. However rigorously one tries to work, errors are made, because of pressure, lack of time for adequate testing, and ambiguous specifications. The only errors that can bring irredeemable failure are those linked to the design of the database and to the choice of the global architecture—two topics that are closely related and that are the foundation of a system. If the foundation is not sturdy enough, you need to pull the whole building down before reconstructing. Other mistakes may require a more or less deep overhaul of what is in place. Most crises, however, need not happen. You must anticipate volume increases when coding. And you must quickly identify and rewrite a query that deteriorates in performance too quickly in the face of increasing data volumes.

Sensitivity of Operations to Volume Increases

All SQL operations are not equally susceptible to variations in performance when the number of rows to be processed increases. Some SQL operations are insensitive to volume increases, some see performance decrease linearly with volume, and some perform very badly with large volumes of data.

Insensitivity to volume increase

Typically, there will be no noticeable difference in a search on the primary key, whether you are looking for one particular key among 1,000 or one among 1,000,000. The common B-tree indexes are rather flat and efficient structures, and the size of the underlying table doesn't matter for a single-row, primary-key search.

But insensitivity to volume increase doesn't mean that single primary-key searches are the ultimate SQL search method. When you are looking for a large number of rows, the "transactional" single-row operation can be significantly inefficient. Just consider the following, somewhat artificial, Oracle examples, each showing a range scan on a sequence-generated primary key:

```
SQL> declare
      n_id          number;
      cursor c is select customer_id
                  from orders
                  where order_id between 10000 and 20000;
    begin
      open c;
      loop
        fetch c into n_id;
        exit when c%notfound;
      end loop;
      close c;
    end;
    /

PL/SQL procedure successfully completed.

Elapsed: 00:00:00.27

SQL> declare
      n_id      number;
      begin
        for i in 10000 .. 20000
        loop
          select customer_id
          into n_id
          from orders
          where order_id = i;
      end loop;
    end;
    /
```

```
PL/SQL procedure successfully completed.

Elapsed: 00:00:00.63
```

The cursor in the first example, which does an explicit range scan, runs twice as fast as the iteration on a single row. Why? There are multiple technical reasons ("soft parsing," a fast acknowledgement at each iteration that the DBMS engine has already met this statement and knows how to execute it, is one of them), but the single most important one is that in the first example the B-tree is descended once, and then the ordered list of keys is scanned and row addresses found and used to access the table; while in the second example, the B-tree is descended for each searched value in the `order_id` column. The most efficient way to process a large number of rows is *not* to iterate and apply the single-row process.

Linear sensitivity to volume increases

End users usually understand well that if twice as many rows are returned, a query will take more time to run; but many SQL operations double in time when operating on double the number of rows without the underlying work being as obvious to the end user, as in the case of a full table scan returning rows one after the other. Consider the case of aggregate functions; if you compute a `max( )`, that aggregation will always return a single row, but the number of rows the DBMS will have to operate on may vary wildly over the life of the application. Perfectly understandable, but end users will always see a single-row returned, so they may complain of performance degradation over time. The only way to ensure that the situation will not go from bad to worse is to put an *upper bound* on the number of rows processed by using another criterion such as a date range. Placing an upper bound keeps data volumes under control. In the case of `max( )`, the idea might be to look for the maximum since a given date, and not necessarily since the beginning of time. Adding a criterion to a query is not a simple technical issue and definitely depends on business requirements, but limiting the scope of queries is an option that certainly deserves to be pointed out to, and debated with, the people who draft specifications.

Non-linear sensitivity to volume increases

Operations that perform sorts suffer more from volume increases than operations that just perform a scan, because sorts are complex and require on average a little more than a single pass. Sorting 100 randomly ordered rows is not 10 times costlier than sorting 10 rows, but about 20 times costlier—and sorting 1,000 rows is, on average, something like 300 times costlier than sorting 10 rows.

In real life, however, rows are rarely randomly stored, even when techniques such as clustering indexes (Chapter 5) are not used. A DBMS can sometimes use sorted indexes for retrieving rows in the expected order instead of sorting rows after having fetched them, and performance degradation resulting from retrieving a larger sorted set, although real, is rarely shocking. Be careful though. Performance degradation from sorts often proceeds by fits and starts, because smaller sorts will be fully executed in memory, while larger sorts will result from the merge of several sorted subsets that have each been processed in memory before being written to temporary storage. There are, therefore, some "dangerous surroundings" where one switches from a relatively fast full-memory mode to a much slower memory-plus-temporary-storage mode. Adjusting the amount of memory allocated to sorts is a frequent and efficient tuning technique to improve sort-heavy operations when flirting with the dangerous limit.

By way of example, Figure 10-2 shows how the fetch rate (number of rows fetched per unit of time) of a number of queries evolves as a table grows. The table used in the test is a very simple orders table defined as follows:

```
order_id         bigint(20) (primary key)
customer_id      bigint(20)
order_date       datetime
order_shipping   char(1)
order_comment    varchar(50)
```

The queries are first a simple primary key–based search:

```
select order_date
from orders
where order_id = ?
```

then a simple sort:

```
select customer_id
from orders
order by order_date
```

then a grouping:

```
select customer_id, count(*)
from orders
group by customer_id
having count(*) > 3
```

then the selection of the maximum value in a nonindexed column:

```
select max(order_date)
from orders
```

and finally, the selection of the "top 5" customers by number of orders:

```
select customer_id
from (select customer_id, count(*)
          from orders
```

```
        group by customer_id
        order by 2 desc) as sorted_customers
limit 5
```

(SQL Server would replace the closing `limit 5` with an opening `select top 5`, and Oracle would replace `limit 5` with `where rownum <= 5`.)

The number of rows in the table has varied between 8,000 and around 1,000,000, while the number of distinct `customer_id` values remained constant at about 3,000. As you can see in Figure 10-2, the primary key search performs almost as well with one million rows as with 8,000. There seems to be some very slight degradation at the higher number, but the query is so fast that the degradation is hardly noticeable. By contrast, the sort suffers. The performance (measured by rows returned by unit of time, and therefore independent of the actual number of rows fetched) of the sorting query decreases by 40% when the number of rows goes from 8,000 to over one million.

The degradation of performance, though, is even more noticeable for all the queries that, while returning the very same number of aggregated rows, have a great deal more rows to visit to get the relatively few rows to be returned. These queries are typically the type of queries that are going to draw the most complaints from end users. Note that the DBMS doesn't perform that badly: the performance decrease is very close to proportional to the number of rows, even for the two queries that require a sort (the queries labeled "Group by" and "Top" in Figure 10-2). But end users simply see the same amount of data—just returned much more slowly.

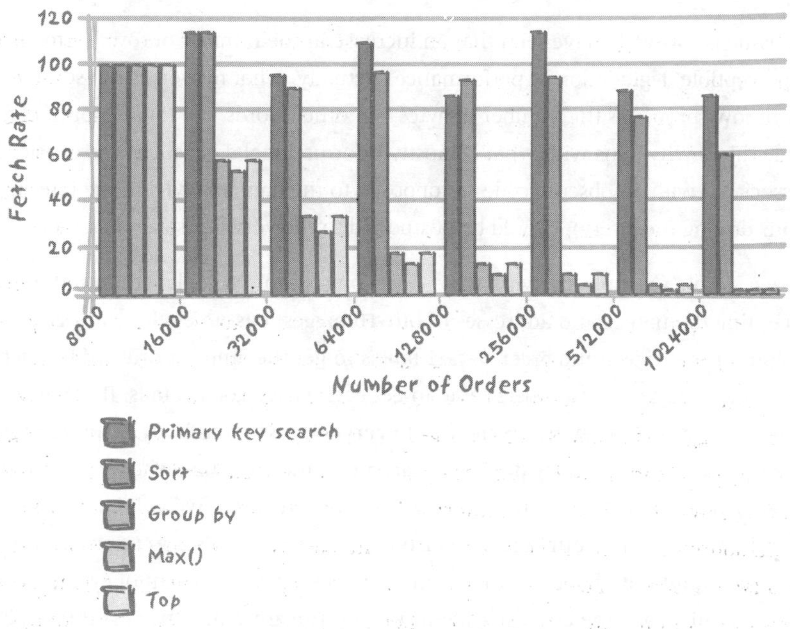

FIGURE 10-2. *How some simple queries behave when the queried table grows*

All database operations are not equally sensitive to volume increases. Anticipate how queries will perform on target volumes.

Putting it all together

The main difficulty in estimating how a query will behave when data volumes increase is that high sensitivity to volume may be hidden deep inside the query. Typically, a query that finds the "current value" of an item by running a subquery that looks for the last time the price was changed, and then performs a `max()` over the price history, is highly sensitive. If we accumulate a large number of price changes, we shall probably suffer a slow performance degradation of the subquery, and by extension of the outer query as well. The degradation will be much less sensitive with an uncorrelated subquery, executed only once, than with a correlated subquery that will compound the effect by its being fired each time it is evaluated. Such degradation may be barely perceptible in a single-item operation, but will be much more so in batch programs.

> **NOTE**
>
> The situation will be totally different if we are tracking, for instance, the current status of orders in a merchant system, because `max()` will apply to a narrow number of possible states. Even if the number of orders doubles, `max()` will in that case always operate on about the same number of rows for one order.

Another issue is sorts. We have seen that an increase in the number of rows sorted leads to a quite perceptible degradation of performance. Actually, what matters is not so much the number of rows proper as the number of bytes—in other words, the total amount of data to be sorted. This is why joins with what is mostly informational data, such as user-friendly labels associated with an obscure code (as opposed to the data involved in the filtering conditions driving the query), should be postponed to the very last stage of a query.

Let's take a simple example showing why some joins should be delayed until the end of a query. Getting the names and addresses of our 10 biggest customers for the past year will require joining the `orders` and `order_detail` tables to get the amount ordered by each customer, and joining to a `customers` table to get each customer's details. If we only want to get our 10 biggest customers, we must get everybody who has bought something from us in the past year, sort them by decreasing amount, and then limit the output to the first ten resulting rows. If we join all the information from the start, we will have to sort the names and addresses of *all* our customers from the past year. We don't need to operate on such a large amount of data. What we must do is keep the amount of data to be sorted to the strict minimum—the customer identifier and the amount. Once everything is sorted, we can join the 10 customer_ids we are left with to the customers table to return all the information that is required. In other words, we mustn't write something like:

```
select *
from (select c.customer_name,
             c.customer_address,
             c.customer_postal_code,
             c.customer_state,
             c.customer_country
             sum(d.amount)
      from customers c,
           orders_o,
           order_detail d
      where c.customer_id = o.customer_id
        and o.order_date >= some date expression
        and o.order_id = d.order_id
      group by c.customer_name,
               c.customer_address,
               c.customer_postal_code,
               c.customer_state,
               c.customer_country
       order by 6 desc) as A
limit 10
```

but rather something like:

```
select c.customer_name,
       c.customer_address,
       c.customer_postal_code,
       c.customer_state,
       c.customer_country
       b.amount
from (select a.customer_id,
             a.amount
      from (select o.customer_id,
                   sum(d.amount) as amount
            from orders_o,
                 order_detail d
            where o.order_date >= some date expression
              and o.order_id = d.order_id
            group by o.customer_id
            order by 2 desc) as a
      limit 10) as b,
      customers c
where c.customer_id = b.customer_id
order by b.amount desc
```

The second sort is a safeguard in case the join modifies the order of the rows resulting from the inner subquery (remember that relational theory knows nothing about sorts and that the DBMS engine is perfectly entitled to process the join as the optimizer finds most efficient). We have two sorts instead of one, but the inner sort operates on "narrower" rows, while the outer one operates on only 10 rows.

Remember what was said in Chapter 4: we must limit the "thickness" of the non-relational layer of SQL queries. The thickness depends on the number and complexity of operations, but also on the amount of data involved. Since sorts and limits of all kinds are non-relational operations, the optimizer will probably not rewrite a query to execute a join after having cut the number of customer identifiers to the bare minimum. Although an attentive reading of two queries may make it obvious that they will return the same result, mathematically *proving* that they always return the same result borders on mission impossible. An optimizer always plays it safe; a DBMS cannot afford to return wrong results by attempting daring rewrites, especially since it knows hardly anything about semantics. Our example is therefore a case in which the optimizer will limit its action to perform the join in inner queries as efficiently as possible. But ordering and aggregates put a stop to mingling inner and outer queries, and therefore the query will for the most part run as it is written. The query that performs the sort of amounts before the joins is, no doubt, very ugly. But this ugly SQL code is the way to write it, because it is the way the SQL engine *should* execute it if we want resilience to a strong increase in the number of customers and orders.

To reduce the sensitivity of your queries to increases in the volume of data, operate only on the data that is strictly necessary at the deeper levels of a query. Keep ancillary joins for the outer level.

Disentangling subqueries

As I have said more than once, correlated subqueries must be fired for each row that requires their evaluation. They are often a major issue when volume increases transform a few shots into sustained rounds of fire. In this section, a real-life example will illustrate both how ill-used correlated subqueries can bog a process down and how one can attempt to save such a situation.

The issue at hand, in an Oracle context, is a query that belongs to an hourly batch to update a security management table. Note that this mechanism is already in itself a fudge to speed up security clearance checks on the system in question. Over time, the process takes more and more time, until reaching, on the production server, 15 minutes—which for an hourly process that suspends application availability is a bit too much. The situation sends all bells ringing and all whistles blowing. Red alert!

The slowness of the process has been narrowed down to the following statement:

```
insert /*+ append */ into fast_scrty
 ( emplid,
   rowsecclass,
   access_cd,
   empl_rcd,
   name,
```

```
    last_name_srch,
    setid_dept,
    deptid,
    name_ac,
    per_status,
    scrty_ovrd_type)
  select distinct
        emplid,
        rowsecclass,
        access_cd,
        empl_rcd,
        name,
        last_name_srch,
        setid_dept,
        deptid,
        name_ac,
        per_status,
       'N'
  from pers_search_fast
```

Statistics are up to date, so we must focus our attack on the query. As it happens, the ill-named pers_search_fast is a view defined by the following query:

```
select a.emplid,
       sec.rowsecclass,
       sec.access_cd,
       job.empl_rcd,
       b.name,
       b.last_name_srch,
       job.setid_dept,
       job.deptid,
       b.name_ac,
       a.per_status
from person a,
     person_name b,
     job,
     scrty_tbl_dept sec
where a.emplid = b.emplid
  and b.emplid = job.emplid
  and (job.effdt=
         ( select max(job2.effdt)
           from job job2
           where job.emplid = job2.emplid
             and job.empl-rcd = job2.empl_rcd
             and job2.effdt <= to_date(to_char(sysdate,
                                        'YYYY-MM-DD'),'YYYY-MM-DD'))
     and job.effseq =
           ( select max(job3.effseq)
             from job job3
             where job.emplid = job3.emplid
               and job.empl_rcd = job3.empl_rcd
               and job.effdt = job3.effdt ) )
  and sec.access_cd = 'Y'
  and exists
          ( select 'X'
            from treenode tn
```

```
34             where tn.setid = sec.setid
35               and tn.setid = job.setid_dept
36               and tn.tree_name = 'DEPT_SECURITY'
37               and tn.effdt = sec.tree_effdt
38               and tn.tree_node = job.deptid
39               and tn.tree_node_num between sec.tree_node_num
40                                         and sec.tree_node_num_end
41               and not exists
42                    ( select 'X'
43                      from scrty_tbl_dept sec2
44                      where sec.rowsecclass = sec2.rowsecclass
45                        and sec.setid = sec2.setid
46                        and sec.tree_node_num <> sec2.tree_node_num
47                        and tn.tree_node_num between sec2.tree_node_num
48                                                 and sec2.tree_node_num_end
49                        and sec2.tree_node_num between sec.tree_node_num
50                                                   and sec.tree_node_num_end ))
```

This type of "query of death" is, of course, too complicated for us to understand at a glance! As an exercise, though, it would be interesting for you to pause at this point, consider carefully the query, try to broadly define its characteristics, and try to identify possible performance stumbling blocks.

If you are done pondering the query, let's compare notes. There are a number of interesting patterns that you may have noticed:

- A high number of subqueries. One subquery is even nested, and all are correlated.
- No criterion likely to be very selective. The only constant expressions are an unbounded comparison with the current date at line 22, which is likely to filter hardly anything at all; a comparison to a Y/N field at line 30; and a condition on `tree_name` at line 36 that looks like a broad categorization. And since the `insert` statement that has been brought to our attention contains no `where` clause, we can expect a good many rows to be processed by the query.
- Expressions such as `between sec.tree_node_num and sec.tree_node_num_end` ring a familiar bell. This looks like our old acquaintance from Chapter 7, Celko's nested sets! Finding them in an Oracle context is rather unusual, but commercial off-the-shelf (COTS) packages often make admirable, if not always totally successful, attempts at being portable and therefore often shun the useful features of a particular DBMS.
- More subtly perhaps, when we consider the four tables (actually, one of them, `person_name`, is a view) in the outer `from` clause, only three of them, `person`, `person_name`, and `job`, are cleanly joined. There is a condition on `scrty_tbl_dept`, but the join proper is indirect and hidden inside one of the subqueries, lines 34 to 38. This is not a recipe for efficiency.

One of the very first things to do is to try to get an idea about the volumes involved; `person_name` is a view, but querying it indicates no performance issue. The data dictionary tells us how many rows we have:

```
TABLE_NAME                     NUM_ROWS
------------------------------ ----------
TREENODE                           107831
JOB                                 67660
PERSON                              13884
SCRTY_TBL_DEPT                        568
```

None of these tables is really large; it is interesting to notice that one need not deal with hundreds of millions of rows to perceive a significant degradation of performance as tables grow. The killing factor is how we are visiting tables. Finding out on the development server (obviously not as fast as the server used in production) how many rows are returned by the view is not very difficult but requires steel nerves:

```
SQL> select count(*) from PERS_SEARCH_FAST;

 COUNT(*)
----------
 264185

Elapsed: 01:35:36.88
```

A quick look at indexes shows that both `treenode` and `job` are over-indexed, a common flaw of COTS packages. We do not have here a case of the "obviously missing index."

Where must we look to find the reason that the query is so slow? We should look mostly at the lethal combination of a reasonably large number of rows and of correlated subqueries. The cascading `exists/not exists` in particular, is probably what does us in.

NOTE

In real life, all this analysis took me far more time than it is taking you now to read about it. Please understand that the paragraphs that follow summarize several hours of work and that inspiration didn't come as a flashing illumination!

Take a closer look at the `exists/not exists` expression. The first level subquery introduces table `treenode`. The second level subquery again hits table `scrty_tbl_dept`, already present in the outer query, and compares it both to the current row of the first level subquery (lines 47 and 48) and to the current row of the outer subquery (lines 44, 45, 46, 49, and 50)! If we want to get tolerable performance, we absolutely must disentangle these queries.

Can we understand what the query is about? As it happens, `treenode`, in spite of its misleading name, doesn't seem to be the table that stores the "nested sets." The references to a range of numbers are all related to `scrty_tbl_dept`; `treenode` looks more like a denormalized flat list (sad words to use in a supposedly relational context) of the "nodes" described in `scrty_tbl_dept`. Remember that in the nested set implementation of tree structures, two values are associated with each node and computed in such a way that the values associated with a child node are always between the values associated with the parent node. If the two values immediately follow each other, then we necessarily have a leaf node (the reverse is not true, because a subtree may have been pruned and value recomputation skipped, for obvious performance reasons). If we try to translate the meaning of lines 31 to 50 in English (sort of), we can say something like:

> There is in `treenode` a row with a particular `tree_name` that matches `job` on both `setid_dept` and `deptid`, as well as matching `scrty_tbl_dept` on `setid` and `tree_effdt`, and that points to either the current "node" in `scrty_tbl_dept` or to one of its descendents. There is no other node (or descendent) in `scrty_tbl_dept` that the current `treenode` row points to, that matches the current one on `setid` and `rowsecclass`, and that is a descendent of that node.

Dreadful jargon, especially when one has not the slightest idea of what the data is about. Can we try to express the same thing in a more intelligible way, in the hope that it will lead us to more intelligible and efficient SQL? The key point is probably in the *there is no other node* part. If there is no descendent node, then we are at the bottom of the tree for the node identified by the value of `tree_node_num` in `treenode`. The subqueries in the initial view text are hopelessly mingled with the outer queries. But we can write a single contained query that "forgets" for the time being about the link between `treenode` and `job` and computes, for every node of interest in `scrty_tbl_dept` (a small table, under 600 rows), the number of children that match it on `setid` and `rowsecclass`:

```
select s1.rowsecclass,
       s1.setid,
       s1.tree_node_num,
       tn.tree_node,
       count(*) - 1 children
from scrty_tbl_dept s1,
     scrty_tbl_dept s2,
     treenode tn
where s1.rowsecclass = s2.rowsecclass
  and s1.setid = s2.setid
  and s1.access_cd = 'Y'
  and tn.tree_name = 'DEPT_SECURITY'
  and tn.setid = s1.setid
  and tn.effdt = s1.tree_effdt
  and s2.tree_node_num between s1.tree_node_num
                           and s1.tree_node_num_end
  and tn.tree_node_num between s2.tree_node_num
                           and s2.tree_node_num_end
group by s1.rowsecclass,
         s1.setid,
         s1.tree_node_num,
         tn.tree_node
```

(The `count(*) - 1` is for not counting the current row.) The resulting set will be, of course, small, at most a few hundred rows. We shall filter out nodes that are not leaf nodes (in our context) by using the preceding query as an inline view, and applying a filter:

```
and children = 0
```

From here, and only from here, we can join to job and properly determine the final set. Giving the final text of the view would not be extremely interesting. Let's just point out that the first succession of exists:

```
and (job.effdt=
        ( select max(job2.effdt)
          from job job2
          where job.emplid = job2.emplid
            and job.empl-rcd = job2.empl_rcd
            and job2.effdt <= to_date(to_char(sysdate,'YYYY-MM-DD'),
                                                  'YYYY-MM-DD'))
      and job.effseq =
          ( select max(job3.effseq)
            from job job3
            where job.emplid = job3.emplid
              and job.empl_rcd = job3.empl_rcd
              and job.effdt = job3.effdt ) )
```

is meant to find, for the most recent effdt for the current (emplid, empl_rcd) pair, the row with the highest effseq value. This condition is not, particularly in comparison to the other nested subquery, so terrible. Nevertheless, OLAP (or should we say *analytical*, since we are in an Oracle context?) functions can handle, when they are available, this type of "top of the top" case slightly more efficiently. A query such as:

```
select emplid,
       empl_rcd,
       effdt,
       effseq
from (select emplid,
             empl_rcd,
             effdt,
             effseq
             row_number() over (partition by emplid, empl_rcd
                                order by effdt desc, effseq desc) rn
      from job
      where effdt <= to_date(to_char(sysdate,'YYYY-MM-DD'),'YYYY-MM-DD'))
where rn = 1
```

will easily select the (emplid, empl_rcd) values that we are really interested in and will be easily reinjected into the main query as an inline view that will be joined to the rest. In real life, after rewriting this query, the hourly process that had been constantly lengthening fell from 15 to under 2 minutes.

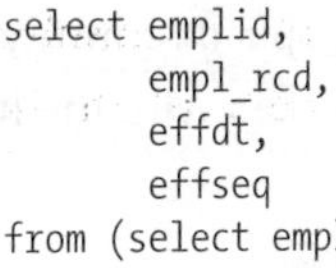

Minimize the dependencies of correlated subqueries on elements from outer queries.

Partitioning to the Rescue

When the number of rows to process is on the increase, index searches that work wonders on relatively small volumes become progressively inefficient. A typical primary key search requires the DBMS engine to visit 3 or 4 pages, descending the index, and then the DBMS must visit the table page. A range scan will be rather efficient, especially when applied to a clustering index that constrains the table rows to be stored in the same order as the index keys. Nevertheless, there is a point at which the constant to-and-fro between index page and table page becomes costlier than a plain linear search of the table. Such a linear search can take advantage of parallelism and read-ahead facilities made available by the underlying operating system and hardware. Index-searches that rely on key comparisons are more sequential by nature. Large numbers of rows to inspect exemplify the case when accesses should be thought of in terms of sweeping scans, not isolated incursions, and joins performed through hashes or merges, not loops (all this was discussed in Chapter 6).

Table scans are all the more efficient when the ratio of rows that belong to the result set to rows inspected is high. If we can split our table, using the data-driven partitioning introduced in Chapter 5, in such a way that our search criteria can operate on a well defined *physical* subset of the table, we maximize scan efficiency. In such a context, operations on a large range of values are much more efficient when applied brutishly to a well-isolated part of a table than when the boundaries have to be checked with the help of an index.

Of course, data-driven partitioning doesn't miraculously solve all volume issues:

- For one thing, the repartition of the partitioning keys must be more or less uniform; if we can find one single value of the partitioning key in 90% of rows, then scanning the table rather than the partition will hardly make any difference for that key; and for the others, they will probably be accessed more efficiently by index. The benefit of using an index that operates against a partitioned table will be slight for selective values. Uniformity of distribution is the reason why dates are so well suited to partitioning, and why range partitioning by date is by far the most popular method of partitioning.
- A second point, possibly less obvious but no less important, is that the boundaries of ranges must be well defined, in both their lower value *and* upper values. This isn't a peculiarity of partitioned tables, because the same can be said of index range scans. A half-bounded range, unless we are looking for values greater than a value close to the maximum in the table or lesser than a value close to the minimum, will provide no help in significantly reducing the rows we have to inspect. Similarly, a range defined as:

```
where date_column_1 >= some value
  and date_column_2 <= some other value
```

will not enable us to use either partitioning or indexing any more efficiently than if only one of the conditions was specified. It's by specifying a `between` (or any semantic equivalent) encompassing a small number of partitions that we shall make best usage of partitioning.

Half-bounded conditions make a poor use of both indexes and partitions.

Data Purges

Archival and data purges are too often considered ancillary matters, until they are seen as the very last hope for retrieving those by-and-large satisfactory response times of six months ago. Actually, they are extremely sensitive operations that, poorly handled, can put much strain on a system and contribute to pushing a precarious situation closer to implosion.

The ideal case is when tables are partitioned (true partitioning or partitioned view) and when archival and purges operate on partitions. If partitions can be simply detached, in one way or another, then an archival (or purge) operation is trivial: a partition is archived and a new empty one possibly created. If not, we are still in a relatively strong position: the query that selects rows for archival will be a simple one, and afterwards it will be possible to `truncate` a partition—`truncate` being a way of emptying a table or partition that bypasses most of the usual mechanisms and is therefore much faster than regular `delete`s.

> **NOTE**
>
> **Because `truncate` bypasses so much of the work that `delete` performs, you should use caution. The use of `truncate` may impact your backups, and it may also have other side effects, such as the invalidation of some indexes. Any use of `truncate` should always be discussed with your DBAs.**

The less-than-ideal, but oh-so-common case is when archival is triggered by age *and* other conditions. Accountants, for instance, are often reluctant to archive unpaid invoices, even when rather old. This makes the rather simple and elegant partition shuffling or truncation look too crude. Must we fall back on the dull-but-trusted `delete`?

It is at this point interesting to try to rank data manipulation operations (inserts, updates, and deletes) in terms of overall cost. We have seen that inserts are pretty costly, in large part because when you insert a new row, all indexes on the table have to be maintained. Updates require only maintenance of the indexes on the updated columns. Their weakness, compared to inserts, is two-fold: first, they are associated with a search (a `where` clause) that can be as disastrous as with a `select`, with the aggravating circumstance that in the meanwhile locks are held. Second, the previous value, inexistent in the case of an insert, must be saved somewhere so as to be available in case of rollback. Deletes combine all the shortcomings: they affect all indexes, are usually associated with a `where` clause that can be slow, and need to save the values for a possible transaction rollback.

Of all operations that change data, deletes offer the greatest potential for trouble.

If we can therefore save on deletes, even at the price of other operations, we are likely to end up on the winning side. When a table is partitioned and archival and purge are dependent mostly on a date condition with strings attached, we can consider a three stage purge:

1. Insert into a temporary table those old rows that we want to keep.
2. Truncate partitions.
3. Insert back from the temporary table those rows that should be retained.

Without partitioning, the situation is much more difficult. In order to limit lock duration—and assuming of course that once a row has attained the "ready for archival" state, no operation whatsoever can put it back to the "no, wait, I have second thought" state—we can consider a two-step operation. This two-step operation will be all the more advantageous given that the query that identifies rows for archiving is a slow-running one. What we may do in that case is:

1. Build a list of the identifiers of the rows to archive.
2. Join on this list for both archival and purge, rather than running the same slow `where` clause twice, once in a `select` statement and once in a `delete` statement.

A major justification for temporary tables is to enable massive, table-oriented operations that would outperform row-wise operations.

Data Warehousing

The purpose of this book is not to devote half a chapter to covering the complex issues linked to data warehousing. Many books on the topic of data warehousing have been written, some of them generic (Ralph Kimball's *The Data Warehouse Toolkit* and Bill Inmon's *Building the Data Warehouse*, both published by John Wiley & Sons, are probably the two best-known titles), some of them specific to a DBMS engine. There has been something of a religious war between the followers of Inmon, who advocates a clean 3NF design of enormous data repositories used by decision-support systems, and the supporters of Kimball, who believes that data warehouses are a different world with different needs, and that therefore the 3NF model, in spite of its qualities in the operational world, is better replaced with *dimensional modeling*, in which reference data is happily denormalized.

As most of this book advocates and assumes a clean 3NF design, I will deal hereafter more specifically with dimensional models, to study their strengths and the reason for their popularity, but also their weaknesses. I will, in particular, examine the interactions between *operational data stores* ("production databases" to the less enlightened) and decision-support systems, since data doesn't fall from heaven, unless you are working for NASA or a satellite operating company, and what you load into dimensional models has to come from somewhere. Understand that it is *not* because one is using the SQL language against "tables" that one is operating in the relational world.

Facts and Dimensions: the Star Schema

The principle of dimensional modeling is to store measurement values, whether they are quantities, amounts, or whatever you can imagine into big *fact tables*. Reference data is stored into *dimension tables* that mostly contain self-explanatory labels and that are heavily denormalized. There are typically 5 to 15 dimensions, each with a system-generated primary key, and the fact table contains all the foreign keys. Typically, the date associated with a series of measures (a row) in the fact table will not be stored as a date column in the fact table, but as a system-generated number that will reference a row in the `date_dimension` table in which the date will be *declined* under all possible forms. If we take, for instance, the traditional starting date of the Unix world, January 1, 1970, it would typically be stored in `date_dimension` as:

date_key	date_value	date_description	day	month	year	quarter	holiday
12345	01/01/1970	January 1, 1970	Thursday	January	1970	Q1 1970	Holiday

Every row that refers to something having occurred on January 1, 1970 in the fact table would simply store the `12345` key. The rationale behind such an obviously non-normalized way of storing data is that, although normalization is highly important in environments where data is changed, because it is the only way to ensure data integrity, the overhead of storing redundant information in a data warehouse is relatively negligible since dimension tables contain very few rows compared to the normalized fact table. For instance, a one-century date dimension would only hold 36,525 rows. Moreover, argues Dr. Kimball, having only a fact table surrounded by dimension tables as in Figure 10-3 (hence the "star schema" name) makes querying that data extremely simple. Queries against the data tend to require very few joins, and therefore are very fast to execute.

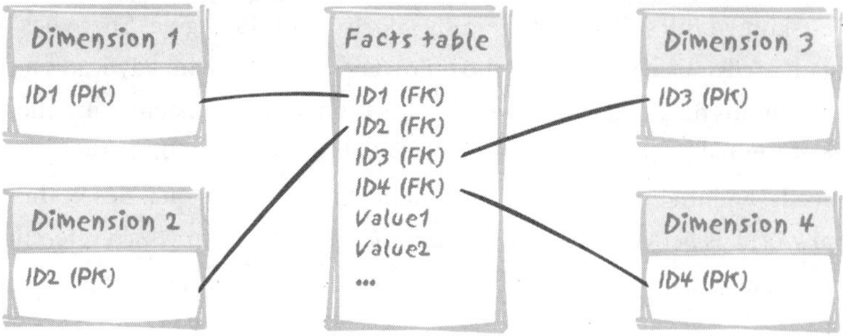

FIGURE 10-3. *A simple star schema, showing primary keys (PK) and foreign keys (FK)*

Anybody with a little knowledge of SQL will probably be startled by the implication that the fewer the joins, the faster a query runs. Jumping to the defense of joins is not, of course, to recommend joining indiscriminately dozens of tables, but unless you have had a traumatic early childhood experience with nested loops on big, unindexed tables, it is hard to assert seriously that joins are the reason queries are slow. The slowness comes from the way queries are written; in this light, dimensional modeling can make a lot of sense, and you'll see why as you progress through this chapter.

The design constraints of dimensional modeling are deliberately read-oriented, and consequently they frequently ignore the precepts of relational design.

Query Tools

The problem with decision-support systems is that their primary users have not the slightest idea how to write an SQL query, not even a terrible one. They therefore have to use query tools for that purpose, query tools that present them with a friendly interface and build queries for them. You saw in Chapter 8 that dynamically generating an efficient query from a fixed set of criteria is a difficult task, requiring careful thought and even more careful coding. It is easy to understand that when the query can actually be anything, a tool can only generate a decent query when complexity is low.

The following piece of code is one that I saw actually generated by a query tool (it shows some of the columns returned by a subquery in a `from` clause):

```
...
FROM (SELECT ((((((((((((t2."FOREIGN_CURRENCY"
                        || CASE
                             WHEN 'tfp' = 'div' THEN t2."CODDIV"
                             WHEN 'tfp' = 'ac' THEN t2."CODACT"
                             WHEN 'tfp' = 'gsd' THEN t2."GSD_MNE"
                             WHEN 'tfp' = 'tfp' THEN t2."TFP_MNE"
                             ELSE NULL
```

```
              END
            )
          || CASE
              WHEN 'Y' = 'Y' THEN TO_CHAR (
                      TRUNC (
                             t2."ACC_PCI"
                            )
                     )
              ELSE NULL
             END
           )
        || CASE
             WHEN 'N' = 'Y' THEN t2."ACC_E2K"
             ELSE NULL
           END
          )
       || CASE
            WHEN 'N' = 'Y' THEN t2."ACC_EXT"
            ELSE NULL
          END
         )
       || CASE ...
```

It seems obvious from this sample's `select` list that at least some "business intelligence" tools invest so much intelligence on the business side that they have nothing left for generating SQL queries. And when the `where` clause ceases to be trivial—forget about it! Declaring that it is better to avoid joins for performance reasons is quite sensible in this context. Actually, the nearer you are to the "text search in a file" (a.k.a. *grep*) model, the better. And one understands why having a "date dimension" makes sense, because having a date column in the fact table and expecting that the query tool will transform references to "Q1" into "between January 1 and March 31" to perform an index range scan requires the kind of faith you usually lose when you stop believing in the Tooth Fairy. By explicitly laying out all format variations that end users are likely to use, and by indexing all of them, risks are limited. Denormalized dimensions, simple joins, and all-round indexing increase the odds that most queries will execute in a tolerable amount of time, which is usually the case.

Weakly designed queries may perform acceptably against dimensional models because the design complexity is much lower than in a typical transactional model.

Extraction, Transformation, and Loading

In order for business users to be able to proactively leverage strategic cost-generating opportunities (if data warehousing literature is to be believed), it falls on some poor souls to ensure the mundane task of feeding the decision-support system. And even if tools are available, this feeding is rarely an easy task.

Data extraction

Data extraction is not usually handled through SQL queries. In the general case, purpose-built tools are used: either utilities or special features provided by the DBMS, or dedicated third-party products. In the unlikely event that you would want to run your own SQL queries to extract information to load into a data warehouse, you typically fall into the case of having large volumes of information, where full table scans are the safest tactic. You must do your best in such a case to operate on arrays (if your DBMS supports an array interface—that is fetching into arrays or passing multiple values as a single array), so as to limit round-trips between the DBMS kernel and the downloading program.

Transformation

Depending on your SQL skills, the source of the data, the impact on production systems, and the degree of transformation required, you can use the SQL language to perform a complex `select` that will return ready-to-load data, use SQL to modify the data in a staging area, or use SQL to perform the transformation at the same time as the data is uploaded into the data warehouse.

Transformations often include aggregates, because the granularity required by decision support systems is usually coarser than the level of detail provided by production databases. Typically, values may be aggregated by day. If transformation is not more complicated than aggregation, there is no reason for performing it as a separate operation. Writing to the database is much costlier than reading from it, and updating the staging area before updating the data warehouse proper may be adding an unwanted costly step.

Such an extra step may be unavoidable, though, when data has to be compounded from several distinct operational systems; I can list several possible reasons for having to get data from different unrelated sources:

- Acute warlordism within the corporation
- A recently absorbed division still using its pre-acquisition information system
- A migration spread over time, meaning that at some point you have, for instance, domestic operations still running on an old information system while international ones are already using a new system that will later be used everywhere

The assemblage of data from several sources should be done, as much as possible, in a single step, using a combination of set operators such as `union` and of in-line views—subqueries in the `from` clause. Multiple passes carry a number of risks and should not be directly applied to the target data warehouse. The several-step update of tables, with `null` columns being suddenly assigned values is an excellent recipe for wreaking havoc at the physical level. When data is stored in variable length, as is often the case with character information and sometimes with numeric information as well (Oracle is an example of such a storage strategy), it will invariably lead to some of the data being relegated to overflow pages, thus compromising the efficiency of both full scans and indexed accesses, since indexes usually point to the head part of a row. Any pointer to an overflow area will mean visiting more pages than would otherwise be necessary to answer a given question, and will be costly. If the prepared data is very simply inserted into the target data warehouse tables, data will be properly reorganized in the process.

It is also quite common to see several updates applied to different columns of the same table in turn. Whenever possible, perhaps with help from the case construct, always update as many columns in one statement as possible.

Multiple massive updates applied to a table often wreak havoc at the physical level.

Loading

If you build your data warehouse (or data mart, as others prefer to say) according to the rules of dimensional modeling, all dimensions will use artificial, system-generated keys for the purpose of keeping a logical track over time of items that may be technically different but logically identical. For instance, if you manufacture consumer electronics, a new model with a new reference may have been designed to replace an older model, now discontinued. By using the same artificial key for both, you can consider them as a single logical entity for analysis.

The snag is that the primary keys in your operational database will usually have different values from the dimension identifiers used in the decision support system, which becomes an issue not with dimension tables but with fact tables. You have no reason to use surrogate keys for dates in your operational system. In the same way, the operational system doesn't necessarily need to record which electronic device model is the successor to another. Dimension tables are, for the most part, loaded once and rarely updated. Dimensional modeling rests partly on the assumption that the fast-changing values are the ones stored in fact tables. As a result, for every row you need to insert into the fact table, you must retrieve (from the operational database primary key) the value of the corresponding surrogate, system-generated key for each of the dimensions—which necessarily means as many joins as there are different dimensions. Queries against the decision support system may require fewer joins, but loading into the decision support system will require many more joins because of the mapping between operational and dimensional keys.

The advantage of simpler queries against dimensional models is paid for by the disadvantage of complex preparation and loading of the data.

Integrity constraints and indexes

When a DBMS implements referential integrity checking, it is sensible to disable that checking during data load operations. If the DBMS engine needs to check for each row that the foreign keys exist, the engine does double the amount of work, because any statement that uploads the fact table *has* to look for the parent surrogate key anyway. You might also significantly speed up loading by dropping most indexes and rebuilding them after the load, unless the rows loaded represent a small percentage of the size of the table that you are loading, as rebuilding indexes on very large tables can be prohibitively expensive in terms of resources and time. It would however be a potentially lethal mistake to disable *all* constraints, and particularly primary keys. Even if the data being loaded has been cleaned and is above all reproach, it is very easy to make a mistake and load the same data twice—much easier than trying to remove duplicates afterwards.

The massive upload of decision-support systems is one of the rare cases when temporarily altering a schema may be tolerated.

Querying Dimensions and Facts: Ad Hoc Reports

If query tools are seriously helped by removing anything that can get in their way, such as evil joins and sophisticated subqueries, there usually comes a day when business users require answers that a simplistic schema cannot provide. The dimensional model is then therefore duly "embellished" with *mini-dimensions, outriggers, bridge tables,* and all kinds of bells and whistles until it begins to resemble a clean 3NF schema, at which point query tools are beginning to suffer. One day, a high-ranking user tries something daring—and the next day the problem is on the desk of a developer, while the tool-generated query is still running. Time for ad hoc queries and *shock SQL!*

It is when you have to write ad hoc queries that it is time to get back to dimensional modeling and see the SQL implications. Basically, dimensions represent the breaks in a report. If an end user often wants to see sales by product, by store, and by month, then we have three dimensions involved: the date dimension that has been previously introduced, the product dimension, and the store dimension. Product and store can be denormalized to include information such as product line, brand, and category in one case, and region, surface, or whatever criterion is deemed to be relevant in the other case. Sales amounts are, obviously, facts.

A key characteristic of the star schema is that we are supposed to attack the fact table through the dimensions such as in Figure 10-4; in the previous example, we might for instance want to see sales by product, store, and month for *dairy products* in the stores located in the *Southwest* and for the *third quarter*. Contrarily to the generally recommended practice in normalized operational databases, dimension tables are not only denormalized, but are also strongly indexed. Indexing all columns means that, whatever the degree of detail required (the various columns in a location dimension, such as `city`, `state`, `region`, `country`, `area`, can be seen as various levels of detail, and the same is true of a date dimension), an end user who is executing a query will hit an index. Remember that dimensions are reference tables that are rarely if ever updated, and therefore there is no frightful maintenance cost associated with heavy indexing. If all of your criteria refer to data stored in dimension tables, and if they are indexed so as to make any type of search fast, you should logically hit dimension tables first and then locate the relevant values in the fact table.

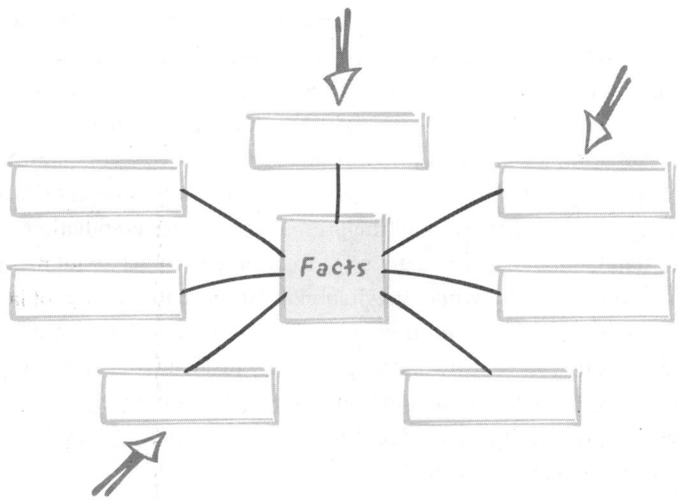

FIGURE 10-4. *The usual way of querying tables in the dimensional model*

Hitting dimensions first has very strong SQL implications that we must well understand. Normally, one accesses particular rows in a table through search criteria, finds some foreign keys in those rows, and uses those foreign keys to pull information from the tables those keys reference. To take a simple example, if we want to find the phone number of the assistant in the department where Owens works, we shall query the table of employees basing our search on the "Owens" name, find the department number, and use the primary key on the table of departments to find the phone number. This is a classic, nested-loop join case.

With dimensional modeling, the picture totally changes. Instead of going from the referencing table (the employees) to the referenced table (the departments), naturally following foreign keys, we start from the reference tables—the dimensions. To go where? There is no foreign key linking a dimension to the fact table: the opposite is true. It is like looking for the names of all the employees in a department when all you know is the phone number of the assistant. When joining the fact table to the dimension, the DBMS engine will have to go through a mechanism other than the usual nested loop—perhaps something such as a hash join.

Another peculiarity of queries on dimensional models is that they often are perfect examples of the association of criteria that's not too specific, with a relatively narrow intersection to obtain a result set that is not, usually, enormous. The optimizer can use a couple of tactics for handling such queries. For instance:

Determining which is the most selective of all these not-very-selective criteria, joining the associated dimension to the fact table, and then checking each of the other dimensions
: Such a tactic is fraught with difficulties. First of all, the way dimensions are built may give the optimizer wrong ideas about selectivity. Suppose we have a date dimension that is used as the reference for many different dates: the sales date, but also, for instance, the date on which each store was first opened, a fact that may be useful to compare how each store is doing after a given number of months of activity. Since the date dimension will never be a giant table, we may have decided to fill it from the start with seventy years' worth of dates. Seventy years give us, on one hand, enough "historical" dates to be able to refer to even the opening of the humble store of the present chairman's grandfather and, on the other hand, enough future dates so as to be able to forget about maintaining this dimension for quite a while. Inevitably, a reference to the sales of last year's third quarter will make the criterion look much more selective than it really is. The problem is that if we truly had a "sales date" inside the fact table, it would be straightforward to determine the useful range of dates. If we just have a "date reference" pointing to the date dimension, the starting point for evaluation is the dimension, not the fact table.

Scanning the fact table and discarding any row that doesn't satisfy any of the various criteria
: Since fact tables contain all the measurement or metrics, they are very large. If they are partitioned, it will necessarily be against a single dimension (two if you use subpartitioning). Any query involving three or more dimensions will require a full scan of a table that can contain millions of rows. Scanning the fact table isn't the most attractive of options.

In such a case, visiting the fact table at an early stage, which also means after a first dimension, may be a mistake. Some products such as Oracle implement an interesting algorithm, known in Oracle's case as the "star transformation." We are going to look next at this transformation in some detail, including characteristics that are peculiar to Oracle, before discussing how such an algorithm may be emulated in non-Oracle environments.

Dimensional modeling is built on the premise that dimensions are the entry points. Facts must be accessed last.

The star transformation

The principle behind the star transformation is, as a very first step, to separately join the fact table to each of the dimensions for which we have a filtering condition. The transformation makes it appear that we are joining several times to the fact table, but appearances are deceiving. What we really want is to get the *addresses* of rows from the fact table that match the condition on each dimension. Such an address, also known as a *rowid* (accessible as a pseudo-column with Oracle; Postgres has a functionally equivalent *oid*) is stored in indexes. All we need to join, therefore, are three objects:

- The index on the column from the dimension table that we use as a filtering condition—for instance, the `quarters` column in `date_dimension`
- The `date_dimension` itself, in which we find the system-generated artificial primary key `date_key`
- The index on the column in the fact table that is defined as a foreign key referencing `date_key` (star transformations work best when the foreign keys in the fact table are indexed)

Even though the fact table appears several times in a star query, we will not hit the same data or index pages repeatedly. All the separate joins will involve different indexes, and all storing rowids referring to the same table—but otherwise those indexes are perfectly distinct objects.

As soon as we have the result of two joins, we can combine the two resulting sets of rowids, discarding everything that doesn't belong to the intersection of the two sets for an and condition or retaining everything for an or condition. This step is further simplified if we are using *bitmap indexes*, for which simple bit-wise operations are all that is required to select our final set of rowids that refer to rows satisfying our conditions. Once we have our final, relatively small set of resulting rowids, then we can fetch the corresponding rows from the fact table that we are actually visiting for the very first time.

Bitmap indexes, as their name says, index values by keeping bitmaps telling which rows contain a particular value and which do not. Bitmap indexes are particularly appropriate to index low-cardinality columns; in other words, columns in which there are few distinct values, even if the distribution of those values is not particularly skewed. Bitmap indexes were not mentioned in previous chapters for an excellent reason: they are totally inappropriate for general database operations. There is a major reason for avoiding them in a database that incurs normal update activity: when you update a bitmap, you have to lock it. Since this type of index is designed for columns with few distinct values, you end up preventing changes to many, many rows, and you get a behavior that lies somewhere between page locking and table locking, but much closer to table locking. For read-only databases, however, bitmap indexes may prove useful. Bitmap indexes are quickly built during bulk loads and take much less storage than regular indexes.

Emulating the star transformation

Although automated star transformation is a feature that enables even poorly generated queries to perform efficiently, it is quite possible to write a query in a way that will induce the DBMS kernel to execute it in a similar, if not exactly identical, fashion. I must plead guilty to writing SQL statements that are geared at one particular result. From a relational point of view, I would deserve to be hanged high. On the other hand, dimensional modeling has nothing to do with the relational theory. I am therefore using SQL in a shamelessly unrelational way.

Let's suppose that we have a number of dimension tables named `dim1`, `dim2`, ... `dim`*n*. These dimension tables surround our fact table that we shall imaginatively call `facts`. Each row in `facts` is composed of `key1`, `key2`, ... `key`*n*, foreign keys respectively pointing to one dimension table, plus a number of values (the facts) `val1`, `val2`, ... `val`*p*. The primary key of `facts` is defined as a composite key, and is simply made of `key1` to `key`*n*.

Let's further imagine that we need to execute a query that satisfies conditions on some columns from `dim1`, `dim2`, and `dim3` (they may, for instance, represent a class of products, a store location, and a time period). For simplicity, say that we have a series of `and` conditions, involving `col1` in `dim1`, `col2` in `dim2` and `col3` in `dim3`. We shall ignore any transformation, aggregate or whatever, and limit our creative exercise to returning the appropriate set of rows in as effective a way as possible.

The star transformation mostly aims to obtain in an efficient way the identifiers of the rows from the fact table that will belong to our result set, which may be the final result set or an intermediate result set vowed to further ordeals. If we start with joining `dim2` to `facts`, for instance:

```
select ...
from dim2,
     facts
where dim2.key2 = facts.key2
  and dim2.col2 = some value
```

then we have a major issue if we have no Oracle *rowid*, because the identifiers of the appropriate rows from `facts` are precisely what we want to see returned. Must we return the primary key from `facts` to properly identify the rows? If we do, we hit not only the index on `facts(key2)`, but also table `facts` itself, which defeats our initial purpose. Remember that the frequently used technique to avoid an additional visit to the table is to store the information we need in the index by adding to the index the columns we want to return. So, must we turn our index on facts(key2) into an index on facts(key2, key3 ... keyn)? If we do that, then we must apply the same recipe to all foreign keys! We will end up with *n* indexes that will each be of a size in the same order of magnitude as the facts table itself, something that is not acceptable and that forces us to read large amounts of data while scanning those indexes, thus jeopardizing performance.

What we need for our facts table is a relatively small row identifier—a surrogate key that we may call fact_id. Although our facts table has a perfectly good primary key, and although it is not referenced by any other table, we still need a compact technical identifier—not to use in other tables, but to use in indexes.

With our system-generated fact_id column, we can have indexes on (key1, fact_id), (key2, fact_id) ... (keyn, fact_id) instead of on the foreign keys alone. We can now fully write our previous query as:

```
select facts.fact_id
from dim2,
     facts
where dim2.key2 = facts.key2
  and dim2.col2 = some value
```

This version of the query no longer needs the DBMS engine to visit anything but the index on col2, the dimension table dim2, and the facts index on (key2, fact_id). Note that by applying the same trick to dim2 (and of course the other dimension tables), systematically appending the key to indexes on every column, the query can be executed by only visiting indexes.

Repeating the query for dim1 and dim3 provides us with identifiers of facts that satisfy the conditions associated with these dimensions. The final set of identifiers satisfying all conditions can easily be obtained by joining all the queries:

```
select facts1.fact_id
from (select facts.fact_id
      from dim1,
           facts
      where dim1.key1 = facts.key1
        and dim1.col1 = some value) facts1,
      (select facts.fact_id
       from dim2,
            facts
       where dim2.key2 = facts.key2
         and dim2.col2 = some other value) facts2,
       (select facts.fact_id
        from dim3,
             facts
        where dim3.key3 = facts.key3
          and dim3.col3 = still another value) facts3
where facts1.fact_id = facts2.fact_id
   and facts2.fact_id = facts3.fact_id
```

Afterwards, we only have to collect from `facts` the rows, the identifiers of which are returned by the previous query.

The technique just described is, of course, not specific to decision-support systems. But I must point out that we have assumed some very heavy indexing, a standard fixture of data marts and, generally speaking, read-only databases. In such a context, putting more information into indexes and adding a surrogate key column can be considered as "no impact" changes. You should be most reluctant in normal (including in the relational sense!) circumstances to modify a schema so significantly to accommodate queries. But if most of the required elements are already in place, as in a data warehousing environment, you can certainly take advantage of them.

Querying a star schema the way it is not intended to be queried

As you have seen, the dimensional model is designed to be queried through dimensions. But what happens when, as in Figure 10-5, our input criteria refer to some facts (for instance, that the sales amount is greater than a given value) as well as to dimensions?

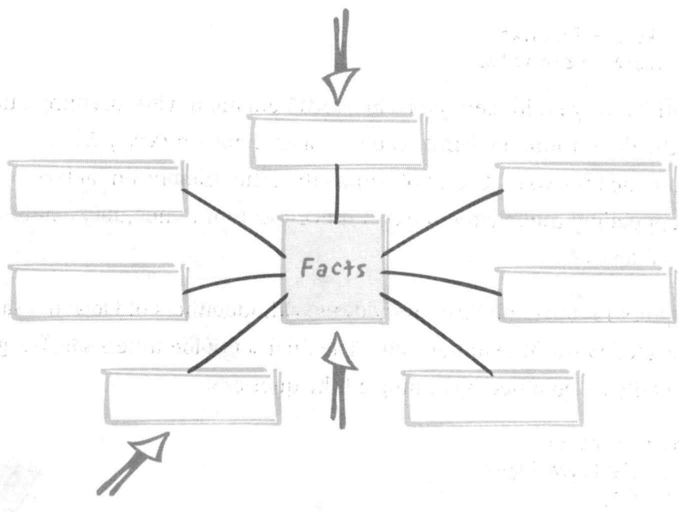

FIGURE 10-5. *A maverick usage of the dimension model*

We can compare such a case to the use of a `group by`. If the condition on the fact table applies to an aggregate (typically a sum or average), we are in the same situation as with a `having` clause: we cannot provide a result before processing all the data, and the condition on the fact table is nothing more than an additional step over what we might call regular dimensional model processing. The situation *looks* different, but it isn't.

If, on the contrary, the condition applies to individual rows from the fact table, we should consider whether it would be more efficient to discard unwanted facts rows earlier in the process, in the same way that it is advisable to filter out unwanted rows in the `where` clause of a query, before the group by, rather than in the having clause that is evaluated after the group by. In such a case, we should carefully study how to proceed. Unless the fact column that is subjected to a condition is indexed—a condition that is both unlikely and unadvisable—our entry point will still be through one of the dimensions. The choice of the proper dimension to use depends on several factors; selectivity is one of them, but not necessarily the most important one. Remember the clustering factor of indexes, and how much an index that corresponds to the actual, physical order of rows in the table outperforms other indexes (whether the correspondence is just a happy accident of the data input process, or whether the index has been defined as constraining the storage of rows in the table). The same phenomenon happens between the fact table and the dimensions. The order of fact rows may happen to match a particular date, simply because new fact rows are appended on a daily basis, and therefore those rows have a strong affinity to the date dimension. Or the order of rows may be strongly correlated to the "location dimension" because data is provided by numerous sites and processed and loaded on a site-by-site basis. The star schema may look symmetrical, just as the relational model knows nothing of order. But implementation hazards and operational processes often result in a break-up of the star schema's theoretical symmetry. It's important to be able to take advantage of this hidden dissymmetry whenever possible.

If there is a particular affinity between one of the dimensions to which a search filter must be applied and to the fact table, the best way to proceed is probably to join that dimension to the fact table, especially if the criterion that is applied to the fact table is reasonably selective. Note that in this particular case we must join to the actual fact table, obviously through the foreign key index, but not limit our access to the index. This will allow us to directly get a superset of our target collection of rows from the fact table at a minimum cost in terms of visited pages, and check the condition that directly applies to fact rows early. The other criteria will come later.

The way data is loaded to a star schema can favor one dimension over all others.

A (Strong) Word of Caution

Dimensional modeling is a technique, not a theory, and it is popular because it is well-suited to the less-than-perfect (from an SQL* perspective) tools that are commonly used in decision support systems, and because the carpet-indexing (as in "carpet-bombing") it requires is tolerable in a read-only system—read-only after the loading phase, that is. The

* Some will say—with some reason—that SQL itself is not above reproach.

problem is that when you have 10 to 15 dimensions, then you have 10 to 15 foreign keys in your fact table, and you must index all those keys if you want queries to perform tolerably well. You have seen that dimensions are mostly static and not enormous, so indexing all columns in all dimensions is no real issue. But indexing all columns may be much more worrisome with a fact table, which can grow very big: just imagine a large chain of grocery stores recording one fact each time they sell one article. New rows have to be inserted into the fact table very regularly. You saw in Chapter 3 that indexes are extremely costly when inserting; 15 indexes, then, will very significantly slow down loading. A common technique to load faster is to drop indexes and then recreate them (if possible in parallel) once the data is loaded. That technique may work for a while, but re-indexing will inexorably take more time as the base table grows. Indexing requires sorting, and (as you might remember from the beginning of this chapter) sorts belong to the category of operations that significantly suffer when the number of rows increases. Sooner or later, you will discover that the re-creation of indexes takes way too much time, and you may well also be told that you have users who live far, far away who would like to access the data warehouse in the middle of the night.

Users that want the database to be accessible during a part of the night mean a smaller maintenance window for loading the decision support system. Meanwhile, because recreating indexes takes longer as data accumulates into the decision support database, loading times have a tendency to increase. Instead of loading once every night, wouldn't it be possible to have a continuous flow of data from operational systems to the data warehouse? But then, denormalization can become an issue, because the closer we get to a continuous flow, the closer we are to a transactional model, with all the integrity issues that only proper normalization can protect against. Compromising on normalization is acceptable in a carefully controlled environment, an ivory tower. When the headquarters are too close to the battlefield, they are submitted to the same rules.

CHAPTER ELEVEN

Stratagems

Trying to Salvage Response Times

But my doctrines and I begin to part company.

—*Thomas Hardy (1840–1928)*

Jude The Obscure, IV, ii

I hope to have convinced you in Chapters 1 and 2 about the extent to which performance depends, first and foremost, on a sound database design, and second, on a clear strategy and well-designed programs. The sad truth is that when you are beginning to be acknowledged as a skilled SQL tuner, people will not seek your advice until they discover that they have performance problems. This happens—at best—during the final stages of acceptance testing, after man-months of haphazard development. You are then expected to work wonders on queries when table designs, program architectures, or sometimes even the requirements themselves may all be grossly inappropriate. Some of the most sensitive areas are related to interfacing *legacy* systems—in other words loading the database or downloading data to files.

If there is one chapter in this book that should leave a small imprint on your memory, it should probably be this one. If you really want to remember something, I hope it will not be the *recipes* (those tricky and sometimes entertaining SQL queries of death) in this chapter, but the reasoning behind each recipe, which I have tried my best to make as explicit as possible. Nothing is better than getting things right from the very start; but there is some virtue in trying to get the best out of a rotten situation.

You will also find some possible answers to common problems that, sometimes surprisingly, seem to induce developers to resort to contorted procedures. These procedures are not only far less efficient, but also commonly far more obscure and harder to maintain than SQL statements, even complex ones.

I shall end this chapter with a number of remarks about a commonly used stratagem indirectly linked to SQL proper, that of optimizer directives.

Welcome to the heart of darkness.

Turning Data Around

The most common difficulty that you may encounter when trying to solve SQL problems is when you have to program against what might charitably be called an "unconventional" design. Writing a query that performs well is often the most visible challenge. However, I must underline that the complex SQL queries that are forced upon developers by a poor design only mirror the complication of programs (including triggers and stored procedures) that the same poor design requires in order to perform basic operations such as integrity checking. By contrast, a sound design allows you to *declare* constraints and let the DBMS check them for you, removing much of the risk associated with complexity. After all, ensuring data integrity is exactly what a DBMS, a rather fine piece of software, has been engineered to achieve. Unfortunately, haphazard designs will force you to spend days coding application controls. As a bonus, you get very high odds of letting software bugs creep in. Unlike popular software systems that are in daily use by millions of users, where bugs are rapidly exposed and fixed, your home-grown software can hide bugs for weeks or months before they are discovered.

Rows That Should Have Been Columns

Rows that should have been originally specified as columns are most often encountered with that appalling "design" having the magical four attributes—`entity_id`, `attribute_name`, `attribute_type`, `attribute_value`—that are supposed to solve all schema evolution issues. Frighteningly, many supporters of this model seem to genuinely believe that it represents the ultimate sophistication in terms of normalization. You will find it under various, usually flattering, names—such as *meta-design*, or *fact dimension* with data warehouse designers.

Proponents of the magical four attributes praise the "flexibility" of this model. There is an obvious confusion of flexibility with flabbiness. Being able to add "attributes" on the fly is not flexibility; those attributes need to be retrieved and processed meaningfully. The dubious benefit of inserting rows instead of painstakingly designing the database in the first place is absolutely negligible compared to the major coding effort that is required, first, to process those new rows, and second, to insure some minimal degree of integrity and data consistency. The proper way to deal with varying numbers of attributes is to define *subtypes*, as explained in Chapter 1. Subtypes let you define clean referential integrity constraints—checks that you will not need to code and maintain. A database should not be a mere repository where data is dumped without any thought to its semantic integrity.

The predominant characteristic of queries against *meta-design* tables, as tables designed around our magical four attributes are sometimes called, is that you find the same table invoked a very high number of times in the `from` clause. Typically, queries will resemble something like:

```
select emp_last_name.entity_id        employee_id,
       emp_last_name.attribute_value  last_name,
       emp_first_name.attribute_value first_name,
       emp_job.attribute_value        job_description,
       emp_dept.attribute_value       department,
       emp_sal.attribute_value        salary
from employee_attributes emp_last_name,
     employee_attributes emp_first_name,
     employee_attributes emp_job,
     employee_attributes emp_dept,
     employee_attributes emp_sal
where emp_last_name.entity_id = emp_first_name.entity_id
  and emp_last_name.entity_id = emp_job.entity_id
  and emp_last_name.entity_id = emp_dept.entity_id
  and emp_last_name.entity_id = emp_sal.entity_id
  and emp_last_name.attribute_name = 'LASTNAME'
  and emp_first_name.attribute_name = 'FIRSTNAME'
  and emp_job.attribute_name = 'JOB'
  and emp_dept.attribute_name = 'DEPARTMENT'
  and emp_sal.attribute_sal = 'SALARY'
order by emp_last_name.attribute_value
```

Note how the same table is referenced five times in the from clause. The number of self-joins is usually much higher than in this simple example. Furthermore, such queries are frequently spiced up with outer joins as well.

A query with a high number of self-joins performs extremely badly on large volumes; it is clear that the only reason for the numerous conditions in the where clause is to patch all the various "attributes" together. Had the table been defined as the more logical employees(employee_id, last_name, first_name, job_description, department, salary), our query would have been as simple as:

```
select *
from employees
order by last_name
```

And the best course for executing *this* query is obviously a plain table scan. The multiple joins and associated index accesses of the query against employee_attributes are performance killers.

We can never succeed in making a query run as fast against a rotten design as it will run against a clean design. Any clever rewriting of a SQL query against badly designed tables will be nothing more than a wooden leg, returning only some degree of agility to a crippled query. However, we can often obtain spectacular results in comparison to the multiple joins approach by trying to achieve a single pass on the attribute table.

We basically want one row with several attributes (reflecting what the table design should have been in the first place) instead of multiple rows, each with only one attribute of interest per row. Consolidating a multi-row result into a single row is a feat we know how to perform: aggregate functions do precisely this. The idea is therefore to proceed in two steps, as shown in Figure 11-1:

1. Complete each row that contains only one value of interest, with as many dummy values as required to obtain the total number of attributes that we ultimately want.
2. Aggregate the different rows so as to keep only the single value of interest from each (the single value in each column). A function such as max( ), that has the advantage of being applicable to most data types, is perfect for this kind of operation.

To be certain that max( ) will only retain meaningful values, we must use dummy values that will necessarily be smaller than any legitimate value we may have in a given column. It is probably better to use an explicit value rather than null as a dummy value, even though max( ) ignores null values according to the standard.

If we apply the "recipe" illustrated in Figure 11-1 to our previous example, we can get rid of the numerous joins by writing:

```
select employee_id,
       max(last_name)         last_name,
       max(first_name)        first_name,
```

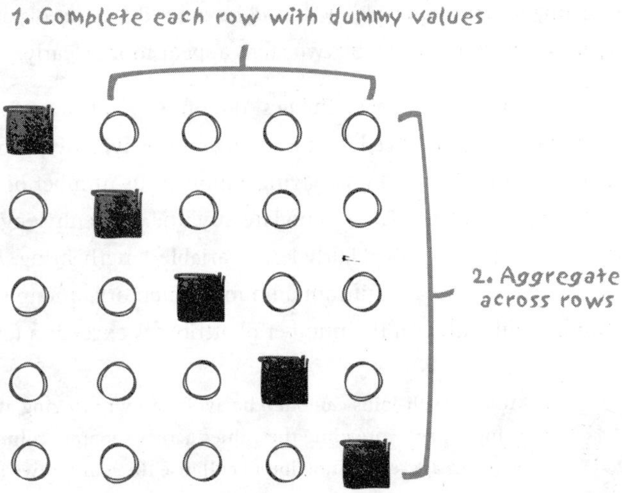

FIGURE 11-1. *Transmogrification of several rows into one row*

```
         max(job_description) job_desription,
         max(department)      department,
         max(salary)          salary
  from  -- select all the rows of interest, returning
        -- as many columns as we have rows, one column
        -- of interest per row and values smaller
        -- than any value of interest everywhere else
       (select entity_id                  employee_id,
               case attribute_name
                 when 'LASTNAME' then attribute_value
                 else ''
               end                        last_name,
               case attribute_name
                 when 'FIRSTNAME' then attribute_value
                 else ''
               end                        first_name,
               case attribute_name
                 when 'JOB' then attribute_value
                 else ''
               end                        job_description,
               case attribute_name
                 when 'DEPARTMENT' then attribute_value
                 else -1
               end                        department,
               case attribute_name
                 when 'SALARY' then attribute_value
                 else -1
               end                        salary
        from employee_attributes
        where attribute_name in ('LASTNAME',
                                 'FIRSTNAME',
                                 'JOB',
                                 'DEPARTMENT',
                                 'SALARY')) as inner
  group by inner.employee_id
  order by 2
```

The inner query is not strictly required—we could have used a series of `max(case when ... end)`—but the query as written makes the two steps appear more clearly.

An aggregate is not, as you might expect, the best option in terms of performance. But in the kingdom of the blind, the one-eyed man is king, and this type of query just shown usually has no trouble outperforming one having a monstrous number of self-joins. A word of caution, though: in order to accommodate any unexpectedly lengthy attribute, the `attribute_value` column is usually a fairly large variable-length string. As a result, the aggregation process may require a significant amount of memory, and in some extreme cases you may run into difficulties if the number of attributes exceeds a few dozen.

Multiple self-joins can often be avoided by retrieving all rows in a single pass, spreading the values across separate columns, and using an aggregate function to collapse the many rows into one.

Columns That Should Have Been Rows

In contrast to the previous design in which rows have been defined for each attribute, another example of poor design occurs where columns are created instead of individual rows. The classic design mistake made by many beginners is to predefine a fixed number of columns for a number of variables, with some of the columns set to null when values are missing. A typical example is illustrated in Figure 11-2, with a very poorly designed movie database (compare this design to the correct design of Figure 8-3 in Chapter 8).

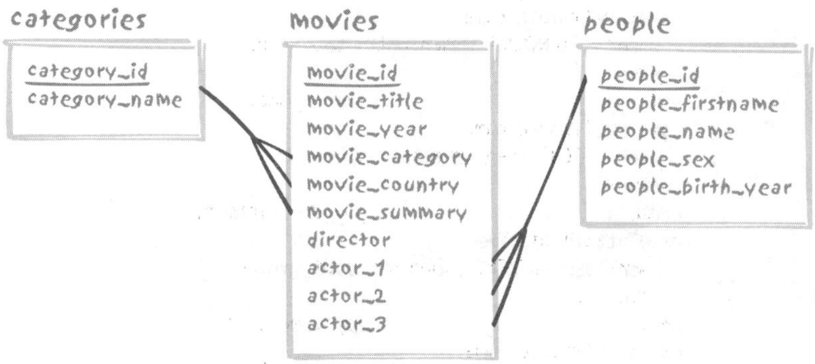

FIGURE 11-2. *A badly designed movie database*

Instead of using a `movie_credits` table as we did in Chapter 8 to link the `movies` table to the `people` table and record the nature of each individual's involvement, the poor design shown in Figure 11-2 assumes that we will never need to record more than a fixed number of lead actors and one director. The first assumption is blatantly wrong and so is the second one since many sketch comedies have had multiple directors. As a representation of reality, this model is plainly flawed, which should already be sufficient reason to discard it. To make matters worse, a poor design, in which data is stored as columns and yet reporting output obviously requires data to be presented as rows, often results in rather confusing queries. Unfortunately, writing queries against poor database designs seems to be as unavoidable as taxes and death in the world of SQL development.

When you want different columns to be displayed as rows, you need a *pivot table*. Pivot tables are used to *pivot*, or turn sideways, tables where we want to see columns as rows. A pivot table is, in the context of SQL databases, a utility table that contains only one column, filled with incrementing values from 1 to whatever is needed. It can be a true table or a view—or even a query embedded in the from clause of a query. Using such a utility table is a favorite old trick of experienced SQL developers, and the next few subsections show how to create and use them.

Creating a pivot table

The constructs you have seen in Chapter 7 for walking trees are usually quite convenient for generating pivot table values; for instance, we can use a recursive with action with those database systems that support it. Here is a DB2 example to generate numbers from 1 to 50:

```
with pivot(row_num)
   -- Generate 50 values
   -- 1 to 50, one value per row
   as (select 1 row_num
      from sysibm.sysdummy1
      union all
      select row_num + 1
      from pivot
      where row_num < 50)
select row_num
from pivot;
```

Similar tricks are of course possible with Oracle's connect by; for instance:*

```
select level
from dual
connect by level <= 50
```

Using one of these constructs inside the from clause of a query can make that query particularly illegible, and it is therefore often advisable to use a regular table as pivot. But a recursive query can be useful to fill the pivot table (an alternate solution to fill a pivot table is to use Cartesian joins between existing tables). Typically, a pivot table would hold something like 1,000 rows.

* Beware that such a construct may not work with some older versions of Oracle.

Multiplying rows with a pivot table

Now that we have a pivot table, what can we do with it? One way to look at a pivot table is to view it as a row-multiplying device. By combining a pivot to a table we want to see pivoted, we repeat each of the rows of the table to be transformed as many times as we wish. Specifying the number of times we want to see one row repeated is simply a matter of adding to the join a limiting condition on the pivot table, for instance:

```
where pivot.row_num <= multiplying value
```

We can thus multiply the three rows in a test `employees` table in a very simple way. First, here are the three rows:

```
SQL> select name, job
  2  from employees;

NAME       JOB
---------- ------------------------------
Tom        Manager
Dick       Software engineer
Harry      Software engineer
```

And now, here is the multiplication, by three, of those rows:

```
SQL> select e.name, e.job, p.row_num
  2  from employees e,
  3       pivot    p
  4  where p.row_num <= 3;

NAME       JOB                               ROW_NUM
---------- ------------------------------ ----------
Tom        Manager                                 1
Dick       Software engineer                       1
Harry      Software engineer                       1
Tom        Manager                                 2
Dick       Software engineer                       2
Harry      Software engineer                       2
Tom        Manager                                 3
Dick       Software engineer                       3
Harry      Software engineer                       3

9 rows selected.
```

It's best to index the only column in the pivot table so as not to fully scan this table when you need to use very few rows from it (as in the preceding example).

Using pivot table values

Besides the mere multiplying effect, the Cartesian join also allows us to associate a unique number in the range 1 to *multiplying value* for every copy of a row of the table we want to pivot. This value is simply the `row_num` column contributed by the `pivot` table, and it will enable us in turn to pick from each copy of a row only partial data. The full process of multiplication of the source rows and selection is illustrated, with a single row, in Figure 11-3. If we want the initial row to finally appear as a single column (which by the way implicitly requires the data types of `col1` ... `coln` to be consistent), we must pick just one column into each of the rows generated by the Cartesian product. By checking the number coming from the `pivot` table, we can specify with a `case` for each resulting row which column is to be displayed to the exclusion of all the others. For instance, we can decide to display `col1` if the value coming from the pivot table is `1`, `col2` if it is `2`, and so on.

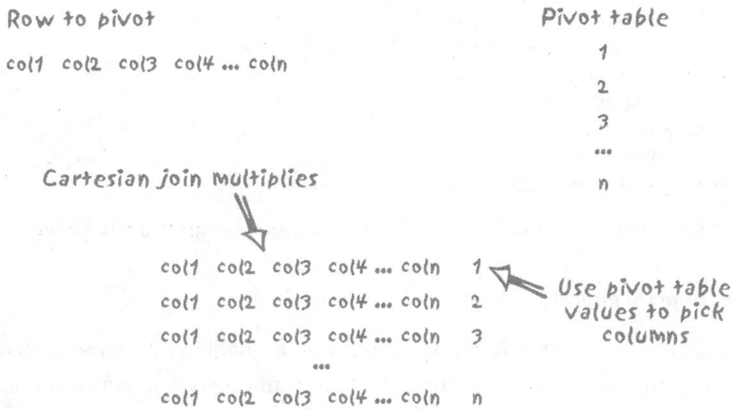

FIGURE 11-3. *Pivoting a row*

Needless to say, multiplying rows and discarding most of the columns we are dealing with is not the most efficient way of processing data; keep in mind that we are rowing upstream. An ideal database design would avoid the need for such multiplication and discarding.

Interestingly, and still in the hypothetical situation of a poor (to put it mildly) database design, a pivot table can in some circumstances bring direct performance benefits. Let's suppose that, in our badly designed movie database, we want to count how many different actors are recorded (note that none of the `actor_...` columns are indexed, and that we therefore have to fetch the values from the table). One way to write this query is to use a `union`:

```
select count(*)
from (select actor_1
      from movies
      union
      select actor_2
      from movies
      union
      select actor_3
      from movies) as m
```

But we can also pivot the table to obtain something that looks more like a select on the movie_credits table of the properly designed database:

```
select count(distinct actor_id)
from --  Use a 3-row pivot to multiply
     --  the number of rows by 3
     --  and return actor_1 the first row in each
     --  set of 3, actor_2 for the second one
     --  and actor_3 for the third one
     (select case pv.row_num
               when 1 then actor_1
               when 2 then actor_2
               else actor_3
             end actor_id
      from movies as m,
           pivot as pv
      where pv.row_num <= 3) as m
```

The second version runs about twice as fast as the first one—significantly faster.

The pivot and unpivot operators

As a possibly sad acknowledgment of the generally poor quality of database designs, SQL Server 2005 has introduced two operators called pivot and unpivot to perform the toppling of rows into columns and vice-versa, respectively. The previous employee_attributes example can be written as follows using the pivot operator:

```
select entity_id as employee_id,
       [lastname],
       [firstname],
       [job],
       [department],
       [salary]
from employee_attributes as employees
     pivot (max(attribute_value)
            for attribute_name in ([lastname],
                                   [firstname],
                                   [job],
                                   [department],
                                   [salary])
               as pivoted_employees
order by 2
```

The specific values in the attribute_name column that we want to appear as columns are listed in the for ... in clause, using a particular syntax that transforms the character data into column identifiers. There is an implicit group by applied to all the columns from employee_attributes that are not referenced in the pivot clause; we must be careful if we have other columns (for instance, an attribute_type column) than entity_id, as they may require an additional aggregation layer.

The unpivot operator performs the reverse operation, and allows us to see the link between movie and actor as a more logical collection of (movie_id, actor_id) pairs by writing:

```
select movie_id, actor_type, actor_id
from movies
     unpivot (actor_id for actor_type in ([actor_1],
                                          [actor_2],
                                          [actor_3])) as movie_actors
```

Note that this query doesn't exactly produce the result we want, since it introduces the name of the original column as a virtual actor_type column. There is no need to qualify actors as actor_1, actor_2, or actor_3, and once again the query may need to be wrapped into another query that only returns movie_id and actor_id.

The use of a pivot table, or of the pivot and unpivot operators, is a very interesting technique that can help extricate us from more than one quagmire. The support for pivoting operators by major database systems is not, of course, to be interpreted as an endorsement of bad design, but as an example of *realpolitik*.

Pivot tables and operators can be a useful technique in their own right, but they should never be used as a means of glossing over the inadequacies of a bad design.

Single Columns That Should Have Been Something Else

Some designers of our movie database may well have been sensitive to the limitation on the number of actors we may associate with one movie. Trying to solve design issues with a creative use of irrelevant techniques, someone may have come up with a "bright idea": what about storing the actor identifiers as a comma-separated string in one wide actors column? For instance:

```
first actor id, second actor id, ...
```

And so much for the first normal form.... The big design mistake here is to store several pieces of data that we need to handle one by one into one column. There would be no issue if a complex string—for instance a lengthy XML message—were considered as an opaque object by the DBMS and handled as if it were an atomic item. But that's not the case here. Here we have several values in one column, and we *do* want to treat and manipulate each value individually. We are in trouble.

There are only two workable solutions with a creative design of this sort:

- Scrapping it and rewriting everything. This is, of course, by far the best solution.
- When delays, costs, and politics require a fast solution, the only way out may be to apply a creative SQL solution; once again, let me state that "solution" is probably not the best choice of words in this case, "fix" would be a better description.

I'll also point out that a more elaborate version of the same mistake could use an "XML type" column; I am going to use simple character-string manipulation functions in my example, but they could as well be XML-extracting functions.

> **NOTE**
>
> Be warned: "creative SQL" is often a euphemism for ugly SQL!

First normal form on the fly

Our problem is to extract various individual components from a string of characters and return them one by one on separate rows. This is easier with some database systems (for instance, Oracle has a very rich set of string functions that noticeably eases the work) than with others. Conventions such as systematically starting or ending the string with a comma may further help us. We are not wimps, but real SQL developers, and we are therefore going to take the north face route and assume the worst:

1. First, let's assume that our lists of identifiers are in the following form:

   ```
   id1,id2,id3, ..., idn
   ```
2. Second, we shall also assume that the only sets of functions at our disposal are those common to the major database systems. We shall use Transact-SQL for our example and only use built-in functions. As you will see, a well-designed user function might ease both the writing and the performance of the resulting query.

Let's start with a (very small) `movies` table in which a list of actor identifiers is (wrongly) stored as an attribute of the movie:

```
1> select movie_id, actors
2> from movies
3> go
 movie_id             actors
 -------------------- ---------------------------------------
                    1 123,456,78,96
                    2 23,67,97
                    3 67,456

(3 rows affected)
```

The first step is to use as many rows from our pivot table as we may have characters in the `actors` string—arbitrarily set to a maximum length of 50 characters. We are going to multiply the number of rows in the `movies` table by this number, 50. We would naturally be rather reluctant to do something similar on millions of rows (as an aside, a function allowing us to return the position of the *n*th separator or the *n*th item in the string would make it necessary to multiply only by the maximum number of identifiers we can encounter, instead of by the maximum string length).

Our next move is to use the substring( ) function to successively get subsets (that can be null) of actors, starting at the first character, then moving to the second, and so forth, up to the last character (at most, the 50th character). We just have to use the row_num value from the pivot table to find the starting character of each substring. If we take for instance the string from the actors column that is associated to the movie identified by the value 1 for movie_id, we shall get something like:

```
123,456,78,96  associated to the row_num value 1
23,456,78,96   associated to the row_num value 2
3,456,78,96    associated to the row_num value 3
,456,78,96      ....
456,78,96
56,78,96
6,78,96
,78,96
78,96
....
```

We'll compute these subsets in a column that we'll call substring1. Having these successive substrings, we can now check the position of the first comma in them. Our next move is to return as a column called substring2 the content of substring1 shifted by one position. We also locate the position of the first comma in substring2. These operations are illustrated in Figure 11-4. Among the various resulting rows, the only ones to be of interest are those marking the beginning of a new identifier in the string: the first row in the series that is associated with the row_num value of 1, and all the rows for which we find a comma in first position of substring1. For all these rows, the position of the comma in substring2 tells us the length of the identifier that we are trying to isolate.

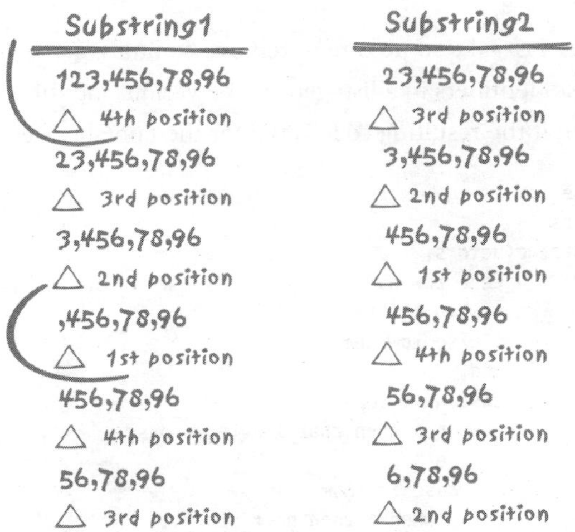

FIGURE 11-4. *Splitting-up a comma separated list*

Translated into SQL code, here is what we get:

```
1> select row_num,
2>        movie_id,
3>        actors,
4>        first_sep,
5>        next_sep
6> from (select row_num,
7>              movie_id,
8>              actors,
9>              charindex(',', substring(actors, row_num,
10>                                      char_length(actors))) first_sep,
11>             charindex(',', substring(actors, row_num + 1,
12>                                    char_length(actors))) + 1 next_sep
13>      from movies,
14>           pivot
15>     where row_num <= 50) as q
16> where row_num = 1
17>    or first_sep = 1
18> go
 row_num     movie_id       actors              first_sep   next_sep
 ----------- -------------- ------------------- ----------- -----------
           1              1 123,456,78,96                 4           4
           4              1 123,456,78,96                 1           5
           8              1 123,456,78,96                 1           4
          11              1 123,456,78,96                 1           1
           1              2 23,67,97                      3           3
           3              2 23,67,97                      1           4
           6              2 23,67,97                      1           1
           1              3 67,456                        3           3
           3              3 67,456                        1           1

(9 rows affected)
```

If we accept that we must take some care to remove commas, and the particular cases of both the first and last identifiers in a list, getting the various identifiers is then reasonably straightforward, even if the resulting code is not for the faint-hearted:

```
1> select movie_id,
2>        actors,
3>        substring(actors,
4>                  case row_num
5>                    when 1 then 1
6>                    else row_num + 1
7>                  end,
8>                  case next_sep
9>                    when 1 then char_length(actors)
10>                   else
11>                     case row_num
12>                       when 1 then next_sep - 1
13>                       else next_sep - 2
14>                     end
15>                 end) as id
16> from (select row_num,
```

```
                 movie_id,
                 actors,
                 first_sep,
                 next_sep
          from (select row_num,
                       movie_id,
                       actors,
                       charindex(',', substring(actors, row_num,
                                 char_length(actors))) first_sep,
                       charindex(',', substring(actors, row_num + 1,
                                 char_length(actors))) + 1 next_sep
                from movies,
                     pivot
                where row_num <= 50) as q
          where row_num = 1
             or first_sep = 1) as q2
go
 movie_id         actors                          id
 ---------------- ------------------------------- -----------------
                1 123,456,78,96                   123
                1 123,456,78,96                   456
                1 123,456,78,96                   78
                1 123,456,78,96                   96
                2 23,67,97                        23
                2 23,67,97                        67
                2 23,67,97                        97
                3 67,456                          67
                3 67,456                          456

(9 rows affected)
```

We could have made the code slightly simpler by prepending and appending a comma to the actors column. I leave doing that as an exercise for the undaunted reader. Note that as the left alignment shows, the resulting id column is a string and should be explicitly converted to numeric before joining to the table that stores the actors' names.

The preceding case, besides being an interesting example of solving a SQL problem by successively wrapping queries, also comes as a healthy warning of what awaits us on the SQL side of things when tables are poorly designed.

Lifting the veil on the Chapter 7 mystery path explosion

You may remember that in Chapter 7 I described the materialized path model for tree representations. In that chapter I noted that it would be extremely convenient if we could "explode" a materialized path into the different materialized paths of all its ancestors. The advantage of this method is that when we want to walk a hierarchy from the bottom up, we can make efficient use of the index that should hopefully exist on the materialized path. If we don't "explode" the materialized path, the only way we have to find the ancestors of a given row is to specify a condition such as:

```
and offspring.materialized_path
    like concat(ancestor.materialized_path, '%')
```

Sadly, this is a construct that cannot use the index (for reasons that are quite similar to those in the credit card prefix problem of Chapter 8).

How can we "explode" the materialized path? The time has come to explain how we can pull that rabbit out of the hat. Since our node will have, in the general case, several ancestors, the very first thing we have to do is to multiply the rows by the number of preceding generations. In this way we'll be able to extract from the materialized path of our initial row (for example the row that represents the Hussar regiment under the command of Colonel de Marbot) the paths of the various ancestors. As always, the solution for multiplying rows is to use a pivot table. If we do it this time with MySQL, there is a function called `substring_index( )` that very conveniently returns the substring of its first argument from the beginning up to the third argument occurrence of the second argument (hopefully, the example is easier to understand). To know how many rows we need from the `pivot` table, we just compute how many elements we have in the path in exactly the same way that we computed the depth in Chapter 7, namely by comparing the length of the path to the length of the same when separators have been stripped off. Here is the query, and the results:

```
mysql>  select mp.materialized_path,
    ->         substring_index( mp.materialized_path, '.', p.row_num )
    ->                                  as ancestor_path
    -> from materialized_path_model as mp,
    ->      pivot as p
    -> where mp.commander = 'Colonel de Marbot'
    ->   and p.row_num <= 1 + length( mp.materialized_path )
    ->                   - length(replace(mp.materialized_path, '.', ''));
+-------------------+---------------+
| materialized_path | ancestor_path |
+-------------------+---------------+
| F.1.5.1.1         | F             |
| F.1.5.1.1         | F.1           |
| F.1.5.1.1         | F.1.5         |
| F.1.5.1.1         | F.1.5.1       |
| F.1.5.1.1         | F.1.5.1.1     |
+-------------------+---------------+
5 rows in set (0.00 sec)
```

Querying with a Variable in List

There is another, and rather important, use of pivot tables that I must now mention. In previous chapters I have underlined the importance of *binding variables*, in other words of passing parameters to SQL queries. Variable binding allows the DBMS kernel to skip the parsing phase (in other words, the compilation of the statement) after it has done it once. Keep in mind that parsing includes steps as potentially costly as the search for the best execution path. Even when SQL statements are dynamically constructed, it is quite possible, as you have seen in Chapter 8, to pass variables to them. There is, however, one difficult case: when the end user can make multiple choices out of a combo box and pass a variable number of parameters for use in an in list. The selection of multiple values raises several issues:

- Dynamically binding a variable number of parameters may not be possible with all languages (often you must bind all variables at once, not one by one) and will, in any case, be rather difficult to code.
- If the number of parameters is different for almost every call, two statements that only differ by the number of bind variables will be considered to be different statements by the DBMS, and we shall lose the benefit of variable binding.

The ability provided by pivot tables to split a string allows us to pass a list of values as a single string to the statement, irrespective of the actual number of values. This is what I am going to demonstrate with Oracle in this section.

The following example shows how most developers would approach the problem of passing a list of values to an in list when that list of values is contained within a single string. In our case the string is v_list, and most developers would concatenate several strings together, including v_list, to produce a complete select statement:

```
v_statement := 'select count(order_id)'
               || ' from order_detail'
               || ' where article_id in ('
               || v_list || ')';
execute immediate v_statement into n_count;
```

This example looks dynamic, but for the DBMS it's in fact all hardcoded. Two successive executions will each be different statements, both of which will have to be parsed before execution. Can we pass v_list as a parameter to the statement, instead of concatenating it into the statement? We can, by applying exactly the same techniques to the comma-separated value stored in variable v_list as we have applied to the comma-separated value stored in column actors in the example of on-the-fly normalization. A pivot table allows us to write the following somewhat wilder SQL statement:

```
select count(od.order_id)
into n_count
from order_detail od,
     (  -- Return at many rows as we have items in the list
        -- and use character functions to return the nth item
        -- on the nth row
      select to_number(substr(v_list,
                              case row_num
                                when 1 then 1
                                else 1 + instr(v_list, ',', 1, row_num - 1)
                              end,
                              case instr(v_list, ',', 1, row_num)
                                when 0 then length(v_list)
                                else
```

```
                                    case row_num
                                      when 1  then instr(v_list, ',',
                                                         1, row_num) - 1
                                      else instr(v_list, ',', 1, row_num) - 1
                                           - instr(v_list, ',',
                                                   1, row_num - 1)
                                    end
                                  end)) article_id
          from pivot
          where instr(v_list||',', ',', 1, row_num) > 0
            and row_num <= 250) x
    where od.article_id = x.article_id;
```

You may need, if you are really motivated, to study this query a bit to figure out how it all works. The mechanism is all based on repeated use of the Oracle function `instr()`. Let me just say that this function `instr(`*`haystack`*`, `*`needle`*`, `*`from_pos`*`, `*`count`*`)` returns the *`count`*th occurrence of *`needle`* in *`haystack`* starting at position *`from_pos`* (`0` is returned when nothing is found), but the logic is exactly the same as with the previous examples.

I have run the pivot and hardcoded versions of the query successively 1, 10, 100, 1,000, 10,000, and 100,000 times. Each time, I randomly generated a list of from 1 to 250 `v_list` values. The results are shown in Figure 11-5, and they are telling: the "pivoted" list is 30% faster as soon as the query is repeatedly executed.

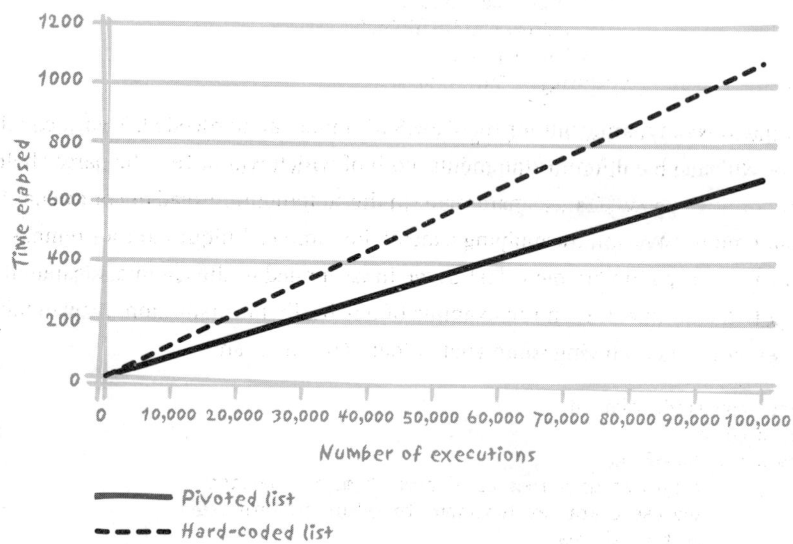

FIGURE 11-5. *Performance of a hardcoded list versus a list transformed with a pivot table*

Remember that the execution of a hardcoded query requires parsing and then execution, while a query that takes parameters (bind variables) can be re-executed subsequently for only a marginal cost of the first execution. Even if this later query is noticeably more complicated, as long as the execution is faster than execution *plus* parsing for the hardcoded query, the later query wins hands-down in terms of performance.

There are actually two other benefits that don't show up in Figure 11-5:

- Parsing is a very CPU-intensive operation. If CPU happens to be the bottleneck, hard-coded queries can be extremely detrimental to other queries.
- SQL statements are cached whether they contain parameters or whether they are totally hardcoded, because you can imagine having hardcoded statements that are repeatedly executed by different users, and it makes sense for the SQL engine to anticipate such a situation. To take, once again, the movie database example, even if the names of actors are hardcoded, a query referring to a very popular actor or actress could be executed a large number of times.* The SQL engine will therefore cache hardcoded statements like the others. Unfortunately, a repeatedly executed hardcoded statement is the exception rather than the rule. As a result, a succession of dynamically built hardcoded statements that may each be executed only once or a very few times will all accumulate in the cache before being overwritten as a result of the normal cache management activity. This cache management will require more work and is therefore an additional price to pay.

Aggregating by Range (Bands)

Some people have trouble writing SQL queries that return aggregates for bands. Such queries are actually quite easy to write using the `case` construct. By way of example, look at the problem of reporting on the distribution of tables by their total row counts. For instance, how many tables contain fewer than 100 rows, how many contain 100 to 10,000 rows, how many 10,000 to 1,000,000 rows, and how many tables store more than 1,000,000 rows?

Information about tables is usually accessible through data dictionary views: for instance, `INFORMATION_SCHEMA.TABLES`, `pg_statistic`, and `pg_tables`, `dba_tables`, `syscat.tables`, `sysobjects` and `systabstats`, and so on. In my explanation here, I'll assume the general case of a view named `table_info`, containing, among other things, the columns `table_name` and `row_count`. Using this table, a simple use of `case` and the suitable `group by` can give us the distribution by `row_count` that we are after:

```
select case
         when row_count < 100
              then 'Under 100 rows'
          when row_count >= 100 and row_count < 10000
              then '100 to 10000'
          when row_count >= 10000 and row_count < 1000000
              then '10000 to 1000000'
          else
              'Over 1000000 rows'
        end as range,
        count(*) as table_count
from table_info
```

* Actually, the best optimization tactic in this particular case would be to cache the result of the query rather than the query.

```
where row_count is not null
group by case
          when row_count < 100
               then 'Under 100 rows'
          when row_count >= 100 and row_count < 10000
               then '100 to 10000'
          when row_count >= 10000 and row_count < 1000000
               then '10000 to 1000000'
          else
               'Over 1000000 rows'
        end
```

There is only one snag here: group by performs a sort before aggregating data. Since we are associating a label with each of our aggregates, the result is, by default, alphabetically sorted on that label:

```
RANGE             TABLE_COUNT
----------------- ------------
100 to 10000                18
10000 to 1000000            15
Over 1000000 rows            6
Under 100 rows              24
```

The ordering that would be logical to a human eye in such a case is to see *Under 100 rows* appear first, and then each band by increasing number of rows, with *Over 1,000,000 rows* coming last. Rather than trying to be creative with labels, the stratagem to solve this problem consists of two steps:

1. Performing the group by on two, instead of one, columns, associating with each label a dummy column, the only purpose of which is to serve as a sort key
2. Wrapping up the query as a query within the from clause, so as to mask the sort key thus created and ensure that only the data of interest is returned

Here is the query that results from applying the preceding two steps:

```
select row_range, table_count
from ( -- Build a sort key to have bands suitably ordered
       -- and hide it inside a subquery
       select case
                when row_count < 100
                  then 1
                when row_count >= 100 and row_count < 10000
                  then 2
                when row_count >= 10000 and row_count < 1000000
                  then 3
                else
                  4
              end as sortkey,
              case
                when row_count < 100
                  then 'Under 100 rows'
                when row_count >= 100 and row_count < 10000
                  then '100 to 10000'
```

```
                when row_count >= 10000 and row_count < 1000000
                  then '10000 to 1000000'
                else
                  'Over 1000000 rows'
              end  as row_range,
              count(*) as table_count
      from table_info
      where row_count is not null
      group by case
                 when row_count < 100
                   then 'Under 100 rows'
                 when row_count >= 100 and row_count < 10000
                   then '100 to 10000'
                 when row_count >= 10000 and row_count < 1000000
                   then '10000 to 1000000'
                 else
                   'Over 1000000 rows'
               end,
               case
                 when row_count < 100
                   then 1
                 when row_count >= 100 and row_count < 10000
                   then 2
                 when row_count >= 10000 and row_count < 1000000
                   then 3
                 else
                   4
               end) dummy
order by sortkey;
```

And following are the results from executing that query:

```
ROW_RANGE         TABLE_COUNT
----------------- -----------
Under 100 rows             24
100 to 10000               18
10000 to 1000000           15
Over 1000000 rows           6
```

Aggregating by range (bands) requires building an artificial sort key to display results in desired order.

Superseding a General Case

The technique of hiding a sort key within a query in the `from` clause, which I used in the previous section to display bands, can also be helpful in other situations. A particularly important case is when a table contains the definition of a general rule that happens to be superseded from time to time by a particular case defined in another table. I'll illustrate by example.

I mentioned in Chapter 1 that the handling of various addresses is a difficult issue. Let's take the case of an online retailer, one that knows at most two addresses for each customer: a billing address and a shipping address. In most cases, the two addresses are the same. The retailer has decided to store the mandatory billing address in the customers table and to associate the customer_id identifier with the various components of the address (line_1, line_2, city, state, postal_code, country) in a different shipping_addresses table for those few customers for whom the two addresses differ.

The wrong way to get the shipping address when you know the customer identifier is to execute two queries:

1. Look for a row in shipping_addresses.
2. If nothing is found, then query customers.

An alternate way to approach this problem is to apply an outer join on shipping_addresses and customers. You will then get two addresses, one of which will in most cases be a suite of null values. Either you check programmatically if you indeed have a valid shipping address, which is a bad solution, or you might imagine using the coalesce( ) function that returns its first non-null argument:

```
select ... coalesce(shipping_address.line_1, customers.line_1), ...
```

Such a use of coalesce( ) would be a very dangerous idea, because it implicitly assumes that all addresses have exactly the same number of non-null components. If you suppose that you do indeed have a different shipping address, but that its line_2 component is null while the line_2 component of the billing address is not, you may end up with a resulting invalid address that borrows components from both the shipping and billing addresses. A correct approach is to use case to check for a mandatory component from the address—which admittedly can result in a somewhat difficult to read query. An even better solution is probably to use the "hidden sort key" technique, combined with a limit on the number of rows returned (select top 1 ..., limit 1, where rownum = 1 or similar, depending on the DBMS) and write the query as follows:

```
select *
from (select 1 as sortkey,
             line_1,
             line_2,
             city,
             state,
             postal_code,
             country
      from shipping_addresses
      where customer_id = ?
      union
      select 2 as sortkey,
             line_1,
```

```
                line_2,
                city,
                state,
                postal_code,
                country
          from customers
          where customer_id = ?
          order by 1) actual_shipping_address
    limit 1
```

The basic idea is to use the sort key as a preference indicator. The limit set on the number of rows returned will therefore ensure that we'll always get the "best match" (note that similar ideas can be applied to several rows when a `row_number()` OLAP function is available). This approach greatly simplifies processing on the application program side, since what is retrieved from the DBMS is "certified correct" data.

The technique I've just described can also be used in multilanguage applications where not everything has been translated into all languages. When you need to fetch a message, you can define a default language and be assured that you will always get at least some message, thus removing the need for additional coding on the application side.

Selecting Rows That Match Several Items in a List

An interesting problem is that of how to write queries based on some criteria referring to a varying list of values. This case is best illustrated by looking for employees who have certain skills, using the three tables shown in Figure 11-6. The `skillset` table links employees to skills, associating a 1 to 3 `skill_level` value to distinguish between honest competency, strong experience, and outright wizardry.

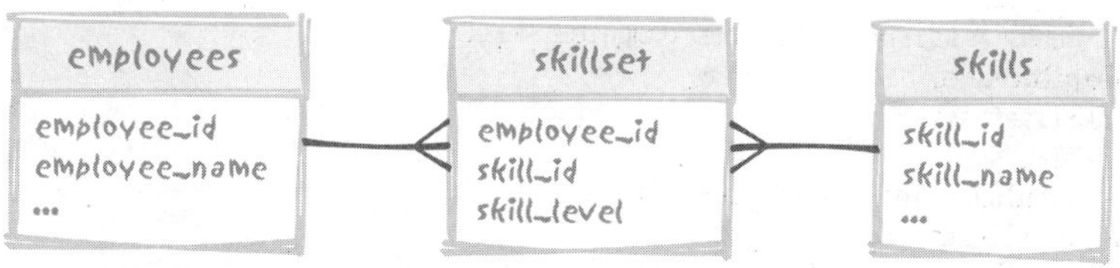

FIGURE 11-6. *Tables used for querying employee skills*

Finding employees that have a level 2 or 3 SQL skill is easy enough:

```
select e.employee_name
from employees e
where e.employee_id in
     (select ss.employee_id
      from skillset ss,
           skills s
      where s.skill_id = ss.skill_id
        and s.skill_name = 'SQL'
        and ss.skill_level >= 2)
order by e.employee_name
```

(We can also write the preceding query with a simple join.) If we want to retrieve the employees who are competent with Oracle or DB2, all we need to do is write:

```
select e.employee_name, s.skill_name, ss.skill_level
from employees e,
     skillset ss,
     skills s
where e.employee_id = ss.employee_id
  and s.skill_id = ss.skill_id
  and s.skill_name in ('ORACLE', 'DB2')
order by e.employee_name
```

No need to test for the skill level, since we will accept any level. However, we do need to display the skill name; otherwise, we won't be able to tell why a particular employee was returned by the query. We also encounter a first difficulty, namely that people who are competent in both Oracle and DB2 will appear twice. What we can try to do is to aggregate skills by employee. Unfortunately, not all SQL dialects provide an aggregate function for concatenating strings (you can sometimes write it as a user-defined aggregate function, though). We can nevertheless perform a skill aggregate by using the simple stratagem of a *double conversion*. First we convert our value from string to number, then from number back to string once we have aggregated numbers.

Skill levels are in the 1 through 3 range. We can therefore confidently represent any combination of Oracle and DB2 skills by a two-digit number, assigning for instance the first digit to DB2 and the second one to Oracle. This is easily done as follows:

```
select e.employee_name,
       (case s.skill_name
          when 'DB2' then 10
          else 1
        end) * ss.skill_level as computed_skill_level
from employees e,
     skillset ss,
     skills s
where e.employee_id = ss.employee_id
  and s.skill_id = ss.skill_id
  and s.skill_name in ('ORACLE', 'DB2')
```

computed_skill_level will result in 10, 20, or 30 for DB2 skill levels, while Oracle skill levels will remain 1, 2, and 3. We then can very easily aggregate our skill levels, and convert them back to a more friendly description:

```
select employee_name,
       -- Decode the numerically encoded skill + skill level combination
       -- Tens are DB2 skill levels, and units Oracle skill levels
      case
        when aggr_skill_level >= 10
          then 'DB2:' + str(round(aggr_skill_level/10,0)) + ' '
      end
      + case
          when aggr_skill_level % 10 > 0
           then 'Oracle:' + str(aggr_skill_level % 10)
       end as skills
```

```
from (select e.employee_name,
             -- Numerically encode skill + skill level
             -- so that we can aggregate them
             sum((case s.skill_name
                    when 'DB2' then 10
                    else 1
                  end) * ss.skill_level)  as aggr_skill_level
      from employees e,
           skillset ss,
           skills s
      where e.employee_id = ss.employee_id
        and s.skill_id = ss.skill_id
        and s.skill_name in ('ORACLE', 'DB2')
     group by e.employee_name) as encoded_skills
order by employee_name
```

But now let's try to answer a more difficult question. Suppose that the project we want to staff happens to be a migration from one DBMS to another one. Instead of finding people who know Oracle or DB2, we want people who know both Oracle and DB2.

We have several ways to answer such a question. If the SQL dialect we are using supports it, the `intersect` operator is one solution: we find people who are skilled on Oracle on one hand, people who are skilled on DB2 on the other hand, and keep the happy few that belong to both sets. We certainly can also write the very same query with an `in()`:

```
select e.employee_name
from employees e,
     skillset ss,
     skills s
where s.skill_name = 'ORACLE'
  and s.skill_id = ss.skill_id
  and ss.employee_id = e.employee_id
  and e.employee_id in (select ss2.employee_id
                        from skillset ss2,
                             skills s2
                        where s2.skill_name = 'DB2'
                          and s2.skill_id = ss2.skill_id)
```

We can also use the *double conversion* solution and filter on the numerical aggregate by using the same expressions as we have been using for decoding the `encoded_skills` computed column. The double conversion stratagem has other advantages:

- It hits tables only once.
- It makes it easier to handle more complicated questions such as "people who know Oracle and Java, or MySQL and PHP."
- As we are only using a list of skills, we can use a pivot table and bind the list, thus improving performance of oft-repeated queries. The `row_num` pivot table column can help us encode since, if the list is reasonably short, we can multiply the `skill_level` value by 10 raised to the (`row_num` –1)th power. If we don't care about the exact value of the skill level, and our DBMS implements bit-wise aggregate functions, we can even try to dynamically build a bit-map.

Finding the Best Match

Let's conclude our adventures in the SQL wilderness by combining several of the techniques shown in this chapter and try to select employees on the basis of some rather complex and fuzzy conditions. We want to find, from among our employees, that one member of staff who happens to be the best candidate for a project that requires a range of skills across several different environments (for example, Java, .NET, PHP, and SQL Server). The ideal candidate is a guru in all environments; but if we issue a query asking for the highest skill level everywhere it shall probably return no row. In the absence of the ideal candidate, we are usually left with imperfect candidates, and we must identify someone who has the best competency in as many of our environments as possible and is therefore the best suited for the project. For instance, if our Java guru is a world expert, but knows nothing of PHP, that person is unlikely to be selected.

"Best suited" implies a comparison between the various employees, or, in other words, a sort, from which the winner will emerge. Since we want only one winner, we shall have to limit the output of our list of candidates to the first row. You should already be beginning to see the query as a `select ... from (select ... order by) limit 1` or whatever your SQL dialect permits.

The big question is, of course, how we are going to order the employees. Who is going to get the preference between one who has a decent knowledge of three of the specified topics, and one who is an acknowledged guru of two subjects? It is likely, in a case such as we are discussing, that the width of knowledge is what matters more to us than the depth of knowledge. We can use a major sort key on the number of skills from the requirement list that are mastered, and a minor sort key on the sum of the various `skill_level` values by employee for the skills in the requirement list. Our inner query comes quite naturally:

```
select e.employee_name,
       count(ss.skill_id) as major_key,
       sum(ss.skill_level) as minor_key
from employees e,
     skillset ss,
     skills s
where s.skill_name in ('JAVA', '.NET', 'PHP', 'SQL SERVER')
  and s.skill_id = ss.skill_id
  and ss.employee_id = e.employee_id
group by e.employee_name
order by 2, 3
```

This query, however, doesn't tell us anything about the actual skill level of our best candidate. We should therefore combine this query with a double conversion to get an encoding of skills. I leave doing that as an exercise, assuming that you have not yet reached a semi-comatose state.

You should also note, from a performance standpoint, that we need not refer to the employees table in the inner query. The employee name is information that we need only when we display the final result. We should therefore handle only employee_id values, and do the bulk of the processing using the tables skills and skillset. You should also think about the rare situation in which two candidates have exactly the same skills—do you really want to restrict output to one row?

> **NOTE**
>
> To paraphrase General Robert E. Lee, "It is well that SQL is so terrible, or we should grow too fond of it."

Optimizer Directives

I shall conclude this chapter with a cautionary note about optimizer directives. An SQL optimizer can be compared to the program that computes shutter speed and exposure in an automated camera. There are conditions when the "auto" mode is no longer appropriate—for instance, when the subject of the picture is backlit or for the shooting of night scenes. Similarly, all database systems provide one way or another to override or at least direct decisions taken by the query optimizer in its quest for the Dream Execution Path. There are basically two techniques to constrain the optimizer:

- Special settings in the session environment that are applied to all queries executed in the session until further notice.
- Local directives explicitly written into individual statements.

In the latter case the syntax between products varies, since you may have these directives written as an inherent part of the SQL statement (for instance `force index(...)` with MySQL or `option loop join` with Transact-SQL), or written as a special syntax comment (such as `/*+ all_rows */` with Oracle).

Optimizer directives have so far been mostly absent from this book, and for good reasons. Repeatedly executing queries against living data is, to some degree, similar to repeatedly photographing the same subject at various times of day: what is backlit in the morning may be in full light in the afternoon. Directives are destined to override particular quirks in the behavior of the optimizer and are better left alone. The most admissible directives are those directives specifying either the expected outcome, such as `sql_small_result` or `sql_big_result` with MySQL, or whether we are more interested in a fast answer, as is generally the case in transactional processing, with directives such as `option fast 100` with SQL Server or `/*+ first_rows(100) */` with Oracle. These directives, which we could compare to the "landscape" or "sports" mode of a camera, provide the optimizer with information that it would not otherwise be able to gather. They are directives that don't depend on the volume or distribution of data; they are therefore stable in time, and they do add value. In any case, even directives that add value should not be employed unless they are required. The optimizer is able to determine a great deal about the best way to proceed when it is given a properly written query in the first place. The best and most simple example of implicit guidance of the optimizer is possibly the use of correlated versus uncorrelated subqueries. They are to be used under dissimilar circumstances to achieve functionally identical results.

One of the nicest features of database optimizers is their ability to adapt to changing circumstances. Freezing their behavior by using constraining directives is indicative of a very short-term view that can be potentially damaging to performance in the future. Some directives are real time-bombs, such as those specifying indexes by name. If, for one reason or another a DBA renames an index used in a directive, the result can be disastrous. We can get a similarly catastrophic effect when a directive specifies a composite index, and this index is rebuilt one day with a different column order.

NOTE

Optimizer directives must be considered the private territory of database administrators. The DBA should use them to cope with the shortcomings of a particular DBMS release and then remove them if at all possible after the next upgrade.

Let me add that it is common to see inexperienced developers trying to derive a query from an existing one. When the original query contains directives, beginners rarely bother to question whether these directives are appropriate to their new case. Beginners simply apply what they see as minor changes to the select list and the search criteria. As a result, you end up with queries that look like they have been fine-tuned, but that often follow a totally irrelevant execution path.

The good plan that is forced upon a query today may be disastrous tomorrow.

CHAPTER TWELVE

Employment of Spies

Monitoring Performance

And he that walketh in darkness knoweth not whither he goeth.

Gospel according to St. John, 12:35

Intelligence gathering has always been an essential part of war. All database systems include monitoring facilities, each with varying degrees of sophistication. Third-party offerings are also available in some cases. All these monitoring facilities are primarily aimed at database administrators. However, when they allow you to really see what is going on inside the SQL engine, they can become formidable spies in the service of the performance-conscious developer. I should note that when monitoring facilities lack the level of detail we require, it is usually possible to obtain additional information by turning on logging or tracing. Logging or tracing necessarily entails a significant overhead, which may not be a very desirable extra load on a busy production server that is already painfully clunking along. But during performance testing, logging can provide us with a wealth of information on what to expect in production.

Detailing all or even some of the various monitoring facilities available would be both tedious and product-specific. Furthermore, such an inventory would be rapidly outdated. I shall concentrate instead on what we should monitor and why. This will provide you with an excellent opportunity for a final review of some of the key concepts introduced in previous chapters.

The Database Is Slow

Let's first try to define the major categories of performance issues that we are likely to encounter in production—since our goal, as developers, is to anticipate and, if possible, avoid these situations. The very first manifestation of a performance issue on a production database is often a call to the database administrators' desk to say that "the database is slow" (a useful piece of information for database administrators who may have hundreds of database servers in their care...). In a well-organized shop, the DBA will be able to check whether a monitoring tool does indeed report something unusual, and if that is the case, will be able to answer confidently "I know. We are working on the case." In a poorly organized shop, the DBA may well give the same answer, lying diplomatically.

In all cases, the end of the call will mean the beginning of a frantic scramble for clues.

Such communications stating that "the database is slow" will usually have been motivated by one of the five following reasons:

It's not the database

The network is stuttering or the host is totally overloaded by something else. Thanks for calling.

Sudden global sluggishness

All tasks slow down, suddenly, for all users. There are two cases to consider here:

- Either the performance degradation is really sudden, in which case it can often be traced to some system or DBMS change (software upgrade, parameter adjustment, or hardware configuration modification).
- Or it results from a sudden inflow of queries.

The first case is not a development issue, just one of those hazards that make the life of a systems engineer or DBA so exciting. The second case *is* a development or specifications issue. Remember the post office of Chapter 9: when customers arrive faster than they can be serviced, queues lengthen and performance tumbles down all of a sudden. Either the original specifications were tailored too tightly and the system is facing a load it wasn't designed for, or the application has been insufficiently stress-tested. In many cases, improving some key queries will massively decrease the average service time and may improve the situation for a negligible fraction of the cost of a hardware upgrade. Sudden global sluggishness is usually characterized by the first phone call being followed by many others.

Sudden localized slowness

If one particular task slows down all of a sudden, locking issues should be considered. Database administrators can monitor locks and confirm that several tasks are competing for the same resources. This situation is a development and task-scheduling issue that can be improved by trying to release locks faster.

A slow degradation of performance reaching a threshold

The threshold may first be felt by one hypersensitive user. If the load has been steadily increasing over time, the crossing of the threshold may be a warning sign of an impending catastrophe and may relate to the lengthening service queues of a sudden global sluggishness. The crossing of a threshold may also be linked to the size increase of badly indexed tables or to a degradation of physical storage after heavy delete/update operations (hanging high-water mark of a table that has inflated then deflated, a Swiss cheese–like effect resulting in much too many pages or blocks to store the data, or chaining to overflow areas). If the problem is with indexes or physical storage (or outdated statistics taking the optimizer down a wrong path), a DBA may be able to help, but the necessity for a rescue operation on a regular basis is usually the sign of poorly designed processes.

One particularly slow query

If the application was properly tested, then the case to watch for is a dynamically built query provided with a highly unusual set of criteria. This is most likely to be a pure development issue.

Many of these events can be foreseen and prevented. If you are able to identify what loads your server, and if you are able to relate database activity to business activity, you have all the required elements to identify the weakest spots in an application. You can then focus on those weak spots during performance testing and improve them.

To anticipate live application performance, you must monitor activity very closely during stress tests and user acceptance trials.

The Components of Server Load

Load, in information technology, ultimately boils down to a combination of excessive CPU consumption, too many input/output operations and insufficient network speed or bandwidth. It's quite similar to the "critical tasks" of project management, where one bottleneck can result in the whole system grinding not to a halt, but to an unnaceptable level of slowness. If processes that are ready to run must wait for some other processes to release the CPU, the system is overloaded. If the CPU is idle, waiting for data to be sent across the network or to be fetched from persistent storage, the system is overloaded too.

"Overloaded," though, mustn't be understood as an absolute notion. Systems may be compared to human beings in respect of the fact that load is not always directly proportional to the work accomplished. As C. Northcote Parkinson remarked in *Parkinson's Law*, his famous satire of bureaucratic institutions:

> Thus, an elderly lady of leisure can spend the entire day in writing and dispatching a postcard [...]. The total effort that would occupy a busy man for three minutes all told may in this fashion leave another person prostrate after a day of doubt, anxiety, and toil.

Poorly developed SQL applications can very easily bring a server to its knees and yet not achieve very much. Here are a few examples (there are many others) illustrating different ways to increase the load without providing any useful work:

Hardcoding all queries
: This will force the DBMS to run parser and optimizer code for every execution, before actually performing any data access. This technique is remarkably efficient for swamping the CPU.

Running useless queries
: This is a situation more common than one would believe. It includes queries that are absolutely useless, such as a dummy query to check that the DBMS is up and running before every statement (true story), or issuing a `count(*)` to check whether a row should be updated or inserted. Other useless queries also include repeatedly fetching information that is stable for the entire duration of a session, or issuing 400,000 times a day a query to fetch a currency exchange rate that is updated once every night.

Multiplying round-trips
: Operating row-by-row, extensively using cursor loops, and banishing stored procedures are all excellent ways to increase the level of "chatting" between the

application side and the SQL engine, wasting time on protocol issues, multiplying packets on the network and of course, as a side benefit, preventing the database optimizer from doing its work efficiently by keeping most of the mysteries of data navigation firmly hidden in the application.

Let me underline that these examples of bad use of the DBMS don't specifically include the "bad SQL query" that represents the typical SQL performance issue for many people. The queries described in the preceding list often run fast. But even when they run at lightning speed, useless queries are always too slow: they waste resources that may be in short supply during peak activity.

There are two components that affect the load on a database server. The visible component is made up of the slow "bad SQL queries" that people are desperate to have tuned. The invisible component is the background noise of a number of queries each of acceptable speed, perhaps even including some very fast ones, that are executed over and over again. The cumulative cost of the load generated by all this background noise routinely dwarfs the individual load of most of the big bad queries. As Sir Arthur Conan Doyle put in the mouth of Sherlock Holmes:

> It has long been an axiom of mine that the little things are infinitely the most important.

As the background noise is spread over time, instead of happening all of a sudden, it passes unnoticed. It may nevertheless contribute significantly to reducing the "power reserve" that may be needed during occasional bursts of activity.

Repetitive short-duration mediocre statements often load a server more than the big bad SQL queries that take a long time to run.

Defining Good Performance

Load is one thing, performance another. Good performance proves an elusive notion to define. Using CPU or performing a large number of I/O operations is not wrong in itself; your company, presumably, didn't buy powerful hardware with the idea of keeping it idle.

When the time comes to assess performance, there is a striking similarity between the world of databases and the world of corporate finance. You find in both worlds some longing for "key performance indicators" and magical ratio—and in both worlds, global indicators and ratios can be extremely misleading. A good average can hide distressing results during the peaks, and a significant part of the load may perhaps be traced back to a batch program that is far from optimal but that runs at a time of night when no one cares what the load is. To get a true appreciation of the real state of affairs, you must drill down to a lower level of detail.

To a large extent, getting down to the details is an exercise similar to that which is known in managerial circles as "activity-based costing." In a company, knowing in some detail how much you spend is relatively easy. However, relating costs to benefits is an exercise fraught with difficulties, notoriously for transverse operations such as information technology. Determining if you spend the right amount on hardware, software, and staff, as well as the rubber bands and duct tape required to hold everything together is extremely difficult, particularly when the people who actually earn money are "customers" of the IT department.

Assessing whether you do indeed spend what you should has three prerequisites:

- Knowing what you spend
- Knowing what you get for the money
- Knowing how your return on investment compares with acknowledged standards

In the following subsections, I shall consider each of these points in turn in the context of database systems.

Knowing What You Spend

In the case of database performance, what we spend means, first and foremost, how many data pages we are hitting. The physical I/Os that some people tend to focus on are an ancillary matter. If you hit a very large number of different data pages, this will necessarily entail sustained I/O activity unless your database entirely fits in memory. But CPU load is also often a direct consequence of hitting the same data pages in memory again and again. Reducing the number of data pages accessed is not a panacea, as there are cases when the global throughput is higher when some queries hit a few more pages than is strictly necessary. But as far as single indicators go, the number of data pages hit is probably the most significant one. The other cost to watch is excessive SQL statement parsing, an activity that can consume an inordinate amount of CPU (massive hardcoded insertions can easily take 75% of the CPU available for parsing alone).

The two most significant indicators of database load are the amount of CPU spent on statement parsing and the number of data pages visited when executing queries.

Knowing What You Get

There is a quote that is famous among advertisers, a quip attributed to John Wanamaker, a 19th-century American retailer:

> Half the money I spend on advertising is wasted; the trouble is I don't know which half.

The situation is slightly better with database applications, but only superficially. You define what you get in terms of the number of rows (or bytes) returned by select statements; and similarly the number of rows affected by change operations. But such an apparently factual assessment is far from providing a true measure of the work performed on your behalf by the SQL engine, for a number of reasons:

- First, from a practical point of view, all products don't provide you with such statistics.
- Second, the effort required to obtain a result set may not be in proportion to the size of the result set. As a general rule you can be suspicious of a very large number of data page hits when only a few rows are returned. However such a proportion may be perfectly legitimate when data is aggregated. It is impossible to give a hard-and-fast rule in this area.
- Third, should data returned from the database for the sole purpose of using it as input to other queries be counted as useful work? What about systematically updating to `N` a column in a table without using a `where` clause when `N` already happens to be the value stored in most rows? In both cases, the DBMS engine performs work that can be measured in terms of bytes returned or changed. Unfortunately, most of the work performed can be avoided.

There are times when scanning large tables or executing a long-running query may be perfectly justified (or indeed inescapable). For instance, when you run summary reports on very large volumes of data, you cannot expect an immediate answer. If an immediate answer is required, then it is likely that the data model (the database representation of reality) is inappropriate to the questions you want to see answered. This is a typical case when a decision support database that doesn't necessarily require the level of detail of the main operational database may be suitable. Remember what you saw in Chapter 1: correct modeling depends both on the data and what you want to do with the data. You may share data with your suppliers or customers and yet have a totally different database model than they do. Naturally, feeding a decision support system will require long and costly operations both on the source operational database and the target decision support database.

Because what you do with the data matters so much, you cannot judge performance if you don't relate the load to the execution of particular SQL statements. The global picture that may be available through monitoring utilities (that most often provide cumulative counters) is not of much interest if you cannot *assign* to each statement its fair share of the load.

As a first stage in the process of load analysis, you must therefore capture and collect SQL statements, and try to determine how much each one contributes to the overall cost. It may not be important to capture absolutely every statement. Database activity is one of those areas where the 80/20 rule, the empirical assessment that 80% of the consequences result from 20% of the causes, often describes the situation rather well. Usually, much of the load comes from a small number of SQL statements. We must be careful not to overlook the fact that hardcoded SQL statements may distort the picture. With hardcoded statements, the DBMS may record thousands of distinct statements where a properly coded query would be referenced only once, even though it might be called thousands of times, each time with differing parameters. Such a situation can usually be spotted quite easily by the great number of SQL statements, and sometimes by global statistics. For instance, a procedure such as `sp_trace_setevent` in Transact-SQL lets you obtain a precise count of executed cursors, reexecutions of prepared cursors, and so on.

If nothing else is available and if you can access the SQL engine cache, a snapshot taken at a relatively low frequency of once every few minutes may in many cases prove quite useful. Big bad queries are usually hard to miss, as also are queries that are being executed dozens of times a minute. Global costs should in any case be checked in order to validate the hypothesis that what has been missed contributes only marginally to the global load. It's when SQL statements are hardcoded that taking snapshots will probably give less satisfactory results; you should then try to get a more complete picture, either through logging (as already mentioned a high-overhead solution), or by use of less intrusive "sniffer" utilities. I should note that even if you catch all hardcoded statements, then they have to be "reverse soft-coded" by taking constant values out of the SQL text before being able to estimate the relative load, not of a single SQL statement, but of one particular SQL statement pattern.

Identifying the statements that keep the DBMS busy, though, is only part of the story. You will miss much if you don't then relate SQL activity to the essential business activity of the organization that is supported by the database. Having an idea of how many SQL statements are issued on average each time you are processing a customer order is more important to SQL performance than knowing the disk transfer rate or the CPU speed under standard conditions of temperature and pressure. For one thing, it helps you anticipate the effect of the next advertising campaign; and if the said number of SQL statements is in the hundreds, you can raise interesting questions about the program (could there be, by chance, SQL statements executed inside loops that fetch the results of other statements? Could there be a statement that is repeatedly executed when it needs to be executed only once?). Similarly, costly massive updates of one column in a table accompanied by near identical numbers of equally massive updates of other columns from the same table with similar `where` clauses immediately raises the question of whether a single pass over the table wouldn't have been enough.

Load figures must be related to SQL statements. SQL statements must be related to business activity. Business activity must be related to business requirements.

Checking Against Acknowledged Standards

Collecting SQL statements, evaluating their cost and roughly relating them to what makes a company or agency tick is an exercise that usually points you directly to the parts of the code that require in-depth review. The questionable code may be SQL statements, algorithms, or both. But knowing what you can expect in terms of improvement or how far you could or should go is a very difficult part of the SQL expert's craft; experience helps, but even the seasoned practitioner can be left with a degree of uncertainty.

It can be useful to establish a baseline, for instance by carrying out simple insertion tests and having an idea about the rate of insertion that is sustainable on your hardware. Similarly, you should check the fetch rate that can be obtained when performing those dreaded full scans on some of the biggest tables. Comparing bare-bones rates to what some applications manage to accomplish is often illuminating: there may be an order of magnitude or more between the fetch or insert speed that the SQL engine can attain and what is achieved by application programs.

Know the limits of your environment. Measure how many rows you can insert, fetch, update, or delete per unit of time on your machines.

Once you have defined a few landmarks, you can identify where you will obtain the best "return on improvement," in terms of both relevance to business activities and technical feasibility. You can then focus on those parts of your programs and get results where it matters.

Some practitioners tend to think that as long as end users don't complain about performance, there is no issue and therefore no time to waste on trying to make operations go faster. There is some wisdom in this attitude; but there is also some shortsightedness as well, for two reasons:

- First, end users often have a surprisingly high level of tolerance for poor performance; or perhaps it would be more appropriate to say that their perception of slowness differs widely from that of someone who has a better understanding of what happens behind the scenes. End users may complain loudly about the performance of those processes of death that cannot possibly do better, and express a mild dissatisfaction about other processes when I would have long gone ballistic. A low level of complaint doesn't necessarily mean that everything is fine, nor does vocal dissatisfaction necessarily mean that there is anything wrong with an application except perhaps trying to do too much.

- Second, a slight increase in the load on a server may mean that performance will deteriorate from acceptable to unacceptable very quickly. If the environment is perfectly stable, there is indeed nothing to fear from a slight increase in load. But if your activity records a very high peak during one particular month of the year, the same program that looks satisfactory for 11 months can suddenly be the reason for riots. Here the background noise matters a lot. An already overloaded machine cannot keep on providing the same level of service when activity increases. There is always a threshold that sees mediocre performance tumbling down all of a sudden. It is therefore important to study an entire system before a burst of activity is encountered to see whether the load can be reduced by improving the code. If improving the code isn't enough to warrant acceptable performance, it may be time to switch to bigger iron and upgrade the hardware.

Do not forget that "return on improvement" is not simply a technical matter. The perception of end users should be given the highest priority, even if it is biased and sometimes disconnected from the most severe technical issues. They have to work with the program, and ergonomics have to be taken into account. It is not unusual to meet well-meaning individuals concentrating on improving statistics rather than program throughput, let alone end-user satisfaction. These well-intentioned engineers can feel somewhat frustrated and misunderstood when end users, who only see a very local improvement, welcome the result of mighty technical efforts with lukewarm enthusiasm. An eighteenth-century author reports that somebody once said to a physician, "Well, Mr. X has died, in spite of the promise you had made to cure him." The splendid answer from the physician was, "You were away, and didn't check the progress of the treatment: he died cured."

A database with excellent statistics and yet unsatisfactory performance from an end-user point of view is like a patient cured of one ailment, but who died of another. Improving performance usually means *both* delivering a highly visible improvement to end users, even if it affects a query that is run only once a month but that is business-critical, and the more humble, longer-term work of streamlining programs, lowering the background noise, and ensuring that the server will be able to deliver that power boost when it is needed.

Performance improvement as perceived by end users is what matters most, but never forget the narrow margin between acceptable and unacceptable performance in a loaded environment.

Defining Performance Goals

Performance goals are often defined in terms of elapsed time, for example, "this program must run in under 2 hours." It is better though to define them primarily in terms of business items processed by unit of time, such as "50,000 invoices per hour" or "100 loans per minute," for several reasons:

- It gives a better idea of the service actually provided by a given program.
- It makes a decrease in performance more understandable to end users when it can be linked to an increase in activity. This makes meetings less stormy.
- Psychologically speaking, it is slightly more exciting when trying to improve a process to boost throughput rather than diminish the elapsed time. An upward curve makes a better chart in management presentations than a downward one.

More than anything else, improved performance means first, doing more work in the same time, and second, doing it in even less time.

Thinking in Business Tasks

Before focusing on one particular query, don't forget its context. Queries executed in loops are a very bad indicator of the quality of code, as are program variables with no other purpose than storing information returned from the database before passing it to another query. Database accesses are costly, and should be kept to a minimum. When you consider the way some programs are written, you are left with the impression that when their authors go shopping, they jump into their car, drive to a supermarket, park their car, walk up and down the aisles, pick a few bottles of milk, head for the checkout, get in line, pay, put the milk in the car, drive home, store the milk into the fridge, then check the next item on the shopping list before returning to the supermarket. And when a spouse complains about the time spent on shopping, the excuses given are usually the dense traffic on the road, the poor signposting of the food department, and the insufficient number of cashiers. All are valid reasons in their own right that may indeed contribute to some extent to shopping time, but possibly they are not the first issues to fix.

I have met developers who were genuinely persuaded that from a performance standpoint, multiplying simple queries was the proper thing to do; showing them that the opposite is true was extremely easy. I have also heard that very simple SQL statements that avoid joins make maintenance easier. The truth is that simplistic SQL makes it easier to use totally inexperienced (read cheaper) developers for maintenance, but that's the only thing that can be said in defense of very elementary SQL statements. By making the most basic usage of SQL, you end up with programs full of statements that, taken one by one, look efficient, except perhaps for a handful of particularly poor performers, hastily pointed to as "the SQL statements that require tuning." Very often, some of the statements identified as "slow" (and which may indeed be slow) are responsible for only a fraction of performance issues.

Brilliantly tuned statements in a bad program operating against a badly designed database are no more effective than brilliant tactics at the service of a feeble strategy; all they can do is postpone the day of reckoning.

You cannot design efficient programs if you don't understand that the SQL language applies to a whole subsystem of data management, and isn't simply a set of primitives to move data between long-term and short-term memory. Database accesses are often the most performance-critical components of a program, and must be incorporated to the overall design.

In trying to make programs simpler by multiplying SQL statements, you succumb to a dangerous illusion. Complexity doesn't originate in languages, but in business requirements. With the exclusive use of simple SQL statements, complexity doesn't vanish, it just migrates from the SQL side to the application side, with a much increased risk of data inconsistency when the logic that should belong to the DBMS side is imbedded into the application. Moreover, it puts a significant part of processing out of reach of the DBMS optimizer.

I am not advocating the indiscriminate use of long, complex SQL statements, or a "single statement" policy. For example, the following is a case where there should have been several distinct statements, and not a single one:

```
insert into custdet (custcode, custcodedet, usr, seq, inddet)
select case ?
         when 'GRP' then b.codgrp
         when 'GSR' then b.codgsr
         when 'NIT' then b.codnit
         when 'GLB' then 'GLOBAL'
         else b.codetb
       end,
       b.custcode,
       ?,
       ?,
       'O'
from edic00 a,
     clidet bT
where ((b.codgrp = a.custcode
        and ? = 'GRP')
       or (b.codgsr = a.custcode
           and ? = 'GSR')
       or (b.codnit = a.custcode
           and ? = 'NIT')
       or (a.custcode = 'GLOBAL'
           and ? = 'GLB'))
   and a.seq = ?
   and b.custlvl = ?
   and b.histdat = ?
```

A statement where a run-time parameter is compared to a constant is usually a statement that should have been split into several simpler statements. In the preceding example, the value that intervenes in the `case` construct is the same one that is successively compared to `GRP`, `GSR`, `NIT`, and `GLB` in the `where` clause. It makes no sense to force the SQL engine into making numerous mutually exclusive tests and sort out a situation that could have been cleared on the application side. In such a case, an `if ... elsif ... elsif` structure (preferably in order of decreasing probability of occurrence) and four distinct `insert ... select` statements would have been much better.

When a complex SQL statement allows you to obtain more quickly the data you ultimately need, with a small number of accesses, the situation is completely different from the preceding case. Long, complex queries are not necessarily slow; it all depends on how they are written. A developer should obviously not exceed their personal SQL skill level, and not necessarily write 300-line statements head on; but packing as much action as possible into each SQL statement should be a prerequisite to improving individual statements.

Tuning SQL statements before improving programs and minimizing database accesses means that you are ignoring some of the major means of tuning improvements.

Execution Plans

When our spies (whether they are users or monitoring facilities) have directed our attention to a number of SQL statements, we need to inspect these statements more closely. Scrutinizing execution plans is one of the favorite activities of many SQL tuners, if we are to believe the high number of posts in forums or mailing lists in the form of "I have a SQL query that is particularly slow; here is the execution plan...."

Execution plans are usually displayed either as an indented list of the various steps involved in the processing of a (usually complex) SQL statements, or under a graphical form, as in Figure 12-1. This figure displays the execution plan for one of the queries from Chapter 7. Text execution plans are far less sexy but are easier to post on forums, which must account for the enduring popularity of such plans. Knowing how to correctly read and interpret an execution plan, whether it is represented graphically or as text, is in itself a valued skill.

So far in this book, I have had very little to say on the topic of execution plans, except for a couple of examples presented here and there without any particular comment. Execution plans are tools, and different individuals have different preferences for various

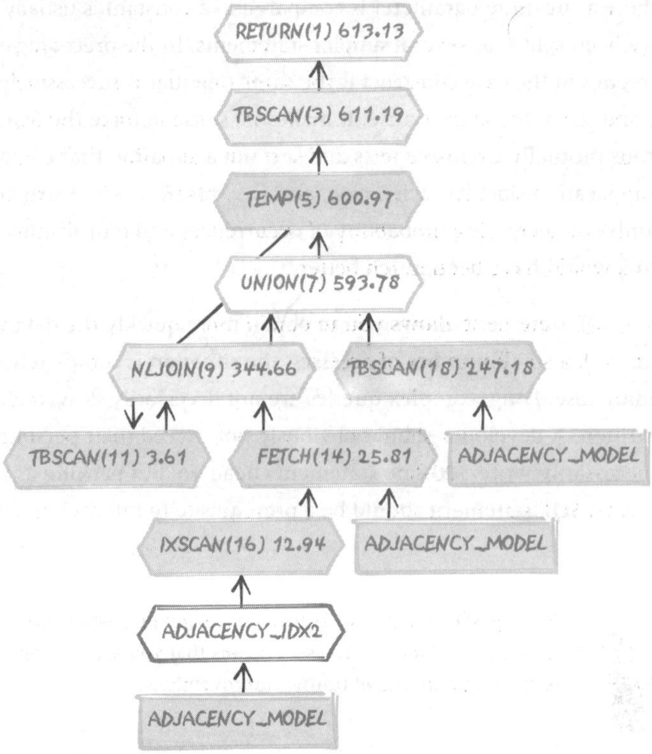

FIGURE 12-1. *A DB2 execution plan*

tools; you are perfectly allowed to have a different opinion, but I usually attach a secondary importance to execution plans. Some developers consider execution plans as the ultimate key to the understanding of performance issues. Two real-life examples will show that one may have some reasons to be less than sanguine about using execution plans as the tool of choice for improving a query.

Identifying the Fastest Execution Plan

In this section, I am going to test your skills as an interpreter of execution plans. I'm going to show three execution plans and ask you to choose which is the fastest. Ready? Go, and good luck!

Our contestants

The following execution plans show how three variants of the same query are executed:

Plan 1

```
Execution Plan
----------------------------------------------------------
   0      SELECT STATEMENT
   1    0   SORT (ORDER BY)
   2    1     CONCATENATION
   3    2       NESTED LOOPS
```

```
   4    3          HASH JOIN
   5    4            HASH JOIN
   6    5              TABLE ACCESS (FULL) OF 'TCTRP'
   7    5              TABLE ACCESS (BY INDEX ROWID) OF 'TTRAN'
   8    7                INDEX (RANGE SCAN) OF 'TTRANTRADE_DATE' (NON-UNIQUE)
   9    4            TABLE ACCESS (BY INDEX ROWID) OF 'TMMKT'
  10    9              INDEX (RANGE SCAN) OF 'TMMKTCCY_NAME' (NON-UNIQUE) ...
  11    3          TABLE ACCESS (BY INDEX ROWID) OF 'TFLOW'
  12   11            INDEX (RANGE SCAN) OF 'TFLOWMAIN' (UNIQUE)
  13    2        NESTED LOOPS
  14   13          HASH JOIN
  15   14            HASH JOIN
  16   15              TABLE ACCESS (FULL) OF 'TCTRP'
  17   15              TABLE ACCESS (BY INDEX ROWID) OF 'TTRAN'
  18   17                INDEX (RANGE SCAN) OF 'TTRANLAST_UPDATED' (NON-UNIQUE)
  19   14            TABLE ACCESS (BY INDEX ROWID) OF 'TMMKT'
  20   19              INDEX (RANGE SCAN) OF 'TMMKTCCY_NAME' (NON-UNIQUE)
  21   13          TABLE ACCESS (BY INDEX ROWID) OF 'TFLOW'
  22   21            INDEX (RANGE SCAN) OF 'TFLOWMAIN' (UNIQUE)
```

Plan 2

```
Execution Plan
----------------------------------------------------------
   0      SELECT STATEMENT
   1    0   SORT (ORDER BY)
   2    1     CONCATENATION
   3    2       NESTED LOOPS
   4    3         NESTED LOOPS
   5    4           NESTED LOOPS
   6    5             TABLE ACCESS (BY INDEX ROWID) OF 'TTRAN'
   7    6               INDEX (RANGE SCAN) OF 'TTRANTRADE_DATE' (NON-UNIQUE)
   8    5             TABLE ACCESS (BY INDEX ROWID) OF 'TMMKT'
   9    8               INDEX (UNIQUE SCAN) OF 'TMMKTMAIN' (UNIQUE)
  10    4           TABLE ACCESS (BY INDEX ROWID) OF 'TFLOW'
  11   10             INDEX (RANGE SCAN) OF 'TFLOWMAIN' (UNIQUE)
  12    3         TABLE ACCESS (BY INDEX ROWID) OF 'TCTRP'
  13   12           INDEX (UNIQUE SCAN) OF 'TCTRPMAIN' (UNIQUE)
  14    2       NESTED LOOPS
  15   14         NESTED LOOPS
  16   15           NESTED LOOPS
  17   16             TABLE ACCESS (BY INDEX ROWID) OF 'TTRAN'
  18   17               INDEX (RANGE SCAN) OF 'TTRANLAST_UPDATED' (NON-UNIQUE)
  19   16             TABLE ACCESS (BY INDEX ROWID) OF 'TMMKT'
  20   19               INDEX (UNIQUE SCAN) OF 'TMMKTMAIN' (UNIQUE)
  21   15           TABLE ACCESS (BY INDEX ROWID) OF 'TFLOW'
  22   21             INDEX (RANGE SCAN) OF 'TFLOWMAIN' (UNIQUE)
  23   14         TABLE ACCESS (BY INDEX ROWID) OF 'TCTRP'
  24   23           INDEX (UNIQUE SCAN) OF 'TCTRPMAIN' (UNIQUE)
```

Plan 3

```
Execution Plan
----------------------------------------------------------
   0      SELECT STATEMENT
   1    0   SORT (ORDER BY)
   2    1     NESTED LOOPS
   3    2       NESTED LOOPS
   4    3         NESTED LOOPS
```

```
 5   4           TABLE ACCESS (BY INDEX ROWID) OF 'TMMKT'
 6   5             INDEX (RANGE SCAN) OF 'TMMKTCCY_NAME' (NON-UNIQUE)
 7   4           TABLE ACCESS (BY INDEX ROWID) OF 'TTRAN'
 8   7             INDEX (UNIQUE SCAN) OF 'TTRANMAIN' (UNIQUE)
 9   3         TABLE ACCESS (BY INDEX ROWID) OF 'TCTRP'
10   9           INDEX (UNIQUE SCAN) OF 'TCTRPMAIN' (UNIQUE)
11   2       TABLE ACCESS (BY INDEX ROWID) OF 'TFLOW'
12  11         INDEX (RANGE SCAN) OF 'TFLOWMAIN' (UNIQUE)
```

Our battle field

The result set of the query consists of 860 rows, and the four following tables are involved:

Table name	Row count (rounded)
tctrp	18,000
ttran	1,500,000
tmmkt	1,400,000
tflow	5,400,000

All tables are heavily indexed, no index was created, dropped or rebuilt, and no change was applied to the data structures. Only the text of the query changed between plans, and optimizer directives were sometimes applied.

Consider the three execution plans, try to rank them in order of likely speed, and if you feel like it you may even venture an opinion about the improvement factor.

And the winner is...

The answer is that Plan 1 took 27 seconds, Plan 2 one second, and Plan 3 (the initial execution plan of the query) one minute and 12 seconds. You will be forgiven for choosing the wrong plan. In fact, with the information that I provided, it would be sheer luck for you to have correctly guessed at the fastest plan (or the result of a well-founded suspicion that there must be a catch somewhere). You can take note that the slowest execution plan is by far the shortest, and that it contains no reference to anything other than indexed accesses. By contrast, Plan 1 demonstrates that you can have two full scans of the same table and yet execute the query almost three times faster than a shorter, index-only plan such as Plan 3.

The point of this exercise was to demonstrate that the length of an execution plan is not very meaningful, and that exclusive access to tables through indexes doesn't guarantee that performance is the best you can achieve. True, if you have a 300-line plan for a query that returns 19 rows, then you might have a problem, but you mustn't assume that shorter is better.

Forcing the Right Execution Plan

The second example is the weird behavior exhibited by one query issued by a commercial off-the-shelf software package. When run against one database, the query takes 4 minutes, returning 40,000 rows. Against another database, running the same version of the same DBMS, the very same query responds in 11 minutes on comparable hardware although all tables involved are much smaller. The comparison of execution plans shows that they are wildly different. Statistics are up-to-date on both databases, and the optimizer is instructed to use them everywhere. The question immediately becomes one of how to force the query to take the right execution path on the smaller database. DBAs are asked to do whatever is in their power to get the same execution plan on both databases. The vendor's technical team works closely with the customer's team to try to solve the problem.

A stubborn query

Following is the text of the query,* followed by the plan associated to the fastest execution. Take note that the good plan only accesses indexes, not tables:

```
select o.id_outstanding,
       ap.cde_portfolio,
       ap.cde_expense,
       ap.branch_code,
       to_char(sum(ap.amt_book_round
          + ap.amt_book_acr_ad - ap.amt_acr_nt_pst)),
       to_char(sum(ap.amt_mnl_bk_adj)),
       o.cde_outstd_typ
from accrual_port ap,
     accrual_cycle ac,
     outstanding o,
     deal d,
     facility f,
     branch b
where ac.id_owner = o.id_outstandng
  and ac.id_acr_cycle = ap.id_owner
  and o.cde_outstd_typ in ('LOAN', 'DCTLN', 'ITRLN',
                           'DEPOS', 'SLOAN', 'REPOL')
  and d.id_deal = o.id_deal
  and d.acct_enabl_ind = 'Y'
  and (o.cde_ob_st_ctg = 'ACTUA'
       or o.id_outstanding in (select id_owner
                               from subledger))
  and o.id_facility = f.id_facility
  and f.branch_code = b.branch_code
  and b.cde_tme_region = 'ZONE2'
group by o.id_outstanding,
```

* Object names have been slightly changed to protect both the innocent and the culprit.

```
        ap.cde_portfolio,
        ap.cde_expense,
        ap.branch_code,
        o.cde_outstd_typ
having sum(ap.amt_book_round
         + ap.amt_book_acr_ad - ap.amt_acr_nt_pst) <> 0
    or (sum(ap.amt_mnl_bk_adj) is not null
        and sum(ap.amt_mnl_bk_adj) <> 0)


Execution Plan
----------------------------------------------------------
   0      SELECT STATEMENT Optimizer=CHOOSE
   1    0   FILTER
   2    1     SORT (GROUP BY)
   3    2       FILTER
   4    3         HASH JOIN
   5    4           HASH JOIN
   6    5             HASH JOIN
   7    6               INDEX (FAST FULL SCAN) OF 'XDEAUN08' (UNIQUE)
   8    6               HASH JOIN
   9    8                 NESTED LOOPS
  10    9                   INDEX (FAST FULL SCAN) OF 'XBRNNN02' (NON-UNIQUE)
  11    9                   INDEX (RANGE SCAN) OF 'XFACNN05' (NON-UNIQUE)
  12    8                 INDEX (FAST FULL SCAN) OF 'XOSTNN06' (NON-UNIQUE)
  13    5             INDEX (FAST FULL SCAN) OF 'XACCNN05' (NON-UNIQUE)
  14    4           INDEX (FAST FULL SCAN) OF 'XAPONN05' (NON-UNIQUE)
  15    3         INDEX (SKIP SCAN) OF 'XBSGNN03' (NON-UNIQUE)
```

The addition of indexes to the smaller database leads nowhere. Existing indexes were initially identical on both databases, and creating different indexes on the smaller database brings no change to the execution plan. Three weeks after the problem was first spotted, attention is now turning to disk striping, without much hope. Constraining optimizer directives are beginning to look unpleasantly like the only escape route.

Before using directives, it is wise to have a fair idea of the right angle of attack. Finding the proper angle, as you have seen in Chapters 4 and 6, requires an assessment of the relative precision of the various input criteria, even though in this case the reasonably large result set (of some 40,000 rows on the larger database and a little over 3,000 on the smaller database) gives us little hope of seeing one criterion coming forward as *the* key criterion.

Study of search criteria

When we use as the only criterion the condition on what looks like a time zone, the query returns 17% more rows than with all filtering conditions put together, but it does it blazingly fast:

```
SQL> select count(*) "FAC"
  2  from outstanding
  3  where id_facility in (select f.id_facility
```

```
                        from facility f,
                             branch b
                        where f.branch_code = b.branch_code
                          and b.cde_tme_region = 'ZONE2');

       FAC
----------
     55797

Elapsed: 00:00:00.66
```

The flag condition alone filters three times our number of rows, but it does it very fast, too:

```
SQL> select count(*) "DEA"
     from outstanding
     where id_deal in (select id_deal
                       from deal
                       where acct_enabl_ind = 'Y');

       DEA
----------
    123970

Elapsed: 00:00:00.63
```

What about our or condition on the `outstanding` table? Following are the results from that condition:

```
SQL> select count(*) "ACTUA/SUBLEDGER"
     from outstanding
     where (cde_ob_st_ctg = 'ACTUA'
            or id_outstanding in (select id_owner
                                  from subledger));

ACTUA/SUBLEDGER
---------------
          32757

Elapsed: 00:15:00.64
```

Looking at these results, it is clear that we have pinpointed the problem. This or condition causes a huge increase in the query's execution time.

The execution plan for the preceding query shows only index accesses:

```
Execution Plan
----------------------------------------------------------
   0      SELECT STATEMENT Optimizer=CHOOSE
   1    0   SORT (AGGREGATE)
   2    1     FILTER
   3    2       INDEX (FAST FULL SCAN) OF 'XOSTNN06' (NON-UNIQUE)
   4    2       INDEX (SKIP SCAN) OF 'XBSGNN03' (NON-UNIQUE)
```

Notice that both index accesses are not exactly the usual type of index descent; there is no need to get into arcane details here, but a FAST FULL SCAN is in fact the choice of using the smaller index rather than the larger associated table to perform a scan, and the choice of a SKIP SCAN comes from a similar evaluation by the optimizer. In other words, the choice of the access method is not exactly driven by the evidence of an excellent path, but proceeds from a kind of "by and large, it should be better" optimizer assessment. If the execution time is to be believed, a SKIP SCAN is not the best of choices.

Let's have a look at the indexes on outstanding (the numbers of distinct index keys and distinct column values are estimates, which accounts for the slightly inconsistent figures). Indexes in bold are the indexes that appear in the execution plan:

INDEX_NAME	DIST KEYS	COLUMN_NAME	DIST VAL
XOSTNC03	25378	ID_DEAL	1253
		ID_FACILITY	1507
XOSTNN05	134875	ID_OUTSTANDING	126657
		ID_DEAL	1253
		IND_AUTO_EXTND	2
		CDE_OUTSTD_TYP	5
		ID_FACILITY	1507
		UID_REC_CREATE	161
		NME_ALIAS	126657
XOSTNN06		**ID_OUTSTANDING**	**126657**
		CDE_OUTSTD_TYP	**5**
		ID_DEAL	**1253**
		CDE_OB_ST_CTG	**3**
		ID_FACILITY	**1507**
XOSTUN01 (U)	121939	ID_OUTSTANDING	126657
XOSTUN02 (U)	111055	NME_ALIAS	126657

The other index (xbsgnn03) is associated with subledger:

INDEX_NAME	DIST KEYS	COLUMN_NAME	DIST VAL
XBSGNN03	**101298**	**BRANCH_CODE**	**8**
		CDE_PORTFOLIO	**5**
		CDE_EXPENSE	**56**
		ID_OWNER	**52664**
		CID_CUSTOMER	**171**
XBSGNN04	59542	ID_DEAL	4205
		ID_FACILITY	4608
		ID_OWNER	52664
XBSGNN05	49694	BRANCH_CODE	8
		ID_FACILITY	4608
		ID_OWNER	52664
XBSGUC02 (U)	147034	CDE_GL_ACCOUNT	9
		CDE_GL_SHTNAME	9
		BRANCH_CODE	8
		CDE_PORTFOLIO	5
		CDE_EXPENSE	56
		ID_OWNER	52664
		CID_CUSTOMER	171
XBSGUN01 (U)	134581	ID_SUBLEDGER	154362

As is too often the case with COTS packages, we have here an excellent example of carpet-indexing.

The indexes on `outstanding` raise a couple of questions.

- Why does `id_outstanding`, the primary key of the outstanding table, also appears as the lead column of two other indexes? This requires some justification, and very persuasive justification too. Even if those indexes were built with the purpose of fetching all values from them and avoiding table access, one might arguably have relegated `id_oustanding` to a less prominent position; on the other hand, since few columns seem to have a high number of distinct values, the very existence of some of the indexes would need to be reassessed.
- All is not quiet on the `subledger` front either. One of the most selective values happens to be `id_owner`. Why does `id_owner` appear in 4 of the 5 indexes, but nowhere as the lead column? Such a situation is surprising for an often referenced selective column. Incidentally, finding `id_owner` as the lead column of an index would have been helpful with our problem query.

Modifying indexes is a delicate business that requires a careful study of all the possible side-effects. We have here a number of questionable indexes, but we also have an urgent problem to solve. Let's therefore refrain from making any changes to the existing indexes and concentrate on the SQL code.

As the numbers of distinct keys of our unique indexes show, we are not dealing here with large tables; and in fact the two other criteria we have tried to apply to `outstanding` both gave excellent response times, in spite of being rather weak criteria. The pathetic result we have with the `or` construct results from an attempt to merge data which was painfully extracted from the two indexes. Let's try something else:

```
SQL> select count(*) "ACTUA/SUBLEDGER"
     from (select id_outstanding
           from outstanding
           where cde_ob_st_ctg = 'ACTUA'
           union
           select o.id_outstanding
           from outstanding o,
                subledger sl
           where o.id_outstanding = sl.id_owner)
     /

ACTUA/SUBLEDGER
---------------
          32757

Elapsed: 00:00:01.82
```

No change to the indexes, and yet the optimizer suddenly sees the light even if we hit the table `outstanding` twice. Execution is much, much faster now.

Replacing the "problem condition" and slightly reshuffling some of the other remaining conditions, cause the query to run in 13 seconds where it used to take 4 minutes (reputedly the "good case"); and only 3.4 seconds on the other database, where it used to take 11 minutes to return 3,200 rows.

A moral to the story

It is likely that a more careful study and some work at the index level would allow the query to run considerably faster than 13 seconds. On the other hand, since everybody appeared to be quite happy with 4 minutes, 13 seconds is probably a good enough improvement.

What is fascinating in this true story (and many examples in this book are taken from real life), is how the people involved focused (for several weeks) on the wrong issue. There was indeed a glaring problem on the smaller database. The comparison of the two different execution plans led to the immediate conclusion that the execution plan corresponding to the slower execution was wrong (true) and therefore, implicitly, that the execution plan corresponding to the faster execution was right (false). This was a major logical mistake, and it misled several people into concentrating on trying to reproduce a bad execution plan instead of improving the query.

I must add a final note as a conclusion to the story. Once the query has been rewritten, the execution plan is *still* different on the two databases—a situation that, given the discrepancy of volumes, only proves that the optimizer is doing its job.

The only yardstick of query performance is how long one takes to run, not whether the execution plan conforms to prejudices.

Using Execution Plans Properly

Execution plans *are* useful, but mostly to check that the DBMS engine is indeed proceeding as intended. The report from the field that an execution plan represents is a great tool to compare what has been realized to the tactics that were planned, and can reveal tactical flaws or overlooked details.

How Not to Execute a Query

Execution plans can be useful even when one has not the slightest idea about what a proper execution plan should be. The reason is that, by definition, the execution plan of a problem query is a bad one, even if it may not look so terrible. Knowing that the plan is bad allows us to discover ways to improve the query, through the use of one of the most sophisticated tools of formal logic, the *syllogism*, an argument with two premises and one conclusion.

This reasoning is as follows:

> (Premise 1) The query is dreadfully slow.
> (Premise 2) The execution plan displays mostly one type of action—for example: full table scans, hash joins, indexed accesses, nested loops, and so forth.

(Conclusion) We should rewrite the query and/or possibly change indexes so as to suggest something else to the optimizer.

Coaxing the optimizer into taking a totally different course can be achieved through a number of means:

- When we have few rows returned, it may be a matter of adding one index, or rebuilding a composite index and reversing the order of some of the columns; transforming uncorrelated subqueries into correlated ones can also be helpful.
- When we have a large number of rows returned we can do the opposite, and use parentheses and subqueries in the `from` clause to suggest a different order when joining tables together.
- In doubt, we have quite a number of options besides transforming correlated sub queries into uncorrelated subqueries and vice versa. We can consider operations such as factorizing queries with either a `union` or a `with` clause. The `union` of two complex queries can sometimes be transformed into a simpler `union` inside the `from` clause. Disentangling conditions (trying to make each condition dependent on as few other conditions as possible) is often helpful. Generally speaking, trying to remove as much as possible of whatever imposes a processing order on the query and trying to give as much freedom as possible to the optimizer is the very first thing to do before trying to constrain it. The optimizer must be constrained only when everything else goes wrong.
- As a last resort, we may remember the existence of optimizer directives and use them very carefully.

Hidden Complexity

Execution plans can also prove to be valuable spies in revealing hidden complexity. Queries are not always exactly what a superficial inspection shows. The participation of some database objects in a query can induce additional work that execution plans will bring to light. These database objects are chiefly:

Views

Queries may look deceivingly simple. But sometimes what appears to be a simple table may turn out to be a view defined as a very complex query involving several other views. The names of views may not always be distinctive, and even when they are, the name by itself cannot give any indication of the complexity of the view. The execution plan will show what a casual inspection of the SQL code may have missed, and most importantly, it will also tell you if the same table is being hit repeatedly.

Triggers

Changes to the database may take an anomalous time simply because of the execution of triggers. These may be running very slow code or may even be the true reason for some locking issues. Triggers are easy to miss, execution plans will reveal them.

The essential value of execution plans is to provide a starting point for performance investigations and to reveal the hidden database operations caused by complex views and triggers.

What Really Matters?

What really matters when trying to improve a query has been discussed in the previous chapters, namely:

- The number of rows in the tables involved
- The existing indexes on these tables
- Storage peculiarities, such as partitioning, that can have as strong an impact as indexes on performance
- The quality of the various criteria that were provided
- The size of the resulting set

This information provides us with a solid foundation from which to investigate query performance, and is far more valuable than an execution plan on its own. Once we know were we stand, and what we have to fight against, then we can move, and attack tables, always trying to get rid of unwanted data as quickly as we can. We must always try to leave as much freedom to the optimizer as we can by avoiding any type of intra-statement dependencies that would constrain the order in which tables must be visited.

In conclusion, I would like to remind you that optimizers, which usually prove quite efficient at their job, are unable to work efficiently under the following circumstances:

- If you retrieve data piecemeal through multiple statements. It is one thing for an application to issue a series of related SQL statements. However, the SQL engine can never "know" that such statements are related, and cannot optimize across statement boundaries. The SQL engine can optimize each individual statement, but it cannot optimize the overall process.
- If you use, without any care, the numerous non-relational (and sometimes quite useful) features provided by the various SQL dialects.

Remember that you should apply non-relational features last, when the bulk of data retrieval is done (in the wider acceptance of retrieval; data must be retrieved before being updated or deleted). Non-relational features operate on finite sets (in other words, arrays), not on theoretically infinite relations.

There was a time when you could make a reputation as an SQL expert by identifying missing indexes and rewriting statements so as to remove functions that were applied to indexed columns. This time is, for the most part, gone. Most databases are over-indexed, although sometimes inadequately indexed. Functions applied to indexed columns are still encountered, but functional indexes provide a "quick fix" to that particular problem. However, rewriting a poorly performing query usually means more nowadays than shuffling conditions or merely making cosmetic changes.

The real challenge is more and more to be able to think globally, and to acknowledge that data handling is critical in a world where the amount of stored data increases even faster than the performance of the hardware. For better or for worse, data handling spells S-Q-L. Like all languages, SQL has its idiosyncrasies, its qualities, and numerous flaws. Like all languages, mastering SQL requires time, experience—and personal talent. I hope that on that long road this book will prove helpful to you.

Building optimally performing SQL can be a source of great satisfaction—enjoy!

PHOTO CREDITS

All images were scanned from *Mémorial de Sainte-Hélène* by Comte Emmanuel de Las Cases, illustrated by Charlet (Ernest Bourdin Editeur, Paris, 1842, two volumes), with the following exceptions:

- The illustration for Chapter 6 was made out of a map of the battle of Fredericksburg, found on *http://www.sonofthesouth.net*, and used with the permission of Paul McWhorter who runs that very rich site on the American Civil War.
- The illustration for Chapter 9 comes from *Notre Armée* by de Lonlay, illustrated by the author (Garnier Frères, Paris, 1890, p. 931).
- The illustration for Chapter 12 comes from *Les Guerres de la Révolution* by Camille Pelletan, Paris, Société d'Éditions d'Art (Collection L.-Henry May, G. Mantoux), no date [end 19th–beginning 20th century; first published, Paris, Colas, 1884], p.95 (10th series), coll. Durelle-Marc, and is published courtesy of the Centre d'Histoire du Droit de l'Université Rennes 1 (*http://www.chd.univ-rennes1.fr/Icono/Pelletan/Pelletan.htm*).

INDEX

Symbols

A

B

C

D

E

F

J

K

L

M

N

O

P

Q

R

S

T

U

V

W

X

ABOUT THE AUTHORS

STÉPHANE FAROULT first discovered relational databases and the SQL language back in 1983. He joined Oracle France in their early days (after a brief spell with IBM and a bout of teaching at the University of Ottawa) and soon developed an interest in performance and tuning topics. After leaving Oracle in 1988, he briefly tried to reform and did a bit of operational research, but after one year, he succumbed again to relational databases. He has been continuously performing database consultancy since then, and founded RoughSea Ltd in 1998 (*http://www.roughsea.com*).

Stéphane Faroult has written (in French) *Fortran Structuré et Méthodes Numériques* (Dunod, 1986, with Didier Simon) and a number of articles in English, in magazines such as *Oracle Scene* (the UK Oracle user group magazine) and *Select* (the North American Oracle user group magazine), as well as on the Web (including the online edition of *Oracle Magazine*). He has also been a speaker at a number of user group conferences in the U.S., in the UK, and in Norway.

PETER ROBSON graduated in geology from Durham University (1968), then taught at Edinburgh University, obtaining an M.Phil in geology in 1975. After working in Greece as a geologist, he specialized in both geological and medical databases at the University of Newcastle.

He has worked with databases since 1977, relational databases since 1981, and Oracle since 1985, in roles which included developer, data architect, and database administrator. In 1980, Peter joined the British Geological Survey and was influential in guiding their adoption of relational DBMS. He has specialized in aspects of the SQL system as well as data modeling from corporate architecture down to the departmental level. Peter has presented at various Oracle database conferences in the UK, Europe, and North America, and he has published in various specialist database magazines. Currently, he is a Director on the Board of the UK Oracle User Group; he can be contacted via his own domain at *peter.robson@justsql.com*.

ISBN	Title	Author	Price

Shroff / O'Reilly

TITLES AT REDUCED PRICES

ISBN	Title	Author	Price
8173663661	.NET Framework Essentials, *324 Pages*	Thai	25.00
818404027X	**Access 2003 for Starters: The Missing Manual, *408 Pages***	**Chase**	**75.00**
8173664277	Access Cookbook for 97, 2000 & 2002 **(Book / CD-ROM)**, *724 Pages*	Getz	100.00
8173662231	ActionScriprt: The Definitive Guide, *726 Pages*	Moock	150.00
8173662886	Building Oracle XML Applications **(Book / CD-ROM)**, *824 Pages*	Muench	100.00
8173665621	Building Secure Servers with Linux, *454 Pages*	Bauer	100.00
8173664250	Building Wireless Community Networks, *144 Pages*	Flickenger	50.00
8173662584	Cascading Style Sheets: The Definitive Guide, *476 Pages*	Meyer	75.00
8173669066	**Cascading Style Sheets: The Definitive Guide (Covers CSS2 & CSS 2.1), 2/ed, *538 Pages***	**Meyer**	**100.00**
8173667241	**Cisco Cookbook, *918 Pages***	**Dooley**	**150.00**
8173662878	Developing ASP Components 2/ed, *864 Pages*	Powers	100.00
8173663882	**Designing Large Scale LANs, *408 Pages***	**Dooley**	**75.00**
817366272X	DHCP for Windows 2000, *288 Pages*	Alcott	75.00
8173663580	**Essential SNMP, *338 Pages***	**Mauro**	**75.00**
8173662754	**Excel 2000 In a Nutshell: A Power User's Quick Reference, *560 Pgs***	**Simon**	**50.00**
8173669406	**Excel Annoyances: How to Fix the Most Annoying Things about Your Favorite Spreadsheet , *266 Pages***	**Frye**	**75.00**
8173668612	**Excel Hacks: 100 Industrial Strength Tips & Tools, *316 Pages***	**David**	**75.00**
8173663599	Exim: The Mail Transport Agent, *638 Pages*	Hazel	75.00
8173669325	**Google: The Missing Manual, *312 Pages***	**Milstein**	**75.00**
817366448X	**IPv6 Essentials, 362 Pages**	**Hagen**	**75.00**
8173660573	Java Threads, 2/ed, *336 Pages*	Oaks	100.00
8173664145	Java Cookbook, *890 Pages*	Darwin	150.00
8173664625	**Java Enterprise in a Nutshell: A Desktop Quick Reference, 2/ed, *1,004 Pages***	**Farley**	**100.00**
8173660557	Java Foundation Classes in a Nutshell, *752 Pages*	Flanagan	75.00
8173662711	Java Internationalization, *456 Pages*	Deitsch	75.00
8173663807	Java Programming with Oracle SQLJ, *404 Pages*	Price	75.00
8173661103	JavaScript Application Cookbook, *512 Pages*	Bradenbaugh	75.00
8173661111	JavaScript Pocket Reference, *96 Pages*	Flanagan	25.00
8173662509	Jini in a Nutshell, *420 Pages*	Oaks	75.00
8173665168	**Learning C#, *374 Pages***	**Liberty**	**75.00**
8173662320	Learning Java **(Book / CD-ROM)**, *732 Pages*	Niemeyer	75.00
8173660603	Learning Perl/Tk, *380 Pages*	Walsh	75.00
8173661677	Learning Web Design: A Beginner's Guide to HTML, Graphics & Web Environment (2 Color Book), *432 Pages*	Niederst	100.00
8173663173	Learning WML & WMLScript, *204 Pages*	Frost	50.00
8173663149	Learning XML, *376 Pages*	Ray	75.00
8173662193	MCSD in a Nutshell: The Visual Basic Exams, *636 Pages*	Foxall	75.00
8173662398	MCSE in a Nutshell: The Windows 2000 Exams, *504 Pages*	Moncur	75.00
8173662517	MP3: The Definitive Guide, *408 Pages*	Hacker	75.00
8173665648	MySQL Cookbook (Covers MySQL 4.0), *1,028 Pages*	DuBois	150.00
8173665613	**Object-Oriented Programming with Visual Basic .NET, *306 Pgs***	**Hamilton**	**50.00**
8173663246	**Oracle Net8 Configuration & Troubleshooting, *412 Pages***	**Toledo**	**75.00**
8173660697	Oracle PL/SQL Language Pocket Reference, *80 Pages*	Feuerstein	25.00

ISBN	Title	Author	Price
8173667195	**Perl 6 Essentials, *208 Pages***	**Randal**	**75.00**
8173661243	Perl/Tk Pocket Reference, *104 Pages*	Lidie	25.00
817366269X	PHP Pocket Reference, *124 Pages*	Lerdorf	25.00
8173661251	PNG: The Definitive Guide, *344 Pages*	Roelofs	50.00
817366126X	Practical Internet Groupware, *520 Pages*	Udell	75.00
8173660751	Practical UNIX & Internet Security, 2/ed, *1,008 Pages*	Garfinkel	150.00
8173660190	QuarkXPress in a Nutshell, *552 Pages*	O'Quinn	50.00
8173662487	sed & awk Pocket Reference, *60 Pages*	Robbins	25.00
8173661294	sendmail Desktop Reference, *74 Pages*	Costales	25.00
8173664161	**Server Load Balancing,*198 Pages***	**Bourke**	**50.00**
8173663866	Solaris 8 Administrator's Guide, *308 Pages*	Watters	100.00
8173662924	**SSH: The Secure Shell: The Definitive Guide, *564 Pages***	**Barrett**	**75.00**
8173662606	Tcl/Tk Pocket Reference, *100 Pages*	Raines	25.00
8173664374	**VB .NET Core Classes in a Nutshell: A Desktop Quick Reference (Book / CD-ROM), *584 Pages***	**Kurniawan**	**75.00**
817366501X	**Visual Studio Hacks: Tips & Tools for Turbocharging the IDE, *304 Pages***	**Avery**	**75.00**
8173665931	**WebLogic Server 6.1 Workbook for Enterprise JavaBeans, 3/ed, *264 Pages***	**Nyberg**	**50.00**
8173663475	Web Database Applications with PHP & MySQL, *600 Pages*	Williams	75.00
8173661359	Webmaster in a Nutshell, 2/ed, *540 Pages*	Spainhour	75.00
8173662630	Windows 2000 Active Directory, *624 Pages*	Lowe-Norris	75.00
8173662789	**Windows 2000 Administration in a Nutshell: A Desktop Quick Reference, *1,000 Pages***	**Tulloch**	**50.00**
8173663327	Windows 2000 Performance Guide, *650 Pages*	Friedman	75.00
8173660743	**Windows 2000 Quick Fixes, *304 Pages***	**Boyce**	**50.00**
8173666903	**Windows Server 2003 in a Nutshell: A Desktop Quick Reference, *672 Pgs***	**Tulloch**	**75.00**
8173663564	**Windows XP in a Nutshell: A Desktop Quick Reference, *640 Pages***	**Karp**	**75.00**
8173665915	**Windows XP Unwired: A Guide for Home, Office, and the Road, *316 Pages***	**Lee**	**75.00**
8173662770	**Word 2000 in a Nutshell: A Power User's Quick Reference, *516 Pgs***	**Glenn**	**50.00**
8173666113	**Word Annoyances, *218 Pages***	**Hart**	**75.00**
8173668094	**Xlib Programming Manual (Version 11): Volume One, *824 Pages***	**Nye**	**100.00**
8173668108	**Xlib Reference Manual (Version 11), 3/ed: Volume Two, *948 Pages***	**Nye**	**100.00**
8173668086	**X Protocol Reference Manual (Version X11): Volume Zero, *468 Pgs***	**Nye**	**75.00**
8173662096	XSLT, *486 Pages*	Tidwell	100.00
PUBLISHED TITLES			
8173666539	.NET and XML, *484 Pages*	Bornstein	425.00
8173669201	.NET Compact Framework Pocket Guide, *122 Pages*	Lee	125.00
8173666547	.NET Framework Essentials, 3/ed, *392 Pages*	Thai	325.00
8173665729	.NET Gotchas: 75 Ways to Improve Your C# and VB.NET Programs, *402 Pgs*	Subramaniam	300.00
8173665753	802.11 Security, *200 Pages*	Potter	175.00
8184041632	**802.11 Wireless Networks: The Definitive Guide, 2/ed, *668 Pages***	**Gast**	**550.00**
9788184043099	**A+, Network+, Security+ Exams in a Nutshell (Cover Essentials 220-602,220-603,220-604 N10-00, *826 Pages***	**Bhardwaj**	**600.00**
8173661995	**Access 2003 Personal Trainer (Book / CD-ROM), (2 Color book), *372 Pages***	**CustomGuide**	**400.00**
9788184042573	**Access 2007: The Missing Manual, *776 Pages***	**MacDonald**	**525.00**
9788184042924	**Access 2007 For Starters: The Missing Manual,** *426 Pages*	**MacDonald**	**375.00**
9788184043334	**Access Data Analysis Cookbook, *384 Pages***	**Bluttman**	**375.00**
8173664285	Access Database Design & Programming, 3/ed, *454 Pages*	Roman	325.00
8173666377	Access Hacks: Tips & Tools for Wrangling Your Data, *362 Pgs*	Bluttman	325.00
8173667233	ActionScript Cookbook, *904 Pages*	Lott	675.00
9788184042832	**ActionScript 3.0 Cookbook, *600 Pages***	**Lott**	**475.00**
9788184043747	**ActionScript 3.0 Design Patterns, *548 Pages***	**Sanders**	**450.00**
8173666555	ActionScript for Flash MX Pocket Reference, *152 Pages*	Moock	125.00
8173665761	ActionScript for Flash MX: The Definitive Guide, 2/ed, *904 Pgs*	Colin Moock	750.00
8173667357	Active Directory Cookbook for Windows Server 2003 and Windows 2000, *632 Pages*	Allen	525.00

ISBN	Title	Author	Price
8173666563	Active Directory for Windows Server 2003, 2/ed, *692 Pages*	Allen	575.00
9788184043501	**Adding Ajax, *418 Pages***	**Power**	**400.00**
817366725X	ADO .NET Cookbook, *636 Pages*	Hamilton	500.00
9788184044980	**ADO .NET Cookbook, 2/ed, *996 Pages***	**Hamilton**	**750.00**
8173665222	ADO .NET for Visual Basic .NET 2003 in a Nutshell: A Desktop Quick Reference **(Book / CD-ROM)**, *626 Pages*	Hamilton	500.00
9788184043563	**Adobe Integrated Runtime(AIR) for JavaScript Developers Pocket Reference, *192 Pages***	**Dura**	**150.00**
8173668302	Advanced Perl Programming, 2/ed, *308 Pages*	Cozens	325.00
9788184044409	**Advanced Rails, *374 Pages***	**Ediger**	**325.00**
8173668205	AI for Game Developers, *400 Pages*	Bourg	375.00
8184041578	**Ajax Design Patterns, *668 Pages***	**Mahemoff**	**500.00**
8184041063	**Ajax Hacks: Tips & Tools for Creating Responsive Web Sites, *304 Pages***	**Perry**	**350.00**
9788184043082	**Ajax on Java,** *176 Pages*	**Olson**	**250.00**
9788184042610	**Ajax on Rails, *364 Pages***	**Raymond**	**350.00**
9788184044898	**Ajax The Definitive Guide, *996 Pages***	**Holdener**	**750.00**
8173667292	Amazon Hacks: 100 Industrial Strength Tips & Tricks, *312 Pages*	Bausch	250.00
8173667799	**Analyzing Business Data with Excel, *276 Pages***	**Knight**	**275.00**
8184040806	**ANT: The Definitive Guide, 2/ed (Cover ANT 1.6), *346 Pages***	**Holzner**	**325.00**
8173667446	Apache Cookbook (Covers Apache 2.0 & 1.3), *264 Pages*	Coar	250.00
9788184044416	**Apache Cookbook, 2/ed, *322 Pages***	**Coar**	**375.00**
8173662525	Apache Pocket Reference, *112 Pages*	Ford	75.00
8173662274	Apache Security, *428 Pages*	Ristic	400.00
8173665133	Apache: The Definitive Guide (Covers Apache 2.0 & 1.3) 3/ed, *594 Pgs*	Laurie	500.00
8184040393	Applied Software Project Management, *304 Pages*	Stellman	350.00
9788184043549	**Apollo for Adobe Flex Developers Pocket Guide, *154 Pages***	**Dixon**	**125.00**
9788184044232	**The Art of Agile Development, *446 Pages***	**Shore**	**400.00**
8173667837	The Art of Project Management, *512 Pages*	Berkun	350.00
8184041411	**The Art of SQL, *382 Pages***	**Faroult**	**350.00**
8184041020	**ASP .NET 2.0 Cookbook (Cover ASP .NET 2.0), *1,028 Pages***	**Kittel**	**675.00**
8173664587	**ASP .NET 2.0: Developer's Notebook, *358 Pages***	**Lee**	**325.00**
8173667306	ASP .NET in a Nutshell: A Desktop Quick Reference, 2/ed, *1,008 Pgs*	Duthie	600.00
8173669384	AspectJ Cookbook, *364 Pages*	Miles	350.00
8184040016	Asterisk: The Future of Telephony, *414 Pages*	Meggelen	375.00
9788184042702	**Astronomy Hacks, *420 Pages***	**Thompson**	**450.00**
8173662347	AutoCAD 2000 In a Nutshell: A Command Reference Guide, *592 Pgs*	Kent	325.00
9788184042900	**BacKup & Recovery, *774 Pages***	**Preston**	**600.00**
9788184043471	**Bash Cookbook, *636 Pages***	**Albing**	**500.00**
8173663955	Beginning Perl for Bioinformatics, *390 Pages*	Tisdall	300.00
8173668981	Better, Faster, Lighter Java, *270 Pages*	Tate	250.00
9788184043556	**Beautiful Code: Leading Programmers Explain How They Think, *634 Pgs***	**Wilson**	**500.00**
8184040032	Beyond Java, *206 Pages*	Tate	200.00
9788173666582	BGP, *292 Pages*	van Beijnum	275.00
8184040547	**Blackberry Hacks: Tips & Tools for Your Mobile Office, *350 Pages***	**Mabe**	**350.00**
8173665125	BLAST, *372 Pages*	Korf	325.00
817366899X	BSD Hacks:100 Industrial-Strength Tips & Tools, *458 Pages*	Lavigne	375.00
8173666598	**Building Embedded Linux Systems, *422 Pages***	**Yaghmour**	**350.00**
9780596101367	**Building Extreme PCs, *192 Pages***	**Hardwidge**	**1,200.00**
8173661014	Building Internet Firewalls 2/ed, *904 Pages*	Chapman	650.00
8173662282	Building Java Enterprise Applications: Vol. 1 - Architecture, *324 Pages*	McLaughlin	225.00
8173661391	Building Linux Clusters **(Book / CD-ROM)**, *360 Pages*	Spector	350.00
8184041543	**Building Scalable Web Sites, *362 Pages***	**Henderson**	**325.00**
9788184044393	**Building the Perfect PC, *360 Pages***	**Thompson**	**350.00**
8173664749	**Building a Web 2.0 Portal with ASP.NET 3.5, *324 Pages***	**Zabir**	**325.00**

ISBN	Title	Author	Price
8173664439	C# & VB .NET Conversion Pocket Reference, *156 Pages*	Mojica	75.00
8184040938	**C# Cookbook, 2/ed (Updated for C# 2.0 and .NET 2.0), *1,196 Pgs***	**Hilyard**	**600.00**
9788184044423	**C# 3.0 Cookbook, 3/ed, *902 Pages***	**Teilhet**	**650.00**
8173664293	C# Essentials, 2/ed, *224 Pages*	Albahari	175.00
8173663726	C# in a Nutshell: A Desktop Quick Reference, *864 Pages*	Drayton	600.00
9788184044379	**C# 3.0 Design Patterns , *330 Pages***	**Bishop**	**350.00**
9788184043846	**C# in a Nutshell 3/ed, *874 Pages***	**Albahari**	**600.00**
8173665192	C# Language Pocket Reference, *132 Pages*	Drayton	100.00
8184040490	**C in a Nutshell, *618 Pages***	**Prinz**	**350.00**
8173666601	C Pocket Reference, *142 Pages*	Prinz	100.00
9788184044911	**C# 3.0 2/ed Pockt Reference, *258 Pages***	**Albahari**	**175.00**
8184040369	**C++ Cookbook, *604 Pages***	**Stephens**	**400.00**
8173666628	C++ in a Nutshell, (Cover ISO/IEC 14882 STD) *816 Pages*	Lischner	500.00
8173667101	C++ Pocket Reference, *148 Pages*	Loudon	100.00
8173662266	CDO & MAPI Programming with Visual Basic, *388 Pages*	Grundgeiger	175.00
8173664269	CGI Programming on the World Wide Web, *454 Pages*	Gundavaram	300.00
817366045X	CGI Programming with Perl 2/ed, *476 Pages*	Gundavaram	350.00
9788184042849	**Cisco IOS Cookbook, 2/ed, *1,250 Pages***	**Dooley**	**850.00**
8173669848	Cisco IOS in a Nutshell, 2/ed: A Desktop Quick Reference for IOS on IP Network, *808 Pages*	Boney	500.00
8173668469	Classic Shell Scripting, *568 Pages*	Robbins	425.00
8173663645	COM+ Programming with Visual Basic, *372 Pages*	Mojica	225.00
8173663653	COM & .NET Component Services, *390 Pages*	Lowy	250.00
8184040199	**Computer Privacy Annoyances, *218 Pages***	**Tynan**	**225.00**
8184041586	**Computer Security Basics, 2/ed, *324 Pages***	**Lehtinen**	**325.00**
8173660638	Creating Effective JavaHelp, *196 Pages*	Lewis	125.00
8184040180	**Creating WebSites: The Missing Manual, *559 Pages***	**MacDonald**	**400.00**
8173669163	CSS Cookbook (Cover CSS 2.1), *280 Pages*	Schmitt	275.00
9788184042733	**CSS Cookbook, 2/ed, *552 Pages***	**Schmitt**	**475.00**
8184042000	**CSS: The Missing Manual, *494 Pages***	**McFarland**	**450.00**
9788184042788	**CSS: The Definitive Guide, 3/ed, *550 Pages***	**Meyer**	**500.00**
9788184042658	**CSS Pocket Reference, 2/ed, *142 Pages***	**Meyer**	**125.00**
8173667802	Database In Depth: The Relational Model for Practitioners, *250 Pages*	C.J.Date	250.00
8173662363	Database Nation: The Death of Privacy in the 21st Century, *336 Pages*	Garfinkel	235.00
9788173662898	Database Programming with JDBC & Java 2/ed, *348 Pages*	Reese	150.00
8173665664	Designing Embedded Hardware, *324 Pages*	Catsoulis	250.00
9788184042597	**Designing Embedded Hardware, 2/ed, *406 Pages***	**Catsoulis**	**275.00**
8173662428	Developing Bio-informatics Computer Skills, *504 Pages*	Gibas	225.00
8173669473	Developing Feeds with RSS and Atom, *280 Pages*	Hammersley	300.00
8184040113	Digital Identity, *266 Pages*	Windley	275.00
8173665672	DNS & BIND Cookbook, *248 Pages*	Liu	250.00
8184041969	**DNS & BIND (Covers BIND 9.3), 5/ed, *654 Pages***	**Albitz**	**550.00**
8173663785	DNS on Windows 2000, 2/ed, *376 Pages*	Larson	275.00
8173660506	DNS on Windows NT, *352 Pages*	Albitz	195.00
8184041039	**Dreamweaver 8: The Missing Manual, *964 Pages***	**David**	**600.00**
8184041209	**Dreawweaver 8 Design and Construction, *330 Pages***	**Campbell**	**375.00**
8173662991	Dreamweaver MX: The Missing Manual, *750 Pages*	McFarland	600.00
8173665281	Dynamic HTML: The Definitive Reference, 2/ed, *1,428 Pages*	Goodman	650.00
9788184042771	**Dynamic HTML: The Definitive Reference, 3/ed, *1,336 Pages***	**Goodman**	**800.00**
8173669015	Eclipse (Coverage of 3.0), *344 Pages*	Holzner	325.00
8173669309	Eclipse Cookbook (Cover 3.0), *372 Pages*	Holzner	350.00
8173669945	Eclipse IDE Pocket Guide, *140 Pages*	Burnette	125.00
8173663017	Effective awk Programming, 3/ed, *454 Pages*	Robbins	325.00
8173667268	Enterprise JavaBeans (Covers EJB 2.1 & EJB 2.0 Includes workbook for JBoss 4.0), 4/ed, *798 Pages*	Monson - Haefel	500.00

ISBN	Title	Author	Price
8184041195	**Enterprise JavaBeans 3.0, 5/ed, *774 Pages***	**Monson-Haefel**	**500.00**
9788173668166	Enterprise Service Architecture - O'Reilly SAP Series, *236 Pages*	Woods	225.00
8173666784	Enterprise Service Bus, *284 Pages*	Chappell	300.00
8184041446	**Enterprise SOA, *466 Pages***	**Woods**	**375.00**
8173669317	Essential ActionScript 2.0, *528 Pages*	Moock	400.00
8184040105	Essential Business Process Modeling, *362 Pages*	Havey	350.00
9788184042757	**Essential CVS, 2/ed, *442 Pages***	**Vesperman**	**425.00**
818404092X	**Essential Microsoft Operation Manager, *400 Pages***	**Fox**	**350.00**
8184040245	Essentail PHP Security, *310 Pages*	Shiflett	125.00
8173669430	Essentail SharePoint, *338 Pages*	Webb	325.00
9788184042825	**Essentail SNMP, 2/ed, *480 Pages***	**Mauro**	**400.00**
817366529X	Essential System Administration, 3/ed, *1,178 Pages*	Frisch	525.00
8173666644	Essential System Administration Pocket Reference, *152 Pages*	Frisch	125.00
8173660255	Essential Windows NT System Administration, *488 Pages*	Frisch	225.00
8173662495	Ethernet: The Definitive Guide, *528 Pages*	Spurgeon	300.00
9788173669613	Excel 2003 Personal Trainer **(Book / CD-ROM)**, (2 Color book) *490 Pgs*	CustomGuide	550.00
8173668299	Excel 2003 Programming: A Developer's Notebook, *330 Pages*	Webb	325.00
8184040288	**Excel 2003 for Starters: The Missing Manual, *408 Pages***	**MacDonald**	**275.00**
9788184042559	**Excel 2007: The Missing Manual, *870* Pages**	**MacDonald**	**550.00**
9788184042955	**Excel 2007 For Starters: The Missing Manual, 364 Pages**	**MacDonald**	**350.00**
9788184043518	**Excel Hacks, 2/Ed Tips & Tools for Streamlining Your Spreadsheets, *428 Pages***	**David**	**400.00**
8173668035	Excel: The Missing Manual, *802 Pages*	MacDonald	550.00
8184040849	**Excel Scientific and Engineering Cookbook, *442 Pages***	**Bourg**	**400.00**
8173665257	Exploring the JDS Linux Desktop **(Book / CD-ROM)**, *418 Pages*	Adelstein	400.00
8184042175	**Fedora Linux, *672 Pages***	**Tyler**	**500.00**
9788184045246	**Flex 3 Cookbook, *797 Pages***	**Noble**	**600.00**
8184041365	**Flash 8 Cookbook, *548 Pages***	**Lott**	**400.00**
8184041047	**Flash 8 Project for Learning Animation and Interactivity (Book / CD-ROM), *372 Pages***	**Shupe**	**400.00**
9788184043488	**Flash CS3 the Missing Manual, *544 Pages***	**Veer**	**500.00**
8173667470	Flash Hacks: 100 Industrial Strength Tips & Tools, *504 Pages*	Bhangal	400.00
8173668590	Flash Out of the Box: A User-Centric Beginner's Guide to Flash **(Book / CD-ROM)**, *264 Pages*	Hoekman	300.00
8173667314	Flash Remoting MX: The Definitive Guide, *652 Pages*	Muck	550.00
0596002874	Free As In Freedom: Richard Stallman's Crusade for Free Software, *243 Pgs*	Williams	750.00
8184040504	**FrontPage 2003: The Missing Manual, *446 Pages***	**Mantaro**	**400.00**
817366868X	GDB Pocket Reference, *78 Pages*	Robbins	75.00
9788184045079	**Google Apps Hacks, *395 Pages***	**Lenssen**	**525.00**
9788184042856	**Google: The Missing Manual, 2/ed, *478* Pages**	**Milstein**	**425.00**
8184040857	**Google Advertising Tools, *366 Pages***	**Davis**	**375.00**
817366949X	Google Hacks: Tips & Tools for Smarter Searching 2/ed, *496 Pgs*	Calishain	350.00
9788184044942	**Google Hack 3/ed, *560 Pages***	**Dornfest**	**400.00**
8184040873	**Google Maps Hacks: Tips & Tools for Geographic Searching & Remixing, *366 Pages***	**Gibson**	**350.00**
8173667136	Google Pocket Guide, *144 Pages*	Calishain	125.00
0596006624	Hackers & Painters: Big Ideas from the Computer Age, *272 Pgs*	Graham	700.00
9788184045024	**Harnessing Hibernate, *392 Pages***	**Elliott**	**400.00**
8173668256	Hardcore Java, *354 Pages*	Simmons	300.00
8173663424	Hardening Cisco Routers, *196 Pages*	Akin	150.00
8173668213	Hardware Hacking Projects for Geeks, *358 Pages*	Fullam	350.00
9788184044195	**Head First C#, *794 Pages***	**Stellman**	**550.00**
9788173664663	Head First Design Patterns, *688 Pages*	Sierra	500.00
9788173665264	Head First EJB: Passing the Sun Certified Business Component Developer Exam, *744 Pages*	Sierra	450.00
9788184040821	**Head First HTML with CSS & XHTML, *694 Pages***	**Freeman**	**500.00**

ISBN	Title	Author	Price
9788173666025	Head First Java (Covers Java 5.0) 2/ed, *730 Pages*	Sierra	450.00
9788184044362	**Head First JavaScript, *666 Pages***	**Morrison**	**500.00**
9788184042214	**Head First Object - Oriented Analysis & Design, *648 Pgs***	**McLaughlin**	**425.00**
9788184040418	**Head First PMP, *712 Pages***	**Greene**	**550.00**
9788184044508	**Head First Software Development, *512 Pages***	**Pilone**	**425.00**
9788173664038	Head First Servlets & JSP: Passing the Sun Certified Web Component Developer Exam, *666 Pages*	Sierra	600.00
9788184044973	**Head First Servlets & JSP: 2/ed,New Mock Exam Included, *928 Pages***	**Sierra**	**650.00**
8184041055	**Head Rush Ajax, *464 Pages***	**McLaughlin**	**375.00**
9788173669347	Hibernate: A Developer's Notebook, *190 Pages*	Elliott	200.00
8173669260	High Performance Linux Cluster with OSCAR, Rocks, OpenMosix, and MPI, *380 Pages*	Sloan	350.00
9788184043808	**High Performance Web Sites Essential Knowledge for Frontend Engineers, *184 Pages***	**Souders**	**200.00**
8173669023	High Performance MySQL: Optimization, Backups, Replication & Load Balancing, *304 Pgs*	Zawodny	300.00
8173663165	Home Hacking Projects for Geeks, *346 Pages*	Faulkner	325.00
8173669449	Home Networking Annoyances: How to Fix the Most Annoying Things About Your Home Network, *234 Pages*	Ivens	250.00
8184040202	Home Networking: The Missing Manual, *263 Pages*	Lowe	275.00
8184042140	**HTML & XHTML the Definitive Guide, 6/ed, *692 Pages***	**Musciano**	**500.00**
8173664323	HTML Pocket Reference, 2/ed, *100 Pages*	Niederst	70.00
9788184042696	**HTML & XHTML Pocket Reference, 3/ed, *118 Pages***	**Robbins**	**125.00**
8173665109	Information Architecture for the World Wide Web, 2/ed, *492 Pgs*	Rosenfeld	400.00
9788184042917	Information Architecture for The World Wide Web, 3/ed, 540 Pgs	Morville	500.00
8184040385	Integrating Excel and Access, *232 Pages*	Schmalz	250.00
9788184043600	**Intel Threading Building Blocks Out fitting C++ for Multi-Core Processor Parallelism, *348 Pages***	**Reinders**	**350.00**
8184040997	**Intermediate Perl, *290 Pages***	**Schwartz**	**300.00**
8173669414	Internet Annoyances: How to Fix the Most Annoying Things about Going Online, *266 Pages*	Gralla	250.00
8173661057	Internet Core Protocols: The Definitive Guide **(Book / CD-ROM)**, *476 Pages*	Hall	375.00
8184040156	Internet Forensics, *250 Pages*	Jones	275.00
8173660158	Internet in a Nutshell, *456 Pages*	Quercia	215.00
8184041810	**The Internet: The Missing Manual, *466 Pages***	**Biersdorfer**	**350.00**
8173663378	IP Routing, *244 Pages*	Malhotra	200.00
9788184042818	**IPv6 Essentials, 2/ed, *450 Pages***	**Hagen**	**450.00**
8173663025	IPv6 Network Administration, *316 Pages*	Murphy	325.00
8173667489	IRC Hack: 100 Industrial-Strength Tips & Tools, *442 Pages*	Mutton	400.00
8173667373	J2EE Design Patterns, *390 Pages*	Crawford	325.00
8173663432	J2ME in a Nutshell: A Desktop Quick Reference, *474 Pages*	Topley	400.00
8173669295	Jakarta Commons Cookbook, *412 Pages*	O'Brien	375.00
8173669481	Jakarta Struts Cookbook, *536 Pages*	Siggelkow	400.00
8173667144	Jakarta Struts Pocket Reference, *142 Pages*	Cavaness	125.00
8173664471	Java & SOAP, *286 Pages*	Englander	275.00
8173664498	Java & XML Data Binding, *224 Pages*	McLaughlin	225.00
817366367X	Java & XML, 2/ed, *534 Pages*	McLaughlin	450.00
9788184043068	Java & XML, 3/ed, 496 Pages	McLaughlin	450.00
8173663793	Java & XSLT, *534 Pages*	Burke	350.00
8173668477	Java 1.5 Tiger: A Developer's Notebook, *210 Pages*	McLaughlin	175.00
8173669368	Java Cookbook (Coverage of 1.5), 2/ed, *872 Pages*	Darwin	600.00
8173666679	Java Data Objects, *568 Pages*	Jordan	350.00
8173666660	Java Database Best Practices, *304 Pages*	Eckstein	275.00
817366577X	Java Enterprise Best Practices, *296 Pages*	Eckstein	275.00
9788184042870	**Java Enterprise in a Nutshell, 3/ed, *906* Pages**	**Farley**	**600.00**

ISBN	Title	Author	Price
8173662843	Java Examples in a Nutshell 2/ed, *592 Pages*	Flanagan	225.00
8173668639	Java Examples in a Nutshell: A Tutorial Companion to Java in a Nutshell, 3/ed, *728 Pgs*	Flanagan	400.00
8173666687	Java Extreme Programming Cookbook, *296 Pages*	Burke	225.00
8184042167	**Java Generics and Collections, *308 Pages***	**Naftalin**	**325.00**
817366434X	Java in a Nutshell: A Desktop Quick Reference, 4/ed, *1,000 Pgs*	Flanagan	600.00
9788184042665	**Java in a Nutshell, 5/ed, *1,266* Pages**	**Flanagan**	**650.00**
8184041187	**Java I/O, 2/ed, *740 Pages***	**Harold**	**550.00**
8173664404	Java Management Extensions, *318 Pages*	Perry	275.00
8173663211	Java Message Service, *300 Pages*	Monson-Haefel	225.00
817366353X	Java Network Programming, 3/ed, *770 Pages*	Harold	500.00
8173665117	Java NIO, *308 Pages*	Hitchens	275.00
9788184044881	**Java Pocket Guide, *208 Pages***	**Liguori**	**150.00**
8173665788	Java Performance Tuning, 2/ed, *600 Pages*	Shirazi	450.00
8173663904	Java Programming with Oracle JDBC, *504 Pages*	Bales	300.00
8173663815	Java RMI, *578 Pages*	Grosso	400.00
8173664129	Java Security, 2/ed, *624 Pages*	Oaks	500.00
9788173668227	Java Servlet & JSP Cookbook, *756 Pages*	Perry	500.00
8173662851	Java Servlet Programming 2/ed, *786 Pages*	Hunter	500.00
8173665680	Java Swing, 2/ed, *1,288 Pages*	Loy	750.00
9788173665929	Java Threads (Covers J2SE 5.0), 3/ed, *368 Pages*	Oaks	300.00
9788173663444	Java Web Services, *286 Pages*	Chappell	300.00
8173666695	Java Web Services in a Nutshell: A Desktop Quick Reference (Covers J2EE 1.4 & JWSDP), *696 Pages*	Topley	500.00
8173666709	JavaScript and DHTML Cookbook, *546 Pages*	Goodman	475.00
9788184041941	**JavaScript: The Definitive Guide, 5/ed, *1,032 Pages***	**Flanagan**	**750.00**
9788184045222	**JavaScript: The Good Parts, *186 Pages***	**Crockford**	**200.00**
8173669031	JavaServer Faces, *614 Pages*	Bergsten	450.00
8173665303	JavaServer Pages (Covers JSP 2.0 & JSTL 1.1), 3/ed, *762 Pgs*	Bergsten	550.00
8173663831	JavaServer Pages Pocket Reference, *96 Pages*	Bergsten	65.00
8173669465	JBoss: A Developer's Notebook, *182 Pages*	Richards	200.00
8184040172	JBoss at Work: A Practical Guide, *318 Pages*	Marrs	325.00
8173666717	JDBC Pocket Reference, *160 Pages*	Bales	100.00
8173668604	JUnit Pocket Guide, *100 Pages*	Beck	100.00
9788184045031	**Java Powe Tools, *925 Pages***	**Smart**	**775.00**
8184041160	**JUNOS Cookbook, *682 Pages***	**Garrett**	**450.00**
9788184044997	**JUNOS Enterprise, *828 Pages***	**Marschke**	**8000.00**
059600768X	Just A Geek, *296 Pages*	Wheaton	700.00
817366515X	JXTA in a Nutshell: A Desktop Quick Reference, *422 Pages*	Oaks	225.00
8173665605	Kerberos: The Definitive Guide, *280 Pages*	Garman	275.00
8173669724	Killer Game Programming in Java, *986 Pages*	Davison	675.00
8184040261	Knoppix Pocket Reference, *104 Pages*	Rankin	100.00
8173666725	LDAP System Administration, *318 Pages*	Carter	300.00
9788184042863	**Learning C# 2005, 2/ed, *566 Pages***	**Liberty**	**450.00**
8173669635	Learning GNU Emacs, 3/ed, *544 Pages*	Cameron	450.00
8184040334	**Learning Java,3/ed (Book / CD-ROM) (Cover J2SE 5.0), *986 Pgs***	**Niemeyer**	**650.00**
8184042159	**Learning JavaScript (Covers Ajax & Dcom), *368 Pages***	**Powers**	**350.00**
8184042671	**Learning MySQL, *632 Pages***	**Tahaghoghi**	**525.00**
8173663912	Learning Oracle PL/SQL (Covers Oracle9i), *452 Pages*	Pribyl	325.00
9788184040043	Learning Perl 4/ed, *316 Pages*	Schwartz	300.00
8173667322	Learning PHP 5, *378 Pages*	Sklar	350.00
8184041535	**Learning PHP and MySQL, *390 Pages***	**Davis**	**325.00**
9788184043716	**Learning PHP and MySQL, 2/ed, *444 Pages***	**Davis**	**400.00**
8173667381	Learning Python (Covers Python 2.3), 2/ed, *630 Pages*	Lutz	525.00

ISBN	Title	Author	Price
9788184043341	**Learning Ruby, *272 Pages***	**Fitzgerald**	**300.00**
9788184040128	Learning SQL, *318 Pages*	Beaulieu	200.00
9788184043044	**Learning SQL on SQL Server 2005, *342 Pages***	**Bagui**	**350.00**
8173668051	Learning the Bash Shell, 3/ed, *362 Pages*	Newham	375.00
8173664447	Learning the Korn Shell, 2/ed, *438 Pages*	Rosenblett	325.00
9788173664236	Learning the UNIX Operating System, 5/ed, *174 Pages*	Peek	125.00
8173660611	Learning the vi Editor 6/ed, *352 Pages*	Lamb	250.00
8173666741	Learning UML, *304 Pages*	Si Alhir	150.00
9788184042689	**Learning UML 2.0, *300 Pages***	**Miles**	**275.00**
817366563X	Learning Visual Basic .NET, *326 Pages*	Liberty	250.00
9788184043495	**Learning WCF, *624 Pages***	**Bustamante**	**500.00**
8184040903	**Learning Web Design: A Beginner's Guide to HTML, Graphics and Beyond, 2/ed, *484 Pages (with 16 Color Pages)***	**Niederst**	**375.00**
8173669422	Learning Windows Server 2003, *682 Pages*	Hassell	525.00
817366062X	lex & yacc 2/ed, *392 Pages*	Levine	225.00
8184041438	**Linux Annoyances for Geeks, *516 Pages***	**Jang**	**400.00**
8173668442	Linux Cookbook, *590 Pages*	Schroder	450.00
8184040164	Linux Desktop Pocket Guide, *202 Pages*	Brickner	150.00
8173663602	Linux Device Drivers, 2/ed, *650 Pages*	Rubini	450.00
9788173668494	**Linux Device Drivers (Covers Version 2.6.10 Linux Kernel), 3/ed, *646 Pages***	**Rubini**	**450.00**
8173669627	Linux in a Nutshell, 5/ed: A Desktop Quick Reference, *954 Pages*	Siever	500.00
8173669457	Linux in a Windows World, *504 Pages*	Smith	450.00
8173668507	Linux iptables Pocket Reference, *106 Pages*	Purdy	100.00
9788184043525	**Linux Kernel In A Nutshell, *216 Pages***	**Kroah**	**225.00**
8173662541	Linux Network Administrator's Guide, 2/ed, *510 Pages*	Kirch	400.00
9788184044218	**Linux Network Cookbook, *654 Pages***	**Kirch**	**500.00**
8173664544	Linux Network Administrator's Guide, 3/ed, *372 Pages*	Kirch	350.00
8173668647	Linux Pocket Guide, *212 Pages*	Barrett	150.00
9788184044904	**LINQ Pocket Reference, *188 Pages***	**Albahari**	**150.00**
8173667187	Linux Security Cookbook, *340 Pages*	Barrett	325.00
9788184042887	**Linux Server Security, 2/ed, *556 Pages***	**Bauer**	**450.00**
817366675X	Linux Server Hacks: 100 Industrial - Strength Tips & Tools, *240 Pgs*	Flickenger	225.00
8184040512	**Linux Server Hacks: Volume 2, *490 Pages***	**Hagen**	**400.00**
9788184043105	**Linux System Administration, *310 Pages***	**Adelstein**	**300.00**
9788184043815	**Linux System Programming, *404 Pages***	**Love**	**375.00**
8184040318	**Linux Multimedia Hacks, *342 Pages***	**Rankin**	**350.00**
8173668434	Linux Unwired, *322 Pages*	Weeks	300.00
8184041780	**LPI Linux Certification in a Nutshell, 2/ed, *996 Pages***	**Pritchard**	**650.00**
817366465X	Managing & Using MySQL, 2/ed, *448 Pages*	Reese	325.00
8173662746	Managing IMAP, *412 Pages*	Mullet	200.00
8173660271	Managing IP Networks with Cisco Routers, *352 Pages*	Ballew	200.00
8173663610	Managing NFS & NIS, 2/ed, *518 Pages*	Stern	400.00
8173669589	Managing Projects with GNU Make, 3/ed, *310 Pages*	Mecklenburg	325.00
8173665230	Managing RAID on Linux, *268 Pages*	Vadala	275.00
8173668655	Managing Security with Snort & IDS Tools, *296 Pages*	Cox Ph.D.	300.00
8173662800	Managing the Windows 2000 Registry, *564 Pages*	Robicheaux	325.00
0596007035	Mapping Hacks: Tips & Tools for Electronic Cartography, *574 Pages*	Erle	900.00
8173661162	Mastering Algorithms with C **(Book / DISK)**, *572 Pages*	Loudon	400.00
8173664455	Mastering FreeBSD and OpenBSD Security, *472 Pages*	Korff	425.00
8173664617	Mastering Oracle SQL (Covers Oracle Database10g), 2/ed, *504 Pages*	Mishra	400.00
8173666768	Mastering Perl for Bioinformatics, *406 Pages*	Tisdall	300.00
8173665087	Mastering Regular Expressions, 2/ed, *492 Pages*	Friedl	400.00
9788184043013	Mastering Regular Expressions, 3/ed, 556 Pages	Friedl	450.00

ISBN	Title	Author	Price
8173665702	Mastering Visual Studio .NET 2003, *420 Pages*	Flanders	375.00
8173667918	Maven: A Developer's Notebook, *232 Pages*	Massol	250.00
9788184042184	**MCSE Core Elective Exams in a Nutshell, *604 Pages***	**Bhardwaj**	**500.00**
8184041551	**MCSE Core Required Exams in a Nutshell, 3/ed, *750 Pages***	**Stanek**	**450.00**
8184040520	**Monad, *218 Pages***	**Oakley**	**225.00**
8173667497	Mono: A Developer's Notebook, *312 Pages*	Dumbill	325.00
9788184042801	**MySQL Cookbook, 2/ed, *990 Pages***	**DuBois**	**750.00**
817366806X	MySQL in a Nutshell, *358 Pages*	Dyer	325.00
8173666776	MySQL Pocket Reference, *94 Pages*	Reese	100.00
8184041403	**MySQL Stored Procedure Programming, *650 Pages***	**Harrison**	**450.00**
8173665249	NetBeans: The Definitive Guide, *662 Pages*	Boudreau	500.00
8173668809	Network Security Assessment, *398 Pages*	McNab	400.00
8173663521	Network Security Hacks: 100 Industrial-Strength Tips & Tools, *328 Pages*	Lockhart	325.00
9788184042740	**Network Security Hacks, 2/ed, *492 Pages***	**Lockhart**	**425.00**
8173668396	Network Security Tools: Writing, Hacking, and Modifying Security Tools , *350 Pages*	Dhanjani	350.00
8173663688	Network Troubleshooting Tools, *370 Pages*	Sloan	250.00
9788184043532	**Network Warrior, *614 Pages***	**Donahue**	**450.00**
8173667926	Nokia Smartphone Hacks: Tips & Tools for Your Smallest Computer, *418 Pgs*	Yuan	400.00
8173667845	NUnit Pocket Reference, *100 Pages*	Hamilton	100.00
8173668264	Office 2003 XML, *596 Pages*	Lenz	450.00
9788184043303	**Office 2007 the Missing Manual, *890 Pages***	**Grover**	**550.00**
8184040296	Open Sources 2.0, *488 Pages*	DiBona	425.00
8173667721	Open Source for the Enterprise, *246 Pages*	Woods	250.00
8173667519	OpenOffice.org Writer **(Book / CD-ROM)**, *234 Pages*	Weber	250.00
8173667403	Optimizing Oracle Performance, *426 Pages*	Milsap	375.00
8173669287	Oracle Applications Server 10g Essentials, *292 Pages*	Greenwald	275.00
8173661170	Oracle Built-in Packages **(Book / DISK)**, *956 Pages*	Feuerstein	475.00
8173667071	Oracle Data Dictionary Pocket Reference, *150 Pages*	Kreines	125.00
8173660670	Oracle Database Administration: The Essential Reference, *552 Pgs*	Kreines	325.00
817366417X	Oracle DBA Checklist Pocket Reference, *88 Pages*	RevealNet	65.00
8184040008	Oracle DBA Pocket Guide, *164 Pages*	Kreines	125.00
8173660689	Oracle Distributed Systems **(Book / DISK)**, *552 Pages*	Dye	325.00
8173664110	Oracle Essentials: Oracle9i, Oracle8i & Oracle8, 2/ed, *382 Pages*	Greenwald	250.00
817366935X	Oracle Essentials: Oracle Database 10g, 3/ed, *368 Pages*	Greenwald	275.00
9788184044201	**Oracle Essentials: Oracle Database 11g, 4/ed, *422 Pages***	**Greenwald**	**400.00**
817366580X	Oracle in a Nutshell: A Desktop Quick Reference, *934 Pages*	Greenwald	600.00
8173664560	Oracle Initialization Parameters Pocket Reference (Oracle Database 10g), *128 Pages*	Kreines	125.00
8173663629	Oracle PL/SQL Best Practices, *208 Pages*	Feuerstein	200.00
8173661189	Oracle PL/SQL Built-ins Pocket Reference, *78 Pages*	Feuerstein	60.00
8184040350	Oracle PL/SQL for DBAs, *466 Pages*	Feuerstein	350.00
818404254X	**Oracle PL/SQL Language Pocket Reference, 3/ed, *140 Pgs***	**Feuerstein**	**125.00**
8184040482	**Oracle PL/SQL Programming, 4/ed, *1,210 Pages***	**Feuerstein**	**600.00**
8173662401	Oracle PL/SQL Programming: A Developer's Workbook, *576 Pgs*	Feuerstein	300.00
8173661197	Oracle PL/SQL Programming: Guide to Oracle8i Features **(Book / DISK)**, *264 Pages*	Feuerstein	235.00
8173668116	Oracle Regular Expression Pocket Reference, *74 Pages*	Burcham	75.00
8173661200	Oracle SAP Administration, *208 Pages*	Burleson	175.00
8173660298	Oracle Scripts **(Book / CD-ROM)**, *208 Pages*	Lomansky	250.00
8173660719	Oracle Security, *448 Pages*	Theriault	220.00
8173663637	Oracle SQL* Loader: The Definitive Guide, *278 Pages*	Gennick	175.00
8173669333	Oracle SQL*Plus Pocket Reference, 3/ed, *160 Pages*	Gennick	125.00
8173666067	Oracle SQL*Plus: The Definitive Guide, 2/ed, *592 Pages*	Gennick	400.00

ISBN	Title	Author	Price
8173662916	Oracle SQL: The Essential Reference, *424 Pages*	Kreines	200.00
8173661847	Oracle Utilities Pocket Reference, *136 Pages*	Mishra	100.00
8173661219	Oracle Web Applications: PL/SQL Developer's Intro, *264 Pages*	Odewahn	180.00
817366028X	Oracle8 Design Tips, *136 Pages*	Ensor	120.00
8173668027	PC Annoyances: How to Fix the Most Annoying Thingsabout your Personal Computer, *236 Pgs*	Bass	225.00
9788184042528	PC Annoyances, 2/ed :How To Fix The Most Annoying Things About Your Personal Compter, Wind & More, 268 Pages	Bass	300.00
8173667152	PC Hacks: 100 Industrial-Strength Tips & Tools, *316 Pages*	Aspinwall	300.00
8173669732	PC Hardware Annoyances: How to Fix the Most ANNOYING Things About Your Computer Hardware, *276 Pages*	Bigelow	275.00
817366532X	PC Hardware in a Nutshell: A Desktop Quick Reference, 3/ed, *848 Pgs*	Thompson	325.00
8173668272	PC Pest Control, *296 Pages*	Gralla	300.00
818404139X	**PC's: The Missing Manual, *612 Pages***	**Rathbone**	**450.00**
8173667128	PDF Hacks: 100 Industrial-Strength Tips & Tools, *308 Pages*	Steward	300.00
8173664463	Perl & XML, *224 Pages*	Ray	175.00
8173661073	Perl 5 Pocket Reference, 3/ed, *96 Pages*	Vromans	70.00
8184042760	**Perl 6 and Parrot Essentials, 2/ed, *304 Pages***	**Randal**	**325.00**
8173668280	Perl Best Practices, *554 Pages*	Conway	425.00
9788173667336	Perl Cookbook, 2/ed, *976 Pages*	Christiansen	675.00
8184041381	**Perl Hacks, *310 Pages***	**Chromatic**	**325.00**
8173668043	Perl Template Toolkit, *600 Pages*	Chamberlain	525.00
8173668361	Perl Testing: A Developer's Notebook, *212 Pages*	Langworth	225.00
8173665710	PHP Cookbook, *638 Pages*	Sklar	550.00
9788184043006	PHP Cookbook, 2/ed, 842 Pages	Sklar	550.00
8184040814	**PHP Hacks: Tips & Tools for Creating Dynamic Web Sites, *468 Pages***	**Herrington**	**400.00**
8184040237	PHP in a Nutshell, *370 Pages*	Hudson	325.00
8184040253	PHPUnit Pocket Guide, *88 Pages*	Bergmann	100.00
817366871X	Postfix: The Definitive Guide, *288 Pages*	Dent	275.00
8173669805	Powerpoint 2003 Personal Trainer **(Book / CD-ROM)**, (2 Color book) *242 Pages*	CustomGuide	425.00
9788184042566	**Powerpoint 2007: The Missing Manual, *502 Pages***	**Veer**	**450.00**
9788184042948	**PowerPoint 2007 For Starters: The Missing Manual, 325 Pgs**	**Vander**	**325.00**
8173660301	Practical C Programming 3/ed, *456 Pages*	Oualline	225.00
8173666822	Practical C++ Programming, 2/ed, *582 Pages*	Oualline	225.00
8184040059	Practical Development Environments, *340 Pages*	Doar	325.00
817366711X	Practical mod_perl, *932 Pages*	Bekman	675.00
8184040326	**Practical Perforce, *370 Pages***	**Wingerd**	**375.00**
8173663920	Practical PostgreSQL **(Book / CD-ROM)**, *642 Pgs*	Command Prompt Inc.	450.00
8173666733	Practical RDF, *360 Pages*	Powers	325.00
8173666830	Practical Unix & Internet Security, 3/ed, *994 Pages*	Garfinkel	650.00
8173664390	Practical VoIP Using VOCAL, *532 Pages*	Dang	450.00
8184040091	Prefactoring, *248 Pages*	Pugh	250.00
8184042108	**Process Improvement Essentials, *364 Pages***	**Persse, PhD**	**400.00**
8184040229	Producing Open Sources Software, *302 Pages*	Fogel	325.00
9788184043709	**Programming Collective Intelligence Building Smart Web 2.0 Application, *374 Pgs***	**Segaram**	**375.00**
9788184040340	**Programming .NET Components, 2/ed (Covers .NET 2.0 & Visual Studio 2005), *656 Pages***	**Lowy**	**425.00**
8173667209	Programming .NET Security, *704 Pages*	Freeman	550.00
8173664382	Programming .NET Web Services, *500 Pages*	Ferrara	375.00
8173667411	Programming .NET Windows Applications (Covers .NET 1.1, & Visual Studio .NET 2003), *1,316 Pages*	Liberty	750.00
8184042086	**Programming Atlas, *418 Pages***	**Wenz**	**375.00**
9788184045055	**Programming Amazon Web Services, S3, EC2, SQS, FPS, and SimpleDB, *616 Pages***	**Murty**	**600.00**
8184040970	**Programming ASP.NET (Covers 2.0), 3/ed, *966 Pages***	**Liberty**	**600.00**
9788184043839	**Programming ASP.NET Ajax, *490 Pages***	**Wenz**	**400.00**

ISBN	Title	Author	Price
9788173669651	**Programming C# (Covers C# 2.0, .NET 2.0 & Visual Studio 2005), 4/ed, *680 Pages***	**Liberty**	**525.00**
9788184044386	**Programming C#, 5/ed, *624 Pages***	**Liberty**	**525.00**
817366076X	Programming Embedded Systems in C & C++, *198 Pages*	Barr	150.00
9788184042627	**Programming Embedded Systems with C and GNU Development Tools, 2/ed, *340 Pages***	**Barr**	**250.00**
8184041454	**Programming Excel with VBA and .NET, *1,128 Pages***	**Webb**	**750.00**
8173669694	Programming Flash Communication Server, *842 Pages*	Lesser	600.00
9788184043358	**Programming Flex 2, *518 Pages***	**Kazoun**	**425.00**
8173661278	Programming Internet E-mail, *384 Pages*	Wood	225.00
9788173668180	Programming Jakarta Struts 2/ed, *470 Pages*	Cavaness	400.00
8184040792	**Programming MapPoint in .NET (Book / CD-ROM), *400 Pages***	**Thota**	**350.00**
9788173662652	Programming Perl 3/ed, *1,116 Pages*	Wall	750.00
8173663114	Programming PHP, *530 Pages*	Lerdorf	350.00
9788184042719	**Programming PHP, 2/ed, *425 Pages***	**Lerdorf**	**425.00**
8173667500	Programming Python (Covers Python 2) **(Book / CD-ROM)**, 2/ed, *1,305 Pages*	Lutzf	750.00
9788184043792	**Programming Python, 3/ed, *1582 Pages***	**Lutz**	**800.00**
8173667861	**Programming SQL Server 2005, *600 Pages***	**Wildermuth**	**400.00**
8173662371	Programming the Perl DBI, *372 Pages*	Descartes	200.00
8173667063	Programming Visual Basic .NET 2003, 2/ed, *564 Pages*	Liberty	425.00
8184040377	**Programming Visual Basic 2005, *580 Pages***	**Liberty**	**400.00**
9788184045253	**Programming Visual Basic 2008, *798 Pages***	**Patrick**	**550.00**
9788184043051	**Progamming WCF Services, 600 Pages**	**Lowy**	**500.00**
8173665737	Programming Web Services with Perl, *492 Pages*	Ray	400.00
8173662045	Programming Web Services with SOAP, *268 Pages*	Snell	200.00
817366207X	Programming Web Services with XML-RPC, *240 Pages*	St.Laurent	175.00
8173668175	Programming with QT (Covers Qt 3), 2/ed, *532 Pages*	Dalheimer	450.00
8184041500	**Project 2003 Personal Trainer, (Book / CD-ROM), *246 Pgs***	**CustomGuide**	**300.00**
817366479X	Python Cookbook (Covers Python 2.3 & 2.4), 2/ed, *852 Pages*	Martelli	600.00
8173666857	Python in a Nutshell: A Desktop Quick Reference (Cover Python 2.2), *662 Pages*	Martelli	500.00
8173669708	Python Pocket Reference (Covers Python 2.4), 3/ed, *168 Pages*	Lutz	125.00
8173668485	qmail, *268 Pages*	Levine	275.00
9788184042962	**Rail Cookbook, 600 Pages**	**Orsini**	**450.00**
817366689X	Real World Web Services, *230 Pages*	Iverson	225.00
9788184043327	**Restful Web Services, *462 Pages***	**Richardson**	**400.00**
8184040865	**RFID Essentials, *276 Pages***	**Glover**	**275.00**
8184041985	**The Relational Database Dictionary, *126 Pages***	**Date**	**150.00**
8173667276	Regular Expression Pocket Reference, *112 Pages*	Stubblebine	100.00
9788184043761	Regular Expression Pocket Reference, 2/ed, *132 Pages*	Stubblebine	150.00
8184041373	**Repairing and Upgrading Your PC, *462 Pages***	**Thompson**	**350.00**
8173669686	RT Essentials, *228 Pages*	Vincent	250.00
8184041802	**Ruby Cookbook, *920 Pages***	**Carlson**	**650.00**
8184041993	**Ruby on Rails: Up and Running, *196 Pages***	**Tate**	**225.00**
9780596007195	Revolution in the Valley, *324 Pages*	Hertzfeld	775.00
9788184043624	**Ruby Pocket Reference, *182 Pages***	**Fitzgerald**	**150.00**
8173665206	Running Linux, 4/ed, *702 Pages*	Welsh	425.00
9788184042726	**Running Linux, 5/ed, *986 Pages***	**Welsh**	**600.00**
8173667055	Samba Pocket Reference, 2/ed, *146 Pages*	Eckstein	125.00
8173664226	SAX2 (Simple API for XML), *248 Pages*	Brownell	175.00
9788184044935	**ScreenOS Cookbook, *854 Pages***	**Brunner**	**600.00**
8173667217	Secure Coding: Principles & Practices, *200 Pages*	Graff	225.00
8173667284	Secure Programming Cookbook for C and C++, *800 Pages*	Viega	600.00
9788184043754	**Security Power Tools, *872 Pages***	**Burns**	**650.00**

ISBN	Title	Author	Price
9788184043617	**Securing Ajax Applications, *266 Pages***	**Wells**	**275.00**
8173663262	Securing Windows NT/2000 Servers for the Internet, *200 Pages*	Norberg	125.00
8173669376	Securing Windows Server 2003, *456 Pages*	Danseglio	400.00
8184040083	Security and Usability, *748 Pages*	Cranor	550.00
817366840X	Security Warrior, *562 Pages*	Peikari	500.00
8173660786	sed & awk, 2/ed, *440 Pages*	Dougherty	300.00
817366918X	SELINUX NSA's Open Source Security Enhanced Linux, *264 Pgs*	McCarty	275.00
8173665834	sendmail, 3/ed, *1,238 Pages*	Costales	850.00
9788184044225	**sendmail, 4/ed, *1,324 Pages***	**Costales**	**850.00**
817366823X	sendmail Cookbook, *418 Pages*	Hunt	400.00
8173666865	Sequence Analysis in a Nutshell: A Guide to Common Tools and Databases (Covers EMBOSS 2.5.0), *310 Pages*	Markel	275.00
9788184040449	SharePoint 2007, The Definitive Guide, *836 Pages*	Pyles	600.00
817366983X	SharePoint Office Pocket Guide, *94 Pages*	Webb	100.00
817366739X	SharePoint User's Guide, *158 Pages*	IDC	150.00
8184040679	**Skype Hacks: Tips & Tools for Cheap, Fun, Innovative Phone Service, *354 Pgs***	**Sheppard**	**350.00**
8173669503	Snort Cookbook, *296 Pages*	Orebaugh	300.00
9788184043693	SOA in Practice, *358 Pages*	Josuttis	375.00
8173669198	SpamAssassin (Covers 3.0), *232 Pages*	Schwartz	250.00
8173668191	Spidering Hacks: 100 Industrial - Strength Tips & Tools, *436 Pages*	Hemenway	350.00
9788173668371	Spring: A Developer's Notebook, *202 Pages*	Tate	200.00
9788184040685	**SQL Cookbook (Cover SQL Server, PostgreSQL,Oracle, MySQL, AND DB2), *640 Pages***	**Molinaro**	**475.00**
9788184042207	**SQL Hacks, 424 Pages**	**Cumming**	**400.00**
8173666520	SQL in a Nutshell (Covers SQL Server, DB2, MySQL, Oracle & PostgreSQL), 2/ed, *720 Pages*	Kline	450.00
8173667438	SQL Pocket Guide (Cover Oracle. DB2, SQL Server & MySQL), *170 Pages*	Gennick	125.00
9788173668241	SQL Tunning (Covers Oracle, DB2 & SQL Server), *356 Pages*	Tow	325.00
8173668418	Squid: The Definitive Guide, *472 Pages*	Wessels	450.00
9788184042795	**SSH The Secure Shell: The Definitive Guide, 2/ed, *680 Pages***	**Barrett**	**525.00**
9788184042634	**Statistics Hacks, *380 Pages***	**Frey**	**350.00**
8173668574	STL Pocket Reference, *136 Pages*	Lischner	100.00
8184041799	**SUSE Linux, *460 Pages***	**Brown**	**400.00**
9788184045048	**Subject to Change, Creating great products and services for an uncertain world, *202 Pages***	**Merholz**	**300.00**
8173664811	Swing Hacks, *554 Pages*	Marinacci	425.00
8173665311	Switching to VoIP, *514 Pages*	Wallingford	450.00
8173669511	SWT: A Developer's Notebook, *330 Pages*	Hatton	325.00
8173663254	T1: A Survival Guide, *312 Pages*	Gast	225.00
8184040539	**Talk is Cheap: Switching to Internet Telephones, *278 Pages***	**Gaskin**	**275.00**
817366093X	Tcl/Tk in a Nutshell: A Desktop Quick Reference, *480 Pages*	Raines	240.00
8173664676	TCP/IP Network Administration 3/ed, *756 Pages*	Hunt	500.00
8173666512	Test Driving Linux: From Windows to Linux in 60 Seconds **(Book / CD-ROM)**, *372 Pages*	Brickner	350.00
818404030X	**Time Management for System Administrators, *238 Pages***	**Limoncelli**	**250.00**
8173666032	**TOAD Pocket Reference for Oracle, 2/ed, *136 Pages***	**McGrath**	**125.00**
9788184044928	**The Ruby Programming Language, *460 Pages***	**Flanagan**	**400.00**
8173666873	Tomcat: The Definitive Guide (Cover Tomcat 4), *336 Pages*	Brittain	300.00
9788184044041	**Tomcat: The Definitive Guide 2/ed, *510 Pages***	**Brittain**	**400.00**
8184040210	Twisted Network Programming Essentials, *210 Pages*	Fettig	275.00
8184041594	**Ubuntu Hacks, *462 Pages***	**Oxer**	**350.00**
9788184040029	UML 2.0 in a Nutshell, *246 Pages*	Pilone	200.00
9788184042993	UML 2.0 Pocket Reference, 150 Pages	Pilone	125.00

ISBN	Title	Author	Price
8173667225	UML Pocket Reference, *96 Pages*	Pilone	100.00
8184040768	**Understanding Linux Network Internals, *1,074 Pages***	**Benvenuti**	**600.00**
9788184043198	**Understanding MySQL Internals, *208 Pages***	**Pachey**	**300.00**
8184040830	**Understanding the Linux Kernel (Cover Version 2.6), 3/ed, *954 Pages***	**Bovet**	**550.00**
8184041608	**Unicode Explained, *692 Pages***	**Korpela**	**525.00**
817366627X	Unit Test Frameworks **(Book / CD-ROM)**, *222 Pages*	Hamill	225.00
8184040601	**Unix in a Nutshell, 4/ed, *992 Pages***	**Robbins**	**450.00**
8173665656	Unix Power Tools, 3/ed, *1,162 Pages*	Powers	750.00
8173666202	Upgrading to PHP 5 (Covers MySQL 4.1), *358 Pages*	Trachtenberg	350.00
8173660948	Using & Managing PPP, *464 Pages*	Sun	240.00
8173665842	Using Samba, 2/ed, *570 Pages*	Eckstein	500.00
9788184043037	Using Samba, 3/ed, 464 Pages	Carter	450.00
817366594X	VB .NET Language Pocket Reference, *160 Pages*	Roman	125.00
8173666881	VBScript in a Nutshell: A Desktop Quick Reference, 2/e, *528 Pages*	Lomax	400.00
8173663300	VBScript Pocket Reference, *118 Pages*	Childs	60.00
8173668582	Version Control With Subversion, *332 Pages*	Collins - Sussman	350.00
8173662622	vi Editor Pocket Reference, *76 Pages*	Robbins	60.00
8173661340	Virtual Private Networks, 2/ed, *228 Pages*	Scott	150.00
8173666164	**Visual Basic 2005: A Developer's Notebook, *272 Pages***	**MacDonald**	**250.00**
8184040911	**Visual Basic 2005 in a Nutshell 3/ed, *766 Pages***	**Patrick**	**500.00**
8184040067	**Visual Basic 2005 Jumpstart, *226 Pages***	**Lee**	**225.00**
8173669740	**Visual C# 2005: A Developer's Notebook, *250 Pages***	**Liberty**	**225.00**
8184042094	**Visual Basic 2005 Cookbook, *754 Pages***	**Craig**	**575.00**
8173660964	Visual Basic Controls in a Nutshell, *512 Pages*	Dictor	310.00
8184040695	**VOIP Hacks: Tips & Tools for Internet Telephony, *326 Pgs***	**Wallingford**	**325.00**
0596007337	We the Media: Grassroots Journalism by the People,for the People, *320 Pages*	Gillmor	775.00
9788184045062	**Web 2.0: A Sttrategy Guide, *282 Pages***	**Shuen**	**350.00**
9788173669057	Web Database Application with PHP & MySQL (Covers PEAR, PHP 5 & MySQL 4.1), 2/ed, *828 Pages*	Willaims	600.00
8173663750	Web Design in a Nutshell: A Desktop Quick Reference, 2/ed, *656 Pages*	Niederst	425.00
9788184040982	Web Design in a Nutshell: A Desktop Quick Reference, 3/ed, *826 Pages*	Niederst	450.00
8173664412	Web Performance Tuning, 2/ed, *488 Pages*	Killelea	350.00
8173665214	Web Privacy with P3P, *350 Pages*	Cranor	300.00
8173663947	Web Security, Privacy & Commerce, 2/ed, *768 Pages*	Garfinkel	500.00
8173667624	**Web Site Cookbook, *262 Pages***	**Addison**	**300.00**
8173663394	Web Services Essentials, *320 Pages*	Cerami	200.00
8173669678	Web Site Measurement Hacks: Tips & Tools to Help Optimize Your Online Business, *442 Pages*	Peterson	400.00
8173663092	WebLogic 8.1: The Definitive Guide, *860 Pages*	Mountjoy	600.00
8173661308	The Whole Internet: The Next Generation, *576 Pages*	Conner/Krol	425.00
8173661367	Win32 API Programming with Visual Basic **(Book / CD-ROM)**, *534 Pages*	Roman	400.00
8173663319	Windows 2000 Commands Pocket Reference, *122 Pages*	Frisch	60.00
9788184042603	**Windows Developers Power Tools, *1,322 Pages***	**Avery**	**750.00**
9788184045239	**Windows PowerShell, *191 Pages***	**Holmes**	**150.00**
8173660883	Windows NT TCP/IP Network Administration, *512 Pages*	Hunt	250.00
8184040776	**Windows Server 2003 Security Cookbook, *522 Pages***	**Danseglio**	**475.00**
9788184045000	**Windows Server 2008 The Definitive Guide, *508 Pages***	**Hassell**	**475.00**
8173668833	Windows Server Hacks: 100 Industrial-Strength Tips & Tools , *328 Pages*	Tulloch	325.00
9788184042139	**Windows Vista: The Definitive Guide, *958 Pages***	**Stanek**	**600.00**
9788184042580	**Windows Vista: The Missing Manual, *860 Pages***	**Pogue**	**600.00**
9788184042979	**Windows Vista For Starters: The Missing Manual, *493 Pages***	**Pogue**	**325.00**
9788184042986	**Windows Vista In A Nutshell, *766 Pages***	**Gralla**	**500.00**
9788184043075	**Windows Vista Pocket Reference, *208 Pages***	**Gralla**	**150.00**

ISBN	Title	Author	Price
817366966X	Windows XP Cookbook, *690 Pages*	Allen	500.00
8173667454	Windows XP Hacks: 100 Industrial-Strength Tips & Tools, *294 Pgs*	Gralla	350.00
8173669643	Windows XP Personal Trainer **(Book / CD-ROM)**, *480 Pgs*	CustomGuide	550.00
8173666911	Windows XP Pocket Reference, *196 Pages*	Karp	125.00
8173667462	Wireless Hacks: 100 Industrial-Strength Tips & Tools, *424 Pages*	Flickenger	275.00
9788184043020	Wireless Hacks, 2/ed: Tips & Tools For Building, Extending & Securing Your Network 2/ed, 480 Pages	Flickenger	425.00
9788184042931	Word 2007 For Starters: The Missing Manual, 372 Pages	Grover	350.00
817366692X	Word Pocket Guide, *160 Pages*	Glenn	125.00
8173665354	Writing Excel Macros with VBA, 2/ed, *580 Pages*	Roman	450.00
8173660778	Writing Word Macros, *416 Pages*	Roman	275.00
818404142X	**XAML in a Nutshell, *316 Pages***	**MacVittie**	**300.00**
8173666156	XML Hacks: 100 Industrial-Strength Tips & Tools, *490 Pages*	Fitzgerald	425.00
8173668450	XML in a Nutshell (Covers XML 1.1 & XInclude), 3/ed, *724 Pages*	Harold	500.00
8173663343	XML Pocket Reference, 2/ed, *128 Pages*	Eckstein	100.00
9788184042641	**XML Pocket Reference, 3/ed, *198 Pages***	**Laurent**	**125.00**
9788184044430	**X Power Tools, *286 Pages***	**Tyler**	**325.00**
8173664900	XSLT 1.0 Pocket Reference, *188 Pages*	Lenz	150.00
8184040784	**XSLT Cookbook (Cover XSLT 1.0 & 2.0, 2/ed, *786 Pages***	**Mangano**	**500.00**
9788184043181	**XQuery, *528 Pages***	**Walmsley**	**500.00**
8184040075	Yahoo! Hacks: Tips & Tools for Living on the Web Frontier, *504 Pgs*	Bausch	400.00
8184040881	**Zero Configuration Networking: The Definitive Guide, *252 Pgs***	**Cheshire**	**275.00**

US EDITION AVAILABLE AT INDIA SPECIAL PRICE:

ISBN	Title	Author	Price
0596102364	**Adobe Creative Suite 2 Workflow, *634 Pages***	**Alspach**	**1,625.00**
0596006004	Adobe Encore DVD: In the Studio, *336 Pages*	Dixon	1,225.00
0596100973	**Adobe InDesign CS2 One-on-One (Book / CD-ROM), *420 Pgs***	**McClelland**	**1,375.00**
9780596529758	**Adobe Photoshop CS3 One-On-One (Book / DVD), *544 Pgs***	**McClelland**	**US$40.00**
0596100965	**Adobe Photoshop CS2 One-on-One (Book / DVD), *512 Pgs***	**McClelland**	**1,225.00**
0596001088	The Cathedral & The Bazaar: Musings On Linux and Open Source by an Accidental Revolutionary, Revised & Expanded, *256 Pages*	Raymond	525.00
059600849X	**Commercial Photoshop Retouching: In The Studio, *410 Pages***	**Honiball**	**1,425.00**
0596008589	**Creating Photomontages with Photoshop: A Designer's Notebook, *96 Pages***	**Collandre**	**800.00**
9780596008031	**Designing Interfaces, *352 Pages***	**Tidwell**	**1,800.00**
9780596526801	**Devices of the Soul Batting for Our Selves in an Age of Machines, *302 Pages***	**Talbott**	**US$18.00**
0596005474	Digital Photography: Expert Techniques (Covers Photoshop CS), *496 Pages*	Milburn	1,375.00
0596006667	Digital Photography Hacks: 100 Industrial - Strength Tips & Tools, *336 Pages*	Story	800.00
0596100159	Digital Photography Pocket Guide, 3/ed, *160 Pages*	Story	450.00
0596008414	**Digital Photography: The Missing Manual, *432 Pages***	**Grover**	**1,200.00**
0596009461	Digital Video Hacks: Tips & Tools for Shooting, Editing & Sharing, *426 Pages*	Paul	800.00
0596005237	Digital Video Pocket Guide, *474 Pages*	Story	500.00
9780596006624	**Hackers & Painters: Big Ideas From the Computer Age, *276 Pgs***	**Graham**	**700.00**
0596008597	**Illustrations with Photoshop: A Designer's Notebook, *96 Pgs***	**Rodarmor**	**775.00**
0596100485	**InDesign Production Cookbook, *224 Pages***	**Dabbs**	**1,200.00**
9780596527051	**Myths of Innovation, *196 Pages***	**Berkun**	**US$20.00**
0596008600	**Photo Retouching with Photoshop: A Designer's Notebook, *96 Pgs***	**CLEC'H**	**775.00**
9780596100209	**Photoshop Blending Modes Cookbook for Digital Photographers, *176 Pages***	**Beardsworth**	**1,025.00**

ISBN	Title	Author	Price
0596008511	**Photoshop CS2 Raw: Using Adobe Camera Raw, Bridge, and Photoshop to Get the Most Out of Your Digital Camera, *206 Pages***	**Aaland**	**1,075.00**
0596100213	**Photoshop Filter Effects Encyclopedia, *176 Pages***	**Pring**	**1,050.00**
0596100620	**Photoshop Fine Art Effects Cookbook, *176 Pages***	**Beardsworth**	**1,050.00**
0596100221	**Photoshop Photo Effects Cookbook, *176 Pages***	**Shelbourne**	**1,025.00**
0596100302	**Photoshop Retouching Cookbook for Digital Photographers, *176 Pages***	**Huggins**	**1,025.00**
9780596101138	**Programming Windows Presentation Foundation, *430 Pages***	**Sells**	**1,100.00**
9780596523701	**Stephen Johnson on Digital Photography, *320 Pages***	**Johnson**	**1,500.00**
0596100833	**Windows Seat, *152 Pages***	**Kost**	**1,600.00**

FORTHCOMING TITLES

June 2008

ISBN	Title	Author	Price
9788184043648	Mastering Perl, 358 Pages	Schwartz	350.00
0596100310	Digital Video Production Cookbook, *192 Pages*	Kenworthy	1,200.00
8184043171	Flash 8: The Missing Manual, *460 Pages*	Moore	500.00
8184043244	Fonts & Encodings, *992 Pages*	Haralambous	675.00
8184043198	Information Dashboard Design, *223 Pages*	Few	250.00
0596101686	Photoshop Workflow Setups, *207 Pages*	Tapp	1,170.00
0596527683	Practical Color Management: Eddie Tapp on Digital Photography, *168 Pages*	Tapp	1,170.00

July 2008

ISBN	Title	Author	Price
8184043473	Adobe Photoshop Lightroom Adventure, *304 Pages*	Aaland	300.00
8184043481	Asterisk Cookbook, *504 Pages*	Meggelen	575.00
818404349X	Developing Databases with Access, *504 Pages*	Freeze	495.00
8184043503	Head First Algebra, *664 Pages*	Davis	500.00
8184043511	Head First Web Design, *600 Pages*	Barr	575.00
818404352X	Linux System Administration, *600 Pages*	Thompson	595.00
8184043546	Ruby in a Nutshell, 2/ed, *304 Pages*	Matsumoto	300.00
8184043554	XSLT, 2/ed, *800 Pages*	Tidwell	675.00
8184043368	Windows Vista Annoyances for Geeks, *704 Pages*	Karp	675.00

- **Dates & Prices of forthcoming titles are tentative and subject to change without notice.**
- **All Prices are in Indian Rupees.**
- **TITLES RELEASED AFTER January 2007 ARE MARKED IN BOLD.**